MW00572533

AND NONE SHALL MAKE THEM AFRAID

AND NONE SHALL MAKE THEM AFRAID

EIGHT STORIES OF THE MODERN STATE OF ISRAEL

RICK RICHMAN

Author of *Racing Against History: The 1940 Campaign for a Jewish Army to Fight Hitler*

New York • London

First American edition published in 2023 by Encounter Books, an activity of Encounter for Culture and Education, Inc., a nonprofit, tax-exempt corporation.
Encounter Books website address: www.encounterbooks.com

Manufactured in the United States and printed on acid-free paper. The paper used in this publication meets the minimum requirements of ANSI/NISO Z39.48–1992 (R 1997) (*Permanence of Paper*).

FIRST AMERICAN EDITION

LIBRARY OF CONGRESS CATALOGING-IN-PUBLICATION DATA

Names: Richman, Rick, 1945– author.
Title: And none shall make them afraid: eight stories of the modern state of Israel / Rick Richman.
Description: First American edition. | New York: Encounter Books, 2023. | Includes bibliographical references and index. |
Identifiers: LCCN 2022021731 (print) | LCCN 2022021732 (ebook) | ISBN 9781641772747 (hardcover) | ISBN 9781641772754 (ebook)
Subjects: LCSH: Zionists—Europe—Biography. | Zionists—United States—Biography. | Zionism—History. | Jews—Europe—Biography. | Jews—United States—Biography. | United States—Relations—Israel. | Israel—Relations—United States. | LCGFT: Biographies.
Classification: LCC DS151.A2 R49 2023 (print) | LCC DS151.A2 (ebook) | DDC 320.54095694—dc23/eng/20220726
LC record available at https://lccn.loc.gov/2022021731
LC ebook record available at https://lccn.loc.gov/2022021732

1 2 3 4 5 6 7 8 9 20 23

To my beloved wife of more than fifty years,
Judy Richman,
whose mind and heart have been a lifelong blessing.
And to our sons,
Robert Richman and David Richman,
gifts from beyond the stars.

What is the probability that the people of Israel driven, as Moses put it, out to the farthest parts under heaven, would, in fact, come back to their ancient land to rejoin the remnant that remained from the corners of the earth, after 2000 years of exile, of persecution, of destruction, of expulsion, and of near elimination? That a people so despised would survive and thrive? These are earthly miracles just as amazing as the parting of the Red Sea. We should be telling that epic story, especially to the younger generation.

Bari Weiss, *How to Fight Anti-Semitism*

[T]he astonishing power of the Jewish past and present is not merely this culture's endurance, or even its objective achievements, but . . . its constant reinvention, its demonstration of what might be possible. That reinvention was not foreordained or predictable; it required hard work and harder optimism . . .

Dara Horn, "Dreams for Living Jews"

[T]hey shall sit every man under his vine and under his fig tree;
And none shall make them afraid.

Micah 4:4

CONTENTS

ACKNOWLEDGMENTS

The popular conception is that writing a book is a solitary endeavor. I have found instead that to conceive, research, write, edit, design, prepare, publish, publicize, and market a book, it takes a *shtetl.* I am deeply indebted to the many people who have made this book possible.

My incomparable editor and agent, Anne Mandelbaum, brought her extraordinary erudition, expertise, and experience to this project. No book—and no author—could have a better friend. The idea for this book was hers, and she presented it to Roger Kimball, President and Publisher of Encounter Books, with her critically important personal endorsement. She made invaluable editorial and structural suggestions over the course of many drafts, and she co-designed the book's striking cover. Without her inspiration and initiative, there would have been no book; with her peerless editing and wise counsel, it became immeasurably better.

Portions of this book appeared, in shorter and different form, in *Mosaic, The Jewish Review of Books, Commentary,* and the Israel Project's *Tower Magazine.* I have had the rare good fortune to work with Neal Kozodoy and Jonathan Silver of *Mosaic,* John Podhoretz of *Commentary,* Abraham Socher of *The Jewish Review of Books,* and David Hazony of *The Tower.*

Chapter 1 began as a Monthly Essay on Herzl in *Mosaic.* Chapter 2 combines and expands essays on Brandeis from *Mosaic* and *What America Owes the Jews, What Jews Owe America* (Mosaic Books and The Straus Center for Torah and Western Thought). Chapter 3 is based on two essays in *The Jewish Review of Books*: "Chaim of Arabia" and "Lawrence of Judea." Chapter 4 extends several essays on Jabotinsky that appeared in *The Tower, Mosaic,* and *Commentary.* Chapter 5, which tells the story of Golda Meir, appeared in part in *Commentary.* Chapters 6 and 7, which center on Ben Hecht and Abba Eban respectively, appeared in part or in a different form in *Mosaic.* Chapter 8, which focuses on Ron Dermer, reflects a key observation by Belladonna Rogers in an essay in *Real Clear Politics.*

I wrote most of this book while a resident scholar at American Jewish University (AJU). I am indebted to President Emeritus Robert Wexler for my research office there, and to President Jeffrey Herbst, Chief Academic Officer Dr. Robbie Totten, and Distinguished Professor of Jewish Studies Michael Berenbaum for my appointment as a resident scholar. Professor Berenbaum made me the beneficiary of many incisive conversations and dissenting engagements, gave me important leads, and graciously reviewed the manuscript. AJU's Ostrow Academic Library, with nearly 300,000 print and e-book titles and extensive electronic sources, was essential to my research, and the dedicated librarians there, Rabbi Patricia Fenton and Jackie Ben-Efraim, assisted me on innumerable occasions. I am, of course, solely responsible for any errors of fact, judgment, or omission in this book.

I am indebted to the biographies by Daniel Mark Epstein (of Aimee Semple McPherson and Edna St. Vincent Millay) and Susan Hertog (of Anne Morrow Lindbergh and Dorothy Thompson), which made me realize that the stories of individuals can convey the depth and nuance of history in a way that a general narrative cannot. These magisterial works gave me something to reach for, even if it exceeded my grasp.

It is an exceptional honor to be included among the authors published by Encounter Books. It has been a pleasure to work with Roger Kimball and his extraordinary team, including Amanda DeMatto (Director of Production), Lauren Miklos (Director of Publicity), and Sam Schneider (Director of Marketing). I thank Mazi Aghalarpour of Village Photo and Digital Imaging in Pacific Palisades for essential assistance in preparing high resolution versions of various photographs and images in this book. I appreciate the work of Chris Crochetière and Julia "Illana" Illana of BW&A Books, Inc. in Oxford, North Carolina, for their expert interior design. I am grateful to Joan Matthews for her close reading and skillful copyediting of the manuscript, and to Carol Staswick for her excellent review and expert indexing.

Over the past decade, I have had the opportunity to converse with many public intellectuals, outstanding teachers, and committed individuals, who added to my understanding and appreciation of Jewish and American history. I am grateful to Roger Hertog, Neal Kozodoy, Seth Lipsky, Norman Podhoretz, John Podhoretz, Jonathan Silver, Rabbi Dr. Robert Wexler, Rabbi David Wolpe, Ruth R. Wisse, Anne Mandelbaum, Anne Lieberman, Doris Wise Montrose, Gary Bialis, Curt Biren,

Larry Greenfield (z"l), Mark Haloossim, Efrem Harkham, Cary Lerman, Hallie Lerman, Elie Alyeshmerni, Tom Barad, Richard Baehr, Richard Becker, Miri Belsky, Carolyn Blashek, Ben Breslauer, Linda Camras, Omri Ceren, Eric Cohen, Jane Z. Cohen, Malcolm Cosgrove, Rabbi Zvi Dershowitz, Dovid Efune, Tom Flesh, Abner Goldstine, Roz Goldstine, Louis Gordon, Rabbi Mark Gottlieb, Gloria Greenfield, Rabbi Nicole Guzik, David Hazony, Dr. Phyllis K. Herman, Rabbi Sherre Hirsch, Ed Lasky, Rabbi Nolan Lebovitz, Andrea Levin, Ken Levin, Rick Lieberman, Angela Maddahi, Martin Mendelsohn (z"l), Jerry Nagin, Sharon Nazarian, Norman Pell (z"l), Andrew Pessin, Daniel Pipes, Daniel Polisar, Bruce Powell, Farshad Rafii, Maura Resnick, Jonathan Sarna, Samuel W. Schaul, Rabbi Erez Sherman, Michael Silberstein, Abraham Socher, David Suissa, Janey Sweet, Dov Waxman, Joel Weinstein, Francine Kahan Weiss, and Pam Wohl.

Finally, I thank my family, who gave me encouragement, suggestions, and assistance—my brother James D. Richman and sister Katherine Margaret Richman and her husband James Thornhill; my sisters- and brothers-in-law Angie and Dr. Bill Cloke and Steven and Alyce Rados; my mother-in-law Magda Rados; my sons Robert Richman and David Richman, and most of all, my brilliant wife, Judy Richman, who provided her invaluable perspective, read drafts with a perceptive and critical eye, and continually challenged my ideas to make them stronger. This book, like my life, has been blessed by her intelligence and love.

October 1, 2022
Los Angeles, California

INTRODUCTION

"Our past is not only behind us; it is in our very being."

—DAVID BEN-GURION

In "Everyman His Own Historian"—the 1931 keynote address to the American Historical Association—Cornell University professor Carl Becker defined history not as "the things said and done," but rather as "the *memory* of the things said and done."[1] Historical research, he said, was "of little import except insofar as it is transmuted into common knowledge." If it "lies inert" in libraries, it "does no work in the world."

In the twentieth century, *Americanism* (the civil religion of freedom and democracy) and *Zionism* (the movement to create a free and democratic Jewish state) were the two most successful "isms" of an ideological age.[2] The others—communism, fascism, national socialism, and antisemitism—murdered millions. But the stories of those involved in the historic work of Zionism and Americanism have in some cases been forgotten, or misrepresented, or not yet given their full due.

This book portrays eight individuals—four from Europe (Herzl, Weizmann, Jabotinsky, Eban) and four from America (Brandeis, Meir, Hecht, Dermer)—who reflect the intellectual and social revolutions that Zionism and Americanism brought to the world. The stories are important not only as individual tales, but even more so as a collective narrative. They illustrate the central ideological saga of the twentieth century—the struggle between free societies and their totalitarian enemies—and the relevance of that struggle to the emerging story of the twenty-first. The historic drama of Americanism and Zionism is a continuing one.

This book thus seeks to bring some seminal Jewish and American stories back into common knowledge, so they can do some work in the world.[3]

Modern Jewish history begins in 1895, when an assimilated Viennese journalist named ***Theodor Herzl*** resolved to lead his people out of Europe, into a land of their own. Covering the treason trial of Alfred Dreyfus in Paris, he heard the Parisian crowds shouting—or so the story goes—"Death to the Jews," which led him to write *The Jewish State*, his history-changing pamphlet. But that story is untrue. The Dreyfus trial played no role in Herzl's sudden conversion to Zionism. The actual story is more complicated, more captivating, and more consequential.

If Herzl was the key to the emergence of Zionism in Europe, the key in America was ***Louis D. Brandeis***—another assimilated Jew who ignored his Jewish heritage for the first fifty years of his life. But in 1914—two years before President Wilson nominated him to the Supreme Court—Brandeis agreed to lead the small American Zionist movement, after a chance meeting with one of Herzl's closest associates. Brandeis proceeded to connect Zionism to American ideals; articulated that connection in a series of landmark speeches; and played a key role in the issuance of the 1917 Balfour Declaration—the British commitment to a Jewish national home in Palestine.

The key to the Balfour Declaration in Britain was ***Chaim Weizmann***, born in 1876 in a *shtetl* in Russia, where he spent his first eleven years. In 1887, he left the *shtetl* for secondary school in Pinsk, eventually earned a doctorate in chemistry in Germany, and moved to Britain in 1904 to teach. In 1917, he represented the Jewish community in discussions with the British government about its draft Declaration. The following year, as World War I raged in the Middle East, he made an arduous five-day trip to the plains of Transjordan to meet Emir Faisal—the commander-in-chief of the Arab Revolt against the Ottoman Empire. In Faisal's tent, they forged a mutual understanding about the post-war liberation of their respective peoples, which they formalized in a 1919 agreement brokered by T. E. Lawrence (the legendary "Lawrence of Arabia"). The story not only illuminates the roots of Israel, but also the history of the Arabs in the twentieth century.

Vladimir Jabotinsky gave up a promising career as a journalist, essayist, and playwright in Odessa to devote his life to Zionism, becoming its most powerful orator and the founder of the Jewish Legion in 1917—the most significant Jewish military force in nearly two millennia. In the 1930s, he repeatedly warned Jews to leave Eastern Europe, while other leaders urged them to stay. In 1937, his testimony before British authorities and Members of Parliament—and his crucial meeting with Winston Churchill—were essential moments in Zionist history.

Golda Meir served as Israel's prime minister from 1967 to 1974—becoming the first woman ever to lead a Western government. She was born in Russia in 1898, grew up in Wisconsin, and moved at age twenty-three from the comfort of America to the frontier of Palestine. The story of her presence in 1938 at a little-remembered international conference in France marked both a personal turning point and a harbinger of a coming world war.

The story of ***Ben Hecht***—the highest-paid Hollywood screenwriter in the 1940s—is another tale of someone who disregarded his Jewish heritage for the first forty years of his life. But in 1941 he was—as he later put it—"walking down the street and bumped into history," when he met Peter Bergson, one of Jabotinsky's young followers. That meeting ultimately inspired him to stage dramas, organize rallies, and make public appeals to save the European Jews, while prominent leaders of American Jewry cautioned silence. With plays, books, and speeches, Hecht became a one-man multimedia operation, speaking and writing words that still reverberate today.

In 1948—one week after it declared its independence—Israel named a thirty-three-year-old former Cambridge University Fellow in Hebrew, Arabic, and Persian literature, ***Aubrey (Abba) Eban***, as its UN representative. Five days later, he appeared before the UN Security Council as Israel was being attacked by Arab armies on three sides, and he proceeded to deliver the first of his many addresses that would lead observers to compare him to Churchill. Eban's speeches still speak to us—not only because of their historic eloquence, but because some of the issues he addressed are still with us.

The return of a people to history—and the role in history that a single individual can play—is illustrated by the story of ***Ron Dermer***, born and raised in the United States, educated in the Ivy League, member of a politically prominent family in Florida—who relinquished his American citizenship to become an Israeli diplomat. To the one-page State Department document, "DS-4080 Oath of Renunciation," Dermer attached an extraordinary essay, entitled "Proud to Have Been an American." It articulated in memorable words the connection between Americanism and Zionism. Thereafter, as Israel's ambassador, he gave speeches that recalled those of Eban, and he played a key role in Washington in 2015, at a moment that linked twentieth-century history to the developing story of the twenty-first century.

Most contemporary readers know the story of David Ben-Gurion, who led Israel in its War of Independence and served as its first prime minister.[4] There are many other stories, however, less known but no less central to the miraculous recovery of the Jewish people in the twentieth century. Eight of them form this book, reflecting the history of Zionism and its relationship to Americanism from 1895 to the present.

These stories deserve to be restored to common memory—to *history*, as Professor Becker defined it. They make us realize that to create a history of our own, worthy of the one we have inherited, we must first become historians.

ONE

The Mystery of Theodor Herzl

"Perhaps a fair-minded historian will find that it was after all something that a Jewish journalist without means, in the midst of the deepest degradation of the Jewish people, in a time of the most sickening anti-Semitism, was able to create a flag out of rag-cloth and a nation out of a foundering rabble—a nation that flocked to this flag with straightened backs."

—HERZL IN HIS DIARY, JUNE 1, 1901[1]

Theodor Herzl in 1897

NOT SINCE MOSES LED the forty-year Exodus from Egypt did anyone transform Jewish history as fundamentally as Theodor Herzl did in seven years—from the publication in 1896 of his pamphlet *The Jewish State* to his historic pledge about Jerusalem at the Sixth Zionist Congress in 1903. Then he died suddenly in 1904, at the age of forty-four.

In 2017, on the centennial of the 1917 Balfour Declaration—Britain's promise to facilitate a Jewish national home in Palestine—Israel's Prime Minister Benjamin Netanyahu said the Declaration resulted "largely thanks to Herzl's brilliant appearances in England."

> Herzl created something out of nothing. He turned Zionism into a mass movement. He created the organizational and economic tools for the World Zionist Organization. Perhaps above all, he gained access to kings and counts . . . and this was no small thing [because a Jewish statesman] did not exist at the time, . . . certainly not one who was a journalist and playwright, and who was only thirty-six years old. It was unthinkable.[2]

An early Zionist and later historian, Oskar K. Rabinowicz, described the situation of the Jews at the end of the nineteenth century as follows:

> Jewry politically and nationally was a disorganized conglomeration of individuals, an amorphous, leaderless mass, oppressed in this or that part of the world, and despised in almost all strata of society in others. On the other hand, Great Britain, at the time, was the most powerful empire on earth. . . . And there he stood, Theodore Herzl, unknown in the English-speaking world, an individual, a Jew from Budapest, a man without a State behind him, without an organized people, without . . . [any] . . . of the

> means of power with which practical politics are made, dreaming of cooperation between Britain and Jewry.[3]

How did a young writer with no political connections, no ties to Jewish organizations, and no financial backing beyond his own resources, negotiate with leading figures in the Western world's ruling empires, engaging in what Netanyahu called "inconceivable diplomatic actions" that were, more than a century later, still "astonishing," and which would lead to the Balfour Declaration and eventually the creation of the modern state of Israel?[4]

How did a man opposed by Orthodox rabbis (who believed a Jewish state should await the messiah), Reform rabbis (who wanted a Jewish state relegated permanently to the past), assimilated Jews (who feared accusations of dual loyalty), Jewish socialists (who considered any type of nationalism reactionary), and Jewish public figures (who thought the whole idea absurd) create a worldwide movement?

Moreover, why did Herzl do all this, given his minimal ties to Judaism and the Jewish people during his early adulthood? He had a bar mitzvah and attended a predominantly Jewish high school, but he had sought assimilation ever since his days as a university student in Vienna.[5] Nor was he religiously observant as an adult: When his son was born in 1891, he did not have him circumcised. On December 24, 1895, six weeks before the publication of *The Jewish State*, Herzl was at home lighting a Christmas tree for his three children.[6]

For many years, the common belief was that Herzl became a Zionist as a result of covering the Dreyfus trial in 1894 in Paris for a Viennese newspaper. More recently, scholars have shown that Herzl's embrace of Zionism had nothing to do with that case.[7]

The story of Herzl thus presents a mystery. He came, seemingly, out of nowhere. At the beginning of 1895, no one would have predicted that the thirty-five-year-old literary editor of Vienna's *Neue Freie Presse* would propose the formation of a Jewish state; present the idea to London's Jewish elite; publish his historic pamphlet; establish the political, financial, and intellectual institutions for a state-in-waiting; negotiate with emperors, kings, dukes, ministers, the Pope, and the Sultan; hold six Zionist congresses attracting hundreds of delegates from more than twenty countries and regions around the world (their numbers increasing each year); produce two remarkable diplomatic achievements in 1903 that set the stage

David Ben-Gurion reading Israel's Declaration of Independence, May 14, 1948

for the Balfour Declaration—and then die heartbroken and impoverished in 1904, less than a decade after he began.

In 1897, a few days after the First Zionist Congress concluded in Basel, Herzl wrote in his diary that he had "founded the Jewish state":

> If I said this out loud today, I would be answered by universal laughter. Perhaps in five years, and certainly in 50, everyone will know it.[8]

In 1947—fifty years later—the United Nations endorsed a Jewish state in Palestine. Six months after that, David Ben-Gurion proclaimed its independence in Tel Aviv—a city that did not exist in 1897—under a massive photograph of Herzl, flanked by two flags identical to the one Herzl hung in Basel.

Ben-Gurion later wrote that Herzl, in the final years of his brief life, had "transformed a pulverized people."[9] He single-handedly turned Zionism—a movement that was, in the words of the early American Zionist Richard J. H. Gottheil, "[f]or the Reform Jews . . . too orthodox; for the Orthodox . . . not sufficiently religious; for the No-nothings . . . too Jewish"—into a movement that commanded the attention of every world power with an interest in the Middle East.[10]

In the long history of the Jewish people since their formation in the barren wilderness of the Sinai, no one had done so much, of such consequence, in so little time.

How and why did that happen?

At the First Zionist Congress in 1897, Herzl's principal ally, Max Nordau—one of the leading public intellectuals in the world—devoted his opening address to a worldwide survey of the condition of the Jewish people.[11] In Eastern Europe, North Africa, and the Middle East—where Nordau said "the overwhelming majority dwells, probably nine-tenths of all Jews"—Jewish life was "a daily affliction of the body; anxiety about the next day, an agonizing struggle to maintain a bare existence."

For the remaining ten percent of the Jewish people, living in the West, Nordau said there was a different, but no less serious, existential distress. Although they generally had food, shelter, and security, the Western Jews suffered from what he called a "distress of the spirit," one even more debilitating than physical deprivation:

> It consists in the harsh repression of [the Jews'] pursuit of higher satisfactions, the striving toward which no Gentile ever need deny himself. . . . This is the moral deprivation of Jews [in the West]. . . . The emancipated Jew is rootless, insecure in his relationship to his neighbors, fearful in his contact with strangers, distrustful of the secret feelings even of his friends.

For the Jewish people, the nineteenth century was ending at a low point, after a very recent historical high. The nineteenth century was the best century Jews had experienced since the destruction of the Temple.[12] They had been given equal rights throughout Europe; universities and professions were opened to them; even life in Russia had improved, as the enlightened Tsar Alexander II freed the serfs in 1861 and allowed Jews significant new personal and professional freedoms.[13]

But in the last two decades of the nineteenth century, a new political movement, with a new name—"antisemitism"—appeared in Germany and spread throughout Eastern Europe.

Growing up, Herzl was the quintessential product of the new Jewish age. Indeed, he embodied the assimilationist ideal.[14] Born in 1860 in Budapest to cultured, upper-middle-class Jewish parents, he grew up in the decade that saw emancipation of the Jews enacted into Hungarian law. His family was, in historian Carl Schorske's words, "economically established, religiously 'enlightened,' politically liberal, and culturally German."[15] Young Jews living in cities such as Warsaw, Berlin, and Vienna had unprecedented opportunities in European society. In 1878, at eighteen, Herzl entered the University of Vienna to study law.

In early 1881, Herzl was admitted to Albia, a selective dueling fraternity that was part of the German nationalist student movement. At the time, German nationalism was not a threat for a Jewish student such as Herzl, but rather an attraction. The movement endorsed liberal values; it was a brand of progressive politics, opposed in Austria to the conservative rule of the Hapsburg Empire—although anti-Jewish elements were present that would eventually overwhelm the movement. A number of illustrious Jews in the 1870s and early 1880s belonged to German nationalist student societies, including Gustav Mahler, Sigmund Freud, and Arthur Schnitzler.

With his admission into Albia, Herzl was joining the sons of aristocrats and professionals in a distinctive elite, its members wearing special insignia.[16] Herzl's entry into the top echelon of student society was the kind of achievement Jews had sought for their children for more than a century.[17] Dueling was an important social institution, a ritual for students to demonstrate their courage. After joining Albia, Herzl took fencing lessons for four hours a day (two from Albia and two privately); in his initiation duel, he received a small scar on his cheek as his badge of honor.

Herzl took "Tancred" as his fraternity name—the title character of Benjamin Disraeli's novel, *Tancred, or the New Crusade*. In 1881, Disraeli had just completed his service as the first Jewish-born British prime minister. In his novel, Tancred is a young Christian aristocrat who studies at Oxford and then travels to the Holy Land, where he meets Eva, a young Jewish woman, who defends "the splendor and superiority" of the Jews, and changes Tancred's view of them. *Tancred* was Disraeli's effort to express his view that the ideal faith was one that recognized both Christianity and Judaism.[18] In taking the name "Tancred"—an enlightened Christian who learned firsthand about the Jews and came to admire them—Herzl chose a name to make a point.[19]

Over the next two years, however, things began to change for both the Jews as a people and Herzl as an individual.

In 1881–82, two seminal books appeared, only one of which the twenty-one-year-old Herzl read. The unread one was *Auto-Emancipation: An Appeal to His People by a Russian Jew,* written anonymously by Leo Pinsker, a well-educated Jewish physician in Odessa.[20] Pinsker wrote it after pogroms swept through Russia in more than a hundred towns following the assassination of Tsar Alexander II by an anarchist group that included a Jew.[21]

Pinsker argued—in a book Herzl would not discover until after he wrote *The Jewish State*—that the "Jewish Question" could be solved only by national independence. The book had both intellectual force and literary grace, and it would become, in David Ben-Gurion's words in 1953, "the classic and most remarkable work of Zionist literature."[22] But it was not treated that way at the time. Pinsker wrote it in German, seeking to appeal to the educated Jews of the West. He traveled to Austria and Germany in search of Jewish leaders to support his ideas—and found none. The chief rabbi of Vienna dismissed him as crazy.[23] Faced with no Western support for his book, Pinsker concluded dispiritedly in 1884 that it would take the messiah—or "a whole legion of prophets"—to arouse the Jews. He called them a "half-alive people."[24]

What Herzl did read in 1882 was Eugen Dühring's highly influential book, *The Jewish Problem as a Problem of Race, Morals, and Culture,* which was an extended pseudo-scientific argument for antisemitism—a word first coined three years earlier by Wilhelm Marr, a German agitator who believed "the Semitic race" was trying to destroy Germany.[25] But unlike Marr, Dühring was a renowned intellectual and philosopher, who drew on Charles Darwin's influential ideas about the role of "favored races" in "the struggle for life." Dühring argued that Jews were an inferior race that must be purged, and his book was widely read not only by intellectuals and students, but also by the wider Austro-Hungarian public, making antisemitism broadly acceptable in Central European society.[26]

Herzl was stunned by the book.[27] It was, he wrote in his diary, "so well-written, [in] excellent German" by "a mind so well trained," and he even agreed with some of Dühring's criticisms of Jewish manners and social characteristics—although, unlike Dühring, he thought they were the result of centuries of social segregation rather than inherent Jewish qualities. He described Dühring's claims about the "Judaization of the press" as the "ancient accusation of Jewish poisoning of wells" expressed in "modern talk," and he believed Dühring had fundamentally misjudged the Jews: They had survived, Herzl noted in his diary, "1,500 years of inhuman pressure" through the "heroic loyalty of this wandering people to its God."[28]

Herzl later said his concern about the Jewish Question began when he read Dühring's book, more than a decade before the Dreyfus affair.[29] At the time, however, Herzl was confident that antisemitism was a passing phenomenon. He predicted "these nursery tales of the Jewish people will disappear, and a new age will follow, in which a passionless and clear-headed humanity will look back upon our errors even as the enlightened men of our time look back upon the Middle Ages."[30]

Herzl's progressive assumptions about the ineluctable progress of European morals, however, would be dispelled by something that soon took place in his own fraternity. It was there, in the heart of the society that had nominally accepted him, that Herzl would have his world turned upside down.

Herzl was among the last three Jews admitted to Albia, reflecting the growing influence of antisemitism. On March 5, 1883, the issue came to a head for Herzl after a memorial for the antisemitic composer Richard Wagner, held by the League of German Students, attended by 4,000 students. Several speakers gave, in the words of a contemporary press report, "coarse anti-Semitic utterances."[31] One of them was a representative of Albia.

After reading the newspaper account of the tirades, Herzl resigned from Albia. He wrote to the fraternity to protest the "benighted tendency which has now become fashionable," called it a threat to liberalism, and upbraided the fraternity's failure to oppose racial antisemitism.[32] Affronted by Herzl's letter, the fraternity instructed him to surrender his insignia at once. In his reply, Herzl wrote that "the decision to resign has not been an easy one."[33]

It was also a lonely one: Albia had several Jews among its members and a significant number of Jewish alumni, but only Herzl resigned.[34]

The new antisemitism, backed by pseudo-science, would be politicized in the following decade, resulting in opposition to any Jewish participation in public or social life.[35] It was fundamentally different from the old religious hatred. Racial antisemitism considered Jews literally a lower form of life and a biological threat to society, which could not be expunged merely by renunciation of Judaism, embrace of Christianity, or devotion to secular society—and certainly not simply by demonstrating personal honor through dueling.[36] It was an antisemitism based on blood.

Herzl received his Doctor of Laws degree in May 1884 and was admitted to the bar in July. He clerked in the courts for a year, grew bored with the work, and decided to pursue his real interest: playwriting. He would go on to write eleven plays—mostly light comedies—in the decade before he published *The Jewish State*. Some were produced on the stages of Vienna, Prague, Berlin, and in one case a German theater in New York. But most received disappointing reviews, or did not find a theater interested at all, and Herzl supported himself instead as a journalist. He became an accomplished writer of *feuilletons*—the short ironic essays that were one of the principal journalistic genres of the time—and he traveled throughout Europe seeking material. In 1887, he traveled to Rome, visiting the Jewish ghetto there (which remained in existence until 1889) and wrote about seeing the "pallid and worn-out faces" of the Jews:

> With what base and malicious hatred these unfortunate people have been tortured and persecuted for the sole crime of loyalty to their faith. We have traveled a long way since. Nowadays Jews are harangued only for having crooked noses, or for being rich even when they are poor.[37]

In 1889, at the age of twenty-nine, Herzl married Julie Naschauer, eight years his junior, the daughter of a wealthy Jewish businessman. The marriage was troubled from the start, and as success as a playwright eluded Herzl and relations with his wife worsened, he suffered from depression. But his *feuilletons* were widely admired, and in 1891, the *Neue Freie Presse*—one of Vienna's most respected newspapers, owned by two assimilated Jewish editors—asked him to become its Paris correspondent.

In Paris, Herzl did not personally experience antisemitism, but he remained troubled by the Jewish Question. In 1883, he considered challenging prominent anti-Semites to duels to demonstrate the honor of the Jewish people. In his diary, he wrote about an idea he thought could "solve the Jewish Question, at least in Austria, with the help of the Catholic Church."[38] He would meet the Pope and propose a "great movement for the free and honorable conversion of [young] Jews to Christianity," in ceremonies "in broad daylight, Sundays at noon, in Saint Stephen's Cathedral, with festive processions"—in exchange for a papal promise to fight antisemitism. His editors not only rejected the idea, but told him he had no right to suggest it.

At the end of 1894, Herzl addressed the Jewish Question for the first time in a play he ultimately called *The New Ghetto*, which he wrote in what he called "three blessed weeks of heat and labor." It featured a young liberal Jewish lawyer named Jacob Samuel—a stand-in for him—who rejects both Jewish materialism and Christian antisemitism. Samuel tells a rabbi that while the "outward barrier" of the Jewish ghetto is gone, Jews still had "inner barriers" that "we must clear away for ourselves." He dies defending Jewish honor in a duel with an Austrian nobleman, and his dying words are: "O Jews, my brethren, . . . get out! Out—of—the—Ghetto!"[39]

Despite months of effort, Herzl was unable to find a theater to stage the play. It would not be produced until three years later, after he had achieved fame as a Zionist, and even then it received only modestly favorable reviews. But after writing it, Herzl told a friend it had opened a "new path" for him—and "something blessed lies in it." In his diary, Herzl wrote:

> I had thought that through this eruption of playwriting I had written myself free of the matter. But on the contrary, I got more and more deeply involved with it. The thought grew stronger in me that I must do something for the Jews. For the first time I went to the synagogue in the Rue de la Victoire and once again found the services festive and moving. Many things reminded me of my youth and the Tabak Street Temple in Pest.[40]

The following year, Herzl wrote *The Jewish State*, after an extraordinary experience in June 1895 that both consumed and confounded him. The experience had an unmistakably biblical echo from the Book of Samuel—one that Herzl seemed to recognize near the end of his life. But it did not involve the trial of Alfred Dreyfus.

Alfred Dreyfus, a Jewish captain in the French army, was arrested for providing secret documents to Germany on October 15, 1894, the week before Herzl began writing *The New Ghetto*. Dreyfus's four-day closed court-martial ended in late December with a unanimous conviction by military judges after an hour of deliberation. They sentenced Dreyfus to life imprisonment and "degradation" (public shaming by stripping his insignia and breaking his sword). Only in 1898—nearly four years after the trial—when Emile Zola published "*J'Accuse*," accusing the government of framing Dreyfus to cover up a senior officer's treason, did the affair become the subject of public debate.

In 1894, almost everyone thought Dreyfus was guilty, an opinion Herzl shared—as evidenced by the articles he filed at the time. Herzl never suggested in his press reports that he thought the case had any particular significance, nor did he make any reference to it in his diary during June 1895, when his historic transformation into a Zionist occurred. Indeed, in the four volumes and 1,631 pages of his Zionist diaries, covering the nine-year period from 1895 to 1904, there are only twelve brief mentions of Dreyfus, none suggesting that the case played any role in Herzl's conversion to Zionism.

What happened to Herzl in June 1895, leading him to reject the assimilation to which he had, to that point, devoted his life, came from a different source.

In early 1895, Theodor Herzl was living alone in Paris at the Hotel Castille. When he became a foreign correspondent in 1891, his parents had moved to Paris to be near him. But they disliked the city (and his wife), and they moved back to Vienna in mid-1894. Herzl's tempestuous marriage had worsened even further, and in November 1894, Julie moved back to Vienna with their children.

At the age of thirty-four, Herzl was at a personal crossroads. After his initial, modest success as a playwright, his literary career had declined. He was a journalist and writer of light essays for a respected newspaper, but the work did not strike him as meaningful. Neither his plays nor his journalism had brought him the kind of success he had craved since his student days in Vienna. A third path, however, would open before him. He was about to become—in the words of his first English biographer, Jacob de Haas—"the chief actor in a world drama." Herzl himself would be mystified by how it happened.

At the end of March 1895, Herzl spent four days in Vienna visiting his family, and there he witnessed Vienna's April 1 municipal elections, in which Karl Lueger's Christian Social Party finished first. Lueger's movement wasn't simply anti-Semitic; its antisemitism was a central plank of its platform. It was the beginning of a process by which Vienna would soon become the first major European city with an overtly anti-Semitic government.

Vienna was Herzl's home, the capital of the Hapsburg Empire, the heart of Central Europe's high culture, the place where a Jewish population nearly twice as large as that of all of France flourished. In Vienna, political antisemitism could not be dismissed as "a salon for the castoffs," as Herzl had described the Parisian version. Austrian Jews were being accused of polluting the culture they had longed to join for a century, and not simply by a benighted clergy but by politicians and the population at large, in a democratic election.

Later that year, Herzl would witness Lueger's party win an even greater electoral victory, recording in his diary that he had observed "the hatred and the anger" at a polling station, when Lueger had suddenly appeared and been met with thunderous acclaim:

> Wild cheering; women waving white kerchiefs from the windows. The police held the people back. A man next to me said with loving fervor . . . "That is our *Führer*." More than all the declamation and abuse, these few words told me how deeply anti-Semitism is rooted in the heart of the people.[41]

Returning to Paris after his visit to Vienna, Herzl was overwhelmed with thoughts about the Jewish Question. They came to him while he was "walking, standing, lying down; in the street, at table, in the dead of night when I was driven from sleep." He wrote innumerable notes to himself, feeling a mystical compulsion to do so: "How I proceeded . . . is already a mystery to me, although it happened in the last few weeks. It is in the realm of the Unconscious."[42]

At first, Herzl thought he would write a novel about the Jewish situation. The French novelist Alphonse Daudet encouraged him to do so, suggesting it could galvanize readers in the way *Uncle Tom's Cabin* had. But Herzl decided instead to send a letter to Baron Maurice de Hirsch, one of the wealthiest men of the era, who had been financing settlements in Argentina for Russian Jews after the pogroms of 1881–82. As of 1894, however, the project had proved a failure, producing a total of four colonies and 3,000 settlers. In his letter, Herzl asked Hirsch—twenty-nine years his senior, whom he had never met—"to discuss the Jewish Question," assuring him that:

> I do not want to interview you nor to talk about a disguised or undisguised financial matter. . . . I simply wish to have a discussion with you about Jewish political matters, a discussion that may have an effect on times that neither you nor I will live to see.[43]

Herzl received a polite but dismissive reply, with Hirsch saying he would be in London for the following two months and thus unable to meet Herzl. He suggested Herzl tell him "in a letter what you were going to say to me in person." The response offended Herzl, who wrote back that "at the moment I am too busy to be brief, as the old saying goes," but "[a]s soon as I find the time, I shall submit to you a plan for a new Jewish policy." Then Herzl added a paragraph that apparently caused Hirsch to change his mind about meeting Herzl:

> What you have undertaken till now has been as magnanimous as it has been misapplied, as costly as it has been pointless. You have hitherto been only a philanthropist. . . . I want to show you the way to become something more.[44]

Two days later, Hirsch wrote to Herzl that in fact he would be in Paris for forty-eight hours during the coming week, and that they could meet on Sunday, June 2, at 10:30 a.m., at Hirsch's palatial home at 2 rue de l'Élysée.[45]

Herzl prepared twenty-two pages of notes for the meeting. He began by asking Hirsch to commit to "at least an hour" for the conversation; Hirsch smiled and said, "Just go ahead." Herzl told Hirsch that pure philanthropy was a mistake—"it debases the character of our people"—and that small-scale colonization was ineffective. Asked what he advised instead, Herzl said the morale of the Jewish people "must first of all be uplifted," and that then they would have to emigrate—whereupon Hirsch terminated the meeting.

Herzl had covered only the first six pages of his notes. He wrote to the Baron the next day, blaming himself for the truncated meeting:

> I still lack the aplomb which will come with time and which I shall need in order to break down opposition, shatter indifference, console distress, inspire a craven, demoralized people, and traffic with the masters of the earth.[46]

It was a single-sentence description of what the thirty-five-year-old Herzl would proceed to do over the next eight years.

Shortly after the meeting with Hirsch, Herzl began to keep a diary devoted to his new project. The first paragraph recorded how an all-consuming idea had taken over his life, a "work of infinite grandeur" that "accompanies me wherever I go, hovers behind my ordinary talk, looks over my shoulder at my comically trivial journalistic work, overwhelms me and intoxicates me." He felt he was in the grip of something beyond himself, writing in his entry on June 12: "Am I working it out? No! It is working itself out in me."

In that initial diary entry, Herzl recorded his fundamental ideas: (a) the new antisemitism "is a consequence of the emancipation of the Jews"—a reaction by those who perceived the Jews' new political and economic rights as a threat to their own; (b) it was a mistake to believe "that men can be made equal simply by publishing a law to that effect"; and (c) the Jews were still psychologically "Ghetto Jews," even though they had physically left the ghetto. They needed, Herzl believed, to change their minds—to recover their honor as Jews, to recognize that assimilation in Europe could not succeed, and to embrace a new Exodus.

The initial phase of Herzl's intellectual frenzy ran from June 5 to June 16, with about 150 diary entries during that time, covering eighty-three pages in printed form. He wrote every day (except Thursday, June 13), composing between eight and fifty-seven entries each day, ranging from single sentences in length to several pages each.

Herzl's diary entries would eventually become the basis of *The Jewish State*, the pamphlet he published eight months later. They covered every aspect of a planned and orderly exodus. He outlined new economic and political institutions ("the Jewish Company" and "the Society of Jews," the forerunners of what would become the Jewish National Fund and the Jewish Agency). He proposed large-scale public works, education "for one and all," creation of inspiring songs ("a *Marseillaise* of the Jews"), and an enlightened seven-hour workday (with two shifts, so each workday would have fourteen hours of work by two sets of workers). He noted that his project had aspects that were not only "moral-political" and "financial," but "technical, military, diplomatic, administrative, economic, artistic, etc." He wrote in his diary that he had made plans for them all.

At several points in these entries, Herzl noted both the simplicity of his idea and the magnitude of his concept: "It took at least thirteen years for me to conceive this simple idea. Only now do I realize how often I went right past it." But its execution would be a world-historical event that would eclipse its predecessor: "The Exodus under Moses bears the same relation to this project as does a [minor play] to a Wagner opera."[47]

Herzl's friends and acquaintances worried that he had gone mad. He confessed in his diary that he sometimes shared their concern:

> During these days, I have more than once been afraid I was losing my mind. This is how tempestuously the trains of thought have raced through my soul. A lifetime will not suffice to carry it all out. But I shall leave behind a spiritual legacy. To whom? To all men. I believe I shall be named among the greatest benefactors of mankind. Or is this belief already megalomania? . . . I think life for me has ended and world history begun.

Herzl comforted himself with the thought that "[t]he man who pointed to the cover of a teakettle lifted by steam and said, 'This is how I shall move people, animals, and freight, and give the world a new appearance,' was derided as a lunatic."[48] He wrote that his project "would be an obsession if it were not so rational from beginning to end," and he suggested that the better term for what he was experiencing was "inspiration." His continual fear, he wrote, was captured in a poem he copied into his diary by Paul Johann Ludwig von Heyse, a German writer who later received the Nobel Prize: "*I shudder to think that I could depart overnight / Depart before I have completed this work*."[49] Herzl was concerned not only because of the magnitude of his project, but because of something he had disclosed to no one outside his family: He had a serious heart condition.

On June 17, Herzl wrote to the chief rabbi of Vienna to assure him that he was "neither completely nor even partially mad":

> My plan is actually as serious as the situation of the Jews itself, and I feel that the Jews in their torpor do not realize this seri-

> ousness clearly enough. . . . [Y]ou cannot even suspect the degree of heat which this interest has reached [in me]. . . . [J]ust as antisemitism forces the half-hearted, cowardly, and self-seeking Jews into the arms of Christianity, it powerfully forced my Jewishness to the surface. . . . I have the solution of the Jewish Question. I know it sounds mad; but in the initial period people will often think me mad until they realize with deep emotion the truth of all I have been saying. I have found the solution, and it no longer belongs to me; it belongs to the world.

Herzl told the rabbi he could not account for the derivation of his idea or its hold on him:

> How did I discover it? I do not know. . . . I consider it a great good fortune that I have found it. . . . I confess to you that I have tears in my eyes as I write this; but I shall carry it through with all rigor.[50]

On June 14, Herzl wrote of acquainting the world "with something that has not been considered possible in 2000 years: Jewish honor." He recounted weeping while writing about "the misfortunes of my people" and his vision of a new land for them. He resolved to "take along all beggars, all peddlers"—and also the wealthy, "who are well advised [to] build their palaces over there," in a new Jewish home:

> The Rothschilds have no idea of how endangered their property already is. They live in a phony circle of courtiers, servants, employees, papers, and aristocratic spongers. . . . I will satisfy all: Poor men, rich men, workers, intellectuals, governments, and anti-Semitic peoples.

What possessed Herzl to imagine that he would be leaving a legacy not only to the Jews, but also "to all people everywhere"? How would he be an actor not only in Jewish history, but "world" history? He gave what we may deem his answer in another diary entry the same day:

> [T]he Jewish state will become something remarkable. [It] will be not only a model country, . . . but a miracle country in all civilization. . . . The Jewish state is a world necessity. . . .

What Herzl had in mind was not only to lead the Jews out of Europe, but also to take European liberalism with them—to use it in a land where the Jewish spirit could flourish, as Europe began to destroy liberalism (and eventually itself) with its Jew-hatred. He wanted not only to save the Jews, but also to save liberalism itself, with a single idea: a Jewish homeland that, through its existence, would (i) address the problems of the Jews, (ii) solve the issues the world had with the Jews, and (iii) avoid the emerging threat to European liberalism of antisemitism—all at once.[51]

While Herzl was dreaming of an "experimental land for [all] humanity," some regarded him as mad for dreaming of a state for a minuscule (and powerless) part of humanity. But a case can be made—particularly in light of what came to pass in the following decades to Europe, to European liberalism, and to the European Jews—that Herzl's call for a Jewish state to ward off a world catastrophe affecting all three, and doing so three decades before Adolf Hitler took power in Germany, was a prophetic message.

In mid-June of 1895, Herzl drafted a long address to the Rothschild Family Council, the forum of the other immensely wealthy Jewish family of the time. He outlined his vision of the "Promised Land"—a place, Herzl wrote, where:

> at last we can live as free men on our own soil and die in peace in our own homeland. Where we, too, can expect honor as a reward for great deeds; where we shall live at peace with all the world, which we shall have freed through our own freedom. . . . [W]e shall move out to the Promised Land, the Land of the Seven Hours, the land which God has promised us in His inscrutable goodness, under the bright banner which we shall fashion for ourselves.[52]

But he was unable to elicit any interest from the Rothschilds.

Herzl published *The Jewish State* on February 14, 1896, analyzing antisemitism as a "national question" that could "only be solved by making it a political world-question."[53] It was translated that year from its original German into English, French, Russian, Yiddish, Hebrew, Romanian, and Bulgarian.[54] In an essay in November 1896, entitled "Judaism"—by which Herzl meant something closer to "Jewish identity" than to the religion itself—Herzl supplemented his argument, writing that Judaism was the key to the "lost inner wholeness" of the Jewish people:

> The atrocities of the Middle Ages were unprecedented, and the people who withstood those tortures must have had some great strength, an inner unity which we have lost. A generation which has grown apart from Judaism does not have this unity. It can neither rely upon our past nor look to our future. That is why we shall once more retreat into Judaism and never again permit ourselves to be thrown out of this fortress.[55]

The Jewish State received a cool reaction from the *Jewish Chronicle*, then as now the leading Jewish newspaper in London, which printed Herzl's long prepublication summary of his pamphlet in its issue of January 14, 1896. In an adjoining editorial, the *Chronicle* called it "a scheme hastened, if not dictated, by panic," saying it was notable for coming from "a man of Dr. Herzl's type," one who "does not lay claim to a deep loyalty to [religious] Judaism," and upbraided him for his "dark and discouraging view." The *Chronicle* concluded that "We hardly anticipate a great future for a scheme which is the outcome of despair."[56]

Undeterred, Herzl organized the First Zionist Congress virtually single-handedly, underwriting the cost out of his own pocket.[57] In mid-1897, however, two months before it was scheduled to begin, he faced a professional crisis that almost derailed the entire effort.

Herzl had decided to start a newspaper devoted to the Zionist movement, calling it *Die Welt* ("The World"), and he published the first issue on June 4, 1897.[58] When the publishers of the *Neue Freie Presse*—both vehement anti-Zionists—learned of his endeavor, they urged him to shut it down, complaining that it was a source of "great embarrassment" to them.[59] Herzl realized they were threatening to fire him, but he wrote in his diary that "I face this possibility with composure":

> My heart is pounding, to be sure, but this is only a weakness of the muscle, not of my will. Should the *N. Fr. Pr.* [Herzl's abbreviation for the *Neue Freie Presse*] drive me out, I shall have lost my position, which I acquired through twenty years of hard work, [but] in a manner of which I need not be ashamed.[60]

Herzl told the publishers that "I certainly don't want to cause embarrassment to the *N. Fr. Pr.* I am devoted to the paper . . . I have put part of my life and health into the *N. Fr. Pr.*" But he was unwilling to cease publishing his Zionist newspaper. Two days later, one of the publishers, Moritz Benedikt, called Herzl into his office and again urged him to give up *Die Welt,* and not play a prominent part at the Zionist Congress. In his diary, Herzl wrote, "Of course I remained inflexible."

Proceeding in the face of opposition from his employers carried both professional and personal risks for Herzl. He owed much of his reputation to the *Neue Freie Presse,* with its wide readership not only in Vienna but throughout Europe.[61] He was jeopardizing both his personal finances and his intellectual influence at the same time. But he was undeterred.[62]

The opposition to his Zionist Congress came not only from his employer but also from various elements of the Jewish community. Herzl had planned to hold the Congress in Munich, a city convenient for delegates to reach, with a significant Jewish population and many kosher restaurants. But the Jewish leadership in Munich protested, and Herzl and his organizing committee had to shift the location to Basel.[63]

Herzl worked simultaneously on the Congress and *Die Welt,* in addition to his *Neue Freie Presse* work, "exhausting all my strength." The amount of work, he wrote in August, has been "enormous."[64] On August 23, with the Congress only a week away and the outcome still uncertain, he wrote in his diary that if the Congress did not produce serious results, he would "withdraw from the campaign and confine myself to keeping the flame alive in the *Welt.*"

The First Zionist Congress attracted 204 delegates from twenty countries and regions.[65] About half came from areas within the Russian and Austro-Hungarian empires (where 80 percent of the Jews in the world then lived). The rest came from Germany, Italy, Switzerland, England, France, Bulgaria, the Netherlands, Serbia, Belgium, Sweden, Palestine, and the United States.[66]

The Congress lasted three days and adopted the platform (the "Basel Program") that would govern Zionist efforts for the following twenty years, culminating in the Balfour Declaration. The Basel Program defined the goal of Zionism as "establishing for the Jewish people a publicly and legally assured home in Palestine."[67]

Herzl insisted the delegates dress in formal attire to reflect the dignity of the event, and he hung a flag in the conference hall with a white field (symbolizing a new Jewish future), two blue strips (resembling a *tallit*), and a Star of David at the center (reflecting the centrality of Jewish identity to the movement).[68] Herzl had spent considerable time working on the flag with the Russian Jewish businessman-turned-Zionist activist David Wolffsohn, since he viewed the flag as extremely important. In his letter to Baron Hirsch in 1895, Herzl had written, "Men live and die for a flag; it is indeed the only thing for which they are willing to die. . . . Visions alone grip the souls of men."[69]

Herzl's appearance on the first morning of the Congress caused, according to the annotated translation of the official proceedings, "prolonged and forceful clapping, cheering, foot-stomping, and cane-pounding."[70] In his address, Herzl described the situation of the Jewish people in terms that could have been a summary of his own experience:

> [I]n this era, which is otherwise so sublime, we see and feel ourselves everywhere surrounded by the old hatred. . . . The first reaction the Jews of today had . . . was surprise, which then changed to pain and anger. . . . The feeling of group solidarity, for which we have been so frequently and fiercely reproached, was in the process of complete dissolution when we were attacked by antisemitism.

Herzl discussed the "raising of the people" that he saw as the critical first ingredient of Jewish nationalism:

> We have, so to speak, come home. Zionism means a returning home to Jewish identity before the return to the country of the Jews. . . . A people can only be helped by itself; and if it cannot do that, then it is quite beyond help. We Zionists want to arouse our people to self-help.

Herzl told the delegates that the goal of Zionism was public legal guarantees of "the historic homeland of the [Jewish] nation, precisely because it is the historic homeland":

> In this Congress we are creating for the Jewish people an agency they have not hitherto possessed but which it has needed most urgently for its survival. . . . And our Congress will live on eter-

> nally . . . restoring to all Jews their dignity, and making them worthy of a history whose glory, if perhaps now faded, is nonetheless imperishable.

The official record notes that "passionate applause" lasting fifteen minutes followed Herzl's address.[71]

On the final evening session of the Congress, Arthur Cohn, the thirty-five-year-old Orthodox rabbi of Basel, gave his address. He received, according to the official minutes, "a thunderous welcome." Rabbi Cohn said that "my heart swells with deep emotion" after hearing the speeches of Herzl and Max Nordau, but he said that he was concerned that, "if the Jewish state were to arise now, its party leadership, which we know does not honor [religious Jewry's] views, would attack the Orthodox." He asked for some clarification about this issue.

Herzl responded by thanking him, "our erstwhile opponent," for "the frankness of his request," and told him: "I can assure you, Zionism intends nothing that might violate the religious conviction of any orientation within Jewry," which produced another round of "thunderous applause."

Herzl concluded the Congress with this summary of what it had meant:

> We cannot say how things will turn out in the future. But we have done something significant for our people. . . . [W]e want to put a plow in the hand of the downtrodden . . . [and] on the day when the plow rests once again in the newly strengthened hand of the Jewish farmer, the Jewish question will have been solved.

Just before the Congress dispersed, Professor Max Mandelstamm of Kiev rose to praise "first and foremost . . . the courageous man to whom we principally owe our thanks . . . the highly esteemed president of the Congress, Herr Dr. Theodor Herzl." Mandelstamm asked "earnestly" that:

> the hard labor which he is performing and which still awaits him, and also the irksome things that have befallen him and are yet to befall him—that these should not keep him from bringing to a victorious conclusion the difficult work that has been initiated, in the same way, with the same spirit, and the same joyous self-sacrifice.

It is safe to say that no one guessed the magnitude of the "irksome things" that would soon befall Herzl, or that he had only seven years left to live.

Herzl had created an atmosphere—out of nothing—that made the delegates feel that they were the National Assembly of a Jewish state. One of the delegates, in a letter written soon after the Congress, observed that "attitudes toward Zionism have changed completely. This is true of the rabbis, the intelligentsia, and the community as a whole."[72]

That Zionism had transformed not only the delegates, but Herzl himself, is apparent in a tale he published in *Die Welt* later that year, about an artist who had long ignored his Jewish roots and was living comfortably when "the age-old hatred re-asserted itself under a fashionable slogan." The artist's soul is a "bleeding wound," but he experiences a "mysterious affection" for Jewish identity as the solution to Jewish suffering. A "strange mood came over him"—the memory of Hanukkah as a child. He buys a menorah and tells his children about the Maccabees. The "great radiance" of the menorah, reflected in their eyes, satisfies his "longing for beauty." The artist sees the week-long candle-lighting as "a parable for the kindling of a whole nation":

> First one candle; it is still dark, and the solitary light looks gloomy. Then it finds a companion, then another, and yet another. The darkness must retreat. The young and the poor are the first to see the light; then the others join in, all those who love justice, truth, liberty, progress, humanity, and beauty. When all the candles are ablaze everyone must stop in amazement and rejoice at what has been wrought.

Scholars and biographers have viewed "The Menorah" as a charming autobiographical story, reflecting Herzl's return to his Jewish identity, expressing what he had achieved in only two years. Herzl himself viewed it as reflecting something greater than merely his own personal evolution: He told Jacob de Haas it represented his ability to see in the Menorah the "brilliantly lit-up new Jerusalem" while others saw only melted wax.[73]

Perhaps in retelling the story of Hanukkah, Herzl was also recalling a part of *Tancred*—the Disraeli novel from which he had chosen his fraternity name—which devoted an entire chapter to Sukkot, described by the Jewess Eva as "one of our great national festivals," the "celebration of the Hebrew vintage, the Feast of Tabernacles." Disraeli wrote in *Tancred* that:

> The vineyards of Israel have ceased to exist, but the eternal law enjoins the children of Israel still to celebrate the vintage. A race

> that persist in celebrating their vintage, although they have no fruits to gather, will regain their vineyards.[74]

In 1899, in an article based on an interview with Herzl, a journalist recounted that, as she listened to his "warm, expressive voice" and "vibrant, moving words," she had been reminded of that passage from *Tancred*. Herzl had told her that:

> "you would not believe that even among the Jews my project has many enemies. Some don't understand it, others don't want to understand it, still others seek to interpret my motives, to see in them the calculations of ambition and interest, there where there is an idea which has taken possession of me. . . . But no matter; I go forward with my dream, in my dream, if you will, and for it. It is so dear to me. . . ."[75]

In two years, Herzl had taken his ideas to the major Jewish philanthropic families (who refused to support them); to the Jewish intelligentsia (who generally dismissed them); and then to the Jewish public (who were inspired in numerous countries). He had established a Zionist Congress that formally adopted the goal of a Jewish state. Now came an even greater challenge: whether to hold out for the land of Palestine or to accept a site more readily available—and in either case having to convince the ruling country to permit the Jews to rebuild their national homeland there, while simultaneously trying to persuade the innumerable Jewish skeptics that the whole effort was realistic and worthwhile.

It is frequently noted that Herzl did not originate the idea of a Jewish state—he said so himself in the opening sentence of *The Jewish State*. His contribution to Jewish political thought was rather his understanding of the intellectual transformation necessary to achieve statehood.[76]

He captured his approach in an epigram—"*If you will it, it is no dream.*"[77] Herzl's fundamental insight was that, before the Jewish people would be ready for a state, they would first have to change their character—through a process not unlike what their ancestors had undergone in the desert with Moses—and to revive their will as a people.[78] Herzl's second insight was that it was necessary to convert the Jewish Question from one of philanthropy supported by wealthy Jewish families to an issue of international relations in the world.[79]

Ahad Ha'am, the most prominent Hebrew-language essayist of the time, and a leader of the Russian "Love of Zion" movement that Leo Pinsker had helped to found, attended the First Zionist Congress as a skeptical observer—and he did not come away swayed.[80] Shortly afterwards, he wrote an essay asserting that a Jewish state was "a fantasy bordering on madness."[81] He argued instead for building in Palestine a "center for the spirit of Judaism" that would "breathe new life into the Diaspora." The "secret of our people's persistence," he wrote, was that "the prophets taught to respect only spiritual power, not to worship material power." In contrast to Herzl's slogan, Ahad Ha'am drew his own from the Book of Numbers (24:17): "*I shall see it, but not now; I shall behold it, but not nigh.*"[82]

It was the beginning of a fierce clash between the "cultural Zionism" of Ahad Ha'am and the "political Zionism" of Herzl—between those who wanted a spiritual center to save Judaism, and those who wanted a state to save the Jews.[83] There would eventually be other types of Zionism—Religious Zionism, Chaim Weizmann's practical or "organic" Zionism, Vladimir Jabotinsky's Revisionist Zionism, and David Ben-Gurion's Labor Zionism—each seeking a Jewish home but on different ideological grounds. The sheer breadth of these varying approaches made Zionism an ideology that could attract Jews from left to right, and the intellectual competition among and between them sharpened Zionism as a whole.

Herzl's vision of Zionism through the lens of international relations stemmed from his realization that—as he told the Second Zionist Congress in 1898—Palestine was "by reason of [its] geographical position, of immense importance to the whole of Europe."[84] At the Fourth Zionist Congress in 1900, he elaborated on his view:

> Our reappearance in the land of our fathers, prophesied by Holy Writ, sung by our poets, yearned for amidst tears by our stricken nation, and jeered at by miserable scoffers—that Return is a matter of political moment to the powers that have interests in Asia.[85]

Herzl saw that a Jewish state in Palestine would be of interest to all four empires that ruled the Western world: to Great Britain, as a gateway to India; to the Ottoman Empire, as a way to secure international refinancing of its debilitating debt; to Russia, as a solution for its large and rebellious Jewish population; and to Germany and Austria-Hungary, as a strategic asset in their competition with the other empires.

Finally, Herzl linked the nationalism of the Jews to the wave of nationalist efforts of others. As he told Lord Nathaniel Mayer Rothschild (head of the English branch of the family) in 1902:

> In our own time, Greeks, Romanians, Serbs, Bulgarians have established themselves [in independent states]—and should *we* be incapable of doing so? Our race is more efficient in everything than most other peoples of the earth. This, in fact, is the cause of the great hatred. We have just had no self-confidence up to now. Our moral misery will be at an end on the day when we believe in ourselves.[86]

In the years following the First Zionist Congress, Herzl began to establish a Jewish national bank, traveled to Palestine in 1898 to meet the Kaiser in Jerusalem, met with the president of the Austrian ministry, received an audience with the Grand Duke of Baden, met twice with Sultan Abdul Hamid II in Constantinople, and convened the Congress annually in Basel—except in 1900, when the Congress met in London as part of an effort to engage Britain. In 1902, Herzl testified in London before the British Royal Commission on Alien Immigration, which had been established to investigate the influx of Jewish refugees from Russia and Romania. The British Jewish population had risen to about 100,000, prompting alarm about the continuing inflow.

Three days before his testimony, Herzl met privately with Lord Rothschild, who sat on the Commission and saw Zionism as a threat to the acceptance of British Jews as loyal subjects. He asked Herzl to support the idea of Jews as Englishmen in his testimony—and Herzl flatly refused: "it would be a stupid piece of arrogance . . . to give the Commission a lecture on the characteristics of a real Englishman." Herzl said he would "simply tell them what frightful misery prevails among eastern Jewry, and that the people must either die or get out."[87] A stunned Rothschild asked Herzl *not* to tell the Commission *that*, because the government was already worried about excessive Jewish immigration. Herzl responded that "certainly I shall say it," and he told Rothschild, "Jewish philanthropy had become a machine for stifling the cries of distress."[88]

Three days later, Herzl told the Commission that "the state of Jewry is worse today than it was seven years ago when I published my pamphlet"; that in Eastern Europe—where most of world Jewry lived—things were "becoming worse and worse day by day"; and that the solution was "recognition of Jews as a people, and the finding by them of a legally recognized home," so they would "arrive there as citizens . . . because they are Jews, and not as aliens."[89]

During the questioning, Lord Rothschild asked Herzl to define what he meant by "Zionism"—whether it was a "movement to re-establish a Jewish state in Palestine, or whether . . . you simply mean that some great endeavor should be made to colonize some part of the world entirely with Jews." Herzl knew it was a loaded question: He was being asked whether Zionism sought to establish the Jews as a nation—which produced fears in the Rothschilds and other prominent British Jews of accusations of dual loyalty—or only to build a refuge for Jews somewhere, which Jewish philanthropists could support. Herzl responded by saying it was both:

> [T]he aims of Zionism are to create a legally assured home for the Jewish people in Palestine. . . . [That] is certainly the goal, but there may be moments where immediate help or a step forward is indispensable, and so Zionists believe that, maintaining always their principle and program, they should in the meantime try to alleviate the hard conditions of oppressed Jews by adequate means.[90]

Within that answer lay the dual nature of Zionism in 1902. It had both an ultimate objective (a Jewish state in Palestine) and an immediate need (a refuge for Jews under existential threat). It was not clear if those goals could be pursued together, or whether at some point they would necessitate a choice. Herzl was trying to keep both options open. He informed the Commission that he received "30 or 40 letters" every day from Russia, where Jews lived in "a permanent state of misery [because they] cannot better their condition; they cannot go into another town to find work; they are under a constant pressure," with no one "sure of his life tomorrow," living "in a perpetual fear with the madness of persecution." In Romania, he testified, more than 37,000 starving Jews had petitioned the First Zionist Congress for help, and their conditions had not improved; in Galicia, about 700,000 Jews were in "very deep misery," living in cramped quarters, sometimes four families in the four corners of a single room—compared to which the worst slums in London were, he said, a "paradise."[91]

Herzl's testimony was eloquent, but he felt he had performed poorly, confiding to his diary that he had spoken and understood English badly. The next day he met the chairman of the Commission, Lord James of Hereford, hoping to "repair the bad impression which I felt I had made." Lord James told him a Jewish colony somewhere could only be achieved with the help of Lord Rothschild, and so Herzl met with Rothschild again the following day and promised to send him a plan for an immediate Jewish colony somewhere.[92] Herzl's transmittal letter read:

> You are the most effective force that our people has possessed since their dispersion, and I consider it my duty to place my humble advice at your disposal if you really wish to do something effectual for our unfortunates. . . . A great Jewish settlement in the eastern Mediterranean [such as Cyprus] would strengthen our own efforts for Palestine. . . . I cannot permit myself to turn away on grounds of principle from any source or form of immediate relief for our poorest of the poor.[93]

On July 21, 1902, Herzl wrote to Lord Rothschild once again, in an effort to present the Zionist case in terms of its benefits to British interests, telling him "you may claim high credit from your government if you strengthen British influences in the Near East by a substantial colonization of our people at [a] strategic point." He emphasized that immediate action was necessary, lest the opportunity vanish:

> Then it will turn out that we Jews, we smart but always outsmarted Jews, will once again have missed the boat. The thing can now be done: big and quick, through the [land company] of which I sent you a general outline.[94]

A month later, Lord Rothschild replied, not only rejecting Herzl's plan but also telling him he "view[ed] with horror the establishment of a Jewish Colony pure and simple." All it would mean, he said, was relief for a few thousand Jews. He preferred that Jews "live amongst their Christian brethren" as "good citizens" and warned that everyone should "beware the impossible [dream of a Jewish state]."[95] In his response, Herzl countered that the Greeks, Romanians, Serbs, and Bulgarians had all recently established themselves in their own nation-states, and that there was no reason the Jews could not do so as well. He assured Lord Rothschild that the problems with a Jewish state would be surmounted:

> Naturally there will always be fights and difficulties, internal and external ones. But what country, what state does not have them? And we shall always produce the men to grapple with these difficulties.[96]

Two months after his testimony before the Commission, Herzl began discussions with (as he described him in his diary) "the famous master of England, Joe Chamberlain." Joseph Chamberlain was Britain's colonial secretary and the most influential member of the Cabinet (and father of the future prime minister, Neville Chamberlain). Herzl wanted him to designate territory for a Jewish colony somewhere within Britain's far-flung empire.

On October 23, 1902, Herzl spent an hour with Chamberlain, writing in his diary afterward that "my voice trembled at first, which greatly annoyed me," but after a few minutes, "I was able to talk calmly and incisively, to the extent that my rough-and-ready English permits it." Addressing Chamberlain's "motionless mask," Herzl "presented the whole Jewish Question as I understand it and wish to solve it."

> "I am in negotiation with the Sultan," I said. "But you know what Turkish negotiations are. If you want to buy a carpet, first you must drink half a dozen cups of coffee and smoke a hundred cigarettes; then you discuss family stories, and from time to time you speak again a few words about the carpet. Now, I have time to negotiate, but my people has not. They are starving in the Pale. I must bring them an immediate help."

Chamberlain told Herzl that he sympathized with Zionism. Herzl asked for territory either in sparsely populated Cyprus in the Eastern Mediterranean, or in El Arish on Egypt's Mediterranean coast, which was largely uninhabited. Either location, he told Chamberlain, would be "a rallying point for the Jewish people in the vicinity of Palestine." The next day, Herzl sent a memorandum, outlining a plan for a Jewish colony in El Arish. Chamberlain sent it to Lord Evelyn Cromer, the consul-general in British-ruled Egypt. Herzl noted in his diary that he had so worn himself out that his heart had been "acting up in all sorts of mysterious ways." But he thought his exhaustion might presage something historic: "Is it possible that we stand on the threshold of obtaining a—British—charter and founding the Jewish state?"[97]

Lord Cromer responded on November 22, 1902, noting political and other difficulties, but urging further study. Herzl and the British authorities reviewed the issues over the following months, and Herzl commissioned a draft agreement from the law firm of David Lloyd George. But eventually the Egyptian administration objected, and the project was dropped in mid-1903.[98]

The collapse of Herzl's efforts for El Arish coincided with a horrific pogrom in Kishinev (now called Chisinau in Moldova), about 90 miles northwest of Odessa.[99] Kishinev was not a remote *shtetl*; it was Russia's fifth-largest city, a provincial capital with 110,000 residents, one-third to one-half of whom were Jewish.[100]

The two-day rampage in Kishinev began on April 19, 1903—four months before the Sixth Zionist Congress was scheduled to convene. Forty-nine Jews (including children) were murdered; innumerable women were raped; injuries ran into the hundreds; some one thousand homes were destroyed or damaged. On April 26, in its Sunday edition, the *New York Times* reported, "Scores of Jews Killed: Details of the Anti-Semitic Riots . . . Add to the Horrors."

The pogrom inspired the most influential poem in modern Jewish history, Chaim Nachman Bialik's epic "In the City of Slaughter," translated from Hebrew into Russian by a twenty-four-year-old journalist, Vladimir Jabotinsky, and read even more widely in translation than the original.[101] Dr. Jacob Bernstein-Kohan, the director of the World Zionist Organization's press department, lived in Kishinev, and he used his contacts with the Western media to publicize the pogrom. Reaction spread throughout the United States, with continual press reports and protests.[102] There were demonstrations in 27 states; 80 newspapers published more than 151 scathing editorials; senators, congressmen, and mayors made speeches condemning the atrocities.[103] The Hearst newspapers sent Michael Davitt, a respected journalist, to Kishinev to interview survivors. His vivid reports were turned into a best-selling book.[104]

The B'nai B'rith prepared a formal petition to the Tsar, signed by 12,544 prominent American political figures, publishers, and Christian clergy, and asked President Theodore Roosevelt to submit it to Russia.[105] Secretary of State John J. Hay at first rejected the idea:

> [N]o one hates more energetically than [President Roosevelt] does such acts of cruelty and injustice as those we deplore. But he must carefully consider all the circumstances and then decide whether any official action can be taken in addition to the impressive and most effective expression of public opinion in this country.[106]

Roosevelt eventually directed John W. Riddle, the American chargé d'affaires in St. Peterburg, to seek an audience with the Russian foreign minister and deliver the B'nai B'rith petition to him. But the Russian government refused to accept it, and the Roosevelt administration dropped the issue.[107]

It was Theodor Herzl who took Kishinev beyond protest and petition.

On May 8, 1903, Herzl published an article in *Die Welt* promising that what had happened to "our brothers in distant Bessarabia" (the province where Kishinev was located) would not be forgotten. He vowed that, unlike previous pogroms, this one would generate an effective response, and not merely the usual outpouring of distress:

> Always when Jews are attacked, a current of sympathy passes through the race. One helps, counsels, as the occasion suggests; the fugitives escape from the horde to a safe distance; the dead are buried. When the grass grows over the graves, the event is forgotten—out of mere self-love, because we want to eat our breakfast in peace and contentment, with happy children round about . . . [but] *we will not forget Kishineff.*[108]

Herzl had been seeking a meeting with Russian officials since 1896, both directly and through intermediaries, but his requests had all been rebuffed. In the wake of Kishinev, he wrote again on May 19, 1903, to the powerful Russian minister of the interior, Vyacheslav Plehve, requesting his support for an "organized emigration" of Jews from Russia.[109] Plehve was widely considered to be harshly anti-Jewish. Shortly after the pogrom, the *Times of London* published a letter—shown decades later to have been a forgery—purportedly sent by Plehve to the Kishinev police before the pogrom, signaling government support for the coming violence.[110] Many Zionists thought it was shameful that Herzl would consider meeting with such a man.

But Herzl saw that he and Plehve had a mutual interest: Plehve didn't want Jews in Russia, and Herzl wanted them to be permitted to leave—with a place to go. He believed Russia could influence the Sultan to permit a Jewish homeland in Palestine, and he knew Plehve needed to improve Russia's image in the West. Kishinev would be discussed at the upcoming Zionist Congress in a few weeks, with the international press in attendance.[111]

Plehve and Herzl met on August 8, 1903, and Plehve agreed that Jewish emigration was the answer. He promised to make an "effective intervention" with the Sultan for a charter in Palestine and to permit Zionist activity in Russia. On August 12, Herzl received a formal letter from Plehve, confirming that Russia favored the creation of "an independent state in Palestine." Plehve told him the letter had been reviewed by the Tsar and thus was an official declaration of the Russian government. Herzl published it in *Die Welt* and considered it extremely important: It was the first formal governmental endorsement of a Jewish state, and he could use it as a diplomatic lever elsewhere.[112]

On August 14, 1903, the second major endorsement of a Jewish homeland came when the British made a formal offer of land in East Africa for Jewish settlement, to be named "New Palestine."[113] Herzl thought the British offer was another important step forward: He told his ally Max Nordau that "we have, in our relationship with this gigantic nation, acquired recognition as a state-building power." But most importantly, there had to be, Herzl thought, "an answer to Kishinev, and this is the only one" immediately available. He arranged for a draft charter to be prepared by the law firm of David Lloyd George.[114]

At the Zionist Congress in August, with 592 delegates in attendance, Herzl presented his two great diplomatic triumphs—the official recognition of Zionist goals by both Britain and Russia, two of the world's largest empires. He expected to receive praise for his efforts. But the sizable Russian delegation reacted in a fury, believing Plehve had taken advantage of Herzl and that the British offer was a dangerous diversion from Palestine. Some accused Herzl of a willingness to abandon the Promised Land altogether.[115]

Max Nordau urged the delegates to view East Africa as a *Nachtasyl*, a "shelter for the night," offered by the greatest power on earth. It would be irresponsible, he argued, not to form at least an exploratory delegation.[116] The delegates ultimately approved a committee to visit the region and report to the next Congress, but the resolution passed by only a plurality: 295 in favor and 176 against, with 143 abstentions. Most West European delegates voted yes; most from Russia and Poland voted "no." One of the journalists there, Israel Cohen, wrote that the "scene that followed the announcement [of the vote] was one that I can never forget":

> Amid a tumult of cheers and groans . . . the Russian delegates all marched into an adjoining hall. There they gave vent to indignation and grief without restraint. . . . Herzl went and begged them to return, but they shouted back a defiant "*Nein!*" A little later . . . after tempers had somewhat cooled, the Russian delegates allowed him to address them. . . . He spoke to them calmly, recalled his repeated efforts in Constantinople . . . and appealed to them to appreciate the political significance of the British offer. He assured them that he remained loyal to the Basle Program [of a homeland in Palestine]. . . . The result was that he won them over and on the following morning they returned to their places in the Congress Hall, [but] with faces more sternly set than before.[117]

In his concluding address—the last he would ever deliver to a Zionist Congress—Herzl praised the Congress as "our first institution, and I trust it may ever remain the best, highest, and most worthy until we transplant it to the beautiful land of our fathers, the land which we need not explore to love." He reminded the delegates that "[w]e cannot always follow the crow's flight," and that "if it were possible to proceed by the straight cloud-path, no leader would be required":

> For all our people know where Zion is, nor do I think that our masses need suffer more in order to make them good Zionists. But because many misunderstandings have arisen among us, I must repeat, before we part . . . that not for a single second, not for a single thought, have we departed from the Basel program. When in a difficult moment, which is not an infrequent occurrence, I thought that all hope must be abandoned at least for the

> span of [a] normal life[time], I was about to propose an expedient to you, and having learned to know your hearts I also desire to offer you a word of consolation, which is at once a pledge on my part . . .

Then Herzl raised his right hand and uttered his pledge, in Hebrew, from Psalm 137: "*If I forget thee O Jerusalem may my right hand forget its cunning.*" The gesture, the sentence, and the rendition in Hebrew produced deafening applause.[118]

After the Congress ended, Jacob de Haas escorted Herzl to the train station, where Herzl embraced him and said the next Congress would be "the Congress of the Exodus."[119] In his diary, Herzl wrote that he had told Nordau that, if he lived until the next Congress, "I will by then either have obtained Palestine or have recognized the impossibility of all further effort"—and in the latter case he would "retire from the leadership and advise the creation of two bodies, one for East Africa, one for Palestine," and let the delegates decide which way to go.[120]

The rift between the Eastern and Western Zionists continued after the Congress, and Herzl was castigated in the press for the East Africa proposal. The *Jewish Chronicle* asked editorially "whether the history of Israel was . . . to end in an African swamp [with] the suggestion that Jews are to be vomited forth from Western lands and banished into barbarism."[121] On September 3, 1903, twenty-seven-year-old Chaim Weizmann published a scathing attack on Herzl in the Warsaw Hebrew newspaper *Hatsofeh* ("The Observer"). He claimed that Herzl was not really a Jewish nationalist, but merely a "promoter of projects," who in suggesting East Africa had ignored the "psychology of the people and its living desires."[122]

Herzl left Basel in August exhausted from the extraordinarily emotional debate.[123] "Palestine is the only land where our people can come to rest," he wrote in his diary, "but hundreds of thousands need immediate help." By November 1903, he had made no further progress in his diplomatic efforts to persuade the Ottoman Empire to permit a Jewish home in Palestine. Given the continuing divisive rift in the Zionist movement, he concluded he could no longer serve as its head. On November 11, 1903, he drafted an impassioned "Letter to the Jewish People," resigning as president of the Zionist Organization.

Herzl's letter began with this sentence: "The path splits, and the split goes straight through the leader's heart." He had been only a "Jewish statist" at the beginning, he wrote, but he had eventually become a *Ḥovev Zion* (a "Lover of Zion"), and yet he remained torn between the ultimate goal of a home in Palestine and the immediate need of a Jewish refuge wherever possible:

> For me there is no other solution but Palestine for the great national question which is called the Jewish Question. But I cannot and must not overlook the fact that the Jewish Question also contains an element of bitter distress which the philanthropic organizations have proved incapable of alleviating.

To address this distress, he needed land, and the only land on offer was in East Africa.[124] He described his dilemma in deciding whether to pursue the offer:

> I cannot go [to East Africa], because I am a *Hovev Zion.* Only if all the *Hovev* were to join us could I . . . direct [the] East Africa [project]. If there is a split, my heart will remain with the Zionists [holding out for Palestine] and my head with the Africans [urging an immediate refuge]. This is such a great conflict that I can only solve it by resigning.

Herzl ended his resignation letter with an evaluation of what he believed he had achieved in his six years of leadership:

> In accordance with my modest energies I have created some instruments for the awakened Jewish people. I shall certainly not leave embittered or dissatisfied. . . . I was richly rewarded far beyond what I merited and deserved, by the love of my people—a measure of love such as has seldom been bestowed upon individuals who had a far greater claim to such love than I did. I am not owed anything. The Jews are a good people, but unfortunately also a profoundly unhappy one. May God continue to help them.

Herzl never sent the letter. The handwritten draft was found among his papers after his death eight months later, and it was not published until 1928.[125] In 1903, Herzl remained president of the Zionist Organization even as his health deteriorated, and as further diplomatic success eluded him. In the final eight months of his life, he met with the Pope, the King

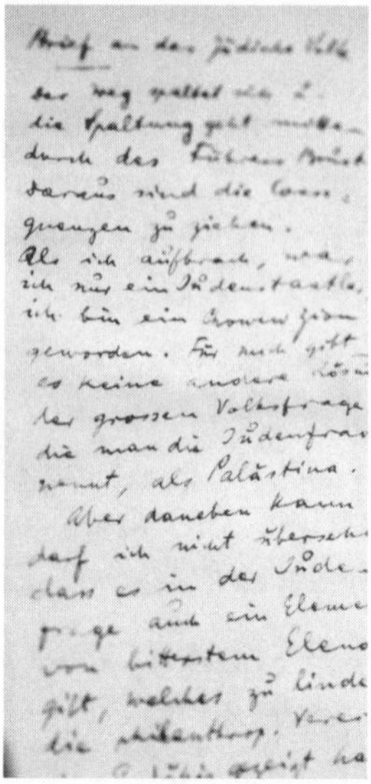

The first page of Herzl's handwritten "Letter to the Jewish People," November 1903

of Italy, the Austrian foreign minister, and others, before dying of his chronic heart condition on July 3, 1904.[126]

In a January 24, 1902, diary entry, Herzl had written that "Zionism was the Sabbath of my life," and he attributed his accomplishments to his principled pursuit of his idea:

> I believe that my effective leadership is to be attributed to the fact that I who, as a man and a writer, have so many faults and have been guilty of so many mistakes and follies, have been in this matter of Zionism pure of heart and wholly unselfish.[127]

At the beginning of 1904, concerned about Herzl's health and finances, some of his Zionist associates had offered to arrange an annuity for him, but Herzl refused, telling David Wolffsohn, "What about my self-respect? Why would I accept money [to] act according to my convictions?" Israel Zangwill assured him it would be kept secret, to which Herzl responded, "You say no one would know. One person would know. I would know."

Herzl died in poverty. His wife and three children would depend on financial support from the movement after his death. Julie died in 1907 at the age of thirty-nine; the three orphaned Herzl children led difficult lives and died at young ages as well, one by a drug overdose, one by suicide, and one in the Holocaust.

Herzl did not live to see the resolution of the East African controversy that split his heart. At the Seventh Zionist Congress in 1905, the delegates formally rejected the East Africa idea. Twelve years later, however, Britain issued the Balfour Declaration, and many historians believe Herzl's efforts involving important British figures—including Arthur Balfour (prime minister at the time of the East Africa negotiation) and David Lloyd George (his lawyer and later the prime minister at the time of the Balfour Declaration)—set the essential stage for the seminal British endorsement in 1917 of a Jewish national home in Palestine.[128]

Herzl's story bears a certain resemblance to that of the prophet Samuel—one that may have struck Herzl himself, as his health began to decline precipitously in late 1903 and early 1904.[129] In the opening chapter of the Book of Samuel, Hannah prays for a child, pledging to dedicate him to the Lord. Her prayer is granted; she names him Samuel ("Samu-El"—"Heard by God"); and she eventually sends him to live with the high priest Eli. Late one night, Samuel hears someone calling his name; he goes to Eli and says, "Here I am." Eli tells him he didn't call him. Samuel goes back to sleep; the Lord calls again; Samuel goes to Eli, and Eli again says he didn't call. When it happens yet again, Eli recognizes it is the Lord calling Samuel, and he advises Samuel to say, if it happened again, "Speak, Lord, for Your servant is listening." The Lord calls again; Samuel says he is listening; and the Lord tells him: "I am about to do something in Israel that will make the ears of everyone who hears of it tingle." Through Samuel, the Lord will prevent Eli from passing the priesthood to his sons and will eventually crown Saul the first King of Israel.

The Book of Samuel played a role in a dream Herzl had when he was twelve years old. He recounted it for the first time about six months before his death, to his Zionist colleague Reuben Brainin. In Herzl's childhood dream, a majestic old man (the "King-Messiah") had taken him into the clouds, where they met Moses. The King-Messiah told Moses, "It is for this child that I have prayed," and then said to Herzl, "Go, declare to the

Jews that I shall come soon and perform great wonders and great deeds for my people and for the whole world." Herzl told Brainin he had never disclosed the dream to anyone.[130]

As a child preparing for his bar mitzvah, Herzl may well have learned the stories of both Samuel and Moses and unconsciously combined them in a dream. His recollection and disclosure, three decades later, reflected not self-importance but rather a certain wistfulness: His health was failing; his heart had been broken at the Sixth Zionist Congress; he was eight years into his project and a Jewish state was nowhere on the horizon; the way forward was unclear; he was thinking of stepping down; and he had already drafted his resignation letter. But at least, through him, the ears of the Jewish people had tingled.

Perhaps the story of Samuel can serve as a parable for Herzl's life: He thought he had a calling as a playwright, but he was wrong; then he thought his calling was as an essayist and reporter, but those writings left him unfulfilled. Then, in June 1895, he was possessed by an all-encompassing idea, coming from a mysterious source, like a voice in the night. On his third attempt, Herzl had found his calling. Or perhaps his Calling found him.

Herzl's life and his achievements were of biblical proportions. In an essay entitled "The Epochal Herzl," published in a collection of essays in 1929 in honor of Herzl's memory, Rabbi Stephen S. Wise wrote—at a time when a Jewish state was still two decades in the future—that Herzl had changed the world:

> We live in a world basically different from that of Herzl, for we are part of a Jewish life which Herzl remade. . . . Those of us who have lived alike in the pre-Herzlian and the post-Herzlian epochs know that this man's coming upon the Jewish scene brought another era into being. . . . After Herzl's day Jews no longer denied their Semitism or concealed their Jewishness. To the former they assented as a fact; the latter they affirmed as their distinction.[131]

As a writer, as an institution builder, and as a diplomat, Herzl bore on his shoulders the weight of the Jewish future. And his prophecy, written on the final page of *The Jewish State*, when he was thirty-six years old, came miraculously true:

> I believe that a wondrous generation of Jews will spring into existence. The Maccabaeans will rise again. . . . The Jews wish to have a State, and they shall have one. . . . And whatever we attempt there to accomplish for our own welfare will react with beneficent force for the good of humanity.[132]

The mystery of Herzl may be insoluble.[133] His appearance in Jewish history was so sudden; his age so young; his time so short; his goal so immense; his approach so new; his efforts so substantial; and his struggle so sustained, that—even a century later—the longest-serving prime minister in Israeli history would continue to describe him in terms of awe and astonishment.

TWO

Louis D. Brandeis: The American Prophet

"My approach to Zionism was through Americanism."

Louis Brandeis in 1915

AT THE DAWN OF THE TWENTIETH CENTURY, Zionism was an unappealing idea to Americans in general and to American Jews in particular. The idea was not only geographically distant, but also cognitively dissonant. The American ideal was the melting pot—the transformation of immigrants into a new American identity, not the preservation of their religious or national distinctions.

A century later, the opposite was true: Zionism had created a Jewish state and the United States had become its major ally. Americans of both political parties supported the creation of Israel, which enjoyed the approval not only of substantially all American Jews, but the vast majority of all Americans.

A century is a short timespan for such a radical and profound change. How did it come to pass? Certainly, the intervening horror of the Holocaust made it clear that the Jews needed a state. But the idea of a modern Jewish state preceded the Holocaust by more than fifty years. The success of Zionism was the triumph of ideas propagated, debated, and refined over the half-century preceding the Holocaust, and of the efforts of exceptional individuals who devoted their lives to the cause.

American Zionism was related to—but also differed significantly from—the Zionism that emerged from Europe and Russia. Zionism in America was a subcategory of the ideology known as "Americanism"—the civil religion that espoused freedom, equality, and democracy at home, and the ambition to extend it to others throughout the world. In 1914, Zionism and Americanism were merged into a single unique philosophical approach, which would prove critical to the formation of the State of Israel a third of a century later.

The person most responsible for the development of the American Zionist ideology was a secular Jew, born and raised in Kentucky, who in his first fifty-five years had shown little interest in Jews or Judaism—and none whatsoever in Zionism.[1]

Louis Dembitz Brandeis was the son of Jewish parents who had emigrated from Prague in 1848 and had prospered in America. They gave their American son, born in Louisville in 1856, no Jewish education at all. He did not have a bar mitzvah, never observed Shabbat, did not attend religious services, and did not celebrate Jewish holidays.[2] His distance from both Jews and Zionism before 1914 was reflected in the fact that, despite his substantial annual income from his law practice and his substantial accumulated wealth, his gifts to Jewish charities were minimal. They averaged about $250 per year (out of about $15,000 total gifts per year) from his income averaging $75,000 per year (more than $2,000,000 in today's dollars) and personal assets exceeding $1 million (about $28 million in today's dollars).[3]

In August 1914, with the outbreak of World War I and the European continent divided by war, the World Zionist headquarters in Berlin could no longer lead the movement. In New York, a group of Zionists established a "Provisional Executive Committee for General Zionist Affairs" to replace the Berlin office. The committee chose as its chairman one of the country's most eminent Jews—the fifty-eight-year-old Brandeis—who in his acceptance speech said:

> I feel my disqualification for this task. Throughout the long years which represent my own life, I have been to a great extent separated from Jews. I am very ignorant in things Jewish.[4]

The emergence of Brandeis in 1914 to lead the American Zionism movement, seemingly out of nowhere, would later be described by the prominent Zionist, Ezekiel Rabinowitz, as "a real miracle."[5]

The distance of American Jews from Zionism at the turn of the century is reflected in the speech of Rabbi Isaac Mayer Wise, the head of Reform Judaism in America, in 1897—the year after Theodor Herzl published *The Jewish State*. Rabbi Wise publicly disparaged and dismissed Zionism. "[A]ll this agitation on the other side of the ocean," he told the Central Conference of American Rabbis (CCAR), "concerns us very little." He called Zionism a "new Messianic movement" appealing to "the fantastic dupes of a thoughtless Utopia." It was a "momentary inebriation of morbid minds," a philosophy that would rob Judaism of its "universal ground."

In its platform, the Reform movement held that Jews were "no longer a nation, but a religious community" and that Judaism was "a progressive religion, ever striving to be in accord with the postulates of reason." The movement thus rejected rituals it believed reflected the "primitive ideas" of an earlier age. The American Jewish Committee, formed in 1906, was a non-Zionist—indeed an anti-Zionist—organization, and the number of American Jews active in Zionist affairs, even in the decade after Herzl galvanized the European Jews, was minuscule. For Jewish immigrants to America—whether in the mid-nineteenth century from Germany or at the turn of the century from Russia—the route to acceptance in America was assimilation.

This was the theme of the speech Brandeis delivered in 1905 to Boston's New Century Club, on the 250th anniversary of the arrival of Jews in America, titled "What Loyalty Demands." He addressed "the obligation which this great privilege of American citizenship involves." American public life, he said, had "no place for what President [Theodore] Roosevelt has called hyphenated Americans"—not for "Protestant-Americans, or Catholic-Americans, or Jewish-Americans, not German-Americans, Irish-Americans, or Russian-Americans." Brandeis said that "[h]abits of living or of thought which tend to keep alive difference of origin or to classify men according to their religious beliefs are inconsistent with the American ideal of brotherhood and are disloyal."

The Jewish people had "found at last in America," Brandeis said, the recognition of the "high ideals" the Jews had first brought to the world many centuries ago, and loyalty to American values was thus "the truest expression of loyalty" to Jewish tradition. For Brandeis, as of 1905, Jewish nationalism—Zionism—was far from his thinking. Only a decade later, however, in another major address in 1915, Brandeis would say that "loyalty to America demands . . . that each American Jew become a Zionist."

In 1916, President Woodrow Wilson named Brandeis to the U.S. Supreme Court, where he would serve for twenty-three years and write a series of landmark opinions that were, in the words of the constitutional historian Jeffrey Rosen, "constitutional poetry." But perhaps Brandeis's most enduring historical writing would be his 1915 address, in which he said that Zionism was essential to Jewish contributions to America:

> [O]nly through the ennobling effect of its strivings can we develop the best that is in us and give to this country the full ben-

> efit of our great inheritance. The Jewish spirit, so long preserved, the character developed by so many centuries of sacrifice, should be preserved and developed further, so that in America as elsewhere the [Jewish descendants] may in the future live lives and do deeds worthy of their ancestors.

How did Zionism—an idea Brandeis would have rejected a decade before—become for him not only a palliative for the despondent Jews of the world but an essential creed for the more prosperous American ones, virtually none of whom desired to go to Palestine themselves, and for whom America was already their new Zion?

The conversion of Brandeis to Zionism sprang from several sources, and biographers still debate which influence was the most important.[6] But one of the most significant ones was surely a meeting, on an unrelated subject, with Jacob de Haas, who had been Herzl's lieutenant in Britain from the beginning and had been elected an officer at the first four Zionist Congresses. He had moved to America in 1902, at Herzl's suggestion, to advance the movement there.[7]

A decade later, de Haas was the editor of *The Jewish Advocate* in Boston. At the end of his interview of Brandeis on a controversy regarding insurance law, de Haas asked Brandeis if he was related to Louis Dembitz, whom de Haas called "a noble Jew." Brandeis replied that Dembitz was his late uncle and asked de Haas to explain his admiration of him.[8] De Haas replied that Dembitz had been one of the earliest supporters of the nascent Zionist movement in America.[9] This led to an hour-long discussion about Herzl, the first of many between Brandeis and de Haas, and it caused Brandeis to spend months researching Zionism. De Haas later wrote:

> [F]rom that first interview [Brandeis] began an earnest quest for knowledge. Probably no other Jew has arrived at the same conclusions and to such deeply stirred self-consciousness by the same process. . . . He studied the footnotes as well as the printed page of Jewish history and made the Zionist idea his own.[10]

We do not know everything Brandeis read as he studied Zionism, but we can surmise it included *Rome and Jerusalem: A Study in Jewish Nationalism* by Moses Hess, a German socialist and former communist whose

1862 book began, "After an estrangement of twenty years, I am back with my people," and Leo Pinsker's 1882 pamphlet, *Auto-Emancipation*, which cited Hillel's aphorism, "If I am not for myself . . ." He definitely read the Zionist essays of Ahad Ha'am, which he later said gave him an understanding of "the history and other things Jewish" that he had lacked. All of these were written with intellectual force, moral passion, and literary grace, and they would have impressed Brandeis on those grounds alone.

Brandeis likely also read Max Nordau's 1905 essay, "Zionism and Anti-Semitism," which was specifically directed at Jewish readers in the West.[11] After Herzl's death in 1904, Nordau—one of the foremost public intellectuals of the day—became the most prominent Zionist figure in Europe and was well known in the United States.[12] In his essay, Nordau wrote that Zionism would realize its goals through "the enthusiasm of modern educated Jews . . . [with an] awakened consciousness . . . and ambition to save the ancient blood . . . to add to the achievements of their forefathers the achievements of their posterity." Nationalism—the dominant principle in international politics since the middle of the nineteenth century—had taught "all peoples . . . to regard their peculiarities as qualities," and he urged Jews "to remember what they had unlearned."

Five-sixths of the twelve million Jews in the world—essentially all those outside the United States—were living lives of physical deprivation and psychological desperation, which Nordau said in his essay confronted Zionism with an unprecedented goal:

> Never before has the effort been made to transplant, peacefully, in a short space of time, to another soil, several million people from various countries. . . . It will be necessary to accustom Jews of different origins to one another, to train them practically to national unity, and at the same time to overcome the superhuman obstacles of difference of language, unequal civilization, and of the manners of thought, prejudices, likes, and dislikes of foreign nations, brought severally from the lands of their birth.

What gave Zionists the courage to undertake "this labor of Hercules," Nordau wrote, was:

> the conviction that they are doing a necessary and useful work, a work of love and civilization, a work of justice and wisdom. They desire to save eight to ten million of their kindred from intoler-

> able suffering. They desire to free the nations among whom they now vegetate from a presence which is considered disagreeable. They wish to deprive anti-Semitism—which everywhere lowers public morals and develops the very worst instincts—of its victim.

Brandeis also became convinced that a Jewish homeland could undertake experiments in democracy and social justice more easily than larger countries. He was impressed that the Bible criticized even the most illustrious ancient leaders—including Moses and David—for their political sins and personal failings. He wondered "whether any government today would risk publishing a document depicting the nation's most favored ruler as the Bible does David."[13]

The texts that Brandeis studied gave him a sense of the Jewish past, present, and future—the civilizational contributions, the contemporary crisis, and the call to the educated Jewish elite of the West to join a historic movement for the future.

On November 8, 1914, Brandeis gave his first major address on Zionism, a speech at Columbia University titled "The Duty of Educated Jews in America," later reprinted as "A Call to the Educated Jew."[14] Brandeis said the Jews had a "treasure which we have acquired by inheritance—and which we are duty bound to transmit unimpaired . . . to coming generations," because the benefits had "not come to us by accident":

> They were developed by 3,000 years of civilization, and nearly 2,000 years of persecution; developed through our religion and spiritual life; through our traditions; and through the social and political conditions under which our ancestors lived. . . .
>
> The fruit of 3,000 years of civilization and a hundred generations of suffering may not be sacrificed by us. . . . [A]ssimilation can be prevented only by preserving national characteristics and life as other peoples, large and small, are preserving and developing *their* national life. . . . And must we not, like them, have a land where the Jewish life may be naturally led, the Jewish language spoken, and the Jewish spirit prevail? Surely we must, and that land is our fathers' land: it is Palestine.

Cover of the pamphlet reprinting Brandeis's 1914 address

Brandeis saw Zionism not as providing a place for American Jews to go—since they needed no physical refuge—but rather as one that would inspire them to preserve their historic heritage. In his view, while millions of Jews in the world needed a Jewish home in Palestine, "[w]e Jews of prosperous America above all need its inspiration."

Brandeis repeated his Columbia address in more extended form in an address in 1915 to the Conference of Eastern Council of Reform Rabbis, which he titled "The Jewish Problem: How to Solve It."[15] For the Jews of the United States, it was as revolutionary a document as Herzl's pamphlet, *The Jewish State*, had been for the Jews of Europe, because Brandeis connected Zionism to the American creed. He maintained that the Jewish experience in Europe demonstrated that while liberalism had protected Jews legally as individuals, it had not protected them as a practical matter as a people, and that the "Jewish Problem" was one of the Jews collectively:

> Obviously, no individual should be subjected anywhere, by reason of the fact that he is a Jew, to a denial of any common right

> or opportunity enjoyed by non-Jews. But Jews collectively should likewise enjoy the same right and opportunity to live and develop as do other groups of people. This right of development on the part of the group is essential to the full enjoyment of rights by the individual.

Brandeis then expressed the same insight that had come to Herzl two decades before: that liberalism alone could not solve the Jewish Question:

> Half a century ago the belief was still general that Jewish disabilities would disappear before growing liberalism. When religious toleration was proclaimed, the solution of the Jewish Problem seemed in sight. When the so-called rights of man became widely recognized, and the equal right of all citizens to life, liberty and the pursuit of happiness began to be enacted into positive law, the complete emancipation of the Jews seemed at hand.
> . . .
> The Ghetto walls crumbled; the ball and chain of restraint were removed in central and western Europe. . . . But the anti-Jewish prejudice was not exterminated even in those countries of Europe in which the triumph of civil liberty and democracy extended fully to Jews "the rights of man." The antisemitic movement arose in Germany a year after the granting of universal suffrage.

Brandeis argued that the solution was national rights for the Jews—in the same way that national rights had been the solution for other peoples in the world. He quoted Giuseppe Mazzini, the intellectual leader of the movement that had united the disparate duchies of Italy into the modern nation of Italy:

> Deeply imbedded in every people is the desire for full development, the longing, as Mazzini phrased it, "To elaborate and express their idea, to contribute their stone also to the pyramid of history." . . . The assertion of nationality raised Ireland from the slough of despondency. It roused Southern Slavs to heroic deeds. It created gallant Belgium. It freed Greece. It gave us united Italy. . . . Each of these peoples developed because, as Mazzini said, they were enabled to proclaim "to the world that they also live, think, love, and labor for the benefit of all."

Brandeis accordingly connected Zionism to the nationalist campaigns that other peoples had conducted in recent decades:

> [Zionism] seeks . . . to make the dream of a Jewish life in a Jewish land come true as other great dreams of the world have been realized. . . . [T]he dream of Italian independence and unity, after centuries of vain hope, came true through the efforts of Mazzini, Garibaldi and Cavour. . . . [T]he dream of Greek, of Bulgarian and of Serbian independence became facts. . . . The movements of the last century have proved that whole peoples have individuality no less marked than that of a single person . . . and that the misnamed internationalism which seeks the obliteration of nationalities or peoples is unattainable.

In American Zionism, as Brandeis articulated it, there was no issue of dual loyalty, because it did not require that American Jews move to Palestine; nor swear allegiance to a different country; nor give up any part of their American identity. It required only that American Jews support the right of other Jews to build their own society in their ancient homeland, as the Italians, Greeks, Bulgarians, and Serbs had done in theirs.[16] Jewish nationalism would contribute to world civilization, because the experience of the Jews, like the experience of other peoples, was unique. Moreover, things could be accomplished in a new small state that could not be accomplished elsewhere:

> Palestine, when the Jews constitute a majority there, may, because of its very smallness, serve as a laboratory for some far-reaching experiments in democracy and social justice. . . . [L]et us teach all peoples that they are all chosen, and that each has a mission for all. . . .
>
> Zionism seeks to establish in Palestine, for such Jews as choose to go . . . a legally secured home, where they may live together and lead a Jewish life, where they may expect ultimately to constitute a majority of the population and may look forward to what we should call home rule. The Zionists . . . are convinced that the undying longing of Jews for Palestine is a fact of deepest significance; that it is a manifestation in the struggle for existence by an ancient people which has established its right to live, a people whose three thousand years of civilization has produced a faith, culture and individuality which enable it to contribute

> largely in the future, as it has in the past, to the advance of civilization; and that it is not a right merely but a duty of the Jewish nationality to survive and develop.

Brandeis summarized the "remarkable achievement" of Zionism after "a few Jewish emigrants from Russia and from Rumania, instead of proceeding westward to this hospitable country where they might easily have secured material prosperity, turned eastward for the purpose of settling in the land of their fathers" and faced obstacles there that appeared "almost insuperable":

> This land, treeless a generation ago, supposed to be sterile and hopelessly arid, has been shown to have been treeless and sterile because of man's misrule. It has been shown to be capable of becoming again a land "flowing with milk and honey."
>
> This material development has been attended by a spiritual and social development no less extraordinary; a development in education, in health and in social order. . . . Perhaps the most extraordinary achievement of Jewish nationalism is the revival of the Hebrew language. . . . [T]he effect of the renaissance of the Hebrew tongue is far greater than that of unifying the Jews. It is a potent factor in reviving the essentially Jewish spirit.
>
> Our Jewish Pilgrim Fathers have laid the foundation. It remains for us to build the superstructure.

Brandeis was using the language of the founding of the United States—the "Pilgrim Fathers," the pioneering "colonies and colonists," the land becoming one "of milk and honey"—to convey the idea that the effort was quintessentially American. He believed that supporting the rights of others to have what Americans enjoyed was part of the American mission in the world, and thus "loyalty to America demands rather that each American Jew become a Zionist."

Brandeis concluded that the duty to resolve the "Jewish Question" in the world fell particularly upon American Jewry, not only because the three million Jews in America were more than a fifth of all the Jews in the world, but also because:

> We are representative of all the Jews in the world; for we are composed of immigrants, or descendants of immigrants coming from every other country. . . . Let us insist that the struggle for

> liberty shall not cease until equality of opportunity is accorded to nationalities as to individuals.

Brandeis thus maintained that a Jewish homeland would further the ideals of Americanism. "My approach to Zionism," he wrote, "was through Americanism":

> In time, practical experience and observation convinced me that Jews were, by reason of their traditions and their character, peculiarly fitted for the attainment of American ideals. Gradually it became clear to me that to be good Americans, we must be better Jews, and to be better Jews, we must become Zionists.

In one sense, Brandeis had made a 180-degree turn in his thinking—from his 1905 speech calling a hyphenated Jewish-American identity "disloyal," to his 1915 speech contending that to be better Americans, American Jews had to be Zionists. But the two views were, in fact, complementary: In 1905, he had seen that Jewish values could be lived in America; in 1915, he realized that the preservation of Jewish values required a Jewish state that would reflect and extend American values—freedom and democracy.

Brandeis's speech was reprinted as the lead essay in the first issue of *The Menorah Journal*, a new magazine of American Jewish thought, in which he asserted that "[p]atriotism to America, as well as loyalty to our past, imposes upon us the obligation of claiming this heritage of the Jewish spirit and of carrying forward noble ideals and traditions through lives and deeds worthy of our ancestors."[17]

The association of Brandeis with Zionism gave it a status in the United States that no other person could have provided. Brandeis contributed not only his name and his eloquence to the movement, but also his money and his time.[18] "He took over with zest and enthusiasm," wrote Louis Lipsky, later the President of the Zionist Organization of America, describing how Brandeis would come to the Zionist offices in New York early in the morning and remain for hours, discussing issues and assigning tasks, "innocent of vanity or conceit . . . [with] a cordiality that won confidence," using "logic, tact and infinite patience."[19]

The ranks of American Zionists surged after Brandeis became their leader. Before Brandeis, there were about 12,000 members in the Federation of American Zionists—out of a total Jewish population in America of three million.[20] Once Brandeis became involved, the membership quintupled over the succeeding five years.[21]

The most significant part of the Brandeis story, however, came in 1917, as Britain debated whether to issue the Balfour Declaration and commit itself to establish a Jewish national home in Palestine, if Britain were to prevail in World War I. In his efforts to encourage the British War Cabinet to issue the declaration, Chaim Weizmann, the Zionist leader in London, was encountering strenuous opposition from a Jewish establishment that feared Zionism could jeopardize their status as loyal British subjects.

At a critical moment, as the British turned to President Woodrow Wilson to determine if America would support the Declaration, Weizmann turned to Brandeis for help.

Brandeis had first met Woodrow Wilson in 1912, when Wilson was the governor of New Jersey and had invited him to lunch to discuss his coming presidential campaign. Despite Brandeis's national reputation, the two had never met: Wilson was a Democrat while Brandeis was a Progressive Republican. Wilson's leading biographer, A. Scott Berg, writes that Brandeis "could not have known [as he traveled from Boston to meet Wilson] that he, as much as anybody, would shape the future of Woodrow Wilson's campaign and career."

Their initial lunch extended into a three-hour meeting, during which Brandeis offered Wilson the ideas that would form the basis of Wilson's "New Freedom" campaign and his subsequent administration. Wilson's main opponent was Theodore Roosevelt, who was running as a third-party candidate of the Progressive Party (the Republican candidate was William Howard Taft) on a platform urging regulation of the monopolistic "trusts" that dominated the American economy. Brandeis told Wilson that rather than *regulating* monopolies (which implicitly accepted them as a valid part of the economy), the government should instead *mandate competition* to prevent them from forming in the first place. Brandeis convinced Wilson that "our industrial freedom and our civic freedom go hand in hand" and this became the theme of Wilson's "New Freedom" campaign.

Brandeis called on all Progressives, irrespective of party, to support Wilson; his nomination, Brandeis said, ranked "among the most encouraging events in American history." The *New York Times* reported the Brandeis endorsement on its front page. After the election, Brandeis served as a key adviser to the new president and worked on the most important parts of Wilson's legislative program. Wilson appointed him to the Supreme Court in 1916 and stood by him during a contentious four-month Senate confirmation hearing—the first hearing on a Supreme Court nomination ever held by the Senate in its 127-year history.[22]

As of 1917, Brandeis was thus both a close friend and an important political confidant of Wilson, who held him in the highest regard.

At the beginning of the war in 1914, President Wilson had promised that America would maintain strict neutrality, and his campaign slogan in 1916 was that "He Kept Us Out of War." But in February 1917, Germany announced it would sink every vessel approaching the ports of Britain and Europe—including American ones—and Britain released the "Zimmermann Telegram," a coded message from Germany's foreign minister, Arthur Zimmermann, to Germany's ambassador to Mexico, offering to give American territory to Mexico after the war if Mexico sided with Germany. The telegram infuriated Wilson and the American public.

On April 2, Wilson addressed a special session of Congress, pronouncing the German submarine actions "a warfare against mankind" and that the "world must be made safe for democracy," with peace "to be planted upon the tested foundations of political liberty" rather than on the autocracy of Germany and its allies. The United States, Wilson said, would wage a war "for democracy . . . for the rights and liberties of small nations . . . and make the world itself at last free"—in accordance with "the principles that gave [America] her birth and happiness." On April 6, 1917, Congress declared war on Germany.

In 1917, the Middle East was an important theater of World War I. The British occupied the Sinai Peninsula in late 1916, and on April 2, 1917, decided to invade Palestine. The British foreign minister, Arthur Balfour, visited the United States soon thereafter. He first encountered Brandeis at a White House reception and the two had breakfast to discuss Palestine. Brandeis discussed the issue on May 6 at the White House with President Wilson to receive instructions from him, and thereafter had further conversations with Balfour on May 7 and 10.

By the summer and early fall of 1917, the British Cabinet was considering successive drafts of a pro-Zionist declaration regarding Palestine, which the British thought would solidify support for its war effort in both Russia and the United States. The Russian Tsar, Nicholas II, had been deposed, rendering Russia's continued participation in the war as Britain's ally uncertain, and the American public's backing for the war was shaky as well. Key members of the British War Cabinet believed an endorsement of Zionist aspirations would appeal to the public in both Russia and the United States, since both had large Jewish populations. The British were also alarmed by rumors that Germany—the headquarters of the world Zionist movement before the war—was actively considering its own pro-Zionist statement to win over Jewish support.

The principal opposition to British support of Zionism came from within the British Jewish community itself, led by Edwin Montagu—the sole Jewish minister in the British government—who vehemently opposed it. On September 3, Montagu submitted a memorandum to the British War Cabinet entitled "On the Anti-Semitism of the Present Government"—a provocative title designed to dramatize Montagu's belief that, as he set forth in his memorandum, Zionism was "a mischievous political creed, untenable by any patriotic citizen of the United Kingdom." He thought Zionism would only generate additional antisemitism, rather than solve it. His opposition was so fierce that he went so far as to write in his memorandum that "I would be almost tempted to proscribe the Zionist organization as illegal and against the national interest."

The Cabinet held multiple meetings regarding the issue and found itself split, in part because of its uncertainty about President Wilson's views. The day before the October 4 Cabinet meeting, Montagu circulated another memorandum, claiming that "every Jew who is prominent in public life in England, with the exception of the present Lord Rothschild, Mr. Herbert Samuel, and a few others," were anti-Zionists. He listed forty-seven names and suggested that American Jews were not in favor of Zionism, quoting a June 28, 1917, statement of the President of the Central Conference of American Rabbis that it "looks with disfavor upon any movement the purpose of which is other than religious." Montagu quoted Jacob Schiff, one of the most eminent American Jews, as opposing a Jewish state and supporting only a place in Palestine where "Jewish religious life, Jewish thought and Jewish learning would develop in all its primitive purity."

At the Cabinet meeting, Montagu made a passionate anti-Zionist speech and the Cabinet instructed Balfour—who had asserted that he knew President Wilson was extremely supportive of the Zionist movement—to solicit Wilson's views directly.

Balfour cabled a draft declaration to Wilson's chief adviser, Colonel Edward M. House, with a request for the President's opinion. Weizmann cabled Brandeis, telling him the matter was urgent and that it would greatly help "if President Wilson and yourself would support [the] text." Brandeis spoke with Wilson again, as did Colonel House, and on October 17, Wilson passed a private message through Colonel House to the British that he supported the declaration. House asked the British to keep Wilson's message private for the time being—"as he has arranged that American Jews shall [later] ask him for his approval which he will give publicly here."

At its meeting on October 31, the British Cabinet—with Wilson's private approval in hand—authorized the issuance and publication of the Balfour Declaration, in the form of a letter to Lord Rothschild.[23]

Foreign Office,
November 2nd, 1917.

Dear Lord Rothschild,

I have much pleasure in conveying to you, on behalf of His Majesty's Government, the following declaration of sympathy with Jewish Zionist aspirations which has been submitted to, and approved by, the Cabinet

"His Majesty's Government view with favour the establishment in Palestine of a national home for the Jewish people, and will use their best endeavours to facilitate the achievement of this object, it being clearly understood that nothing shall be done which may prejudice the civil and religious rights of existing non-Jewish communities in Palestine, or the rights and political status enjoyed by Jews in any other country"

I should be grateful if you would bring this declaration to the knowledge of the Zionist Federation.

Chaim Weizmann wrote to Brandeis that Wilson's message had been "one of the most important individual factors" in breaking the internal British deadlock. Nahum Goldman, later the president of the World Zionist Organization, wrote that without Brandeis's efforts, the Balfour Declaration "would probably never have been issued."[24]

In approving the British move, Wilson had acted without the knowledge of his Department of State. Given the views of Secretary of State Robert Lansing, the Department would undoubtedly have opposed it. Lansing—unaware of Wilson's private communication to Britain—wrote a December 13, 1917, letter to Wilson suggesting that the President refrain from taking any position on the Declaration, citing three reasons:

(1) The U.S. had declared war against Germany but not Germany's ally, the Ottoman empire, which ruled Palestine.
(2) Jews themselves were not unified behind the idea of a Jewish homeland; and
(3) Many Christians would "undoubtedly resent turning the Holy Land over to the absolute control of the race credited with the death of Christ."[25]

Lansing helpfully suggested to Wilson that he need state publicly only the first reason. Wilson responded that he had already assented to the Balfour Declaration.

The issuance of the Balfour Declaration on November 2, 1917, provoked a reaction within the American Jewish establishment similar to that of Edwin Montagu: an anxious concern about being viewed as less than patriotic. On December 11, 1917, Henry Morgenthau, the most recent American ambassador to the Ottoman Empire, published a 1,000-word statement in the *New York Times*, writing that he wanted to "strongly emphasize to all my American fellow citizens . . . that a majority of those of my faith in America . . . are 100-percent Americans and wish to remain so." The "whole world," he wrote, was "now moving away from the emphasis hitherto placed upon extreme nationalism," and:

> What an error it would be, at the very time when the primary message to the world of the Jewish people and their religion should be one of peace, brotherhood, and the international

> mind, to set up a limited nationalist state and thereby appear to create a physical boundary to their religious influence.

On July 4, 1918, the Central Conference of American Rabbis (CCAR) echoed Morgenthau's sentiments in a new resolution that rejected what they saw as the Balfour Declaration's misperception that the Jews were a people without a country. On the contrary, the CCAR declared, Jews "ought to be at home in all lands":

> The ideal of the Jew is not the establishment of a Jewish state—not the reassertion of Jewish nationality which has long been outgrown. We believe our survival as a people is dependent upon the assertion and the maintenance of our historic religious role and not upon the acceptance of Palestine as a homeland of the Jewish people. The mission of the Jew is to witness to God all over the world.

In a letter dated August 31, 1918, to Stephen Wise, President Wilson expressed his satisfaction with the American Zionist movement and the Balfour Declaration—in a letter that Brandeis helped draft—but his letter was not greeted with universal acclaim in the American Jewish community.[26] In his Rosh Hashanah sermon on September 6, 1918, Rabbi Samuel Schulman of New York's Temple Beth-El, in his twentieth year at the synagogue, speaking to a congregation that included Adolph Simon Ochs, the publisher of the *Times*, told his congregation:

> Our destiny is not to become a little Oriental people in Palestine. It is rather to persist in the world as Israel, Priest of God: to witness as God's congregation in the whole world, and therefore, to be a part of every nation, abdicating political nationality as a thing too little.[27]

In contrast, Rabbi H. Pereira Mendes of the Union of Orthodox Congregations of America, together with two former presidents of the New York Board of Jewish Ministers, wrote to Wilson to express their "profound gratification" for his support of the Balfour Declaration. Rabbi Samuel Buchler, on behalf of two other Orthodox organizations representing, he asserted, "the great bulk of Jews throughout the United States," praised Wilson for his approach.

The debate within the Jewish community on the advisability of a Jewish state would continue for the next thirty years—until the question was settled by history. The Holocaust transformed the issue from an intellectual discussion about the role of Jews in the world to a recognition of what was needed for the Jewish people to survive in it. The "international mind" would prove to be a poor protector of Jews; the high-minded Jewish discourse about the religious "mission of the Jew . . . all over the world" verged on self-flattery; and ironically, perhaps the only thing that might have avoided the tragedy for the Jews in the 1930s was precisely what many prominent Jews had disparaged, in the years leading up to it, as a "thing too little."

But what about the Arabs? Did the Balfour Declaration and Jewish nationalism contradict Arab nationalist aspirations?[28] Was Zionism an imperialist colonial project that violated the human or political rights of the Arabs? Did it violate or contradict Britain's pre-war assurances to them?

Or was Zionism a national liberation movement that both complemented and assisted the nascent nationalism of the Arabs? To answer these questions, we need to turn to the story of Chaim Weizmann and Emir Faisal bin Hussein.

THREE

Chaim Weizmann and the First Arab-Zionist Alliance

"We are not coming to Jerusalem; we are returning."

Chaim Weizmann, circa 1918

On JANUARY 3, 1919, a few weeks after World War I ended, Chaim Weizmann, the head of the World Zionist Organization, met with Emir (Prince) Faisal, the commander-in-chief of the Arab Revolt against the Ottoman Empire. They met in a room at the Carlton Hotel in London, where they had come to sign an agreement. In its way, Weizmann's presence in London, and at that meeting, were events in Jewish history as unlikely as the emergence of Herzl and Brandeis.

Faisal's father, Hussein bin Ali, was the King of Hedjaz (today part of Saudi Arabia) and ruled the two holiest sites of Islam—Mecca and Medina. The family traced its lineage to the Prophet Mohammed.[1] Faisal was accompanied to the meeting by his adviser, translator, and friend, T. E. Lawrence ("Lawrence of Arabia"), who had helped him lead the Arab Revolt and who over the preceding month had brokered the agreement. It exchanged Arab acceptance of the Balfour Declaration for Zionist support of an Arab state in the balance of the Ottoman lands.

After the signing, Weizmann, Faisal, and Lawrence crossed the English Channel to attend the Paris Peace Conference, where the victorious Allies were about to redraw the maps of Europe and the Middle East in the wake of the defeat of Germany and its ally, the Ottoman Empire. Weizmann and Faisal made complementary presentations to the Allies on the future of Palestine. A year-and-a-half after the issuance of the Balfour Declaration, the Jews and the Arabs were pursuing their goals together.

Weizmann was forty-two years old. He had been born in a small Russian *shtetl* called Motol—a place he described in his autobiography as a "townlet" ("half-town, half-village")—where he had spent his first eleven years. Motol had no paved roads, no post office, no newspapers, and had a primitive agricultural economy with a one-room school, where a single book was taught—the Hebrew Bible.

How in the world did Weizmann get from there to London, become a Zionist leader in a language he had only recently learned, represent the Zionist movement in discussions with the British Cabinet as it considered the Balfour Declaration and, together with the leader of the Arabs, produce a post-war proposal for Palestine acceptable to both Jews and Arabs?

In 1885, Weizmann's family sent him from Motol on his own to live in Pinsk to attend secondary school. The twenty-five miles between Motol and Pinsk was, Weizmann would later write, "astronomical"—not only in terms of the arduous trip, an all-day journey from the *shtetl* by horse-drawn wagon, but also in intellectual and cultural distance.

Weizmann excelled in the science courses available to him there and, upon graduation, went to Germany for college and graduate study. It would have been more logical for him to enter a Russian university in Moscow, but for a Jewish student, this would involve assuming a false identity (since Jews were generally not permitted to live beyond the Pale of Settlement) and paying a bribe (with money neither Weizmann nor his family had). Weizmann thus went west, and eventually earned a PhD in chemistry, *summa cum laude*, at the University of Freiburg.

Pinsk lacked the sophistication of Warsaw, Vilna, and Odessa, but it was one of the centers of Zionism in Russia. From his fifteenth year forward, Zionism became Weizmann's principal extracurricular interest. He attended the Zionist Congress in 1903 as a twenty-six-year-old Russian delegate—where he led a student faction opposing Herzl's East Africa option. Then he moved to England to accept a teaching position at the University of Manchester—220 miles north of London—speaking little English when he arrived, but a year later delivering his first chemistry lecture in English.

Weizmann had written his doctoral thesis on chemical reactions in dyestuffs, a field that would later have unexpected military application during World War I. His knowledge and skill in the field of chemistry helped to produce a synthetic substitute for acetone that materially assisted Britain's war effort; and his wartime work brought him into contact with key people in the British government—who became personal acquaintances and part of the British War Cabinet in 1917, when he would articulate for them the importance of Palestine to the Jews of the world.

There were several factors that coalesced to produce the Balfour Declaration.[2] The immediate reason for its issuance was Britain's hope that it would generate American and Russian support for the British war effort, as World War I reached a critical stage in 1917. The war was in its fourth year; its outcome was not yet clear; and Britain needed the support of the U.S. and Russia, each of which had a large Jewish population. The War Cabinet thought the Declaration would help keep them as allies in the war against Germany and the Ottoman Empire.[3]

Britain also had a broader war strategy, however, which was designed to bring the Jewish, Arab, and Armenian national movements into an informal alliance with Britain. Two weeks after the Declaration was issued, Sir Mark Sykes—the British diplomat involved in the 1916 Sykes-Picot Agreement that divided the Middle East into British and French spheres of influence—outlined the broader strategy in a letter to the British War Cabinet:

> We are pledged to Zionism, Armenian liberation, and Arabian independence. *Zionism is the key to the lock.* I am sanguine that we can demonstrate to the world that these three elements are prepared to take common action and stand by one another. If once the Turks see the Zionists are prepared to back [the Arabs and Armenians] . . . [the Turks] will come to us to negotiate. . . . [Emphasis added.][4]

To effectuate this alliance, Sykes wrote, "our immediate policy should be by speech and open statement" to promote "Zionist, Armenian, and Arab common action and alliance."

On December 2, 1917—one month after the Balfour Declaration—the British Jewish community held a celebration at the London Opera House, drawing a crowd of more than 4,000, with thousands more outside. Lord Robert Cecil, the British Under Secretary of State for Foreign Affairs, addressed the celebrants, emphasizing that the British policy was "Arabian countries should be for the Arabs, Armenia for the Armenians, Judea for the Jews." Representatives of the Arab and Armenian communities attended the event and gave congratulatory speeches.[5]

In the following months, Weizmann formed a Zionist Commission to travel to Palestine to assist the war-torn Jewish community there; plan new Jewish institutions such as the Hebrew University; and establish relations with the Arabs. He arrived in Palestine in April 1918, and found that the vicious Russian anti-Semitic forgery, "The Protocols of the Elders of Zion," describing a purported Jewish plot to rule the world, had been widely distributed among the Arabs. There were rampant rumors that—as Weizmann wrote caustically to Balfour from Tel Aviv—the British were "going to hand over the poor Arabs to the wealthy Jews, who are . . . ready to swoop down like vultures on an easy prey and to oust everybody from the land."

The British arranged for Weizmann to address the Arab Muslim and Christian leaders in Jerusalem at a dinner on April 27.[6] Weizmann began by saying it was "with a sense of grave responsibility that I rise to speak on this momentous occasion. Here my forefathers stood 2,000 years ago." He told the gathering that the Jews were not "coming" to Palestine, but rather were *returning* to it; that there was room in Palestine for many times more than the existing population; that Zionists endorsed the Arab Revolt against the Ottomans; that the Jews sought "the opportunity of free national development in Palestine, and in justice it cannot be refused." He said that self-government in Palestine should be deferred until Palestine could develop economically and politically, with a Great Power to administer it as a trustee in the meantime.

Weizmann's speech was consistent with the "organic" Zionism he espoused—midway between the "political" Zionism of Herzl (which sought an immediate state for the Jews) and the "cultural" Zionism of Ahad Ha'am (which sought simply a "cultural center" for Judaism). Weizmann wanted a right of unhindered Jewish immigration to Palestine and the opportunity to build Jewish institutions there, which he believed would enable Palestine to evolve slowly into a democratic state with a Jewish majority.[7]

That approach reflected how Balfour—during the October 31, 1917, Cabinet meeting that had approved the final text of the Balfour Declaration—had defined the Jewish "national home" to be endorsed by Britain. Balfour had said that the "national home" would be:

> some form of British, American, or other protectorate, under which full facilities would be given to the Jews to work out their own salvation and to build up, by means of education, agriculture, and industry, a real center of national culture and focus of

> national life. It did not necessarily involve the early establishment of an independent Jewish State, which was a matter for gradual development in accordance with the ordinary laws of political evolution.[8]

Weizmann's speech was well received that evening, and the British next arranged for him to travel to meet Faisal.

In June 1918, Turkish forces occupied the Jordan Valley, and Weizmann thus was unable to travel directly to Faisal's military camp on the Transjordanian plains, a relatively short distance from Jerusalem on the map. His trip to meet with Faisal would necessitate a five-day journey by train, boat, car, camel, and foot. Weizmann went to Tel Aviv, took a train to Suez, circumnavigated the Sinai Peninsula in a dilapidated cargo boat, proceeded north from Aqaba seventy-five miles by car (which broke down), continued by camel from there, and completed the journey on foot. The weather, he wrote later, was "like standing near a red-hot oven."[9]

Weizmann left Tel Aviv on May 30 and reached Faisal's camp on the evening of June 3. On his arrival, he was able to watch Arab military movements in the north through his binoculars, and as he looked west, across the Jordan River, he was profoundly moved, as he realized that he was viewing the land where Moses had led the Israelites from Egypt three millennia earlier:

> I looked down from Moab on the Jordan Valley and the Dead Sea and the Judean hills beyond. . . . [A]s I stood there I suddenly had the feeling that three thousand years had vanished. . . . Here I was, on the identical ground, on the identical errand of my ancestors in the dawn of my people's history . . . that they might return to their home.

The following morning, Weizmann and Faisal met for almost an hour, with a British military attaché, Lieutenant Colonel P. C. Joyce, acting as interpreter. Weizmann explained the goals of Zionism in the same way he had in Jerusalem, and Joyce's minutes of the meeting show that Faisal repeatedly endorsed cooperation between Jews and Arabs. Faisal made no political commitments (saying they could only be made by his father) but, according to Joyce's minutes, said he "personally accepted the possibility of future Jewish claims to territory in Palestine."

Weizmann and Faisal at Faisal's Military Headquarters, June 4, 1918

After the meeting, Faisal suggested they take a photograph together outside his tent.

Joyce sent his minutes to Balfour, who asked him to convey to Weizmann "my appreciation of the tact and skill shown . . . in arriving at a mutual understanding with the Sheikh." After Weizmann returned to Tel Aviv, he wrote to his wife, Vera, that he had found Faisal "quite intelligent," a "very honest man," who was interested in "Damascus and the whole of northern Syria" but—strikingly—"not interested in Palestine."[10] Weizmann later told a Zionist group that the meeting had been "momentous"—that Faisal and he had "fully understood each other."[11]

Faisal's relative indifference to the land of Palestine was understandable, given his larger goals. At the time of the Balfour Declaration, Palestine was an undeveloped, sparsely populated area, with a total population of 600,000 Arabs and 60,000 Jews, living in an area that today has more than 12 million residents.[12] The Arab population there was about 5 percent of all the Arabs living under Ottoman rule. Faisal was primarily interested in Arab sovereignty over—and in the eventual unity of—the key

Arab cities of Damascus, Baghdad, Mecca, and Medina. In Jerusalem, by contrast, most of the population were Jews—and had been ever since the late nineteenth century.[13]

Not only was Palestine unnecessary for Faisal's goal of Arab unity; he and his father believed Zionism would, in fact, be good for the Arabs: It would bring financial resources and technical expertise to Palestine, transforming the Arab economies there and beyond.

On January 4, 1918, D. G. Hogarth, the director of Britain's Arab Bureau in Cairo, had traveled to Jeddah to deliver to King Hussein a formal message outlining British policy: (1) The Arabs would be given "full opportunity of once again forming a nation"; (2) "no obstacle should be put in the way" of the return of the Jews to Palestine; and (3) all holy sites, and the religious and political rights of all residents, would be preserved. The message emphasized the importance of "the friendship of world Jewry" to the Arab cause, and that Zionist leaders were "determined to bring about the success of Zionism by friendship and co-operation with the Arabs."

Hogarth's record of the conversation noted that the King "agreed enthusiastically" with these principles. In an article published on March 23, 1918, in *Al-Qibla*, Mecca's daily newspaper, the King wrote that Palestine was "a sacred and beloved homeland" for the Jews, "its original sons" [*abna'ihi-l-asliyin*], and that the "return of these exiles [*jaliya*] to their homeland" would be "materially and spiritually" beneficial.[14]

As World War I drew to a close, Lawrence submitted a map to the British Cabinet outlining his vision of a five-nation post-war Middle East. At the time, "Palestine" was considered to comprise not only the area west of the Jordan River, but also an equally large area to the east, where two-and-a-half of the ancient Israelite tribes had lived.[15] The land east of the Jordan had significant agricultural value.[16] Lawrence's map assigned (i) a broad swath of land to Faisal (labeled "Arabs"); (ii) a large area to the east labeled "Irak" to Faisal's older brother Emir Abdullah; (iii) a northern area to Faisal's younger brother Emir Zeid; (iv) another area in the northwest for the Armenians; and (v) a small area labeled "Palestine"—comprising the area west of the Jordan River and a very narrow strip of land on the East Bank of the Jordan River—for the Jews.

Lawrence's demarcation of "Palestine" effectively split it in half, assigning the western portion to the Jews and the eastern portion to be part of a large set of Arab states. On December 27, 1918, Faisal met with the British Foreign Office and told them he recognized the moral claims of the Zi-

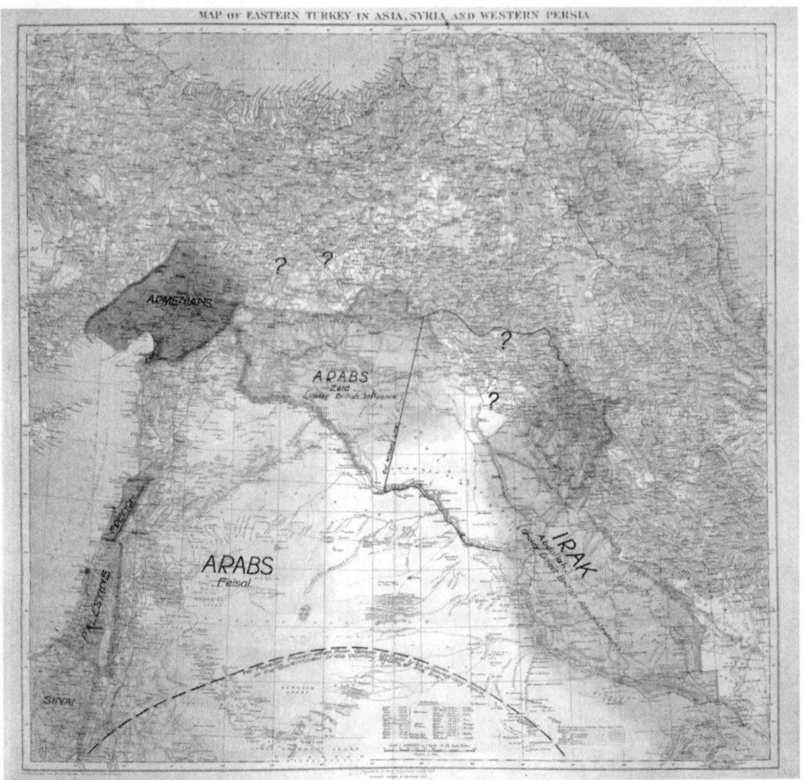

Lawrence's map presented to the British War Cabinet in November 1918

onists in Palestine. He also told Reuters that he was "in entire agreement" with the Zionist program, and that it "did not in the slightest prejudice the claims of the Arab National Movement."

On December 10, Faisal had arrived in London with Lawrence, and they had met with Weizmann at the Carlton Hotel the following day. Weizmann wrote a memorandum summarizing the discussion, noting that Faisal promised that at the Paris Peace Conference he would recognize the national and historical rights of Jews to Palestine and endorse the appointment of Britain as trustee over it, with the Muslim holy places and the economic interests of the Arabs in Palestine protected.

The next day, the *Times of London* published a statement from Faisal affirming that "The two main branches of the Semitic family, Arabs and Jews . . . understand one another, and I hope that as a result of interchange of ideas at the Peace Conference . . . each nation will make definite progress towards the realization of its aspirations." On December 29, Faisal gave a speech (with Lawrence translating) at a banquet given in his honor by Lord Walter Rothschild. In his speech, Faisal said:

> No true Arab can be suspicious or afraid of Jewish nationalism. . . . We are demanding Arab freedom and we would show ourselves unworthy of it, if we did not now, as I do, say to the Jews—welcome back home.

On January 3, 1919, Faisal and Weizmann met again at the Carlton Hotel and signed their agreement, explicitly recognizing "the national aspirations" of both the Jews and the Arabs. The agreement provided that "all measures shall be adopted" to implement the Balfour Declaration, including the "immigration of Jews into Palestine on a large scale," while protecting Arab civil and religious rights and Muslim control of their holy sites. The Zionists promised to support the formation of an Arab state and to provide economic, technical, and other assistance to it.

The agreement was silent on the ultimate political sovereignty over Palestine. At that time, Faisal would not have endorsed a Jewish state, nor would Weizmann have sought one, since the Jews were not yet a majority in Palestine. Weizmann viewed the Balfour Declaration not as a declaration of a Jewish state in Palestine, but rather as a charter giving the Jewish people the right to build one.[17] He envisioned a slow process, with years of immigration and institution-building, to create a society that would evolve naturally into a Jewish majority that would be entitled to a state. On the final page of the agreement, Faisal added a proviso, handwritten in Arabic, conditioning the entire agreement on the achievement of Arab independence beyond Palestine as set forth in a memorandum he had delivered that week to the British Foreign Office.[18] The proviso read:

> "Provided the Arabs obtain their independence as demanded in my Memorandum [to the British] . . . I shall concur in the above articles. But if the slightest modification or departure were to be made, I shall not then be bound by a single word of the present Agreement."[19]

In his memorandum to the British government, Faisal had written that the "aim of the Arab nationalist movements" was to "unite the Arabs eventually into one nation"—but not to seek a single state immediately, since in Faisal's words it was "impossible to constrain" all the Arab prov-

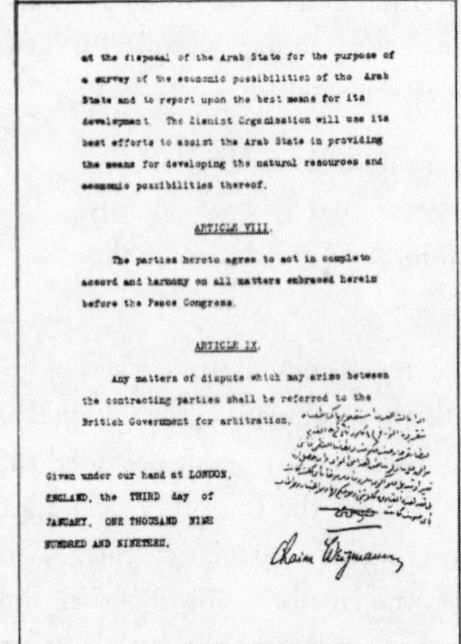

at the disposal of the Arab State for the purpose of a survey of the economic possibilities of the Arab State and to report upon the best means for its development. The Zionist Organisation will use its best efforts to assist the Arab State in providing the means for developing the natural resources and economic possibilities thereof.

ARTICLE VIII.

The parties hereto agree to act in complete accord and harmony on all matters embraced herein before the Peace Congress.

ARTICLE IX.

Any matters of dispute which may arise between the contracting parties shall be referred to the British Government for arbitration.

Given under our hand at LONDON, ENGLAND, the THIRD day of JANUARY, ONE THOUSAND NINE HUNDRED AND NINETEEN.

Chaim Weizmann

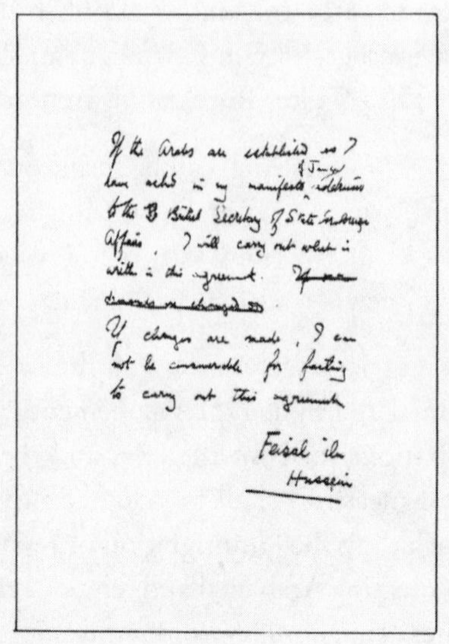

If the Arabs are established as I have asked in my manifesto {January} addressed to the British Secretary of State for Foreign Affairs, I will carry out what is written in this agreement.

If changes are made, I cannot be answerable for failing to carry out this agreement

Faisal ibn Hussein

Last Page of Faisal-Weizmann Agreement with T. E. Lawrence Translation of Faisal's Caveat

inces into "one frame of government," given their "economic and social differences." He stated that Syria was "sufficiently advanced politically to manage her own internal affairs" and should have immediate freedom, and Hedjaz (with Mecca and Medina) should continue as a separate kingdom, to work out its relationship with neighboring Arab areas on its own. Significantly, Faisal dealt with Palestine in a separate paragraph, which did not claim Arab sovereignty over it.

Faisal wrote that "the Arabs cannot risk assuming the responsibility of holding level the scales in the clash of races and religions that have, in this one province, so often involved the world in difficulties." For Palestine, Faisal sought an "effective super-position of a great trustee," with "a representative local administration" to promote "the material prosperity of the country." Faisal's memorandum was consistent with Weizmann's speech in Jerusalem on April 27 and with their meetings on June 4 and December 11.

At the Paris Peace Conference, Faisal's testimony excluded Palestine from his demand for Arab independence.[20] He asked instead that, because of its "universal character," Palestine be "left on one side for the mutual consideration of all parties interested." The Zionist submission to the Con-

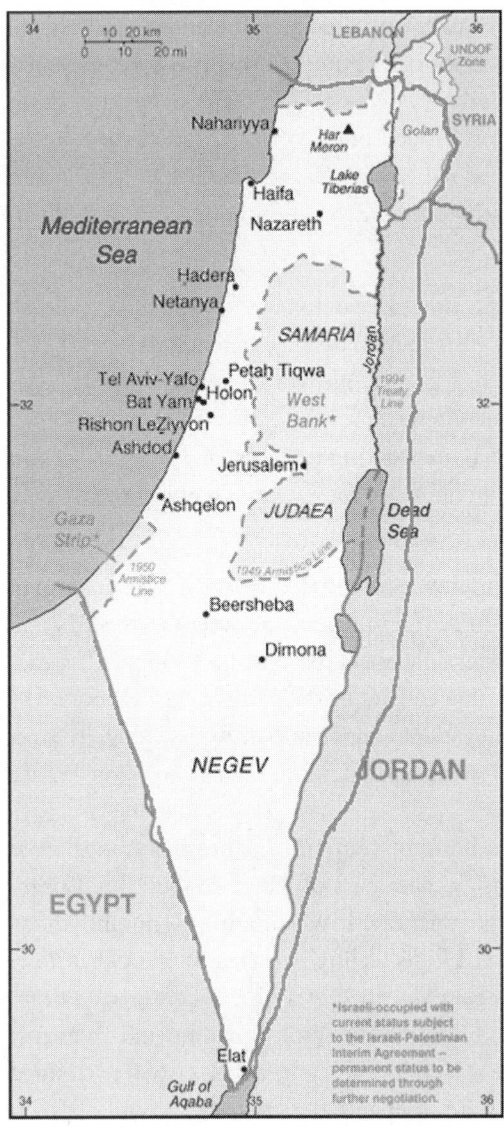

Jewish National Home Boundaries Presented to the 1919 Paris Peace Conference, superimposed on a map of present-day Israel and Jordan

ference specified boundaries for the Jewish national home that left all of Palestine east of the Jordan, except for a narrow strip, to the Arabs, consistent with Lawrence's November 1918 map.[21]

On March 5, 1919, the *New York Times*, in a news story headlined "Prince of Hedjaz Welcomes Zionists," published the text of a letter that Faisal had delivered to Felix Frankfurter, who was a member of the American Zionist delegation to the Peace Conference.[22] The letter was designed to ensure continued Zionist support for Arab nationalism by counteracting a March 1 interview Faisal had given to *Le Matin*, a Parisian daily, which had cast some doubt on his acceptance of the Zionist goals.[23] The letter to Frankfurter, as published in the *Times*, stated that "[w]e Arabs look with the deepest sympathy on the Zionist movement," and said further that:

> Our deputation in Paris is fully acquainted with the proposals submitted by the Zionists to the Peace Conference and regards them as moderate and proper. We will do our best to help them through and wish the Jews a most hearty welcome home. . . . [Dr. Weizmann and I] are working together for a reformed and revived Near East, and our two movements complete each other.[24]

While the Paris Peace Conference recognized Faisal as the spokesman for the Arabs, it failed to endorse the independent Syrian state and Arab control of areas outside Western Palestine that he had sought. Instead, Britain and France split effective control of the Middle East through the mandate system that the Allies would adopt in San Remo, Italy, in 1920, giving Britain control of Palestine and Mesopotamia (Iraq), and France control of Lebanon and Syria.

Britain installed Faisal as King of Iraq and his brother Abdullah as King of Transjordan. Hedjaz became part of Saudi Arabia. But Faisal's handwritten proviso in his agreement with Weizmann was not met in every respect, and Faisal departed Paris feeling betrayed by the Great Powers, especially France. In July 1919, the Syrian Congress, comprised of representatives of prominent Arab families in Syria, Lebanon, and Palestine, reacted by rejecting any French claim to any portion of Syria, claimed that Lebanon and Palestine were inseparable parts of Syria, and opposed Jewish immigration and other Zionist claims.[25]

The French proceeded to expel Faisal from Syria, nullifying the designation of him by the Syrian Congress as King. In the words of Faisal's biographer, Ali A. Allawi, with "the disastrous end to [Faisal's] kingdom in Syria . . . [t]he expectations and hopes raised by the Arab Revolt lay in ruins." The fierce century-long Arab opposition to political Zionism had begun.

Lawrence was deeply disappointed by the outcome in Paris. During

Faisal at the Paris Peace Conference
(T. E. Lawrence stands behind Faisal to his left, wearing a dark Arab headdress)

the Conference, he began drafting *Seven Pillars of Wisdom*, his account of his role in the Arab Revolt with Faisal, which he described as the "procession of Arab freedom from Mecca to Damascus," where they fought "in the naked desert, under the indifferent heaven," as part of an "army without parade or gesture, devoted to freedom." But when "the new world dawned [after World War I], the old men came out again and took our victory to re-make in the likeness of the former world they knew. . . . [W]e stammered that we had worked for a new heaven and a new earth, and they thanked us kindly and made their peace." In *Seven Pillars*, Lawrence warned that the Middle East was a region that no foreigner could rule forever:

> No foreign race had kept a permanent footing, though Egyptians, Hittites, Philistines, Persians, Greeks, Romans, Turks and Franks had variously tried. All had in the end been broken. . . . Semites had sometimes pushed outside this area, and themselves been drowned in the outer world. . . . Only in Tripoli of Africa,

> and in *the everlasting miracle of Jewry*, had distant Semites kept some of their identity and force. [Emphasis added].

The reference by Lawrence to "the everlasting miracle of Jewry" is striking, because he has generally been considered only an Arab partisan. But Lawrence also supported Zionism, and Weizmann considered him a personal friend.[26] After his death in 1935, Lawrence's brother Arnold published *T. E. Lawrence by His Friends*—a collection of essays by those who "knew [my brother] intimately in one aspect or another."[27] Weizmann, by then the leading Zionist of the time, contributed a recollection of the "long and memorable talk" he had with Lawrence about Zionism, and Lawrence's assistance in negotiations with Arab leaders:

> Lawrence readily gave not only his advice, but his personal help in furthering both Zionist aspirations and an understanding with the Arabs. Actuated by the desire to bring about cooperation between the two peoples, he was instrumental in drawing up the treaty between Emir Faisal and myself in 1919. . . .[28]

Lawrence's disillusionment after the 1919 Peace Conference is captured in an unpublished letter he sent to Frederick Claude Stern, Prime Minister David Lloyd George's private secretary, dated May 14, 1920. At the time of the letter, fighting between the Arabs and the French in Syria and Lebanon had begun, and a rebellion against the British was progressing in Iraq.[29] Lawrence wrote to decline Stern's invitation to attend a discussion about Palestine:

> Paris gave me a bad taste in my mouth, and so last May I dropped politics, and have had no touch with the British or Arabs or Zionists since. I'm out of them for good, and so my views on Palestine are merely ancient history. . . . [I]t's rather a sore subject, for since the [1918] armistice our Government has thrown away one chance after another, and now only fighting will put things straight: and I personally don't want to fight on either side this time![30]

But despite his disappointing experience in Paris in 1919, and his seemingly permanent withdrawal from Middle East affairs in 1920, Lawrence agreed in 1921 to join the British government in a new department formed to deal with the Middle East, after he received repeated requests from the new Secretary of State for the Colonies—Winston Churchill.

Churchill was in line to become Secretary of State for the Colonies in early 1921. On December 4, 1920, his private secretary wrote to Lawrence, telling him Churchill "would like very much to have a talk with you."[31] After speaking with Lawrence, Churchill sent a memorandum to Prime Minister David Lloyd George, telling him "[a]ll affairs in the triangle Jerusalem-Aden-Basra must be dealt with in their integrity . . . from one single point of view."[32] Otherwise, Churchill warned, there would be the "same paralysis and confusion of action which has done so much harm during the last two years."[33]

It took Churchill three attempts to recruit Lawrence as his principal Arab affairs adviser, because Lawrence feared "the shallow grave of public duty."[34] But Churchill assured Lawrence he would have a great deal of authority, and Lawrence came to realize it was a "very great chance" to accomplish what he had fought for in the Arab Revolt and at the Paris Peace Conference.[35]

On the weekend of January 8 and 9, 1921, Lawrence held long discussions with Faisal at the English country home of the Earl of Winterton.[36] Lawrence told Churchill afterwards that Faisal agreed with Lawrence's plan to bring both Iraq and Transjordan under Arab jurisdiction and "agreed to abandon all claims of his father to Palestine." Lawrence told Churchill that Faisal's sidelining the question of Syria, and forgoing claims to Palestine, bode well:

> [A]ll questions of pledges and promises, fulfilled or broken, are set aside. You begin a new discussion on the actual positions today and the best way of doing something constructive with them. It's so much more useful than splitting hairs.[37]

Lawrence told Churchill that the new plan would redeem Britain's wartime pledges to both the Arabs and the Jews. As the distinguished historian Sir Martin Gilbert has written:

> In 1915 the Arabs had been promised "British recognition and support for their independence" in the Turkish districts of Damascus, Hama, Homs and Aleppo—each of which was mentioned in the promise—but which did not include Palestine or

> Jerusalem. Two years later Britain had promised a national home for the Jewish people in Palestine, but with no mention of specific borders. If, therefore, the land east of the Jordan became an Arab state, and the land west of the Jordan . . . became the area of the Jewish National Home, Britain's pledges would be fulfilled.[38]

On March 2, 1921, Churchill and Lawrence traveled to Cairo to hold a conference on British policy in the region. About forty leading British authorities on the Middle East attended.[39] Over a nine-day period, Churchill heard from officials, experts, and Arab delegations.[40] At the end, the conference adopted Lawrence's plan, with Palestine partitioned along the Jordan River. In a letter to his friend Robert Graves, the English poet, Lawrence called it "a most ambitious design for the Middle East: a new page in the loosening of the Empire tradition."

The plan paralleled the one Lawrence had brokered with Faisal in 1919—Arab sovereignty everywhere outside a truncated Jewish Palestine, in exchange for Arab support for the smaller version of the Jewish National Home.[41] Churchill telegraphed Lloyd George, advising him that, "fortified by [the] views of Colonel Lawrence," he would meet Abdullah in Jerusalem to discuss establishing him in Transjordan.[42] Churchill then met with Abdullah four times in Jerusalem.

On March 30, 1921, Churchill met with a Palestinian Arab delegation, headed by the British-appointed former mayor of Jerusalem, Musa Kazim Pasha al-Husseini, who demanded that Churchill repudiate the Balfour Declaration. Churchill refused—both on grounds that it was a binding statement of British policy ratified by the Allied powers, and because it was based on justice. He told the Arabs that:

> It is manifestly right that the Jews, who are scattered all over the world, should have a national center and a National Home where some of them may be reunited. And where else could that be but in this land of Palestine, with which for more than three thousand years they have been intimately and profoundly associated?[43]

Britain gave Abdullah control of the Transjordanian region in April 1921.[44] Faisal was installed as the first King of Iraq on August 23, 1921.[45] In *Seven Pillars*, Lawrence summarized his satisfaction with the resolution of the Arab claims:

Churchill, Lawrence, and Abdullah in Jerusalem, 1921

> Mr. Winston Churchill was entrusted by our harassed Cabinet with the settlement of the Middle East; and in a few weeks, at his conference in Cairo, he made straight all the tangle, finding solutions, fulfilling (I think) our promises in letter and spirit (where humanly possible) without sacrificing any interest of our Empire or any interest of the peoples concerned. So we were quit of the war-time Eastern adventure, with clean hands. . . .[46]

In 1927, Lawrence wrote that Churchill and he shared the credit for the successful resolution: "I had the knowledge and the plan. He had the imagination and the courage to adopt it and the knowledge of the political procedure to put it into operation." Lawrence called it "the big achievement of my life," and said he was now satisfied "we kept our promises to the Arab Revolt."[47]

Several years after Lawrence's death in 1935, Churchill told Parliament that Lawrence had been "the truest champion of Arab rights whom modern times have known," that together he and Lawrence had established "vast regions" of independent Arab kingdoms that "had never been known in Arab history before," while also being "continually resolved to close no door upon the ultimate development of a Jewish National Home, fed by continual Jewish immigration into Palestine"—a regional settlement he said Lawrence had considered "fair and just."[48]

Having effectively split Palestine in two, the British prepared to accept the 1922 League of Nations Mandate—the international recognition of the Churchill-Lawrence plan. The principles were incorporated in the Churchill White Paper issued on June 22, 1922, which found that the Jews over several generations had re-created their national community in Palestine, and that:

> it is essential that [the Jewish community] should know that it is in Palestine as of right and not on sufferance. That is the reason why it is necessary that the existence of a Jewish National Home in Palestine should be internationally guaranteed, and . . . rest upon ancient historic connection.[49]

The League of Nations approved the Mandate for Palestine on July 22, 1922, incorporating the Balfour Declaration by reference, noting "the historical connection of the Jewish people with Palestine" and assigning to Britain the responsibility to "secure the establishment of the Jewish national home" there.[50] The Mandate allowed Britain to "postpone or withhold" establishing the Jewish national home "in the territories lying between the Jordan [River] and the eastern boundary of Palestine" (the nation of Jordan today), based on Britain's consideration of "the existing local conditions." The Arabs ultimately received approximately 75 percent of the Palestine Mandate.

With his plan effectuated, Lawrence resigned from the Colonial Office, believing that the respective claims of the Arabs and the Jews had been fairly resolved.[51] On July 8, 1922, Churchill wrote to Lawrence to tell him his assistance had been invaluable:

> I very much regret your decision to quit our small group at the Middle East Department of the Colonial Office. Your help in all matters and guidance in many has been invaluable to me and to your colleagues. I should have been glad if you would have stayed with us longer. I hope you are not unduly sanguine in your belief that our difficulties are largely surmounted. . . .[52]

The endorsement of the Balfour Declaration by France, Italy, and the United States had transformed the Declaration into something that was, as historian Martin Kramer has noted, roughly comparable to a UN Se-

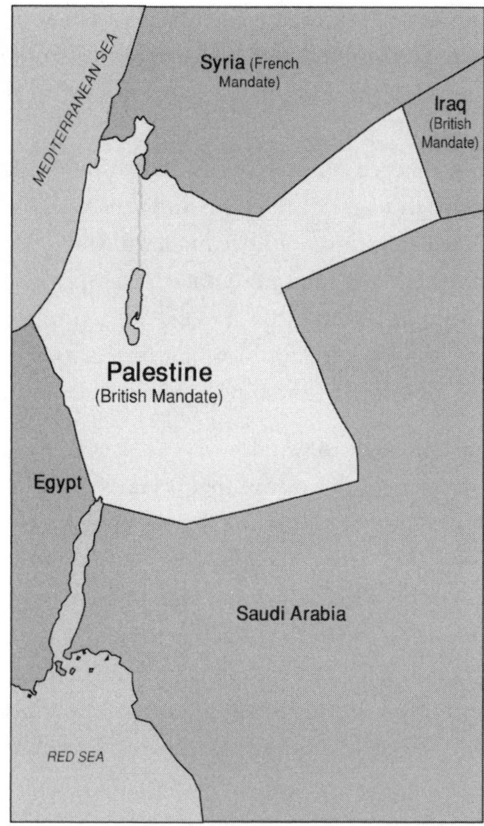

British Mandate for Palestine, 1922

curity Council resolution today. It was now a Great Power agreement as World War I approached its end. In 1920, the victorious Allies formally endorsed the Declaration at their post-war San Remo Conference, and Turkey (as the pre-war ruler of Palestine and post-war successor of the Ottoman Empire) signed the Treaty of Sèvres, which included the Declaration within its terms. After five years of consideration between 1917 and 1922, ending with the League of Nations Mandate, the Balfour Declaration had become an established part of international law.

Thirteen years later, when Lawrence died at the age of forty-six in a motorcycle accident, Britain had still not established Western Palestine as the Jewish national home. In 1937, in the face of Arab violence, Britain's Peel Commission—created to investigate the causes of the violence—proposed that Western Palestine should also be divided—into another sizable Arab state and a minuscule Jewish one, which would comprise about 15 percent of the original area of Palestine. Weizmann, backed by David Ben-Gurion, led the Zionist Congress in 1937 to accept the British partition proposal in principle, but the Arabs categorically rejected it.

In 1939, Britain reneged entirely on its obligation under the Mandate to facilitate the Jewish national home, issuing instead a new plan under which all of Western Palestine would be made an Arab state, with the Jewish population permanently limited to one-third. Speaking in the House of Commons, Churchill called this "a plain breach of a solemn obligation," and he forcefully rejected the idea that the Balfour Declaration had been a promise to a minority Jewish population in Palestine:

> [The pledge] was made to world Jewry. . . . It was in consequence of and on the basis of this pledge that we received important help in the War, and that after the War we received from the Allied and Associated Powers the Mandate for Palestine. . . . [The pledge] was not made to the Jews in Palestine but to the Jews outside Palestine, to that vast, unhappy mass of scattered, persecuted, wandering Jews whose intense, unchanging, unconquerable desire has been for a National Home. . . . That is the pledge which was given, and that is the pledge which we are now asked to break.

Eventually, five independent Arab states—Syria, Lebanon, Jordan, Iraq, and Egypt—covering a total area of 1.2 million square miles, emerged from the defeat of the Ottoman Empire by the Allies. The League of Nations Mandate for the Jewish national home covered fewer than 11,000 square miles, in only a part of Palestine. But Britain increasingly retreated from even the reduced obligation it assumed under that Mandate until, with its 1939 White Paper, it reneged on it entirely.

The House of Commons approved the White Paper by a vote of 268–179. Weizmann called it "a sort of Munich applied to us at a time when Jewry is drowning in its [own] blood." Even with millions of Jews in existential danger, Britain proceeded to forbid Jewish immigration to Palestine entirely. It ultimately returned its mandate to the United Nations in 1948, with its obligation to facilitate the Jewish national home unfulfilled.

In the end, Israel was established not by Great Britain but by the Jews themselves, after the United Nations adopted a two-state resolution in 1947. It was accomplished not only against British opposition but against an invasion by five Arab armies, from countries that owed their own existence to the plan executed by Churchill and Lawrence—one of the underlying principles of which had been a recognition that the Jewish people were entitled to their national home in Palestine as of right, and not by sufferance.

Faisal died in 1933 at the age of fifty, having used his diplomatic skills to build Iraq into a fully independent state. In a 634-page biography, published in 2014 by Yale University Press, the Iraqi scholar Ali A. Allawi wrote that "realistic, purposeful and constructive [Arab] patriotism also died with Faisal, to be replaced with the far more strident, volatile and angry nationalism that swept the Arab world after the end of the Second World War."[53]

In Weizmann's view, the 1919 agreement with Faisal (which he consistently called a "treaty") was a milestone in Arab-Jewish relations, and he repeatedly cited it in later years. In 1936, in testimony before the British Peel Commission on Palestine, he recounted its origins:

> [I]n 1918 there was one distinguished Arab who was the Commander-in-Chief of the Arab armies which were supporting the right flank of Allenby's army, the then Emir Faisal—subsequently King Faisal—and on the suggestion of General Allenby I went to his camp. I frankly put to him our aspirations, our hopes, our desires, our intentions, and I can only say—if any oath of mine could convince my Arab opponents—we found ourselves in full agreement, and this first meeting was the beginning of a lifelong friendship, and our relationship was expressed subsequently in a treaty.

In 1946, when the British again considered the future of Palestine, Weizmann wrote to Prime Minister Clement Attlee, maintaining that the Balfour Declaration was "part of a general Middle Eastern settlement" that had offered:

> a subcontinent to the Arabs and a "small notch"—as Lord Balfour put it—to the Jews. In 1917, it was the protagonists of the Arab revival—Sir Mark Sykes and Colonel T. E. Lawrence—who were among the foremost advocates of the Zionist settlement in Palestine. King Faisal was agreeable to a Jewish Palestine because he realized that it would promote the general progress of the Arab world.

Weizmann testifying in 1947 to the United Nations Special Committee on Palestine

On October 18, 1947, Weizmann addressed the United Nations as it approached its vote on a two-state resolution for Palestine. After noting the Arab achievement of independence in a wide area of the Middle East, he said:

> The Jews are only claiming in small measure what has been conferred upon the Arabs in abundant degree. There was a time when Arab statesmanship was able to see this equity in its true proportions. That was when the eminent leader and liberator of the Arabs, the Emir Faisal, later King of Iraq, made a treaty with me.

Weizmann acknowledged that in 1919 Faisal's handwritten proviso had not been satisfied, but he told the UN that "[t]he condition which [Faisal] then stipulated, the independence of all the territories outside Palestine, has now been fulfilled."

On November 14, 1947, two weeks before the UN voted, Weizmann met Eleanor Roosevelt—who was a member of the American Delegation—in the UN Delegates Lounge. The next day, he sent her copies of (i) "my treaty" with Faisal, (ii) Faisal's 1919 letter to Felix Frankfurter, and (iii) Faisal's formal statement to the Paris Peace Conference, to "dispel the impression," Weizmann wrote, "so assiduously circulated by the Arabs that it was all done without the consent of the Arabs at that time."

On May 16, 1948, Weizmann sent a message—he was too ill to attend in person—to a rally at Madison Square Garden celebrating Israel's Declaration of Independence two days before, as the neighboring Arab states responded by invading Israel. Weizmann's remarks included this passage:

> It is timely to recall the understanding of our cause and of our peaceful purposes which Arab leaders showed after the First World War, and the Treaty, which it was my privilege to sign with Emir, later King, Faisal, who represented the Arab people at the Peace Conference. . . . [The Arab states] will find the Jewish State always ready and eager to enter into neighborly relations and to join with them in a common effort to increase the welfare and prosperity of the Near East.

The Weizmann-Faisal agreement marked a historic moment, a time when Arabs and Zionists worked together, coordinating their diplomatic efforts to further their respective national goals, when the most prominent leader of the Arabs recognized that the Jews were not imperialist colonizers but nationalist allies, returning to a land that had once been theirs, where their religion had been born and where part of their ancient Temple still stood, with the Jews seeking not the entire land from which they had been expelled but only the minimum necessary to save their lives and their culture. They were not building an empire. They were coming home.[54]

A century later, with their respective states in existence but threatened by a new Persian hegemon, as Iran sought to create an Islamist empire across Syria, Lebanon, Iraq, and Yemen and began attacking Saudi Arabia and other Arab states through its proxies, a *de facto* Arab security arrangement with Israel began to take shape, behind the scenes.[55] Then formal diplomatic and economic relationships between Israel and four Arab countries were signed, deemed the "Abraham Accords," beginning with a signing ceremony at the White House on September 15, 2020. The Foreign Ministers of Bahrain and the United Arab Emirates (UAE), the Prime Minister of Israel, and the President of the United States joined together.[56]

In March 2022, an Arab-Israeli "Negev Summit" was held in Israel at Sde Boker—the home of Ben-Gurion—attended by the Foreign Ministers of Israel, Egypt, the United Arab Emirates, Bahrain, and Morocco, and the American Secretary of State, as cooperation continued to expand in the wake of the Accords.[57] The senior foreign policy officials of the five countries posed at the summit for a photograph together, everyone crossing their arms and joining hands with those on either side—a dramatic image that conveyed a message to Iran.[58]

After more than a century, the second Arab-Zionist alliance was being formed.

FOUR

Vladimir Jabotinsky and the Peel Prophecies

"We are facing an elemental calamity.
We have got to save millions, many millions."

Vladimir Jabotinsky in 1926

IN THE 1920S AND 1930S, as the Jews proceeded to rebuild their national home, backed first by Britain's Balfour Declaration and later by the League of Nations Mandate for Palestine, Arab violence against the Jews increased.

In 1920, Arabs in Jerusalem rioted during Passover, believing rumors that the Zionists were planning to install a Jewish-minority government over the Arabs, dispossess them of their property, and occupy the Muslim holy places. Six Jews were killed and two hundred more were injured. The riots were preceded by the distribution of the fraudulent *Protocols of the Elders of Zion*, which alleged a worldwide Jewish conspiracy, and a resolution adopted by the Muslim-Christian Association rejecting "a National Home for the people who did evil unto the Messiah and to the whole world."

In 1921, Arab riots continued over the Jewish presence at the Western Wall of their ancient Temple in Jerusalem, the holiest site of Judaism.[1] Arab opposition continued even after Britain, acting in accordance with an option provided in the Mandate, split Palestine into two parts in 1922 and transferred administrative control of Palestine east of the Jordan River ("Transjordan"—present-day Jordan) to Abdullah, Faisal's brother, and closed it to Jewish immigration.

In 1929, the violence worsened further, after thousands of Jews marched to the Western Wall on August 15, 1929—Tisha B'Av, the day commemorating the destruction of the Temple—to protest British restrictions on Jewish prayer there. The Arab attacks resulted in the death of 133 Jews and 339 injured. There were 116 Arabs killed and 232 others wounded, most of them by the British police attempting to suppress the riots. Seventeen Jewish communities were evacuated, and the Jewish community in Hebron—one of the principal cities of the Hebrew Bible—was massacred.[2]

In 1936, Haj Amin al-Husseini, the Mufti of Jerusalem and head of the "Supreme Arab Committee," called for an Arab general strike. Trains, roads, and telephone wires were sabotaged; widespread violence was visited on the Jews; and Arab guerrilla attacks were carried out against the British. As the violence continued, Britain established the Palestine Royal Commission under the chairmanship of Lord Peel (known colloquially as the Peel Commission), assigned to "ascertain the underlying causes of the disturbances," review the Arab and Jewish grievances, and make recommendations for the future.[3]

Recognizing that the future of their national home was at stake, the Jews presented a major defense of the Zionist cause to the Commission: Their printed memorandum ran 288 pages, with appendices that covered (a) the history of Palestine, (b) the legality of the Mandate, and (c) the Jewish accomplishments in Palestine in the two decades since the Balfour Declaration. The principal Zionist leaders, ranging across the entire Zionist spectrum—Chaim Weizmann, David Ben-Gurion, Vladimir Jabotinsky, and others—all testified before the Commission.[4]

Weizmann appeared first, as the head of the World Zionist Organization, testifying on November 15, 1936, for more than two hours and answering questions for another two. He told the Commission that, for the 6 million Jews in Eastern Europe, "the world is divided into places where they cannot live, and places into which they cannot enter." There ought to be, he said, "one place in the world . . . where we could live and express ourselves in accordance with our character," and that place was Palestine, where the Jews once had their national home, to which they had always maintained their claim—even after being expelled and dispersed around the world—and to which they prayed daily for an eventual return. Weizmann summarized both the Jewish claim and the contemporaneous Jewish rebuilding:

> [S]ince the destruction of Palestine [by the Romans] as a Jewish political entity, there was not a single century in which the Jews did not attempt to come back. . . . [A]t the beginning of the twentieth century, they had "no funds, no experience, no training, a broken-up people; a people which for centuries had been divorced from agricultural pursuits" . . . but we began. After fifteen years we stand before an achievement on which . . . we look with a certain amount of pride. . . . It was the land about which

> the British officials in 1919 said to me that we could not make anything out of.

Ben-Gurion, the head of the Jewish Agency Executive, appeared before the Commission in Jerusalem on January 7, 1937. He said that the Jewish right to Palestine was ultimately based on neither the Balfour Declaration nor the League of Nations Mandate, but rather on the Bible—considered not as a religious document, but rather as a historical one, the written record of centuries of Jewish sovereignty—and that therefore:

> I say on behalf of the Jews that the Bible is our Mandate, the Bible which was written by us, in our own language, in Hebrew, in this very country. . . . Our right is as old as the Jewish people. It was only the recognition of that right which was expressed in the Balfour Declaration and the Mandate.

Nor were the Jewish rights to Palestine, Ben-Gurion continued, based on either the number of Jews living in Palestine at the time of the Balfour Declaration in 1917 or the number in 1937 as the Peel Commission met:

> When the Balfour Declaration was made there were 60,000 Jews here. It was not only the right of those 60,000 [that the Declaration recognized]. Now we are 400,000 [in Palestine] and it is not only the right of these 400,000. It is because . . . [Palestine] is the . . . homeland of the Jewish people that we have rights in this country.

Haj Amin al-Husseini, who had instigated the 1936 riots and the continuing violence, testified on January 12, 1937, five days after Ben-Gurion. He alleged that the Balfour Declaration was the result of "undue Jewish pressure" on the British government, part of a Jewish plan to reconstruct their Temple on Arab holy places. He demanded "abandonment of the experiment of the Jewish National Home," the termination of the Mandate, and the establishment of Palestine as an Arab state. He said a Jewish national home was a physical impossibility, because Palestine was allegedly "already fully populated" and it was "impossible to place two distinct peoples . . . in one and the same country."[5] In his colloquy with the Commissioners, Husseini made it clear that an Arab state in Palestine would expel even the Jewish residents already there:

Q. [I]f the Arabs had [a state in Palestine], would they be prepared to welcome the Jews already in the country?
A. That will be left to the discretion of the government which will be set up . . .
Q. Does His Eminence think that this country can assimilate and digest the 400,000 Jews now in the country?
A. No.
Q. Some of them would have to be removed by a process kindly or painful as the case may be?
A. We must leave all this to the future.

The last Zionist leader to testify before the Commission was Vladimir Jabotinsky, the head of the New Zionist Organization, founded by him in 1935 to seek a Jewish state on both sides of the Jordan River, which was the geographical area of Palestine at the time of the Balfour Declaration and the League of Nations Mandate. Jabotinsky was a Russian journalist, essayist, playwright, novelist, orator, and translator, fluent in seven languages, educated as a lawyer. In 1903, at the age of twenty-three, he had been a delegate from Odessa to the historic Sixth Zionist Congress—where Herzl had presented the East African option offered by the British.[6]

During World War I, Jabotinsky had been the moving force behind the creation of the Jewish Legion, a regiment of 15,000 British, American, Canadian, and Palestinian Jews who fought alongside the British forces under the command of British Lieutenant Colonel John Patterson, helping to free Palestine from the Ottoman Turks.[7] It was the most prominent organized Jewish military force in almost two millennia.[8] Jabotinsky enlisted in the Legion as a private at age thirty-eight, was promoted to lieutenant, and fought in Palestine in 1918. Patterson's 1922 book, *With the Judeans in the Palestine Campaign*, effusively praised both the Legion and Jabotinsky's leadership.[9]

In his own book, *The Story of the Jewish Legion* (1928), Jabotinsky wrote that "half the Balfour Declaration belongs to the Legion," which had been formed in London four months before the Declaration was issued—because the Legion had demonstrated to the British that the Jews, widely derided at the time as mere "tailors," were serious about joining the fight for Palestine. In his book, Jabotinsky repeated the message he had given to his fellow soldiers in 1918:

Jabotinsky (in the center) with soldiers of the Jewish Legion, 1918

> And to each one of the five thousand [members of my own] brigade I say what I once said to my "tailors" [while we were fighting in Palestine] . . . "Far away, in your home, you will one day read glorious news, of a free Jewish life in a free Jewish country—of factories and universities, of farms and theaters, perhaps of MPs and ministers. . . . Then you shall stand up, walk to the mirror, and look yourself proudly in the face . . . and salute yourself—for 'tis you who have made it."[10]

Jabotinsky formed the Haganah defense force in 1920, in response to the Arab violence against the Jews, and in 1923 he wrote two landmark essays about the Zionist movement, "The Iron Wall" and "The Ethics of the Iron Wall," maintaining that the Arabs would never accept a Jewish presence in Palestine until they were convinced that they could not eliminate it by force. He argued that an "Iron Wall" was thus a necessity for peace—since peace was not possible until the Arabs gave up that hope.[11] He also established in 1923 a youth organization called Betar, a Hebrew acronym based on the name of Joseph Trumpeldor, a celebrated Zionist soldier who had died in 1920 fighting to protect Tel Hai, a Jewish settlement in Palestine. Betar was also the name of the place where the Jews in the ancient Bar-Kokhba revolt had made their last stand against the Romans.

The credo of Betar was *hadar*, a Hebrew word with no exact English equivalent, which combined "dignity," "honor," and "majesty." Jabotinsky continually reminded Jews, especially the Jewish youth in Betar, that they were the descendants of royalty. He crystallized his essential message in 1934 in an essay titled "The Idea of Betar":

> Behind every one of us stand 70 generations of ancestors who could read and write, and who spoke about and inquired into God and history, peoples and kingdoms, ideas of justice and integrity, humanity and its future. Every Jew is in this sense a "prince."

Jabotinsky testified before the Peel Commission in London on February 11, 1937, at its final public hearing.[12] Four days earlier, the *New York Times* had published a major article about the horrific situation facing the Jews of Eastern Europe, written by Otto D. Tolischus, one of the *Times'* most experienced European correspondents. His report from Poland covered five columns in the Sunday edition, describing the wave of antisemitism sweeping Eastern Europe, extending far beyond Germany. The first paragraph read:

> Anti-Semitism, raised by Adolf Hitler in Germany to the status of a political religion, is rapidly spreading throughout Eastern Europe and is thereby turning the recurrent Jewish tragedy in that biggest Jewish center in the world into *a final disaster of truly historic magnitude*. [Emphasis added.]

Tolischus reported that the "disaster is now taking place in Latvia, Lithuania, Hungary and Rumania and is approaching a high-water mark in Poland, the country with the biggest Jewish population outside the United States." He described the situation in the starkest terms:

> In all these countries the majority of the Jews, totaling 5,000,000 souls, or 30 percent of the whole Jewish population in the world, are now facing the prospect of either repeating the Exodus on a bigger scale than that chronicled in the bible, and somehow making it through the immigration barriers erected against them

Jabotinsky testifying before the Peel Commission, February 11, 1937

> everywhere, or spending the rest of their lives in an atmosphere of creeping hostility and dying a slow death from economic strangulation.

In Germany, there remained about 400,000 Jews (some 200,000 having left since Hitler took power in 1933). The number at risk in the other countries of Eastern Europe was twelve times that number. They were living, in the words of the chairman of the Joint Distribution Committee, the Jewish relief group, as reported in the *Times*, in "unspeakable degradation and misery," making "a desperate attempt to survive." The Jews remaining in Germany, he said, "face extermination."

In London, the newspapers reported that hundreds of people queued outside the House of Lords for a chance to hear Jabotinsky, with many of them turned away.[13] The audience included William Ormsby-Gore (the British Secretary of State for the Colonies), Dr. Vera Weizmann (a physician and the wife of Chaim Weizmann), Lady Blanche Dugdale (Lord Balfour's niece and biographer, and an ardent Zionist), Lieutenant Colonel John Patterson, and other notables. Jabotinsky would later say it "was the best speech I ever made."

Jabotinsky's testimony consumed an hour and a half, followed by questions from the Commissioners that lasted another forty minutes. The British press—including the *Times of London*, the *News Chronicle, Daily News, Morning Post,* and *Manchester Guardian*—all carried extensive reports of his testimony.[14]

Jabotinsky began by noting that Palestine—with its historic boundaries on both sides of the Jordan River—was the obvious place to settle the homeless and threatened Jews of the world. He testified that Jewish immigration would threaten none of the existing Arab residents: If Palestine, with its population of 1.6 million, were populated in the future at the same density as Sicily, he noted, it would sustain 12 million people; and if populated at the same density as England, 18 million.

There was thus enough room in Palestine for both Jews and Arabs, Jabotinsky testified, as well as for major population increases of both groups in the future. Palestine could hold, he told the Commission:

> the 1,000,000 present Arab population, plus 1,000,000 economic places reserved for their progeny, plus many millions of Jewish immigrants . . . and I think that disposes ultimately of any suspicion that, in our schemes, anybody of any party dreams of displacing or of disturbing the present non-Jewish population. . . .
>
> [T]here is no question of ousting the Arabs. On the contrary, the idea is that Palestine on both sides of the Jordan should hold the Arabs, their progeny *and* many millions of Jews. [Emphasis by Jabotinsky.]

Jabotinsky praised the "purely spiritual aspects of Jewish nationalism"—rebuilding Hebrew culture and creating a model community—but he said that "as compared with our actual needs and our real position in the world today, all that has rather the character of luxury":

> We are facing an elemental calamity, a kind of social earthquake. . . . We have got to save millions, many millions. I do not know whether it is a question of re-housing one-third of the Jewish race, half of the Jewish race, or a quarter of the Jewish race; I do not know, but it is a question of millions. . . .

As for the Arab claims to Palestine, Jabotinsky acknowledged their understandable perspective, but he tried to put the competing claims into a proper balance:

> I have the profoundest feeling for the Arab case, in so far as that Arab case is not exaggerated. . . . It is quite understandable that the Arabs of Palestine would prefer Palestine to be the Arab State No. 4, No. 5, or No. 6—that I quite understand—but when the

> Arab claim is confronted with our Jewish demand to be saved, it is like the claims of appetite versus the claims of starvation.

Jabotinsky maintained that in "the decisive terrible balance of need," the Jewish case was compelling, given the condition of the Jewish people and the absence of Jewish sovereignty anywhere in the world, while other peoples (including the Arabs) already had it in abundance:

> [E]very nation on earth, every normal nation, beginning with the smallest and the humblest, who do not claim any merit, any role in humanity's development, they all have states of their own. That is the normal condition for a people; yet when we, the most abnormal of peoples and therefore the most unfortunate, ask only for the same conditions as the Albanians enjoy, to say nothing of the French and the English, then it is called too much. . . .
>
> [W]ith 1,000,000 more Jews in Palestine today you could already have a Jewish majority, but there are certainly 3,000,000 or 4,000,000 in [Eastern Europe] who are virtually knocking at the door asking for admission—i.e., for salvation.

Jabotinsky expressed his greatest disappointment in Britain's failure, fifteen years after it had sought and received the Mandate for Palestine, to meet its obligation to reestablish the Jewish national home, as it was legally required to do. He castigated Britain's failure to adopt even a plan to do so:

> I always thought, before coming to England, that if a civilized country, a civilized government, assumed a trust, internationally . . . dealing with a people who have so long suffered and who have so long hoped . . . I expected that government to sit down and prepare a blueprint, a plan . . . [starting] with a geological survey of both sides of the Jordan, in order to ascertain what agricultural settlement could be satisfied. Further, a plan of industrial development calculated to provide sustenance for large scale immigration; a plan of what tariff laws and customs measures should be adopted in order to protect that development; a plan for a taxation system . . . [to assist] the new settlers and the newcomers. Finally, a measure for guaranteeing security. . . .

What particularly galled him, Jabotinsky said, was that the British not only had failed to provide security for the Jews, but had even denied them the right to protect themselves:

> And as the Jews never asked to be protected by anyone else, a plan [under the Mandate] should embody the Jewish demand that they should themselves be allowed to form a protecting body in Palestine, or at least a considerable part of it. . . . [T]hat is what everybody expected. I need not tell you how totally disappointed we were . . . . I can only say we have greatly suffered under this . . . deliberate aversion from making plans. . . . We have suffered terribly.

The British failure, Jabotinsky continued, forced the Jews "to prepare by underhand methods, with insufficient equipment, with insufficient drilling, in an amateurish way." The results were pogroms against which the Jews could not adequately defend themselves. He was sitting directly across from the Commissioners as he gave his testimony, and he almost lost his composure as he continued, saying that "I really do not know how a government can allow or tolerate such a state of things after three experiences [in 1920, 1921, and 1929], of which 1929 was a terrible one":

> I am sorry if I am getting excited, and I apologize to the Commission and hope they understand the reason for it. . . . A fortnight ago, before the [new violent] events, on the 6th of April, [1936], a telegram was sent to the High Commissioner informing him disturbances were coming, and we called his attention to the fact that the troops were not sufficient and the police not sufficiently reliable. . . .
>
> My Lord and gentlemen, it is neglect, omission . . . all this tragedy. . . . Sufficient numbers of splendid youth were out there to take their due part, had they been made use of from the beginning, the riots would not have taken these dimensions. . . .
>
> We have been asking, we have been demanding it on our knees, let us defend the country. It was turned down. . . . [B]y mobilizing 5,000 Jewish youths in the course of the months of April and May [of this year] you would have stopped the riots.

Jabotinsky next demanded that another Royal Commission be established to determine the responsibility for the British inaction that had resulted in death and destruction for the Jews in Palestine:

> Because I claim someone is guilty. I claim that a tremendous amount of ammunition for the Arabs has been allowed to percolate into Palestine both before and during the events. I claim there was neglect of duty. . . . Sometimes even a humble man like myself has the right to say the words "*J'accuse*." . . . I submit most respectfully and humbly that some independent Commission, independent of the Colonial Office and independent of the [British officials in Palestine], should inquire and investigate into this question of guilt. . . . [T]he person guilty should be punished and that is what I humbly demand.

Jabotinsky then outlined what he believed would be the only way to implement the League of Nations Mandate: "We call it a Ten-Year Plan . . . [with] agrarian reforms, taxation and custom reforms, a reform of the civil service, opening up Transjordan for Jewish penetration, an assurance of public security by . . . legalization of Jewish self-defense."

Despite the desperate situation he had portrayed, and Britain's abject failure to meet its international obligations, Jabotinsky ended his statement by expressing confidence in the British:

> I believe in England, just as I believed in England twenty years ago, when I went against nearly all Jewish opinion and said, "Give soldiers to Great Britain" [by forming the Jewish Legion] because I believed in her. I still believe. . . . I thank the Commission very much for their kindness and attention. I beg your forgiveness for having kept you for an hour and a half.

Lord Peel responded by telling Jabotinsky that his points had been "particularly forcibly put."

On March 12, 1937, Winston Churchill testified *in camera* before the Commission, as the author of the 1922 British White Paper that had declared the Jews were in Palestine "as a matter of right, not sufferance." He told the Commission that the Balfour Declaration's commitment to the Jews had been important when it was made and could not simply be discarded by Britain fifteen years later:

> I insist upon loyalty and upon the good faith of England to the Jews, to which I attach the most enormous importance, because we gained great advantages in the War. We did not adopt Zionism entirely out of altruistic love of starting a Zionist colony: it was a matter of great importance to this country. It was a potent factor on public opinion in America and we are bound by honor, and I think upon the merits, to push this thing as far we can.

Churchill testified that the Balfour Declaration envisioned "an increasing Jewish population, that that population should not in any way be restricted from reaching a majority position," and that the thought was that "there might well be a great Jewish State there, numbered by millions." One of the commissioners asked him about an "indigenous population" being "subject to the invasion of a foreign race," and Churchill forcefully rejected the premise of the question. He said that while he had "great regard for Arabs," it was "the Arabs, who had been the outsiders, the conquerors," and that under them the land had become "a desert."

Churchill concluded that Britain was bound to uphold its commitment under the Balfour Declaration and the League of Nations Mandate, not only because it was right, but because—if Britain did not—another great power would take over an area of strategic importance:

> My view is that you should go on and persevere with the task, holding the balance in accordance with the Declaration, allowing the influx of new immigrants to take place as fast as can be. . . . But if you cannot do that, give it up and let Mussolini take it on, which he would be very anxious to do. Someone else might come in. You would have to face that. A power like Italy would have no trouble. There are powers in the world which are rising powers which are unmoral powers. . . .

In private, the Peel Commission had been considering the possibility of replacing the Mandate for a Jewish homeland with a partition of Palestine into a Jewish and an Arab state, retaining a British corridor to Jerusalem to keep control of the holy places. The Commission raised the idea with Weizmann *in camera*, the day after Ben-Gurion's testimony. Weizmann welcomed it; then caught himself and cautioned that he lacked the authority to endorse it; and then requested more time to consider it:

> [I]f a tripartite [partition] agreement can be arrived at and this is the price which is demanded from us, our contribution to peace, I do not think you would find us difficult. . . . [But] I am saying it without any authority; I am saying it on my own responsibility. . . . I would not like to close the door on any proposal. . . . Permit me not to give a definite answer now. Let me think of it.

With his initial reaction, however, Weizmann had effectively communicated his approval of a partition plan for Palestine.

On July 5, 1937, the British Cabinet released the 435-page Peel Commission Report, with a partition recommendation that the British government officially endorsed.[15]

The Report traced the 3,000-year Jewish connection to Palestine and found that building the Jewish national home had been advantageous to the Arabs, because they had benefited from the investment of Jewish capital and Jewish economic activity in Palestine, which had raised Arab employment and income. The Report noted the very large increases in the Arab population in Jewish urban areas, contrasted with virtually no population growth in Arab towns such as Nablus and Hebron. It observed that Jewish hospitals and clinics served both Arabs and Jews; and it recognized that Jewish anti-malaria efforts throughout Palestine had benefited everyone.

The Report found that the underlying cause of the ongoing violence was the implacable Arab opposition to any Jewish home in Palestine. The Commission found that the "ugliest element in the picture" was not terrorism against Jews (the Report observed that such violence was "no new thing"), but rather attacks by *Arabs on Arabs*—especially those suspected of insufficient adherence to the virulent anti-Jewish views of Haj Amin al-Husseini, the Mufti of Jerusalem. Arabs who did not support continued violence received visits from "gunmen," the Report noted, such as the one "to the editor of one of the Arabic newspapers last August shortly after he had published articles in favor of [ending violence]":

> Similar visits were paid during our stay in Palestine to wealthy Arab landowners or businessmen who were believed to have made inadequate contributions to the funds which the Arab

> Higher Committee were raising to compensate Arabs for damage suffered during the "disturbances." Nor do the "gunmen" stop at intimidation. It is not known who murdered the Arab Acting Mayor of Hebron last August, but no one doubts that he lost his life because he had dared to differ from the "extremist" policy of the Higher Committee. The attempt to murder the Arab Mayor of Haifa . . . is also, we are told, regarded as political.

The Commission concluded that Arab nationalism in Palestine was "inextricably interwoven with antagonism to the Jews." It did not derive from economics or any "positive national feeling" of the Arabs themselves. Even if the Jewish national home were "far smaller," the Report concluded, "the Arab attitude would be the same." It concluded that Arab "moderates" would not facilitate a peaceful settlement, since in the end they always sided with the extremists. The Commission pronounced itself:

> convinced that no prospect of a lasting settlement can be founded on moderate Arab nationalism. At every successive crisis in the past that hope has been entertained. In each case it has proved illusory.

Accordingly, the Commission proposed a partition plan that would: (a) allocate almost all of Palestine west of the Jordan River to the Arabs, (b) retain Jerusalem and a corridor to it from the Mediterranean for Britain, and (c) restrict the Jews to a minuscule state in a small part of the north—a minor portion of the land originally promised to the Jews by Britain and the League of Nations in 1922 and that had long since become part of international law.

The Peel Commission proposal generated a firestorm of opposition from Churchill and others who had been involved with the Balfour Declaration and the League of Nations Mandate and still supported the establishment of Palestine as the Jewish national home.[16] For their part, Arabs across the board rejected even a small Jewish state. Jewish opinion, as usual, was divided.

Weizmann appreciated the voluminous evidence in the Report of Jewish achievements in Palestine and the Commission's support for a Jewish state. But he believed that the recommendations were completely inconsistent with the facts the Commission had found. In his 1949 autobiography, he would write that:

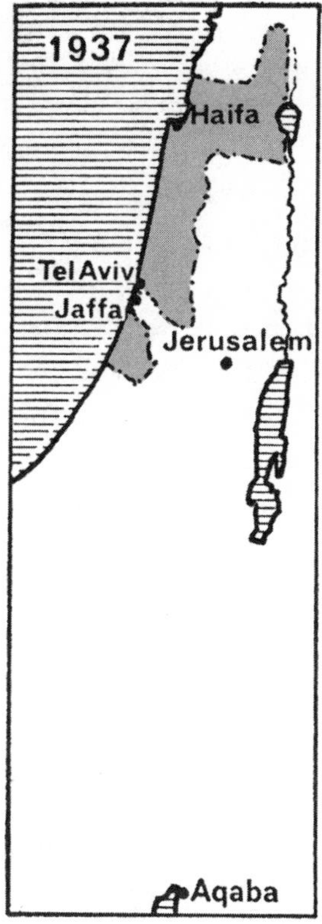

Peel Commission Map of Proposed Jewish State in Palestine (Alamy World History Archive)

> The report put an end to the persistent falsehood that Jewish land purchases and land development had led to the displacement of Arabs; then it recommended severe restrictions on Jewish purchases of land. It asserted that Jewish immigration had brought benefits to the Arab people; then it recommended the severe curtailment of Jewish immigration. . . . [In 1922, the British government had stated that] Jews were in Palestine "as of right and not on sufferance,". . . . Now the Peel Report recommended that . . . "political and psychological factors must be taken into consideration." . . . In other words, our entry into Palestine was made conditional on the mood of the Arabs.

Weizmann realized, as he later wrote, that "Arab terrorism had won its first major victory," because the Mandate "was pronounced unworkable." It was "hard to describe the heartsickness and bitterness of Jews as they watched the larger Hitler terror engulf their kin in Europe, while the gates of Palestine were being shut as a concession to the Arabs." The bulk of the country was being turned over to "the clique of so-called Arab leaders who organized the disturbances of [1936]," and having used violence to destroy the Mandate, they would undoubtedly use the same tactics to undermine the partition proposal as well, lest the Jews obtain sovereignty even in a much-reduced area.

Weizmann nevertheless believed that the Report marked a historic moment—the chance to establish a Jewish state—and he wanted to seize the opportunity, perhaps in part because he had effectively assured the Commissioners in private that he would welcome a partition proposal. Ben-Gurion also supported partition, believing the inadequate boundaries could be expanded later, either through further negotiation or otherwise. Jabotinsky was completely opposed to the partition proposal: He thought it was both unjust, in view of the international assurances the British and the League of Nations had long given the Jews, and unworkable as a practical matter, given the size of the proposed Jewish state, which he thought would be promptly overrun even if it could be established. It would not solve but rather exacerbate the situation of the Jews.

Accordingly, Jabotinsky proceeded to take his position directly to Members of Parliament and then personally to Churchill.[17]

On July 13, 1937, a week after the issuance of the Peel Commission Report, Jabotinsky addressed a meeting of Members of the House of Commons convened by Sir John Haslam of the ruling Conservative Party, who introduced Jabotinsky as a man who was a "friend of this country," who "fought for this country . . . in the War in 1917-1918 under Allenby and was decorated for bravery." Jabotinsky proceeded to illustrate his presentation with three sketches, designed to show that the portion of Palestine allocated to the Jews was "less than a drop in the ocean of our Jewish distress and land hunger."[18]

Jabotinsky's first sketch showed the boundaries of Palestine, as they were understood at the time of the League of Nations Mandate, compared to the small, shaded portion allocated for the Jewish state in the Peel Commission Report—after Palestine had already been partitioned in 1922 by the transfer of Transjordan to the Arabs:

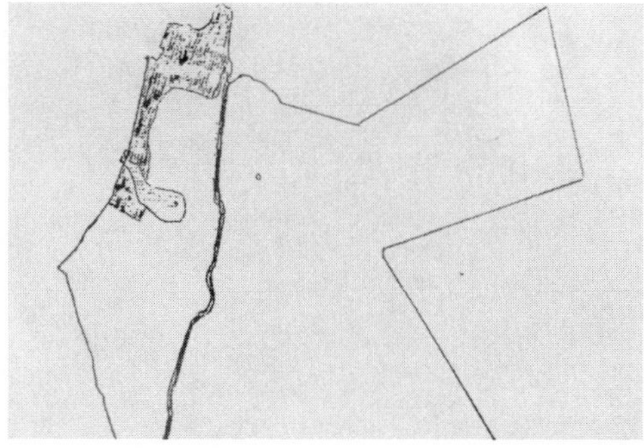

Jabotinsky explained the sketch to the assembled MPs as follows:

> [I]n 1922, Transjordan was cut off . . . an area of 90,000 square kilometers containing even today a population of only 320,000. What was left for us . . . is the western slice . . . and its population is . . . 645,000 inhabitants, or about 140 inhabitants per square kilometer . . . about the same as that of industrial Germany. . . . [T]he hope of settling there large numbers of additional immigrants . . . is rather fantastic.

Jabotinsky's second map showed all of Palestine, as originally defined, compared to the vast amount of land for Syria, Lebanon, Iraq, and Saudi Arabia that had been carved out of the defunct Ottoman Empire, resulting in several new Arab nations of considerable size:

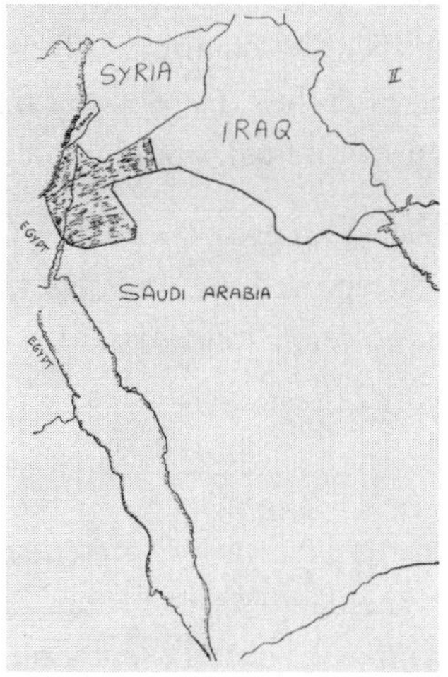

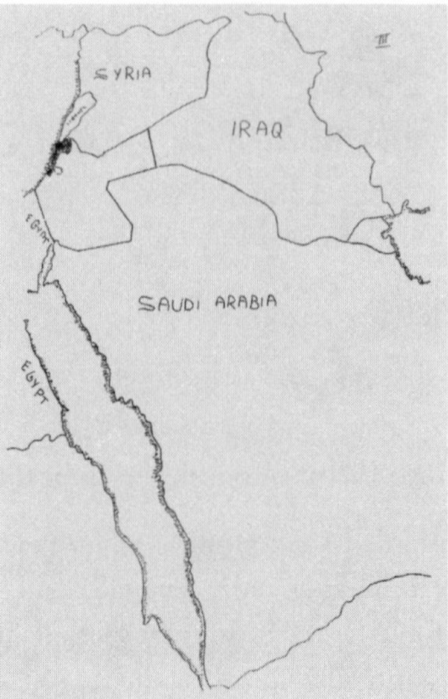

On his third map, Jabotinsky showed the portion of Palestine allocated to the Jews compared to the total area comprising the new Arab states of Lebanon, Syria, Iraq, Saudi Arabia, and Transjordan:

With his maps, Jabotinsky dramatically demonstrated the result for the Jews if the Commission's plan were confirmed by Parliament. For the Jews, Jabotinsky said:

> There will be no room for any immigration even remotely adequate for our needs. For *real* Zionism . . . bent on saving millions of men and women from their distress—for this kind of Zionism, [the Peel] Partition, if final, would mean the doom of death.

When Jabotinsky finished his presentation, the MPs applauded. A week later, the *New York Times* reported that in Poland, where most of the European Jews lived, over 200,000 Zionists paraded to protest the proposed partition.[19]

On July 16—three days after Jabotinsky's presentation to the MPs—Lady Violet Bonham Carter, the daughter of former Prime Minister Herbert Asquith and a close friend of Churchill, sent Churchill a note, enclosing a letter and memorandum from Jabotinsky. "People are so ignorant," she wrote to Churchill, "of the geographical & strategic position of the *tiny* corner now allotted to the Jews." She told him that Jabotinsky's material contained "some very relevant objections to the [partition] scheme," in case "you feel disposed to speak" in the Parliamentary debate scheduled for July 21. Churchill had told her he was not sure if he would participate.[20]

Jabotinsky's letter urged Churchill to address the issue, since the Jews "would be grievously disappointed if your voice were not heard."[21] The proposed Jewish state would be in a "dwarfish area . . . surrounded not by the Arab Palestine only, but by an Arab Federation. . . . It will inevitably be coveted, and inevitably attacked at the first opportunity," destined to be "eventually captured by the neighboring Arab States, the conquest being probably accompanied by destruction and massacre."[22]

Jabotinsky wrote that "the worst feature of the whole business [is] that we shall have no time even to state our case" in opposition to it. He told Churchill that he hoped the opposition "will be stated by friends, in the first place by you," and he emphasized that the plan was being rushed through Parliament:

> Unprecedented pressure is being used to get to final and fateful decisions before even that evidence, on which the Report is supposed to be based, has been read by all concerned, and especially before the Jews, to whom it is a matter of life and death, have had time properly to confer.

Churchill and Jabotinsky met before the debate, and during the debate, Churchill criticized the plan and proposed a substitute resolution, requiring that the government, before seeking Parliamentary approval, bring the plan to the League of Nations for "adequate enquiry"—and then—only if approved by the League—present a more detailed plan to Parliament. Churchill's substitute resolution was adopted, depriving Prime Minister Chamberlain of the approval he had sought for the Peel partition.

On July 25, 1937, Churchill published an op-ed for the Hearst Sunday newspapers, entitled "Can Partition Bring Peace to Palestine," in which he wrote that the "tract of land assigned to the Jews, no bigger than an English county, already bears a population of 140 to a square mile . . . as densely populated as Germany or England, and twice as heavily as France" and that the partition proposal presented "a set of grave strategic problems . . . none of which appear to have been sufficiently envisaged at the present time."[23]

The League of Nations' Permanent Mandates Commission proceeded to conduct a detailed examination of the partition proposal, and it concluded that the Mandate had become "almost unworkable once it was publicly declared to be so by a British Royal Commission."

The Twentieth Zionist Congress, held in Zurich in August 1937, debated the Peel partition proposal at length. It became the most contentious Zionist Congress since 1903, when Herzl had presented the East African offer. For the first time, deliberations among the 484 delegates were held behind closed doors. It was a virtual rerun of 1903: a battle between idealists and realists—but this time not in the shadow of a pogrom in Kishinev, but rather the ongoing Jewish disaster throughout Eastern Europe.

The Congress eventually adopted a compromise resolution, by a vote of 300–158, calling the Peel Commission's partition plan "unacceptable," directing the Zionist leadership "to resist any infringement of the rights of the Jewish people internationally guaranteed by the Balfour Declaration and the Mandate," but expressing "the readiness of the Jewish people to reach a peaceful settlement with the Arabs of Palestine," based on the "mutual recognition of their respective rights." The resolution authorized further negotiations to seek a more realistic plan.

The Arabs refused to recognize any Jewish sovereignty, however—no matter how small the area, no matter how large the area for a new Arab state in addition to the already existing ones, and no matter that Palestine had already been partitioned in 1922. The Arab reaction was—in the words of a royal commission established in 1938 to consider partition boundaries—"immediate and uncompromising," and the Arabs initiated more violence on an even larger scale:

> The outburst of uncompromising disapproval . . . [was] followed by an intensification of the Arab lawlessness which had continued sporadically since the end of the Arab general strike in [1936]. During the last days of July, and throughout August and September [1937], a widespread campaign of murder and intimidation cost many Jews and Arabs their lives.

The Supreme Arab Committee announced that "the only solution" would be "cessation of the experiment" of the Jewish National Home, "cessation of the British Mandate," creation of an independent Arab state, and the immediate end "of all Jewish immigration and of land sales to Jews." The 1938 British commission investigating possible boundaries visited Palestine and reported that "[a]lmost every day brought its record of murder, intimidation and sabotage," and that when it left, after spending three months there, "the tension between the Arab and Jewish communities was probably greater than it had ever been."[24]

At the end of Jabotinsky's session on July 13, 1937, with Members of the House of Commons, James Guy of the Scottish Unionist Party had asked him the "one question which I think is a crucial one":

> If a Mandate [for a Jewish state in Palestine] were put into force, does [Mr. Jabotinsky] consider that, in view of the antagonism of the Arabs, it would be possible to develop any system of self-government for the whole of Palestine by means of a Legislative Council in which the Arabs would co-operate?

Jabotinsky answered as follows:

> My conviction about it is this: give us 10 years to . . . create a Jewish majority, and, together with the Jewish majority to create also Arab prosperity on both sides of the Jordan. And then I can assure you that 10 years hence there will be in Palestine . . . a real Parliament with Jews and Arabs, with members no longer concerned with nationalistic quibbles but concerned with problems of social and economic construction. That is the dream of every Jew and every Zionist without distinction of party.

The premise underlying Jabotinsky's prophecy—a state with a Jewish majority in all of Palestine—never came to pass. Instead, over the following ten years, Arab antagonism to any Jewish homeland only intensified. The Arab war against the Jewish state would begin in 1947, the day after the United Nations General Assembly adopted a new partition plan (Resolution 181), by a two-thirds vote, with the Jewish state larger than the one in the Peel Commission Report but still relegated to roughly 5 to 10 percent of the original area of Palestine on both sides of the Jordan. Most of the land allocated to the Jewish state was located in the arid Negev Desert in the south:

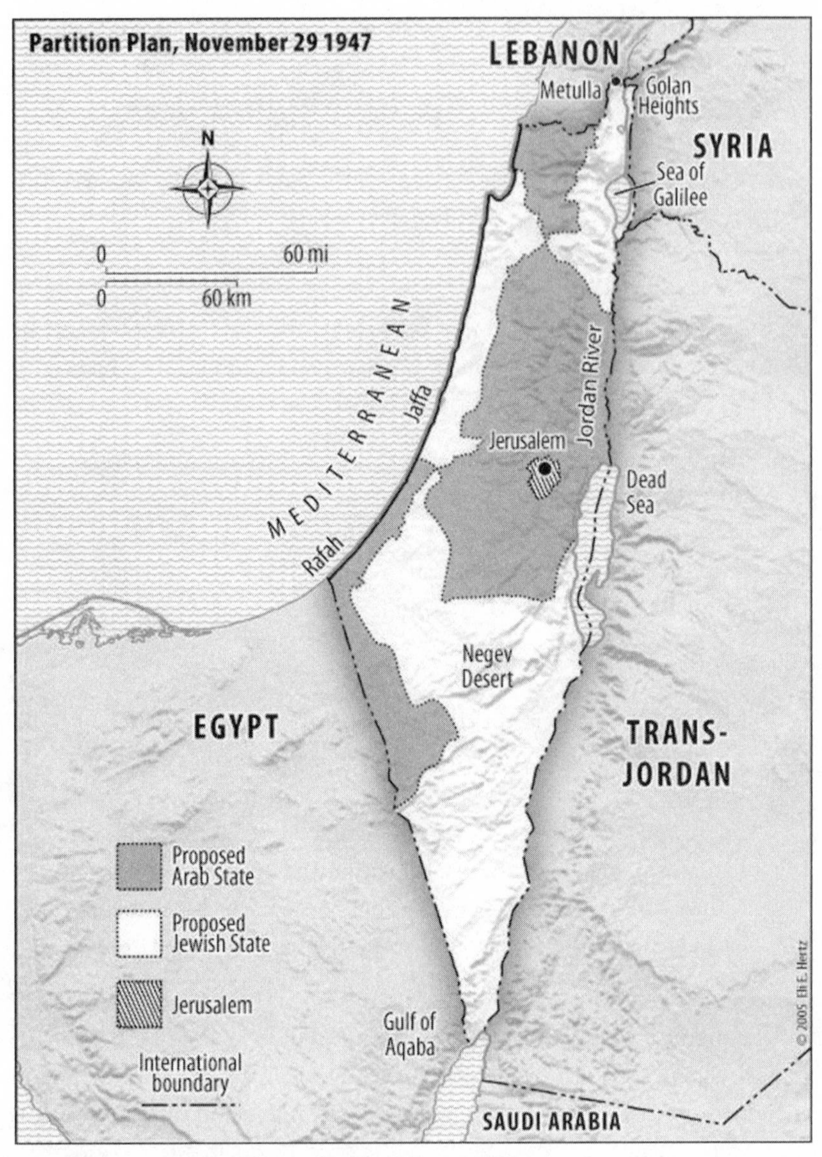

UN Resolution 181 Partition Plan (1947)

Seven months later, in its May 14, 1948, Declaration of Independence, Israel included a direct appeal to its Arab residents:

> WE APPEAL—in the very midst of the onslaught launched against us now for months—to the Arab inhabitants of the State of Israel to preserve peace and participate in the upbuilding of the State on the basis of full and equal citizenship and due representation in all its provisional and permanent institutions.

According to the authoritative review of what happened next—Benny Morris's *The Birth of the Palestinian Refugee Problem Revisited* (2004)—hundreds of thousands of Palestinian Arabs fled Israel in 1948 not because of Jewish expulsion, but because Arab leaders tried to clear the way for an invasion and for their anticipated destruction of the Jewish state. The Arab leaders were:

> encouraging or ordering a great many villages to send away their women, children and old folk, to be out of harm's way. Whole villages, especially in the Jewish-dominated coastal plain, were also ordered to evacuate. There is no doubt that, throughout, the departure of dependents lowered the morale of the remaining males and paved the way for their eventual departure as well. . . .
>
> [T]he problem wasn't created by the Zionists but by the Arabs themselves, and stemmed directly from their violent assault on Israel. Had the Palestinians and the Arab states refrained from launching a war to destroy the emergent Jewish state, there would have been no refugees, and none would exist today.

Despite the orders or encouragements to leave, most of the Arab residents in 1948 remained in Israel. Today, Arabs constitute one-fifth of Israel's population and have more civil and religious rights than Arabs in the surrounding Arab states. Arab Israelis have been elected to every Knesset since 1948, and multiple Arab political parties are present there. Muslim religious sites in Israel remain under Arab control. Arabs have served on the Israeli Supreme Court and as ambassadors and consuls general. There are Arabs in the Israel Defense Forces and the Israeli police. And in 2021, the Arab *Ra-am* Party became part of the Israeli governing coalition—after its leader, Mansour Abbas, rejected what he called seventy years of unproductive victimhood and concluded that the "problems of [Arab] social and economic construction" within Israel were his paramount concern.[25]

Jabotinsky's first prophecy thus came partially true, even in a truncated Jewish state. Today there is "a real Parliament with Jews and Arabs," and a political system that gives Arabs not only free speech and parliamentary participation but significant—and recently determinative—political power in the negotiations to establish an Israeli coalition government.

Jabotinsky's other Peel prophecy—that a Jewish state that was too small would produce not peace, but rather war—unfortunately also came true, more than once.

In 1938, Jabotinsky visited South Africa to deliver a speech titled "*Na'hamu, Na'hamu Ami*" ("Be Ye Comforted My People").[26] It was a biblical phrase, he explained to his audience, teaching that "at the moment of the deepest darkness the Jew should never lose his ability to see the light beyond the horizon and to give comfort to himself and to his brethren." A ship caught in a gale, he said, could go in either direction, because it was not the wind, but the set of the sail, that determined the ship's direction. He ended his speech with an expression of hope:

> I do not believe in the blackness of the horizon. I see light. I think that the good set of the sail can transform that storm into a wind of salvation and of redemption. . . . [Our] Ten-Year Plan of transforming Palestine . . . will save us.[27]

Jabotinsky had an extraordinary ability to see the existential dangers in a situation and yet maintain his optimism at the same time. Later in 1938, in Warsaw on Tisha b'Av (the Ninth of Av), the day memorializing the destruction of the ancient Temples, Jabotinsky set forth both a warning and a vision.[28] This was the warning:

> For three years I have been calling on you, Jews of Poland, the glory of world Jewry . . . I have been ceaselessly warning you that the catastrophe is coming closer. My hair has turned white, and I have aged in these years, because my heart is bleeding for you, dear brothers and sisters, [who] do not see the volcano which will soon begin to spurt out the fire of destruction. I see a terrifying sight.

> I know: you do not see, because you are bothered and rushing about with everyday worries. . . . For God's sake: may each one save his life while there is still time. And time is short.

And this was the vision that he presented in the same speech:

> I want to say one more thing to you on this day of the Ninth of Av: Those who will succeed to escape from the catastrophe will merit a moment of great Jewish joy—the rebirth and rise of a Jewish State. I do not know if I will earn that. My son, yes! I believe in this just as I am sure that tomorrow morning the sun will shine again. I believe in this with total faith.

After the 1939 Nazi-Soviet invasion of Poland, the chance for a new Exodus was gone. Soon enough, the "first rate disaster of truly historic magnitude" that the *Times* had described in 1937 would move well beyond economic strangulation.

On September 3, 1939, two days after Hitler invaded Poland, Jabotinsky called Lieutenant Colonel Patterson, his commander in the Jewish Legion during World War I, and they met that afternoon in London to begin working on a plan to form a Jewish Army to fight Hitler. The following day, Jabotinsky wrote to Prime Minister Chamberlain "[o]n behalf of a movement whose origin is that Jewish regiment which, under Allenby, crossed the Jordan in 1918." Jabotinsky offered to form a Jewish Army to support Britain's "resolve to cut out the cancer choking God's earth." Chamberlain dismissed the offer.[29]

In January 1940, Jabotinsky published a 255-page book in London, entitled *The Jewish War Front*, arguing that world Jewry needed to form a Jewish Army to take an active part in the struggle against Nazism. The Jewish problem in Eastern Europe, he wrote, was of immense importance to world peace, and it was "a problem which means literally life or death to five or six million people." He decided to travel to America—not to enlist American Jews in a Jewish Army, but to try to influence American public opinion to support such an army, to be formed from among the half a million stateless Jews in the world at that time. Jabotinsky was confident he could build such a Jewish military force, because he had done it before, during World War I—and when the Jews were not a target of the war. Now that they were an explicit target in a new war, he wanted Jews to "fight the giant rattlesnake" in Europe. His assistant in New York was the thirty-year-old Benzion Netanyahu.

As he prepared for his trip, Jabotinsky stayed in touch with Churchill, writing him personally on January 23, 1940, about 2,000 Jewish refugees trapped on the Danube River, who could not escape to Palestine because Britain threatened confiscation of ships and imprisonment of their crews if they approached Palestine.[30]

In March 1940, Jabotinsky traveled to America seeking to build public support for a Jewish Army.[31] On June 19, a capacity crowd of 5,000 came to the Manhattan Center to hear him speak. The day before, Churchill had made his "finest hour" address, which the *New York Times* described as given in a "tired voice . . . deadened with grief for the France he loved," an attempt "to awaken his somnolent, complacent countrymen to the reality of the danger facing this island and at the same time convince them that theirs was not a hopeless struggle."[32] Jabotinsky urged his audience not to "forecast historical events on the basis of last week's headlines":

> [I]f there will be an invasion [of Britain] it will not be millions of men nor thousands of heavy tanks. The figures are bound to be on a much smaller scale. And that means that foreign help, to be effective, need not wait till millions of soldiers can be sent over. Every division now may prove decisive . . . [which] has a direct bearing also on the prospects of a Jewish Army. . . .
>
> [T]here is still time ahead of us for changes to come in; there are still immense probabilities for quite decisive changes. One need not name them: enough to say that God's box of tricks is by far not emptied yet. This is why my belief in the ultimate defeat of the rattlesnake is not shattered—provided we all remember the principle by which all great nations live and without which they die, the principle which is the secret of our own Jewish people's survival through all these centuries of torture: No Surrender.

What was needed, Jabotinsky declared, was a Jewish Army to "signify that the Jewish people chooses a cloudy day to renew its demand for recognition as a belligerent on the side of a good cause." With Colonel Patterson onstage with him, Jabotinsky said he wanted to see the "giant rattlesnake" not simply destroyed, but "destroyed with our help":

> There is stuff for well over 100,000 Jewish soldiers even without counting American Jews. . . . [H]ad our request for a Jewish Army been granted early in the war when we first submitted it to the Allies, that source alone would have yielded three to four divisions. Even now it can yield two at least. . . .
>
> There were periods—there still are, there still will be in the months before us—when the impression is that England's plight leaves America only superficially rippled, while the basic attitude of this mighty nation is expressed in the words, "The Yanks are *not* coming." As an observer and a reporter, I contest this impression. . . . [I would say:] "Mr. Churchill, they are coming!" But "they" will be delayed. It takes long to equip a battleship; smaller craft can be delivered quicker. I want the Jews "coming" at once.

The *New York Times* reported the speech in a story quoting both Jabotinsky ("I challenge the Jews, wherever they are still free, to demand the right of fighting the giant rattlesnake . . . as a Jewish Army") and Patterson ("If I were a Jew, nothing would give me greater pleasure than to show the German criminals that the Jews of today are capable of fighting just as their forefathers were when . . . they shook the mighty Roman Empire").

Jabotinsky's speech struck a nerve, invigorating Jews frustrated by the failure of their leaders to respond effectively to the catastrophe facing European Jews. Offers to serve in the prospective Jewish Army poured in; the Canadian foreign ministry offered training camps; Jabotinsky's New Zionist Organization moved to raise funds and conduct grassroots efforts across the country.

Four days before the speech, Jabotinsky and Patterson had sent a joint telegram to Churchill informing him of the forthcoming "great rally [at the] Manhattan Center" and asserting that "American public opinion [is] literally seething" over the "Jewish Army plan."[33] Two days after the speech, Jabotinsky wrote to the British Ambassador in Washington, Lord Lothian, telling him the Manhattan Center event had demonstrated the proposal for a Jewish Army had "caught on with the imagination of Jews and non-Jews, which after all is the main element of final success."

At the end of July, Jabotinsky decided to return to England in August, looking forward to a reunion with his wife (who had been unable to obtain a visa to join him in America) and to resuming discussions with the British government for a Jewish Army under British command. On Au-

Jabotinsky in Poland in 1939, with Menachem Begin in the lower left corner

gust 2, Jabotinsky signed a contract to publish a book on Jewish problems that would follow the war. The next evening, he traveled to the Catskills town of Hunter, New York, to visit the camp of his Betar youth movement there. Betar had had 78,000 members worldwide before World War II began, half of them in Poland, where its leader was a twenty-five-year-old named Menachem Begin.

When he arrived at the Betar camp late that night, Jabotinsky went to his room, where he suffered a fatal heart attack, at age fifty-nine. His last words were, "I am so tired, I am so tired." He had worked for Zionism until the final moment of his life.[34]

Jabotinsky's funeral was held on August 5 in Manhattan at the Gramercy Park Chapel on Second Avenue, attended by prominent Jewish leaders and representatives of the British, Polish, and Czech consulates, and with 750 other invitees and 12,000 people standing outside in the street. Three rabbis officiated and 200 cantors chanted. In accordance with Jabotinsky's wishes, the services followed the precedent of Herzl's funeral in 1904: no speeches, eulogies, or instrumental music. A throng of 25,000 people lined the streets of New York as Jabotinsky's funeral cortege passed.[35]

Crowds lining the streets in New York, ten deep, for Jabotinsky's funeral cortege

Jabotinsky's grave on Mount Herzl, Israel

A decade later, on the day Israel declared its independence and was attacked by the surrounding Arab nations, Menachem Begin addressed his "fighting family" in Jerusalem, with words that evoked the speech Jabotinsky had given in Palestine three decades before to his "tailors." In his address, Begin said:

> [D]o you remember how we started? With what we started? You were alone and persecuted, rejected, despised and . . . tortured but did not surrender; you were cast into prison, but you did not yield; . . . [As we fight], we shall be accompanied by the spirit of those who revived our Nation, [Herzl, Nordau, Trumpeldor] and the father of resurrected Hebrew heroism, [Vladimir] Jabotinsky.

Jabotinsky's story and his influence extended far beyond his life. The leader of Betar in Poland in 1940 (Menachem Begin) became one of the most influential prime ministers in Israel's history. The son of Jabotinsky's assistant in 1940 (Benjamin Netanyahu) became Israel's longest-serving prime minister. The party that adopted Jabotinsky's principles (Herut, which later became the key part of the Likud) became Israel's leading political force after 1977.

Jabotinsky lies today on Mount Herzl in Jerusalem, near the grave of Theodor Herzl.

FIVE

Golda Meir: Portrait of the Lioness as a Young Woman

"There is only one thing I hope to see before I die . . ."

Golda Meir—at that time Golda Mabovitch—
in Milwaukee in 1914

"Lioness" was Henry Kissinger's description of Israel's fourth prime minister, who assumed office in 1969 at the age of seventy-one. She had moved from the United States to Palestine in 1921 at age twenty-three to pursue socialist Zionism; was instrumental in transforming the Jewish community there into a state; was one of the signatories to Israel's Declaration of Independence in 1948; served as its first ambassador to the Soviet Union; then as labor minister for seven years; then as foreign minister for a decade; and finally, as the first female head of state in the Western world.[1]

As prime minister, she led Israel for five years—in the aftermath of the 1967 Six-Day War through the 1973 Yom Kippur War—resigning in 1974 at age seventy-six. Her involvement at the forefront of Zionism and in the leadership of Israel—from 1921 to 1974—extended more than half a century. She became a beloved figure in America, celebrated in books and on stage and screen: Her 1975 autobiography, *My Life*, was a best-seller; Anne Bancroft played her on Broadway in 1977 in a play with a one-word title, *Golda*; Ingrid Bergman portrayed her in the 1982 TV film, *A Woman Called Golda*.

But neither the play nor the film included the story of her searing experience in 1938, when the Jewish community in Palestine sent her to observe a 32-nation conference in Evian, France, convened to address the plight of the European Jews. Although most histories of World War II omit the story of the Evian Conference, it is a key to understanding the advent of that war—and also the temperament that it produced in Israel's future prime minister. It helps explain how she became a lioness.

Before she was Golda Meir in Israel, she was Golda Meyerson in America; and before that, she was Golda Mabovitch in Tsarist Russia. Born in 1898 in Kyiv, she lived her first eight years there. After the horrific 1903

Kishinev pogrom, her father left for America, found work as a carpenter in Milwaukee, and in 1906 sent for his wife and three daughters to join him. The four women escaped from Russia in a harrowing journey, using false identities and paying border bribes. She said later that all she took from Russia was "fear, hunger and fear."

In Milwaukee, Golda Mabovitch was amazed to find that the police on horseback protected her father as he marched in Labor Day parades, instead of trampling him to stop his demonstration. She found socialism in the air.[2] The Milwaukee socialists and the labor movement created a party, the Social-Democrats, whose candidate, Emil Seidel, became the first socialist mayor in the United States. Victor L. Berger, an immigrant from Austria-Hungary who cofounded the Socialist Party of America with Eugene V. Debs, became the first socialist congressman. At eighteen, Mabovitch joined the local chapter of the *Poalei Zion* (Workers of Zion), a movement dedicated to "proletarian Zionism," and she avidly followed the news from Palestine, where Jews were seeking to live out socialist ideals in kibbutzim.

The following year, at the age of nineteen, she married a fellow socialist, Morris Meyerson, in a wedding a few weeks after the Balfour Declaration was issued—and after she had secured Morris's consent to move to Palestine as soon as they could. After World War I ended, the young couple emigrated to Palestine and joined a kibbutz.

In the first two decades of her life, Golda had thus been immersed in some of the strongest currents of history. She had grown up in an anti-Semitic Russian autocracy, lived in unprecedented freedom in America, and watched socialist politicians succeed in Milwaukee. She had experienced both dictatorship and democracy, witnessed socialism at its height at the local level, embraced Zionism at an early age, and decided to help build a democratic socialist Jewish state in Palestine.

In Palestine, her "American expertise" helped her rise in the political circles there. She understood American Jews, spoke their language in unaccented English, and engaged in many fund-raising trips in the United States and Canada in the 1930s, during the depths of the Depression, collecting millions of dollars for the cause. In a single month in 1932, only thirty-four years old, she traveled to Kansas City, Tulsa, Dallas, San Antonio, Los Angeles, San Francisco, and Seattle, and then to three cities in Canada. In the following decades, she would speak at United Jewish Appeal (UJA) and Israel Bonds events, rallies at Madison Square Garden,

Golda Meyerson with her husband, Morris, 1918

and countless dinners. She became the face of Zionism in America—once described as "The First Lady of the Jewish People" on a huge banner behind her as she spoke at an event in Chicago. She was able to connect with American Jews in a way no other envoy from Palestine could. Later, Ben-Gurion would call her the "woman who got the money which made the state possible."[3]

Meyerson lacked a college education, but she had a way of crystallizing issues in plainspoken English. She would become famous for her epigrammatic sayings: "Don't be so humble, you're not that great." "One must not try to erase the past merely because it does not fit the present." "Britain is trying to prevent the growth of the Jewish community in Palestine, but it should remember that Jews were here 2,000 years before the British came."

"We cannot explain [our actions] to the world, [but] if we remain alive, we will explain all sorts of things." And one of her most famous sayings: "There is only one thing I hope to see before I die, and that is that my people should not need expressions of sympathy anymore."

The history underlying her epigrams made them more than simply clever expressions. To understand the one about the expressions of sympathy for the Jews, one needs to know the history of the first three months of 1938, and the international conference that convened in July that year at Evian—with forty-year-old Golda Meyerson, attending as a "Jewish observer from Palestine," seated not with the delegates but with the audience, not allowed to speak. Her autobiography, written four decades later, makes it clear that Evian was a turning point in her life.

As 1938 began, Franklin D. Roosevelt and Adolf Hitler were completing their fifth years in office, both having arrived at their historic roles at the beginning of 1933.

Hitler became the German chancellor on January 30, 1933. Roosevelt was inaugurated as the American president five weeks later, on March 4, 1933. By March, Hitler had assumed absolute power in Germany; before the year was over, he withdrew from the League of Nations; disavowed the Treaty of Versailles that had ended World War I; opened concentration camps for political opponents and "dangerous" others; staged a boycott of Jewish-owned businesses; dramatically reduced the number of Jewish children in public schools; sponsored nationwide book burnings of "un-German" books; and forbade "non-Aryans" from working in journalism. In June 1933, the U.S. consul general George Messersmith wrote to the State Department from Berlin that the persecution of the Jews was:

> . . . one of the most serious and one of the saddest problems that has arisen in a civilized country in modern times. . . . I personally can see no hope for the Jews in Germany for years to come and all those who can possibly get out of the country will wish to do so.[4]

The logical destination for emigration was the United States. Between 1880 and 1920, more than 20 million immigrants had come to America, including 2 million Jews. But the Immigration Act of 1924 applied strict new quotas, limiting visas to 2 percent of each nationality in the 1890

American census (selected because it was the last census before the wave of immigration after the Russian pogroms), and categorically excluding all Asians, with minor exceptions. The law thus made it relatively easy to emigrate to America from Britain; extremely difficult from Eastern Europe; and effectively impossible from Japan and China.

After the quota for Britain, the largest quota was for immigrants from Germany—25,987 per year—but in practice even that relatively low number was not allowed into the United States. As the condition of the Jews in Germany dramatically worsened, about 87,500 Germans applied for immigrant visas in 1934. Fewer than 4,400 were admitted.[5]

In 1935, the German Reichstag passed the Nuremberg Laws, establishing the systematic persecution of the Jews, identifying them not by religion but by blood—one Jewish grandparent sufficed. Hitler rebuilt the German military and occupied the demilitarized zone in the Rhineland in 1936, with minimal protest from the world. In 1937, he opened the Buchenwald concentration camp for political prisoners and sponsored a traveling exhibition entitled "The Eternal Jew," alleging a world Jewish conspiracy. The exhibition toured Berlin, Vienna, and other cities, ultimately viewed by nearly half a million Germans.

By 1938, antisemitism—which young Jews such as Theodor Herzl had initially dismissed in 1882 as a passing, crackpot theory—was pervasive in Europe, enshrined in law, pursued in Germany by an absolute dictator in his increasingly powerful country, with a goal he had explicitly set forth in his 1925 autobiography, *Mein Kampf* (*My Struggle*).[6]

As of 1938, the American newspaper of record, the *New York Times*, viewed these developments with relative equanimity. On January 1, 1938, it published a major article by Frederick T. Birchall, its chief European correspondent and winner of the 1934 Pulitzer Prize, reporting that for Germany, 1937 had been a year of "steady progress, enhanced national prestige and increased strength." Fewer than two decades after its devastating defeat in the Great War, Germany was "now definitely a great power, ranking equally with Great Britain and France."

German unemployment had dropped from 6 million in 1933 to fewer than half a million in 1938, while U.S. unemployment was at 14 percent in 1937, increasing to 18 percent in 1938. Birchall noted that the German economic progress had been achieved at a "triple cost"—a "financial cost" of massive public debt, an "economic cost" from diverting so much national income to the government, and a "spiritual cost"—by which Birchall did not mean the Nazi treatment of the Jews, but rather the "increased regimentation of the German people." Birchall discussed the Jews in a single sentence, offered matter-of-factly:

> The elimination of Jews from commercial and professional life, with virtual confiscation of their assets, goes steadily on.

The *Times* reported that the "large advances" made by the fascist states in 1937 had been encouraged by the "forbearance" of Britain, France, and the United States—which all stood by as Germany threatened its neighbors, Italy annexed Ethiopia, and Japan waged war against China. In the second week of 1938, Hitler declared that his "unalterable goal" in Austria was the one he had set forth in 1925 on the first page of *Mein Kampf*: the "liberation" of the country of his birth by annexing it to Germany.

On January 30, 1938, on the fifth anniversary of Hitler's ascension to power, Birchall published in the *New York Times Magazine* an analysis of Hitler's achievements—entitled "Five Years of Nazism." Birchall described the article as his "attempt to draw a fair and impartial picture of Germany's accomplishments and of her present state." The article began on a lyrical note:

> Five years out of the thousand which Hitler has set as the minimum period of his party's supremacy have rolled away. . . . It seems but yesterday since the tramp of marching Storm Troopers down the torchlit *Wilhelmstrasse* [Berlin's main boulevard] heralded the opening of a new era, yet in the meantime the Reich and Europe have taken on a new complexion.

Birchall noted that rearmament had enabled Germany "to smash the . . . Franco-British hegemony over Europe" and had been "principally responsible for banishing unemployment." There was "almost no crime in Germany" and "[p]eace and order prevail throughout the land." "Regarded dispassionately," Birchall wrote, "the achievements have been more than notable"—and he then proceeded to describe them passionately:

> Germany has built up a wonderful military machine . . . already promising to surpass in striking power the military forces of any other nation. She has constructed 2000 kilometers of the

> most modern motor roads in existence. . . . She has built and is still building great public and party structures, sport fields and recreation centers. She is remodeling some of the largest cities, including Berlin, Hamburg, Munich and Nuremberg. She has promoted vast social welfare enterprises, such as the Strength Through Joy organization, which has its own pleasure resorts . . . and last year provided cheap vacations for six million persons. . . .

The remaining German unemployment, Birchall wrote, was attributable mainly to people who were simply unemployable, because of their "physical or racial disability." The reference to "racial disability" was the closest Birchall came in his long article to mentioning the Nazi treatment of the Jews.

In briefer articles in January 1938, the *Times* reported on the increasingly dire situation of the Jews throughout Eastern Europe. In Poland, the Jews were living in "utter destitution and degradation." In Romania, the premier had insisted they emigrate and warned of "terrible pogroms" if they were not expelled first. James G. McDonald, the former League of Nations High Commissioner for Refugees, said nearly 1 million Jews were facing a situation in Romania even worse than in Germany. As for Germany, a *Times* article under the headline "Jews Seen Doomed as Group in Germany" reported on a speech by a former Hadassah president, Mrs. Samuel W. Halprin, who had just returned from there; she said "[a]ll of German Jewry knows . . . they are doomed."[7]

To read the *New York Times* day-by-day through the first months of 1938 is to observe in real time the steady collapse of British and French opposition to Hitler—and to note from President Roosevelt, five years into his presidency, utter silence.

By the beginning of 1938, it was already clear, wrote Edwin L. James, the managing editor of the *Times* international edition, that the "aggressive nations" knew that the "democratic nations" did "not wish to take up arms to curb [the aggressors], unless there is a direct attack upon their territory." An incident in January 1938, involving the just-retired American ambassador to Germany (William E. Dodd), the German ambassador to the United States (Hans Dieckhoff), and the American secretary of state

(Cordell Hull), exemplified the American position under the Roosevelt administration.

From 1933 until his resignation at the end of 1937, Dodd had become increasingly convinced that Hitler, Goebbels, and Goering were depraved and dangerous. On January 13, 1938, as a former ambassador and now a private citizen, he addressed more than 2,500 people at the Manhattan Opera House in New York, where he said the situation in Germany for the Jews was "worse than at any time in the last hundred years." Later that day, in another speech, he said "[m]ankind is in grave danger, but democratic governments seem not to know what to do." He urged the democracies of the world to unite to oppose the German-Italian-Japanese combination.

Both speeches were reported the next day in the *Times*, and Ambassador Dieckhoff appeared in person at the State Department to lodge an official German protest. The *Times* reported that Secretary of State Hull told him the federal government "had no control over the utterances, public or private, of individual citizens." Then Hull went further: he held a press conference to state publicly that Dodd's views "could in no way be taken as representing the official views" of the Roosevelt administration. According to the *Times* front-page report:

> A reporter asked Mr. Hull whether he meant that Mr. Dodd's views did not "necessarily" represent the views of the government, but the Secretary declined to specify further.[8]

On February 12, 1938, Hitler summoned Austria's Chancellor Kurt Schuschnigg to his mountaintop chalet in Berchtesgaden, Germany, and confronted him with an ultimatum: Give the Nazis control of Austrian internal affairs and appoint a pro-Nazi foreign minister, or face a German invasion. It was another violation of the Treaty of Versailles, which required Germany to respect the "inalienable independence" of Austria. Facing a threat of overwhelming force, Austria yielded late that night. Four days later, the *Times* reported that:

> Privately British Government quarters are infinitely relieved that there has been a "peaceful" capitulation to Chancellor Hitler and not an armed insurrection in Vienna . . . . If Chancellor

> Schuschnigg had turned to London . . . he would have received no help whatever.[9]

The *Times* noted that "already there is talk in Berlin of confronting Austria's neighbor Czechoslovakia"; that Hungary, Yugoslavia, and Romania all lay within Hitler's sights; and that Hitler was confident that Britain and France would "show again the same detachment and aloofness toward any new German moves"—provided "of course, that the German Government plays its hand with caution, and . . . [does] not try to push too far at once." The *Times* reported that the British cabinet had concluded that "there was nothing for Britain to do but push ahead toward agreements with both Germany and Italy even at a heavy cost."[10]

An Austrian official told the *Times*, "We cannot believe that it is really in the interests of [Britain and France] . . . to allow Germany to receive the enormous accession of strength that swallowing Austria would give her," sealing the fate of Czechoslovakia and Hungary and facilitating a German advance toward the Suez Canal. But the *Times* reported that Chamberlain seemed ready "to pay twice or thrice if he could reach a peace agreement" so he could "call a general election this Fall on [his] achievement in 'guaranteeing peace.'"

Within Austria, Schuschnigg tried to rally the public to resist Hitler, with a speech to the Assembly, broadcast throughout the country, saying "Austria must remain Austria" and scheduling a plebiscite on Austrian independence for Sunday, March 13—"evidence of his determination," the *Times* reported, "that Austria shall not be swallowed up without a struggle." But Hitler responded by massing 50,000 troops on the Austrian border, and Schuschnigg—seeing no response from the West—canceled the plebiscite and resigned. On March 12, 65,000 Nazi troops moved into Austria as Nazi bombers roared over Vienna. The *Times* reported that the British were "appalled" by the Reich's methods and had sent a "sharp rebuke" to Berlin.[11]

On March 13, Austria was formally incorporated into the German Reich. The *Times* editorialized that "[n]o event in the recent history of Europe matches in importance Germany's conquest of Austria by force of arms" and that "large developments" might result, which "may in the end overshadow in importance even the conquest of Austria itself." On March 14, Winston Churchill told the House of Commons that "[t]he gravity of the event of March 12 cannot be exaggerated":

> Europe is confronted with a program of aggression . . . unfolding stage by stage, and there is only one choice open, not only to us but to other countries, either to submit like Austria, or else take effective measures while time remains to ward off the danger.

The March 12 *Anschluss* subjected more Jews to Nazi control than the total number who had left Germany in the previous five years. In the following five days, Hitler proceeded to wreak on the 185,000 Austrian Jews what it had taken him five years to do to the Jews in Germany. The *Times* reported that a "wave of suicides is sweeping the country."[12]

During the first week after the *Anschluss*, there were mass arrests of Jews, brutal attacks, closings of Jewish institutions, destruction of Jewish businesses, barring of Jews from all economic life, elimination of their civil rights, widespread seizures of properties, deportations to concentration camps, and rampant Jewish suicides. Vienna's most widely circulated Jewish newspaper appeared with a swastika on its masthead and its Jewish editors were dismissed. On March 14, two days after the *Anschluss*, the *Times* reported that:

> Jews were disappearing from Vienna life. Few, if any, were to be seen on the streets or in the coffee houses. Some were asked to leave street cars. Others were not molested if they gave the Hitler salute. . . . Dr. Herman Oppenheim, head of Young Austrian Jewish Congress, was taken into "protective custody."[13]

On March 14, the *Times* reported that "the Nazification of Austria continued swiftly today under her new German masters." Jewish physicians were barred by the Viennese Emergency Hospital organization and a decree was issued that Jews employed as judges or lawyers in the State legal department be terminated. On March 26, Field Marshall Hermann Goering spoke in Vienna, saying, "Vienna must become German again. The Jew . . . must go."[14]

The stunning events set off an immediate, panicked Jewish search for means of emigration. But the borders were closed, and foreign embassies were unable to process more than a few exit visas, given the laws and quotas of their home countries.

During this entire period, Roosevelt made no public statement about either Hitler or the Jews. On February 21, the *Times* reported the White House was "completely silent" on Hitler but Roosevelt "might soon make known in an informal way the views of his Administration toward the political situation abroad." But no presidential statement, formal or informal, was issued.

The *Times* reported in its headline that "U.S. Will Not Act in Austria Crisis—[Secretary of State] Hull Says There Was Nothing Washington Intended to Do About Move by Hitler." At his regular press conference, Hull declined to comment on the Austrian situation, on grounds that the United States was not involved. He reported, however, that he had kept FDR "well-informed." On March 14, the German ambassador called on Hull at his office to notify him that Austria no longer existed and was now part of the Third Reich. The *Times* reported that Hull received the German note "with hardly a show of reaction." On March 17, Hull delivered a major foreign policy address before the National Press Club, setting forth the administration's "profound conviction" that:

> The most effective contribution which we, as a nation sincerely devoted to the cause of peace, can make—in the tragic conditions with which our people, in common with the rest of mankind, are confronted today—is to have this country respected throughout the world for integrity, justice, goodwill, strength, and unswerving loyalty to principles.

Roosevelt had reviewed Hull's address in advance and had sent him a one-word note about it: "Grand!"

The journalist Dorothy Thompson, whom *Time Magazine* called one of the two "most influential women in the U.S." (the other was Eleanor Roosevelt), had reported on the threat of Hitler from the beginning. She had interviewed him in 1932 and had been expelled from Germany after writing a book warning that, if elected, Hitler would establish a dictatorship with a movement in which "anti-Semitism is the life and soul." The April 1938 issue of *Foreign Affairs* included Thompson's article entitled "Refugees: A World Problem," in which she wrote that:

> In Germany, more and more Jews are being deprived of the means to continue living in the homes they have had for centu-

> ries. . . . Austria has lost her struggle for independence. The victory of the Nazis there creates a vast new problem of refugees. . . . Rumania is experimenting with anti-Semitic laws; the Jewish question in Poland has been acute for some years. In the Danubian Basin alone—in Austria, Czechoslovakia, Rumania, Hungary and Yugoslavia—live some two million Jews. There are over three million more in Poland. . . . Already there are some four million people in the world who are "men without a country." . . . To close one's eyes to it would be "ostrichism" in an acute form.[15]

Roosevelt had been provided with a prepublication copy of Thompson's article. The American president, who had so far said nothing, apparently realized that something, or at least the appearance of something, had to be done.

On March 18, Roosevelt held a cabinet meeting to consider a humanitarian response to the *Anschluss*. The discussion concluded that Congress would not authorize increased quotas, and Roosevelt decided instead to launch an international conference to encourage other countries to admit refugees. He acknowledged privately that the United States could not do much, but a conference could at least "show our sympathy with the victims of those conditions."

On March 23, the United States issued an invitation to thirty countries—nine European countries, twenty countries in the Western Hemisphere, and Australia—to convene in Evian to "consider what steps can be taken to facilitate the settlement in other countries of political refugees from Germany (including Austria)." The text of the invitation included an assurance that no country would be expected to change its laws to admit more refugees or to provide any funds to resettle refugees; any financing, the invitation noted, would have to be provided by private organizations. Roosevelt did not send either Secretary of State Hull or Under Secretary Sumner Welles to the conference, nor any other official member of the administration. Instead, he enlisted his friend Myron C. Taylor, the recently retired CEO of U.S. Steel Corporation, to attend on behalf of the United States, appointing him "ambassador extraordinary and plenipotentiary."

As preparations for the Evian Conference proceeded leisurely over the next three months, the situation of the Jews in Austria, already disastrous, grew steadily worse. On June 20, 1938, two weeks before the conference began, the front-page headline of the *New York Times* read as follows:

> *Vienna Nazis Widen Drive on Jews; Every Family Reported Suffering; Even Children Are Victims in the 'Orgy of Jew-Baiting,' . . . Hopes Put in Parley Called by U. S.*

The article described "the sad fate almost certainly awaiting the Jews still left" in Austria: The Gestapo had established its headquarters in the Jewish quarter of Vienna, wielding "ruthless and unchallengeable power," creating "utter demoralization and destitution of the Jewish population":

> In Vienna and Austria no vestige of decency or humanity has checked the will to destroy, and there has been an unbroken orgy of Jew-baiting such as Europe has not known since the darkest days of the Middle Ages. . . . [W]hat was once a community outstanding in intellect and culture is being turned into a community of beggars.

The Nazis had established, the *Times* continued, a policy of "systematic economic destruction and systematic maintenance of panic for the whole Jewish population":

> Tens of thousands of Jews have been thrown out of employment. All important Jewish business either has been confiscated directly or placed under an Aryan commissar. . . . Jews are charged for the paint used in writing upon their premises that it is a Jewish business.
>
> . . . [M]en and women, young and old, are taken each day and each night from their houses or in the streets and carried off, the more fortunate to Austrian prisons, and the rest to Dachau and other concentration camps in Germany. . . . There can be no Jewish family in the country which has not one or more of its members under arrest. . . . The Jews would welcome evacuation but for most it is impossible. Only a few still own any considerable property and they cannot take out even that. . . . Thousands stand outside the consulates of America, England and other

THE NEW YORK TIMES, SUNDAY, JULY 3, 1938.

WILL THE EVIAN CONFERENCE GUIDE HIM TO FREEDOM?

A British cartoon reflecting the hopes that are placed in the Evian Conference—This meeting, to be at Evian, France, on Wednesday to arrange for the emigration of political refugees, was called at the instigation of the President and Secretary Hull, and only Italy, out of thirty-three nations asked to join, refused to participate. Myron C. Taylor, industrialist, will represent the United States.

> countries, waiting through the night for admission so that they may register their names.

The article concluded by reporting that "the hopes of Jews and non-Aryans in Austria are fixed upon the conference which the United States has convened at Evian at the beginning of July."

In its Sunday, July 3, edition, the *Times* reprinted a British cartoon, showing an elderly, bearded man, wearing a skull cap, sitting at the middle of swastika, under a sign pointing "Go" in all four directions, with a "Stop" posted at the end of each of them. Over the horizon, there was sunlight labeled "Evian Conference."

Hitler openly taunted the Western countries about the conference. Two days after Roosevelt's announcement of it, Hitler said of the Jews:

> I can only hope that the other world which has such deep sympathy for these criminals will at least be generous enough to convert this sympathy into practical aid. We on our part are ready to put all these criminals at the disposal of these countries, for all I care, even on luxury ships.[16]

To ensure the Evian proceedings did not get out of hand, Myron Taylor met beforehand with France's representative, Henri Berenger, a former French ambassador to the United States, to reiterate several points: (1) Evian would be a "confidential meeting . . . and not a public conference where all sorts of ideas will be aired to the press and to the general public"; (2) there would be a public session at the outset for general statements, but other meetings would be held in "executive session"; and (3) the British, French, and Americans would hold "strictly confidential meetings" during the Conference to coordinate the positions of the three governments.[17]

Before the Conference began, the United States took the most logical place for Jews to go—Palestine—off the diplomatic table.[18] The State Department provided a confidential memorandum to the American delegation, instructing it to "reject any attempts to interject" consideration of Jewish immigration into Palestine onto the Conference agenda, advising that any discussion of that issue would "stir up bitter passions and might even lead to a disruption of the Committee's labors."[19]

The Conference agenda anticipated that each government would furnish "for the strictly confidential information of the Committee, a statement of its immigration laws and practices and its present policy regarding the reception of immigrants . . . [and] the number and type of immigrants it is now prepared to receive or that it might consider receiving." No diplomatic action, no change of laws, no provision of funds were contemplated—only secret, nonbinding discussions after a general opening session, with no formal representation by the Jewish Agency, the body designated by the League of Nations to assist the establishment of the Jewish National Home in Palestine, nor any other Jewish representatives.[20]

On July 6, 1938, Chaim Weizmann, on behalf of the Jewish Agency, submitted a memorandum to the Conference, summarizing the problems facing the Jews:

> The impoverishment and degradation of the 600,000 Jews of Germany and Austria need no elaboration. The Jews of Poland, 3,000,000 of them, are regarded as "excess population" and are slowly but surely perishing. In Romania and Hungary, the pressure on the Jewish populations comprising approximately 1,175,000 persons is daily increasing.[21]

The memorandum expressed "the hope that due consideration will be given to the part which Palestine has played, and can play in the future, in the solution of the Jewish problem," and it summarized the Jewish achievements in Palestine since the Balfour Declaration:

> Between 1918 and 1937 the Jewish population of Palestine increased from 60,000 to 416,000, and from 10 per cent to over 30 percent of the total population. . . . In 1922 there were 75 Jewish agricultural settlements with a population of 15,000; in 1938, 223 settlements with a population of 105,000.

The memorandum noted that the British were restricting Jewish immigration because of the alleged lack of economic "absorptive capacity" in Palestine, but that immigration, with its accompanying influx of capital and pioneer energy, served to *enlarge* absorptive capacity. The more immigrants came, the more work was needed (housing, factories, roads, etc.), and the more such economic activity occurred, the more room there was for additional immigrants. There was thus no reason, the memorandum continued, that immigration "should not go on climbing up and up." Jewish immigration had resulted in the expansion of Arab industry, Arab cultivation of citrus and other agricultural products, Arab labor in urban areas, and major new civic institutions, such as hospitals, that served Arabs as well as Jews.

But Jewish immigration during this period had been progressively blocked by Britain, and thus had now *decreased*, from 62,000 in 1935 to 30,000 in 1936 and 10,500 in the first half of 1937. The memorandum urged the Conference to recognize that "Palestine holds a unique position among the countries of Jewish immigration":

> It is the only country to which the Jew comes with international sanction, "as of right and not on sufferance."

On July 4, 1938, two days before the Evian Conference, the *New York Times* reported Rabbi Stephen S. Wise's speech to more than 2,000 people at the Zionist Organization of America's annual convention. Wise asserted that the Conference would be a "dismal failure" unless Britain allowed mass immigration to Palestine, because:

> To other lands Jewish refugees may go as welcome or half-welcome guests. To Palestine they must be free to go as of right,

> and not on sufferance. This is the time for England to . . . return once again to the standards and ideals of Balfour and Lloyd George.

Rabbi Wise read the convention a message from President Roosevelt, who wrote that rebuilding the Jewish homeland was "a noble ideal." Roosevelt did not inform the convention that he had already removed Palestine from any consideration at the Evian Conference.

To read the speeches of the nine-day Evian Conference, which convened on July 6, 1938, in the Hotel Royal's Grand Ballroom with 140 representatives from thirty-two countries, is to see a cascade of euphemisms, all designed to avoid using the words "Jews" (who were the subject of the Conference) and "Hitler" (who had created the problem the Conference was called to address).

Even the word "Palestine" did not appear until the final day—in the final speech of the British delegate, who mentioned it then only to confirm that Palestine, as a potential destination for the mortally endangered Jews, was off the table.

None of those three words—"Jews," "Hitler," "Palestine"—appeared in Myron Taylor's opening address, which began by noting that "millions of people" were "being uprooted from the homes where they have long been established," in a "major forced migration" that was "artificially stimulated by governmental practices in some countries" that had forced "great bodies of reluctant migrants" to be absorbed in "abnormal circumstances."

Taylor cautioned that the Conference could only take preliminary steps that might, "in the long run," contribute to "a practicable amelioration of the condition of the unfortunate human beings with whom we are concerned." He expressed "the firm belief of the American Government" that the Conference should work toward solving the problem "of so many hapless human beings," so that "the forced and chaotic dumping of unfortunate peoples in large numbers" did not create an "obstacle to general appeasement." He said that:

> If the present currents of migration are permitted to continue to push anarchically upon the receiving States and if some Governments are to continue to toss large sections of their popula-

Myron C. Taylor addresses the Evian Conference, July 1937
(Chief adviser James G. McDonald is seated at his right)

> tions lightly upon a distressed and unprepared world, then there is catastrophic human suffering ahead which can only result in general unrest and in general international strain which will not be conducive to the permanent appeasement to which all peoples earnestly aspire.

Britain's Lord Winterton spoke next. He was, in the London *Jewish Chronicle*'s euphemistic language, someone who was "out of sympathy with the Jews in general."[22] The words "Jews," "Hitler," and "Palestine" were absent from his speech as well. He assured the Conference, however, that Britain was "anxious to cooperate" in finding "a practical means of relieving the difficulties which confront the unfortunate people who wish to emigrate." Regrettably, he said, there was not much Britain itself could do to welcome any refugees:

> [T]he United Kingdom is not a country of immigration. It is highly industrialized, fully populated and is still faced with the problem of unemployment. For economic and social reasons, the traditional [British] policy of granting asylum can only be applied within narrow limits.

Lord Winterton delivering a speech at the Evian Conference in 1938

Winterton said Britain was, however, "carefully surveying the prospects of the admission of refugees to [British] colonies and overseas territories." Unfortunately, some places were "already overcrowded, others are wholly or partly unsuitable for European settlement, while in others . . . local political conditions hinder or prevent any considerable immigration." His government was "not unhopeful" that "certain East African territories" might present "possibilities," but "it would be premature for me to make any positive statement on the subject." But he wanted to be sure everyone understood that "any project which may emerge is unlikely to involve the settlement of more than a limited number of selected families." He closed by reiterating Britain's admirable desire to:

> Make a beginning and help to alleviate in some degree the consequences of a situation, the poignancy and gravity of which has struck the imagination and excited the sympathy of people in all countries.

France's Henri Berenger spoke third, claiming that France had taken more of "these unhappy individuals"—who "have been so well called the 'stateless' victims of present-day national revolutions"—than any other country. But France, while continuing to be "faithful to the long-standing tradition of universal hospitality which has characterized her throughout all her history," had now "reached, if not already passed, the extreme point of saturation as regards admission of refugees." France was only "prepared to discuss with the other nations how their emigration can best be directed." He closed by saying that he knew the task would be "difficult, thankless and uncertain" but that:

> [I]t will be useful work, work which will do honor to the American Government. I wish here on behalf of the French Government to signify its fullest agreement in principle with that task . . . always bearing in mind [that France] has already almost exhausted her own resources which unfortunately are not so boundless as her zeal to serve the cause of humanity.

A few minutes later, the opening session of the Conference adjourned, immediately after adopting a resolution, proposed by Myron Taylor, "that we send a message of homage to the President of the United States."[23]

Despite its solemnity, its formal proceedings, its large number of attendees, and its many statements of sympathy for an unnamed group, the nature of the Conference was obvious from the torrent of euphemisms and the "message of homage" that marked its first day—and the absence of any condemnation of Hitler (much less a message to him). William L. Shirer, who would later write the seminal history of the period, *The Rise and Fall of the Third Reich*, witnessed the Conference as a thirty-four-year-old reporter working for CBS and Edward R. Murrow. In his diary for July 7, 1938, after the second day of the Conference, Shirer wrote that:

> I doubt if much will be done. The British, French and Americans seem too anxious not to do anything to offend Hitler. It is an absurd situation. They want to appease the man who was responsible for their problem. . . . I've put [Myron] Taylor on for a [CBS] broadcast, but have no invitation from New York to talk myself on the program of this conference. We are not really covering it at all.[24]

The Conference met from July 6 to July 15. Thirty-nine relief and other organizations were present to observe but did not have the status of delegates and were not allowed to address any public session. They were given five minutes each to make presentations at a nonpublic subcommittee meeting. Latin American countries said they might have room for agricultural workers (there were few if any in Vienna or Berlin). Venezuela emphasized it would have to be "rigorously selective." Colombia cautioned that too much immigration was dangerous: "The bad example of the Old World can spread to other continents and make the planet uninhabitable." The smaller European countries, such as Belgium, Denmark, Sweden, and Switzerland, all stressed their incapacity to admit any more refugees. Australia was even blunter: Its delegate stated that Australia "does not have a racial problem and does not wish to import one."[25]

In a speech on the last day of the Conference, Lord Winterton finally mentioned "Palestine"—but only to make explicit Britain's rejection of it as part of any solution. He said that:

> The [Conference] will perhaps expect me, as representing the Power that holds the Mandate for Palestine, to offer some observations. It has been represented in some quarters that the whole question . . . could be solved if only the gates of Palestine were thrown open to Jewish immigrants without restriction of any kind. I should like to say emphatically as I can, that I regard any such proposition as wholly untenable.[26]

Winterton acknowledged that Britain "has a direct obligation under the terms of the [League of Nations] Mandate to facilitate Jewish immigration into Palestine," but he asserted that Britain had already discharged that obligation because "[t]he number of German Jews admitted during the last few years is, I believe, over 40,000." He reiterated that Britain was investigating "small-scale settlement" in Kenya but emphasized that "[t]here can be no question of mass immigration."[27]

Some scholars have suggested that the word "Jew" was generally avoided, in favor of a generic reference to "refugees," because an emphasis on Jews would have been "grist for the mill of American anti-Semites."[28] The historian Henry L. Feingold writes that the Roosevelt administration reasoned that "[i]f a distinction between Jewish and non-Jewish refugees was made . . . only the latter would be resettled, and Jews would be left stranded."[29] But the careful avoidance of naming the main group at risk did not lead to any significant steps to save any of the refugees, Jewish or otherwise.

Even drafting a final Conference resolution became problematical, be-

Left to right: Henri Berenger (France); Myron C. Taylor (U.S.); Lord Winterton (Britain)

cause the South American countries enjoyed trade agreements and commercial arrangements with Germany and feared German disapproval of any action they might take. They conditioned their approval of a resolution on it being clear that they had no obligation to take any action, and that there be nothing in any way critical of Germany.[30] The resolution as adopted noted that "the fate of the unfortunate people affected" in an unnamed country "may hinder seriously the processes of appeasement in international relations" and called for a "long range program" within "the framework of existing migration laws" for "involuntary emigrants."[31]

In an editorial on July 14, 1938, the day before the Conference ended, the *New York Times* succinctly summarized the results of the nine-day, thirty-two-nation meeting:

> All the delegates professed a sincere desire to do what they could, but none offered to relax the quotas and restrictions that every country has put on immigration.

Weizmann had planned to attend the Evian Conference, and he had purchased tickets to travel there. But he was advised not to come by Nahum Goldmann, the head of the World Jewish Congress, who told him that Myron Taylor was a serious and sympathetic person but was not inclined to allow private organizations to speak publicly.

Weizmann thus stayed home and spent the week meeting with Malcolm MacDonald, the head of Britain's Colonial Office, writing him a sixteen-page typewritten letter, marked "Personal," to summarize the points they had discussed. He told him that, as soon as the British Government had approved the Peel Commission partition recommendation, it should have promptly implemented it. The Peel Report had rejected "the absurd and mendacious charges which Arab agitators had made against us for years." Since the Jews were willing to accept Western Palestine, rather than the entire area contemplated at the time of the Balfour Declaration, Weizmann said the British "should say frankly to the Arabs":

> "We have given you four independent Kingdoms, with an area approximating that of the whole of Western Europe. In the 10,000 square miles of Western Palestine, we propose to keep our pledge to the Jews (with due provision for minorities, and for the Holy Places, of course) and set up a Jewish State."

In Weizmann's view, there were only two places that could immediately absorb large numbers of Jewish immigrants: Palestine ("where the preparatory work has been done during the past sixty years") and America ("where great industrial opportunities undoubtedly exist"). But given the immigration restrictions under American law, Palestine was the "one real prospect of prompt and permanent help."

On July 15, 1938, Weizmann wrote to Rabbi Solomon Goldman in New York to say that Evian "has proved to be a grave disappointment," making it clear that the world's democracies were unwilling to help European Jewry, "although of course everyone had been sympathetic."[32] The message was also clear to the Arabs in Palestine. The journalist Pierre van Paassen, in his award-winning 1939 autobiography, *Days of Our Years*, wrote about the long-running Arab attacks on Jews in Palestine that had begun in 1936 and which had then:

> increased in intensity at the moment the Jewish people's representatives at the [Evian] conference on refugees asked Britain to

> translate her verbal assurances of sympathy for the victims of the Nazi terror into practical, definite, and concrete assistance by opening the doors of Palestine to Jewish immigration.[33]

On July 29, 1938, two weeks after the conclusion of the Conference, the Nazi intelligence organization reported internally on the results:

> The resolutions show that a practical and concrete result that would ease the question of Jewish emigration is not possible. . . . The statements made by delegates of all of the countries have clearly shown that . . . there is extensive aversion to a significant flow of emigrants, either out of social considerations or out of an unexpressed racial abhorrence against Jewish emigrants.[34]

Hitler's Foreign Office gloated publicly that:

> Since in many countries it was recently regarded as wholly incomprehensible why Germany did not wish to preserve in its population an element like the Jews . . . it appears astounding that [those] countries seem in no way anxious to make use of these elements themselves now that the opportunity offers.[35]

On August 14, 1938, the *New York Times* reviewed Dorothy Thompson's new book—*Refugees: Anarchy or Organization?*—with the reviewer summarizing the Evian Conference as follows:

> [T]he conference . . . vanished into the jungle of committees, subcommittees and sub-subcommittees from which so many conferences, setting out bravely from Geneva and adjacent points, have never returned. . . . [It is a] problem the continued existence of which will eventually become almost as much a reproach to democracies failing to solve it as the two dictatorships which have cruelly called it into being.[36]

Most accounts of the origins of World War II make little or no reference to the Evian Conference.[37] Perhaps the reason is that nothing of consequence materialized there. But the lack of action was itself consequential. It sent a signal to Hitler that no nation in the world wanted the Jews, that Palestine had effectively been closed as a place of refuge, and that Germany could deal internally with the Jews as it wished, without fear of even a critical resolution from the West.

Martin Gilbert has written that the "lessons of Evian, as learnt by the Nazi leadership," may have led to a "decisive" change in "anti-Jewish [German] polices from forced emigration to physical destruction." In his 2011 PhD thesis, "The Jewish Trail of Tears: The Evian Conference of July 1938," Dennis R. Laffer concluded that its "hypocritical rhetoric and . . . ineffectiveness" was "clearly recognized by Nazi Germany and ultimately influenced its anti-Jewish policies."[38] It was "not a coincidence," Laffer wrote, "that the pogrom of November 1938, *Kristallnacht*, occurred only four months later." Historian Ernst Marcus concluded that "[t]here is an immutable connection between the . . . Evian Conference and the events of November [1938]"—and what followed after that.[39]

Hitler had witnessed the West's appeasement, the muted response to the brutal annexation of Austria, the self-isolation and silence of the United States, the world's acquiescence in the barbaric treatment of the Jews, and the holding of an ineffectual conference to address the problem, which could barely bring itself, during its nine days of sympathetic consideration, to mention the word "Jews." Two-and-a-half months after the Evian Conference, Britain and France entered into the Munich Agreement with Hitler. The following year, Hitler invaded Poland.

The Evian Conference was a meeting in a luxurious hotel, at a beautiful resort, in an idyllic part of a country that would itself be occupied by German troops less than two years later, in part because of the dramatic display of Western irresolution demonstrated at the Conference.

History is not only the memory of the "things said and done." It is also the story of the things that were not. Silence and inaction can send a message of their own, as clear as a resolution of homage.

Watching the proceedings in Evian, Golda Meir recalled in her autobiography, was a "terrible experience"—one that no one "who didn't live through it can understand." As she sat there, at the back of the room, she felt "a mixture of sorrow, rage, frustration and horror," watching the delegates fail to treat the "numbers [as] human beings." At Evian, she learned that "Jews neither can nor should ever depend on anyone else for permission to stay alive":

> I realized—perhaps for the first time since I was a little girl in Russia listening in terror to the hooves of Cossack horses thundering through town—that it is not enough for a weak people to demonstrate the justice of its demands. . . . Nothing was accomplished at Evian . . . but before I left, I held a press conference. . . . "There is one thing I hope to see before I die," I told the press, "and that is that my people should not need expressions of sympathy anymore."[40]

In 1956, after the world castigated Israel for its retaliation against Egyptian shelling and Arab fedayeen raids, which had lobbed hand grenades into synagogues and attacked buses filled with women and children, Meir said she was uninterested in explaining Israel's actions to the world. She noted that the world would certainly express its sympathy if Israel were destroyed, but that "doesn't interest us." "If we remain alive, we will explain all sorts of things." After the Six-Day War in 1967, she told a rally at Madison Square Garden:

> We're a wonderful people, [the world] tells us. . . . Look at what they can achieve against such odds. Now that they have won this battle, let them go back where they came from so that the hills of Syria will again be open for Syrian guns; so that Jordanian Legionnaires [can] shoot and shell at will. . . .

Sitting at the Evian Conference in 1938, she also recalled the Socialist International conference she had attended a year earlier, where the Spanish delegation had implored their international socialist colleagues for help in the Spanish Civil War—and had been turned down by the British Labor Party, the leading socialist party in the world. She learned that "socialist brotherhood" was an unreliable force for national survival—a lesson she would learn again nearly a half century later as Israel's prime minister during the 1973 Yom Kippur War.

After that war—in which Israel was almost destroyed—she convened a special conference of the Socialist International, attended by twenty heads of state and socialist party leaders, because she wanted "to hear for myself, with my own ears, what it was that kept the heads of these socialist governments from helping us." She told them she wanted to understand—since they had not even permitted "refueling the [American] planes that saved us from destruction"—"what socialism is really about today":

> We are all old comrades, long-standing friends. . . . Believe me, I am the last person to belittle the fact that we are only one tiny Jewish state and that there are over twenty Arab states with vast territories, endless oil, and billions of dollars. But what I want to know from you today is whether these things are the decisive factors in Socialist thinking, too?[41]

The Conference chairman asked whether anyone wanted to reply to Meir's question. No one did, and thus she effectively received her answer. Years later, in 2017, when Israel no longer had a socialist government, the World Socialist movement would desert Israel ideologically as well. On the centenary of the Balfour Declaration, the World Socialist Web Site castigated the landmark document in modern Jewish history as "a sordid deal" that had launched "a nakedly colonial project."[42]

Socialism had been one of the reasons young Golda Meyerson had emigrated to Palestine in 1921. But she saw the socialist nations fail to assist the Spanish socialist government in 1937 and fail again to support the socialist state of Israel in 1973. At Evian, she had learned that Jewish refugees would not be saved by universal sympathy or by a universalist ideology.

A year after the Evian Conference, Golda Meyerson wrote an article pledging that, at least in Palestine, "our children will be safe for the Jewish people." She wrote that:

> I cannot conceive that we shall fail in our work here, in our defense of every single settlement, even the smallest, if we keep before us the picture of the thousands of Jews in the concentration camps of Europe. Therein lies our strength . . . our fundamental faith is alive. What has been done to other peoples and to other countries will not be done to us.[43]

"Little did I know," she later wrote, "that what would be done to the Jews would be indescribably worse."[44]

After the Evian Conference, with Hitler tightening his vise on the Jews and Britain shutting the doors to Palestine, the spotlight of Jewish history turned to the United States.

What was the reaction of the American Jews—a community of 4.9 million living in relative safety—watching what had taken place in Austria and what had not happened in Evian; witnessing two months later the appeasement of Hitler in the Munich Agreement; and then two months after that, the vicious *Kristallnacht* pogrom initiated by Hitler; then the issuance in July 1939 of the new British White Paper reneging on Britain's obligation to facilitate the Jewish national home in Palestine, rejecting even its 1937 Peel recommendation for two states there, and designating Palestine instead to become a single Arab-majority state; and finally, on September 1, 1939, the Nazi invasion of Poland—the center of Jewish civilization in Europe—with a Polish Jewish population as large as that in the United States? At that moment, what did they do?

This brings us to the story of one of the most famous Americans of the time, the screenwriter Ben Hecht.

SIX

Ben Hecht and the Soul of American Jews

"In addition to becoming a Jew in 1939,
I became also an American."

Ben Hecht, circa 1940

WHEN THE WRITER BEN HECHT died suddenly in 1964, at the age of seventy, the *New York Times* carried the news on the front page of its Sunday edition. The 2,100-word obituary continued on an inside page, where it filled four columns.[1]

Hecht, the *Times* wrote, had "chronicled high life and low life in Chicago, New York and Hollywood," writing "novels, short stories, plays and a stream of memoirs." Beginning as a crime reporter and a human-interest columnist in Chicago, Hecht wrote pieces that were later republished in two volumes. His first novel, *Erik Dorn*, published in 1921 when he was twenty-seven years old, "made him a national literary figure."[2] He wrote 250 short stories and 20 plays, including the Broadway sensation *The Front Page*, and he became Hollywood's highest-paid screenwriter, with classics such as *Scarface, Wuthering Heights, His Girl Friday*, and *Notorious* to his credit. He received six Oscar nominations and won two. He wrote thirty-five books, including multiple best-sellers. Saul Bellow reviewed his 525-page autobiography, *A Child of the Century*, on the cover of the *New York Times Book Review*, calling it "intensely interesting . . . independent, forthright and original." *Time* named it one of the most important books since *Time* had begun publishing.[3]

Near the end of the obituary was a brief, unflattering description of Hecht's involvement with Zionism. But it was Hecht's encounter with it in the 1940s—after a lifetime of indifference to Jewish issues—that became as important to him as almost anything in his life. It changed his life and his legacy.[4] In an age of isolationism, he helped define what it meant to be an American and an American Jew in the world.[5]

By 1939, Hecht—only in his mid-forties—had already had an extremely successful career. Born on the Lower East Side of New York in 1894 to

Russian Jewish immigrants, he had grown up in Wisconsin, skipped college, and headed to Chicago to pursue a journalistic and literary career, joining an illustrious salon that included Theodore Dreiser, Edgar Lee Masters, and Carl Sandburg, becoming a friend of Sherwood Anderson and Max Bodenheim, and going to Berlin in 1918–19 to report on political violence in Germany. It was an experience that left him, he later wrote, "with a permanent cynicism toward history."

Back in America, he created new forms of journalism with his crime/human interest columns, innovative stage plays, and groundbreaking motion pictures—becoming an American success story even as the Depression devastated the economy. By 1939, he had been extraordinarily productive, reaching new heights in a variety of different types of writing. Of his Jewish identity, he would later recall that:

> I lived forty years in my country without encountering anti-Semitism or concerning myself even remotely with its existence. This is perhaps a record for a Jew or, more likely, for a country. . . . I attended no synagogue, read no Jewish history or literature, never heard of the Spanish Inquisition, and listened to no discussion of Jewish problems. . . . I went to work as a newspaper reporter . . . [and] met no hint or whisper of anti-Semitism. . . . I remember this world of 1910 to 1925 from almost every point of view but a Jewish one.

In 1926, he received perhaps the most famous telegram in movie history. His friend Herman Mankiewicz, the head of Paramount Pictures, urged him to come to Hollywood to work for $300 a week: "The three hundred is peanuts. Millions are to be grabbed out here and your only competition is idiots. Don't let this get around."

Hecht went, and the following year he wrote a 68-page treatment for the first gangster movie—*Underworld*—over the course of a single week. He received a $10,000 bonus (about $150,000 in 2022 dollars) and won the Oscar for "Best Original Story" at the first Academy Awards ceremony in 1929. His next script was *Scarface*, written over an eleven-day period, starring Paul Muni as a mobster patterned on Al Capone. It established the gangster movie as a significant new film genre.

Hecht later described his screenwriting method as killing off "as many people as I could." He said he "knew audiences adored disaster, sudden death, explosions, much more than they did ideas, points of view or intelligence of any kind."[6] The key, he said, "was that I stuck to doing things that had no thought in them."[7] He also wrote romantic comedies, and eventually more than sixty-five screenplays. Otto Preminger later said that Hecht could "have become one of the greatest writers in the theater and in American literature," but "unfortunately . . . [h]e had no time. He always had jobs in Hollywood." As the 1930s progressed, however, Hecht came to consider his Hollywood career a prostitution of his talent. He thought movies had "corrupted our century" and that he was playing "the literary whore," haunted by "the echo of integrity that still wails in my empty head."[8]

In Hecht's 1936 autobiographical play, *To Quito and Back*, the lead character is a cynical newspaperman who had once witnessed political murders in Germany. Another character observes that "we hover on the sidelines of all passionate events, and are always on the right side of discussions, but never on any side of the barricades." Three years later, after *Kristallnacht*, Hecht would join the Jewish side, and in 1941—after a chance meeting with one of Jabotinsky's followers—he would move to the barricades, seeking to mobilize the English language to support the embattled Jews of Europe and Palestine.

On November 9, 1938, Adolf Hitler and Hermann Goering, a high-ranking Nazi official and Hitler's henchman, initiated a massive two-day pogrom, euphemistically named *Kristallnacht* (Night of Broken Glass). Nazi headquarters issued orders to arrest Jews, disarm them, destroy their stores, deface their cemeteries, post signs reading "Death to International Jewry," and arrest the elite members of the Jewish community. Police stations received written instructions that:

> [A]s many Jews in all districts, especially the rich, as can be accommodated in existing prisons are to be arrested. . . . After the detentions have been carried out, the appropriate concentration camps are to be contacted immediately for the prompt accommodation of the Jews.

The scope of the carnage and the number of arrests were staggering. More than 1,000 synagogues were burned; over 7,000 businesses were gutted; hundreds of Jews died; and 30,000 were arrested and sent to concentration camps at Buchenwald, Dachau, and elsewhere.

Frankfurt Synagogue burning during Kristallnacht

Three days after *Kristallnacht*, the major American Jewish organizations met and formally agreed that "there should be no parades, public demonstrations, or protests by Jews."[9] They adopted a strategy of silence, out of fear that Jewish protests might lead to accusations of special pleading. Rabbi Stephen S. Wise, the head of the World Jewish Congress (WJC), explained the organization's silence as a "well-considered policy" based on a determination that Jewish demonstrations would be "unwise."

Five days after the pogrom, President Roosevelt read a brief prepared statement to reporters. It did not mention the Jews by name. He said the "news of the past few days from Germany" had "deeply shocked public opinion in the United States," as it would, he said, "from any part of the world." He could "scarcely believe that such things could occur in a twentieth century civilization"; he had asked the secretary of state to "order our Ambassador in Berlin to return at once for report and consultation." In response to reporters' questions, he denied it was a "recall" of the ambassador, saying it was only "a summons to come home." He said no American protest to Germany was contemplated, and that American quotas for Jewish refugees would not be increased. Rabbi Wise was satisfied with the statement: "At long last," he wrote, "America has spoken."[10]

In June 1939, seven months after *Kristallnacht*, Hecht published a book of novellas titled *A Book of Miracles,* which the *New York Times* called "the most amazing work of fiction of the year."[11] It was filled, the reviewer wrote, with stories that "Tolstoy himself might have written." The reviewer deemed one of them—"The Little Candle"—"something of a miracle itself." It is a tale of an "International Pogrom" in which Germany and its allies murder half a million Jews, with the narrator recounting how, one July day, "we Jews opened our morning newspapers" and "stared with nausea and disbelief" at the report:

> [W]e found that the cloud we had watched so long and, in a way, so aloofly, had grown suddenly black and dreadful and immense. . . . Like a monster evoked out of the smoking pages of our history, it confronted us, exultant and with the ancient howl of massacre on its lips. . . . [W]e who had gone to sleep the night before on the borrowed pillow of civilization woke in the Dark Ages. . . . [W]e were Jews again, whatever our previous conceptions of ourselves had been.

Hecht's narrator says the report "sent our spirits cowering beside the myriads of unknown Jews in the shambles of Europe," creating a "great devitalizing shame," because:

> As always in the days of all our stricken history, we had no armies to move forward to avenge our murdered selves. . . . We knew that our impotence as a people, forgotten in the noise of our individual triumphs . . . demanded we become . . . a nation—and make a fight of it; demanded we die valorously together, [we] who knew only how to die humbly and apart.

The main character—a rabbi who is the most learned and humble scholar in the community—disperses his congregation so they will not hear him as he castigates God. Then he delivers a stunning speech that recalls the one of Job in the Bible—except that, unlike the biblical story, God does not appear at the end. The story portrays a people seeking comfort in a religion providing solace but no protection in the real world.

As literature, "The Little Candle" compares favorably with the best short stories of Hemingway and Fitzgerald: The plot, the language, and the moral complexity are all extraordinary. But it is the work of a writer watching Germany descend once again into the chaos he first witnessed as a young reporter in 1918—and still, two decades later, standing on the sidelines.

Hecht's move from the sidelines to the barricades came in 1941, when he was, he later wrote, "walking down the street one day [and] bumped into history." He was writing columns for *PM*, a new progressive tabloid, and in April had contributed a column titled "My Tribe Is Called Israel." It called on American Jews to cease hiding behind a non-Jewish identity and to respond to what was happening abroad not only as Americans but as Jews.[12]

Soon thereafter a stranger, a young Palestinian Jew named Peter Bergson, who had come to New York in 1940 as part of Vladimir Jabotinsky's effort to build support for a Jewish Army to join the fight against Hitler, wrote to Hecht.[13] Bergson praised him for expressing the "spiritual heroism which for centuries accumulated in the soul of the genuine and conscious Jew" and told him that "[b]y the creation of a Jewish Army we intend to transform this heroic spirit into heroic deeds." After repeated requests, Hecht finally agreed to have drinks with Bergson at the posh 21 Club in Manhattan, an encounter that turned out to last for hours.

The meeting between the famous forty-six-year-old Hollywood writer and the unknown twenty-seven-year-old Zionist was, in its way, as historic as the Mankiewicz telegram. Hecht would later recall that:

> I had no notion on that April day in 1941 that any such collision [with history] was taking place. . . . [My] column had discussed the attitudes of American Jews toward [Hitler]. I had deplored the fact that America's important social, political and literary Jews were reluctant to speak out as Jews under attack and preferred to conduct themselves as neutral Americans. . . . [Bergson]

told me of the fine Jewish renaissance begun by a man named Vladimir Jabotinsky, of whom I had never heard.[14]

Bergson asked Hecht to become the American leader of their cause, a role for which Hecht considered himself completely unqualified, by both temperament and experience:

> I disliked causes. I disliked public speaking. I could bring myself neither to make orations nor listen to them. I never attended meetings of any sort. I had no interest in Palestine and had always bolted any conversation about a Jewish Homeland. My heart had never turned to Jerusalem. Finally, there was nothing more socially distasteful to me than getting involved in a money-raising campaign.

Hecht reluctantly agreed to be the cochairman of the "Committee for a Jewish Army," and in early 1942 he gave his first speech, to a thousand people at a fundraiser held at Twentieth Century Fox.[15] It was a night that "was to alter my life as completely as if I had changed my name and gone to another land."[16]

As 1942 began, the Middle East was becoming a key strategic area in the war, and the situation of the Jews in Europe was becoming extremely ominous.[17] On March 1, 1942, the *New York Times* reported that "Extinction [Is] Feared by Jews of Poland," where more than 3 million Jews lived, from a "Systematic Nazi Campaign," with "Complete Disaster" on the horizon:

EXTINCTION FEARED BY JEWS IN POLAND

Dr. Henry Shoskes Says Reports From 'Underground' Tell of Systematic Nazi Campaign

HUNGER, DISEASE STRIKE

Death Rate in Ghettos So High Complete Disaster Is Seen Within Next 5 Years

On June 13, the *Times* reported that Goebbels had said that Germany would carry out a mass "extermination" of the Jews in reprisal for heavy damage from Allied bombings of German cities, which he blamed on the "Jewish press" in London and New York.[18] He promised that the extermination would not be limited to Europe:

> "The Jews are playing a frivolous game and they will pay for it with the extermination of their race in all Europe and perhaps even beyond Europe."

Goebbels's declaration came a week before Churchill was scheduled to meet with Roosevelt to review the issues in the war—their first meeting since December 1941, when the Japanese attack on Pearl Harbor and German declaration of war on the United States had brought America into the war. Rabbi Wise met with Under Secretary of State Sumner Welles on June 17, 1942, to discuss the Goebbels threat, and he followed it with a June 19 letter to Welles, reiterating that:

> [T]he unspeakable . . . threat of Goebbels to have the Jews of Europe exterminated . . . is a threat which the United Nations cannot afford to ignore. . . . [I]t is worse than a threat. It is the direst attack upon the whole Jewish people, as if they were responsible for the inevitable bombing of German cities and their military depots.

The reference by Rabbi Wise to the "United Nations" was not to the post-war UN, but rather to the twenty-six nations that had signed an agreement on January 1, 1942, calling themselves the "United Nations," declaring a common cause of "life, liberty, independence, and religious freedom," and promising no separate peace with Germany.[19] In his letter, Wise asked Welles to urge Roosevelt and Churchill, as the leaders of the United Nations, to issue a joint statement about the Goebbels threat:

> It would mean more than I can say if you could move both the President and the Prime Minister to see that, as devoted helpers of the United Nations my people might have that spiritual sustainment which would come from a word fitly spoken by the two great leaders of the United Nations.[20]

But Roosevelt and Churchill said nothing about the genocidal threat to the Jews in their post-meeting communiqué.

On June 16, the *Times* reported that 60,000 Jews had been murdered in Vilna in fewer than two weeks. The story quoted a Polish eyewitness who had escaped:

> On May 7, the executions started, [the eyewitness] said. The Jews, men, women and children, were taken from sundown to dawn in trucks to the suburb of Ponary, where they were mowed down by machine-gun fire. The executions continued every night until May 20, the Pole related.

Two weeks later, the *Times* published an article headlined, "1,000,000 Jews Slain by Nazis," reporting that 1 million Jews had already been murdered since the beginning of the war, "carrying out Adolf Hitler's proclaimed policy of exterminating the people." The report was based on a statement by spokesmen for Rabbi Wise's World Jewish Congress (WJC):

> They said the Nazis had established a "vast slaughterhouse for Jews" in Eastern Europe and that reliable reports showed that 700,000 Jews already had been murdered in Lithuania and Poland, 125,000 in Rumania, 200,000 in Nazi-occupied parts of Russia and 100,000 in the rest of Europe. Thus about one-sixth of the pre-war Jewish population in Europe, estimated at 6,000,000 to 7,000,000 persons, had been wiped out in less than three years.[21]

The following month, the *Times* reported that the WJC had learned that Jews were being deported en masse to Poland from four countries—Germany, Austria, Czechoslovakia, and the Netherlands—and were being murdered by firing squads at the rate of 1,000 daily.[22]

1,000,000 JEWS SLAIN BY NAZIS, REPORT SAYS

'Slaughterhouse' of Europe Under Hitler Described at London

LONDON, June 29 (U.P.) — The Germans have massacred more than 1,000,000 Jews since the war began in carrying out Adolf Hitler's proclaimed policy of exterminating the people, spokesmen for the World Jewish Congress charged

The dire situation of the Jews was thus evident to anyone reading the *New York Times* during the first part of 1942.[23] It was known in even greater detail by Western intelligence services in Europe.[24] And in August, a drama began playing out at the State Department, when it learned that a reliable, well-positioned German informant had warned that the Nazis planned to exterminate 4 million Jews within a few months.

On July 28, 1942, Eduard Schulte, the managing director of one of Germany's largest industrial firms, with contacts within both the German military and the German foreign office, traveled to Switzerland to tell Jewish contacts there that the Nazis were considering a plan to transport 4 million Jews to Eastern Europe and exterminate them with cyanide.[25]

Schulte's report reached Gerhard Riegner, a thirty-year-old German Jew serving as a WJC representative in Geneva. Riegner checked Schulte's background and concluded that a mass extermination was consistent with the large-scale Nazi deportations of Jews from Germany, France, Holland, Austria, and Czechoslovakia. On August 8, he went to the American consulate to ask that it send a message by secure cable to the State Department in Washington, for transmittal to Rabbi Wise. The consulate sent the cable to the State Department, which decided not to inform Wise.[26] Wise only learned of Riegner's report from a separate cable that Riegner had sent through the British consulate to Samuel Silverman, the WJC's London representative.[27] Silverman in turn cabled Wise on August 29:

> Have received through Foreign Office the following message from Riegner Geneva. ["]Received alarming report that in Fuehrer's headquarters a plan discussed and under consideration all Jews in countries occupied or controlled Germany number 3-1/2 to 4 million should after deportation and concentration in East at one blow exterminated to resolve once for all Jewish question in Europe. Action reported planned for autumn methods under discussion including prussic acid. We transmit information with all necessary reservation as exactitude cannot be confirmed. Informant stated to have close connections with highest German authorities and his reports generally reliable.["][28]

Riegner's cable was necessarily cautious, noting that the informant was "stated" to have close German high connections and had provided "generally" reliable reports, and that Riegner was sending the news "with all necessary reservation as exactitude cannot be confirmed." Silverman's transmittal cable added that the British Foreign Office "[h]as no information bearing on or confirming story."[29]

On September 3, five days after receiving Silverman's cable, Wise met with Under Secretary of State Welles to discuss the Riegner report, unaware that the State Department had already received and withheld it nearly a month before. Welles asked Wise to withhold any public statement until the State Department could investigate it, and Wise agreed.[30]

In the meantime, the Nazi persecutions were regularly covered by the *Times*.[31] On September 30, Hitler made a seventy-minute speech in the Berlin Sport Stadium, broadcast on radio and reported extensively in the press, including the *Times*, which printed the entire transcript. In his speech, Hitler recalled his words from September 1, 1939, the day Germany had invaded Poland, when he had told the Reichstag that the Jews would be "eradicated" if any nations responded by declaring war on Germany. Now, three years later, Hitler repeated and reemphasized his threat:

> Anti-Semitism is growing, and every nation that enters this war will come out of it an anti-Semitic state. Jews laughed in Germany when I prophesized something [in 1939]. I don't know if they laugh still. . . . But I can assure them . . . I will be right in this prophecy too.[32]

It would not be known until after the war that Hitler had likely decided on his "final solution" between September and October of 1941; that fifteen high-level Nazis (including Adolf Eichmann) had held a conference at Wannsee on January 20, 1942, to implement it; and that the goal was to make the entire European continent *Judenrein* through mass murder.[33] But even a casual reader of the *New York Times* during 1942 could see that the systematic destruction of European Jews was underway, as Hitler had promised in 1939.[34] What the Riegner telegram cautiously described as being considered was, in fact, already happening; what readers of the *Times* had been reading was evidence that it was in fact accelerating.

The State Department "investigation" of the Riegner report appears to have consisted largely of asking the Vatican if it knew of such a development and receiving additional reports from Rabbi Wise.[35] The Vatican, which maintained a public silence about the treatment of the Jews throughout the war, provided no useful information.[36]

The Department sent an October 5, 1942, cable to Leland Harrison, the highest-ranking American official in Switzerland, asking him to consider "strong new evidence [Rabbi Wise had received] confirming . . . previous reports about extermination."[37] Harrison responded the following day that:

> There are indications that Jews are, without any doubt, being driven out systematically from the countries of Western Europe. Such indications are contained in numerous reports which have come to me from both Jewish and non-Jewish sources, supplemented by reports received from [the consul in Geneva], who has been in communication with Dr. Riegner. Jews are being moved, these reports indicate, to unknown destinations in German-occupied Russia and in Poland. It has been credibly reported to me . . . that ghettos of Warsaw and other large cities are being cleared and the Jews sent eastward to a destiny unknown.[38]

Harrison met with Riegner, received a detailed summary, country-by-country, of the Nazi murders of Jews, and forwarded the documents to the State Department at the end of October.[39] On November 13, Welles wrote to Wise that he would "value the opportunity of seeing you the next time you pass through Washington in order to discuss with you certain information I have received from our Minister in Switzerland after his conversation with . . . Mr. Riegner."[40]

On November 24, 1942—three-and-a-half months after the State Department received the Riegner telegram—Welles told Wise that Riegner had indeed been correct, and that 2 million Jews had already been murdered.[41] Neither Welles nor the State Department made any public statement; they simply authorized Wise to inform the press on his own. Wise held a hurried press conference the same day, saying that the State Department had confirmed that "about half the estimated 4,000,000 Jews in Nazi-occupied Europe had been slain in an 'extermination campaign.'" The *Times* story the next day read that:

> "The State Department finally made available today the documents which have confirmed the stories and rumors of Jewish extermination in all Hitler-ruled Europe," Dr. Wise said.[42]

The State Department, asked by the press to confirm or deny Rabbi Wise's statement, said the Department had "made no statement for publication concerning Rabbi Wise's statement" but had simply provided him with certain material "to facilitate the efforts of his committee in getting at the truth." The Department directed any questions about the material to Rabbi Wise.[43]

On December 2, 1942, Rabbi Wise wrote to President Roosevelt, literally begging him, "as your old friend," for a White House meeting with representatives of the American Jewish Committee, the American Jewish Congress, and B'nai B'rith, to discuss what Wise told Roosevelt was "the most overwhelming disaster of Jewish history." It was now "indisputable," he told him, "that as many as two million civilian Jews have been slain." He said the group wanted to present a memorandum and hear "an expression of the conscience of the American people."[44]

On December 8, 1942, Roosevelt met with the group, which brought a two-page letter and a twenty-page memorandum entitled "Blue Print for Extermination."[45] The group met for half an hour with the President.[46] A contemporary memorandum written by one of the Jewish participants in the meeting noted that Roosevelt had talked for twenty-three of the twenty-nine-minutes in the meeting, and had advised the group of a pithy proverb he had recently heard that counseled waiting until the war was over to do anything.[47]

Rabbi Wise told the press after the meeting that the President had assured the group he would "give full consideration" to a proposal to collect evidence bearing on the Nazis' "criminal acts." The next day, the *Times* reported the presidential "pledge" to make "every effort" to "fix guilt," with the headlines reporting that 2 million Jews had already been murdered—and that the murders by poison gas were continuing every hour.

PRESIDENT RENEWS PLEDGES TO JEWS

He Tells Group Every Effort Will Be Made to Fix Guilt in Axis Crimes Against Race

2,000,000 REPORTED DEAD

Delegation Asserts the Newest Nazi Method Is Poisoning at Rate of 100 an Hour

Special to THE NEW YORK TIMES.

On December 17, 1942, at British urging, the Allies issued a statement on reports "that the German authorities . . . are now carrying into effect Hitler's oft-repeated intention to exterminate the Jewish people in Europe." The statement said Jews were being transported "in conditions of appalling horror and brutality" to Poland—"the principal Nazi slaughterhouse"—where they were "deliberately massacred in mass executions" that were "reckoned" to number "many hundreds of thousands."[48] The statement condemned the "bestial policy of cold-blooded extermination" in "the strongest possible terms," promised "retribution" against "those responsible," and pledged to "press on with the necessary practical measures to this end."

Secretary of State Hull, when asked to specify the "practical measures," said that "the names of the guilty persons" were being collected, to be "properly dealt with." British Foreign Secretary Anthony Eden, when asked in the House of Commons about "what constructive measures of relief are immediately practicable," responded more candidly:

> [M]y honorable Friend knows the immense difficulties in the way of what he suggests, but he may be sure that we shall do all we can to alleviate these horrors, though I fear that what we can do at this stage must inevitably be slight.[49]

The transmittal of the Riegner telegram to the State Department, Rabbi Wise's repeated meetings with Sumner Welles and transmittal of evidence to him, and Rabbi Wise's longtime friendship and meetings with President Roosevelt produced nothing in the way of "practical measures." It would take Ben Hecht—an individual with no connections in the Roosevelt administration and no support from Jewish institutions—to write articles, produce full-page newspaper ads, and stage a nationwide pageant that would finally help induce a belated reaction, in 1944, from the Roosevelt administration.[50]

At the end of 1942, more than half of the 6 million Jews who would ultimately be murdered were still alive. The October 1942 issue of *Esquire* published a powerful essay by Hecht titled "A Champion in Chains," urging that the 200,000 Jews of military age in Palestine be allowed to form an army to fight in Northern Africa, which Hecht noted was becoming "the strategic heart of the battle this year." He described the shock of American Jews as they read the news from Europe:

> Most of the Jews I know are, like myself, a little startled to find themselves Jews. It seems we went to bed one night as integrated Americans full of American ways and dreams, Colonial furniture in our homes and no sense of racial demarcation in our souls. And we woke up one morning to find ourselves Jews. . . .
>
> [T]he discovery that I was a Jew did not set me to lighting any Friday night candles nor did it alter by a phrase any of my attitudes toward life. [My ideas] are American attitudes, born in America, nurtured in American schools and developed through service in American journalism, literature, drama and the movies. . . . [But] the nightmare . . . for millions of defenseless people . . . [is] a miasma in which the faraway American Jew, however "emancipated," however "assimilated," has found it hard to breathe.

The situation, Hecht wrote, "kicked at his soul." In February 1943, the *American Mercury* published Hecht's article, "The Extermination of the Jews," which was then republished in condensed form in the *Reader's Digest*—at that time the most widely read magazine in America.[51] In his article, Hecht predicted that after the war, Germany would face justice from "Englishmen, Americans, Russians, Czechs, Poles, Greeks, Norwegians, Belgians, Frenchmen and Dutchmen," but *not* from the Jews—because they would be a "phantom" by then, with 2 million already dead "and another two million yet to be murdered, according to the most conservative of scorekeepers."

In the next fifteen paragraphs of his article, Hecht ranged from Warsaw to Lublin to Odessa and to a dozen other places, each paragraph beginning with the same chilling refrain:

> "*Remember us!* In the town of Freiburg in the Black Forest, two hundred of us were hanged and left dangling out of our kitchen windows to watch our synagogue burn and our rabbi flogged to death. . . .
>
> "Remember us in Wloclawek. Here also the Germans came when we were at worship [on Yom Kippur, praying for God to forgive us]. . . . Under whips and bayonets, they made us use our

> prayer shawls as mops to clean out German latrines. We were all dead when the sun set. . . .
>
> "Remember us who were put in the freight trains that left France, Holland and Belgium and who rode standing up to the east. We died standing up for there was no food or air or water. . . .
>
> "Remember, too, those of us who were not killed by the Germans "but who killed themselves. Some say there were a hundred thousand of us, some say two hundred thousand. No count was kept."

Hecht then wrote the script for a pageant to be presented at Madison Square Garden on March 9, 1943, entitled "We Will Never Die," with some of the most illustrious names from the Broadway stage—Moss Hart, Kurt Weill, and Billy Rose—enlisted to direct and write the music. In his autobiography, Hecht described a call he received from Rabbi Wise after sending the script to him:

> Rabbi Stephen Wise, head of the Jews of New York, head of the Zionists and, as I knew from reading the papers, head of almost everything noble in American Jewry, telephoned me. . . . Rabbi Wise said he would like to see me immediately in his rectory. His voice, which was sonorous and impressive, irritated me. . . . I explained that I was very busy. . . . "Then I shall tell you now, over the telephone, what I had hoped to tell you in my study. . . . I have read your pageant script and I disapprove of it. I must ask you to cancel this pageant and discontinue all your further activities on behalf of the Jews. If you wish hereafter to work for the Jewish Cause, you will please consult me and let me advise you."
>
> At this point I hung up.[52]

"We Will Never Die" featured a stage with two giant tablets inscribed with the Ten Commandments and a combination of religious music and Zionist hymns. The narrators, Paul Muni and Edward G. Robinson—both European-born Jews—recited the names of 120 Jews who had made major contributions to humanity through the centuries, starting with the "little tribe" in ancient Israel whose creed "was destined to change the soul of man." Actor Jacob Ben-Ami told the audience that:

"We Will Never Die," at Madison Square Garden, March 9, 1943

> We are not here to weep for [those murdered in Europe]. We are here to honor them. . . . For in our Testament are written the words of Habakkuk, prophet of Israel, "They shall never die." They are part of something greater, higher and stronger than the dreams of their executioners. They were unarmed, but not we.[53]

The final scene of the ninety-minute pageant was a dramatization of Hecht's February article, with a peace table placed onstage and a narrator explaining that there would be no Jews left in Europe when peace came. Jewish ghosts testified about the murders in country after country, crying "Remember us!"

There were two sold-out performances on March 9—one at 8:45 p.m. and another at 11:15 p.m. scheduled because of the huge demand for tickets. A total of 40,000 people saw the pageant that night, with thousands listening outside on loudspeakers. The *Times* prominently reported it the next day.

"We Will Never Die" was then performed in Washington, D.C., on April 14, 1943, before an audience that included Eleanor Roosevelt, who wrote in her syndicated column that the "music, singing, narration, and actors all served to make it one of the most impressive and moving pageants I have ever seen," with "unforgettable haunting words: 'Remember us.'"[54] It was next performed in Philadelphia, Boston, Chicago, and at the Hollywood Bowl, where it was broadcast nationwide by NBC Radio. More than 100,000 people saw "We Will Never Die" over the course of 1943, and countless more heard it on the radio or read about it in the newspapers.

In September 1943, the Bergson Group published an advertisement in the *New York Times* featuring a poem by Hecht titled "Ballad of the Doomed Jews of Europe."[55] The first and last stanzas of the poem read as follows:

FOUR MILLION JEWS waiting for death
Oh, hang and burn but—quiet, Jews!
Don't be bothersome; save your breath—
The world is busy with other news.

* * * *

Oh World be patient it will take
Some time before the murder crews
Are done. By Christmas you can make
Your Peace on Earth without the Jews.

Both the American Jewish Committee and the American Jewish Congress opposed the ad's publication when Hecht had proposed it at the end of 1942, fearing it was too provocative. When it was ultimately published a year later, another 1 million Jews had been murdered.

During this period, the Roosevelt administration took no action whatsoever to save the European Jews. But on October 8, 1943, the *Times* published an article headlined, "All-Europe Purge of Jews Reported—Hitler Said to Have Ordered Continent Cleared Before End of the War," informing readers that "[w]ell-informed sources" said Hitler had personally ordered "the removal of all Jews from Europe before the end of the war." Then in January 1944, Treasury Secretary Henry Morgenthau, Jr., informed Roosevelt that the State Department was blocking aid to Jewish refugees—and that FDR faced a potential election-year scandal unless he acted promptly.

Morgenthau's "Personal Memorandum" to the President, presented to him at a White House meeting, detailed State Department actions that had made it (in the words of the memorandum) "guilty not only of gross procrastination and willful failure to act, but even of willful attempts to prevent action from being taken to rescue Jews from Hitler."[56] A week later, on January 22, 1944, Roosevelt established the War Refugee Board, with John Pehle as director, to implement (in the words of the executive order) "immediate rescue and relief of the Jews of Europe and other victims of enemy persecution" through safe havens, evacuations from Nazi-occupied territories, delivery of relief supplies into concentration camps, and other measures.[57]

Hecht's writings and nationwide productions—which brought the issue of Hitler's extermination of the Jews of Europe to widespread public awareness, and thus made it a part of the political situation facing Roosevelt as he prepared to run for a third term—played an important role in the establishment of the War Refugee Board.[58] The Board's efforts saved thousands of lives, perhaps as many as tens of thousands, during the final months of the Holocaust.[59] It was far too little, far too late—more than 5 million Jews had already been murdered when Roosevelt established the Board—but every life saved was a world.[60]

In March 1944, Hecht published *A Guide for the Bedeviled* (an allusion to Maimonides' *Guide for the Perplexed*), his best-selling analysis of anti-semitism. Maxwell Perkins, the legendary book editor known for having discovered and edited Ernest Hemingway, F. Scott Fitzgerald, and Thomas Wolfe, praised it for "its fire and power as literature." Hecht decided to write it after lunch in 1943 with an unnamed "famous lady" who was "full of very high-sounding ideas." They had "gossiped aimlessly for an hour on the stupidity of the movies, the stupidity of the theater, and the stupidity of literature—from which it can be seen that we were avoiding any topics of importance." Then she asked him, as an "expert," to explain why the Jews were so disliked:

> She seemed to be asking me . . . to break down and confess something that would clear up the murder of the three million Jews of Europe and also throw a light on the true secret of anti-Semitism everywhere.

The question struck Hecht as comparable to a policeman questioning a corpse to explain its own murder. He believed the woman "had picked up some anti-Semitism germs. There was yet no fever, but the sneeze was there." His book began by listing the contradictory crimes charged against the Jews, beginning with, on the one hand, "the battle cry that [the Jew] was responsible for the killing of Christ" and, on the other hand, the Nazi charge that the Jew "is responsible for the invention of Christ":

> There is also the charge that the Jew is interested only in the massing of money; and next the charge that he is responsible for a system of economics (Socialism, Communism) that seeks to undermine the whole principle of money-making. Next is the charge that he is ill-bred . . . and alongside this comes the charge that he is concerned too much with the arts. . . . There is the charge that the Jew is an un-martial creature . . . and the charge that the Jew is a dangerous fellow who conspires to drag the world into wars for his own secret ends.

The crimes were so diverse and inconsistent, Hecht wrote, "that it is apparent—and has been always apparent—that the only criminal involved is the accuser."

Hecht considered whether he was writing his book (a) as a Jew, or (b) as an American, or (c) as simply a disinterested author. He wrote that it would please him to think his fervor was "no more than that of a mind trained in the humanities under the beneficent culture of the United States":

> For, truly, I have never been anything else but an American and to find myself at forty-nine writing out of an obstreperous Jewish heritage is as confusing to me as if I had waked up one morning and found an entirely new language in my head. . . . I could make out a case for myself as either or neither [a Jew or an American], which is another way of saying that I am both.

Hecht concluded that:

> If I do not defend myself as a Jew, who, then, will? If I do not attack the enemies of Jews, who will have at them? My fellow Americans busy on other fronts? Why should they, since they are not Jewish and I am? Since I hold my peace, why should they raise their fists? . . .

> If my sense of outrage against the Germans is a Jewish one, do I lessen my Americanism by voicing it? . . . If tyrants flout the laws of human rights, and murder the weak, and I shout against them, am I more Jew than American? . . . [A Jew] cries for the rights of man, and for the decent unperilous operation of government. If he cries more loudly for these than the American next to him, is he not, perhaps, more American?

After World War II, with 6 million murdered Jews now gone, Hecht proceeded to turn his attention to securing a state for the surviving European Jews, with as much energy as he had devoted to his essays, advertisements, and pageants. What he did next turned out to affect the American Jews as well.

Perhaps the best evidence of the psychological state of American Jews immediately after World War II can be found in a confidential memorandum the British embassy in Washington prepared in February 1946, describing the Jews in America as of that year. "The Jewish future," the memorandum stated, "in the opinion of many competent observers, is none too rosy in the United States." American Jewish morale was low, the memorandum explained, because of two related existential shocks: (a) the horrific European mass murders, and (b) the pessimistic prospects for a Jewish state.[61] The established American Jews, according to the report, were generally assimilationists, and American Jews in general were scared:

> The American Jew has never before felt so insecure. Zionism, hitherto supported by him as a philanthropic gesture of assistance toward his less fortunate European coreligionists, has suddenly become a matter of personal concern.

On July 7, 1946, the *New York Times Book Review* published Hecht's review of a collection of stories, *The Old Country*, by Sholom Aleichem.[62] The review was Hecht's appreciation of Yiddish literature and of its most celebrated author, but Hecht wrote that he also found the collection "more than a book":

> It is the epitaph of a vanished world and an almost vanished people. The salty and hilarious folk of whom it tells—the Jews of Europe—are dead. . . . And all the quaint and heartwarming

> villages in which the Jews of Europe lived are no longer on the map. . . . [These tales] are their historical farewell to a civilization that wiped them out.

Hecht's effort to support the creation of a Jewish state at first took the form of his play, *A Flag Is Born*, which opened on Broadway on September 5, 1946. It featured music by Kurt Weill, with Paul Muni and Celia Adler playing the roles of "Tevya and Zelda," who were trying to reach Palestine after surviving the Holocaust. The role of the prototypical young Jew, "David," was played by twenty-two-year-old Marlon Brando.[63]

The music of *HaTikvah* filled the theater as three soldiers, representing the three underground Jewish forces in Palestine—the Irgun, the Haganah, and the Lehi—addressed David: "Don't you hear our guns, David? We battle the English. . . . We fling no more prayers or tears at the world. We fling bullets." At a key moment, David turns to the audience and asks:

> "Where were you, Jews? Where were you when the killing was going on? . . . We heard—your silence—in the gas chambers. And now, now you speak a little. Your hearts squeak—and you have a dollar for the Jews. Thank you. Thank you."[64]

David tells the audience that the soldiers "promise to wrest our Homeland out of British claws, as the Americans once did [in 1776]." They say to him, "Come David, and fight for Palestine. . . . We promise you an end to pleading and proverbs."

The *New York Times* review credited Muni with giving "one of the great performances of his career . . . speaking for the Jewish race" and said Weil had composed "one of the finest [scores] he has written." The *Times* wrote that Hecht's script made its point "with force and vigor" and that the opening-night audience included "more than a few" members of delegations to the United Nations.

A Flag Is Born was staged for $40,000: The lead actors accepted minimum union fees and the other cast and crew waived their usual wages; Hecht and Weill donated their royalties. The profits were dedicated to the Irgun, the Jewish military force formed under Jabotinsky and now led by Menachem Begin. The four-week Broadway run was extended to four months, and the play then toured the country. With its minimal production costs, it raised $275,000 ($4.1 million in 2022 dollars).

In 1947, Hecht wrote a sentence that resulted in his being banned in Britain and shunned in Hollywood. It was part of another one of his full-page advertisements, published over his signature, supporting the Jewish efforts to expel the British from Palestine and establish a Jewish state.

The ad appeared simultaneously on May 14, 1947, in the *New York Post*, the *New York Herald Tribune*, and other newspapers.[65] Ten days earlier, the Irgun had mounted a spectacular operation at the British maximum-security prison at Acre, which had seventy-foot-high walls and internal iron gates, where the British were holding 163 Jews, including a number of Irgun leaders. Astonishingly, the Irgun managed a simultaneous break-in and break-out to rescue and free them, and the daring operation was widely reported in the American press.[66]

Hecht's full-page ad, entitled "Letter to the [Jewish] Terrorists of Palestine," brought to "My Brave Friends" the "glad tidings" that the "Jews of America are for you." It included this especially incendiary sentence: "On my word as an old reporter," Hecht wrote in the ad:

> Every time you blow up a British arsenal, or wreck a British jail, or send a British railroad train sky high, or rob a British bank, or let go with your bombs and guns at the British betrayers and invaders of your homeland, the Jews of America make a little holiday in their hearts.[67]

The impact was immediate—in Palestine, America, and Britain. The Irgun distributed Hecht's message throughout Palestine. On May 16, the *New York Times* quoted Churchill calling Palestine "the most dismal of all quarrels into which we have blundered" and saying "we are making fools of ourselves by keeping 100,000 soldiers" there.[68] A week later, on May 23, the *Times* published an interview with Menachem Begin, who demanded withdrawal of "the British regime from our country and the transfer of government to a provisional Hebrew government."[69] Asked if he thought the Irgun's violence was "morally damaging [to] your cause," Begin responded: "in precisely the same degree as bombing Germany was 'morally damaging' to the Allies."

Hecht suffered a severe blow to his career from the ad, which sparked a formal British protest to the State Department and harsh reproaches from newspaper editors, American Jewish leaders, and others.[70] His films were banned by the British Cinematograph Exhibitors' Association, and he found himself a pariah in Hollywood, which depended on the 3,500 theaters in the British market. Nevertheless, Hecht said he was happy about the reaction: It was "the best press I had ever received—a solid acknowledgment of the work I had been doing with all my might."

In 1948, Hecht raised almost the same amount of money as he had with *A Flag Is Born* with a single speech to a group in Los Angeles assembled by the gangster Meyer Harris ("Mickey") Cohen—who had replaced Bugsy Siegel as king of the West Coast mob rackets.[71] Hecht and Cohen were friends, and Cohen told Hecht: "If you'll make a speech, I'll give a party where you can raise some dough."

The event was held at Slapsy Maxie's Café in Los Angeles, and Cohen's manager and bodyguard told Hecht he didn't have to worry: "Each and everybody here has been told exactly how much to give to the cause of the Jewish heroes." Hecht suggested that maybe he didn't have to give the speech, but the manager told him: "The speech is what Mr. Cohen wants to hear."[72]

Hecht began his speech by saying he had received a cable from Menachem Begin, asking him to "do what I can to arouse among the Jews who are not fighting in the Holy Land, the knowledge that without them the Holy Land will be lost"—and that what will be "lost forever [is] the hope of the Jews taking their place as equals in the human family." Hecht quoted Begin saying they were fighting against great odds, with inadequate equipment, and asking that Hecht speak to the "soul of the Jews of the world."

Hecht then directly addressed the "Jewish soul," which he said was "trained by disaster and calumny to live in caution, to hide itself cozily behind good deeds, to overlook insults, to charm its enemies, and to avoid getting its enemies angrier than they are":

> Thus hidden, thus full of cunning modesties and suicidal graces, it has remained nevertheless a brave soul—when destinies other than its own are at stake. It has fought and died valorously in defense of every cause but its own. Yes, it has the courage to fight and die for others. But it has hardly the guts even to *speak* in its own behalf.

> I know this soul of the Jew because I am part of it. And when the Irgun commander asks that it be wakened, he asks for a miracle. Awaken Jews into espousing their own cause—into believing in themselves—into grasping the battles of Palestine as their own bid for freedom. . . . [T]he Irgun asks for more miracles. It asks for us.

Hecht recounted the Allies' failures during the war to help the Jews and then he brought the lesson into the present:

> In his hour of destruction, the Jew of Europe was without friends. Today in his desperate hour of rebirth the plot is still the same. . . . He fights alone in Palestine—against great odds, against increasing odds. And if we Jews whose souls are being fed and strengthened by his courage—whose status in the eyes of the world—is being forged by his valor—if we dreaming Jews of the four winds believe that any nation will ride to his aid—we are fools. . . . [The Jews in Palestine] wait for us. We are their arsenal.

Hecht said that only a Jewish state could prevent "the mass executions of Jews that have been going on since the year Four Hundred," with the Jews never being able to halt a pogrom:

> All the relationships the Jews made, all the honors won, all the medals hung on them have not been enough to move even our own most civilized of countries to raise a hand in their behalf—when the hour of doom struck in Europe. . . . The slaughter of our kind in Europe has left a wound in our spirits that our victory as Americans in the war has not entirely healed. . . . [D]espite the honors and positions we have won in America, we are no different as Jews than our fathers and grandfathers in Europe. We are like them, as Jews—uncertain, despairing, disenchanted, and always singing ourselves to sleep with the happy news that we have friends in court. The Jews have always had friends in court—but they have never won a verdict.

Hecht then set forth the consequences he envisioned if the American Jews did not mobilize to support Zionism at this critical moment:

> If that battle [for Palestine is] lost—we Jews, all of us, are lost for another seven generations. We will have made our bid for human national status . . . and if this bid fails, we will become a gabby and empty people . . . more so than ever in our history. . . . If our bid for a flag and a homeland fails, we will all of us stand guilty before the world of an unworthiness. And this unworthiness we will, for a change, have deserved—if it comes to us. It is our duty to see that it does not come to us. It is in our power to prevent its coming. We will win—if the long dreaming soul of the Jew is wakened.

Hecht concluded by saying that "Jewish money has poured into a thousand causes, but there was never any cause in Jewish history like this one." If Begin loses, he said, it will be "because we—and not he—were too small for the hour of Jewish destiny." A David stands against Goliath, Hecht concluded, and "I ask you Jews—buy him a stone for his slingshot."

Hecht spoke for forty-five minutes. The audience consisted of what he described in *A Child of the Century* as "a thousand bookies, ex-prize-fighters, gamblers, jockeys, touts and all sorts of lawless and semi-lawless characters," who stood up and called out their contributions, after which Cohen ordered that everyone give double, and "man by man, the 'underworld' stood up and doubled the ante for the Irgun." The event raised $200,000—more than $3 million in 2022 dollars.[73]

All in all, Hecht's post-1939 plays, books, and speeches made him a veritable one-man multimedia operation, with an extraordinary outpouring of writing of moral, cultural, and literary force. But in the half century after his death, he became largely forgotten. A recent biographer of Hecht suggested that "Jewish politics . . . probably played a part in the current amnesia," because Hecht "deeply unsettled the staid American Jewish establishment," for whom his "accusations of gross dereliction by America's most powerful Jews—and by the sainted FDR himself—hit much too close to home."[74]

Another answer, however, may involve the soul of American Jewry itself. In Hecht's riveting nonfiction book *Perfidy,* published in 1961—a page-turning account of a 1954 libel trial in Israel that raised searing questions about the Zionist failure to save the Jews of Hungary in 1944—Hecht described how American Jews had initially rejected Zionism and then subsequently embraced it, with the later acceptance being almost as ignoble as the earlier rejection:

> Their basic reaction [had been] that something absurd and a little sad was going on in Jerusalem. And possibly a little dangerous. This reaction was only natural, for there had been no good tidings for Jews out of Jerusalem since the crucifying of one of their young rabbis—by the Romans. The Jewish hell born of that misreported incident had never cooled off. . . .
>
> How different it is now! With all the Jews of the world who were unaware of Eretz-Israel, who made no personal sacrifices for it, and who denounced the fighters for its freedom—[now] patting themselves on the back for the State of Israel. . . . And not religious or "organization" Jews but assimilated American ones, who usually go to Temple only in a coffin. . . . Their eyes gleam. They used to feel this way when . . . Einstein's name appeared in the newspapers. And all as ignorant of what is going on—or went on—in Israel as if it were a foothold on the moon.[75]

If there were two earlier stages in the story of the American Jewish reaction to Zionism—the first fearful and dismissive, the second thankful and proud—the story may now be in a third stage, with American and Israeli Jews moving in divergent directions.[76] Over the past decade, even as each community has flourished in its own region, in ways unparalleled in Jewish history, the divisions have deepened—exemplified and perhaps exacerbated by the divergent reactions to Presidents Obama and Trump.

Some prominent American Jewish commentators argued that President Obama was "the most Jewish president" ever; many Israelis considered him the most anti-Israel. Similarly, there were deeply contrasting reactions to President Trump between Israeli and American Jews.[77] The divide was perhaps best illustrated by a poll taken as the 2020 presidential campaign approached, by the non-partisan Jewish Electorate Institute, which found that "a [presidential] candidate's stance on Israel ranks at the bottom of a list of sixteen policy priorities of [American] Jewish voters."[78]

The division between American and Israeli Jews is ironic, since in a historical sense they are deeply indebted to each other. In 1948, there was not one, but two miracles: (1) the re-creation of the Jewish state after two millennia, and (2) the transformation of American Jews from a fearful minority into a confident people. The second miracle was fundamentally related to the first: The confidence and pride of American Jews grew as the State of Israel survived and succeeded against overwhelming odds.[79]

Three-quarters of a century later, the two communities, separated by many thousands of miles, living in differing circumstances, facing different kinds of threats, may be more dependent on each other than they realize.[80]

In 1964, Hecht's funeral service was held at Temple Rodeph Sholom in Manhattan, attended by several hundred people and officiated by Rabbi Louis Newman, a prominent Zionist who had been one of Jabotinsky's principal associates in America. Menachem Begin traveled from Israel to deliver a eulogy, describing Hecht as a man who "wielded his pen like a drawn sword" and who did "so much for the Jewish people and for the redemption of Israel."[81]

He was more than simply a writer, journalist, essayist, screenwriter, playwright, novelist, short-story writer, and polemicist.[82] In 1939, he became a prophet, and his fortuitous meeting in 1941 with Peter Bergson at the 21 Club—an event as unlikely and unexpected as the emergence of Herzl and Brandeis, or Weizmann's presence in London, or a young woman leaving her newfound freedom in America to devote herself to Zionism in Eretz Israel for a half century—the year following Jabotinsky's death in America, led to someone with literary and oratorical gifts similar to Jabotinsky's to pick up the baton and continue the efforts to wake the American Jews, to restore their souls.

Once they re-created their state in 1948, the Jewish people faced a new challenge—responding on the world stage to the continuing attacks, both physical and ideological, on Jewish sovereignty even in the place where it had historically begun. No other state faced unending challenges to its "right to exist," nor was any other state subjected to the obsessive attention of the UN, year after year.

The Jewish state needed ambassadors of unusual intelligence and eloquence to articulate its principles and defend its actions. Among the eighteen who served as ambassadors from 1948 to 2021 were many with those qualities—starting with Abba Eban.

SEVEN

The Triumph and Tragedy of Abba Eban

"I have never encountered anyone who matched his command of the English language."

Aubrey S. "Abba" Eban (left) with Foreign Minister Moshe Sharett at the UN, 1949

On May 21, 1948—a week after its Declaration of Independence, fighting an invasion by five Arab armies—Israel designated a thirty-three-year-old scholar of Hebrew, Arabic, and Persian literature named Aubrey ("Abba") Eban as its representative to the United Nations. He was the youngest representative there.

Five days later, Eban appeared before the UN Security Council, responding to the Arab rejection of the UN cease-fire resolution. His words were both eloquent and emphatic: "The sovereignty regained by an ancient people, after its long march through the dark night of exile," he said, will not be "surrendered at pistol point." And so:

> It becomes my duty to make our attitude clear, beyond ambiguity or doubt. If the Arab States want peace with Israel, they can have it. If they want war, they can have that too. But whether they want peace or war, they can have it only with the State of Israel.[1]

By the fall of 1948, the London *Jewish Chronicle* reported that Eban was impressing "friend and foe alike with his quiet and able marshalling of Israel's case."[2] In its September 1948 issue, *Commentary* reported that he had "won respect in all quarters for his intellectual ability, the cogency and precision of his advocacy."[3] On May 5, 1949, Eban came to global attention, when he addressed the General Assembly on Israel's application for admission in the UN. As the *Guardian* later noted:

> His widely reported two-hour appeal for the provisional government of the new state of Israel . . . was given major coverage, and his delivery had journalists and commentators reaching for superlatives. In the United States he became a world figure overnight.[4]

The Security Council had endorsed Israel's application on a 9–1 vote (with Egypt voting against and Britain abstaining).[5] But before the General Assembly's confirming vote, the seven Arab UN members succeeded in having the issue delegated to a new ad hoc committee, where they could continue to fight diplomatically what they had lost the previous year militarily.[6] In his autobiography, Eban described the burden that had suddenly fallen on his shoulders:

> I was now personally directing a political operation that had no precedent in international history. No other state had ever been called upon to secure its membership in the international community through a process of cross-examination, advocacy, and rebuttals.

Before the committee, under television klieg lights, Eban expressed his anger at the spectacle of the Arabs sitting in judgment of the state they had sought to destroy, after it had established itself under the UN's 1947 two-state resolution:

> We are as one who, having been attacked in a dark street by seven men with heavy bludgeons, finds himself dragged into court only to see his assailants sitting on the bench with an air of solemn virtue, delivering homilies on the duties of a peaceful citizen. Here sit representatives of the only states which have deliberately used force against a General Assembly resolution . . . posing as the disinterested judges of their own intended victim.
>
> It is a cynical maneuver. In the name of those who have been killed, maimed, blinded, exiled, or bereaved by that cynicism, I express our most passionate resentment at this insincerity.

Eban placed the full burden of the war on the shoulders of the Arab nations that had decided to wage it: They were responsible, he said, "for every death, for all the bereavement and for all the panic and exile which has resulted from that futile and unnecessary conflict." He sat at the table for a total of nine hours, in a process that never before "happened to any applicant state."[7] He ended by saying that Israel's UN application was a world-historical moment, as ancient Israel had contributed fundamental values to civilization, and now:

> A great wheel of history comes full circle today as Israel, renewed and established, offers itself, with all its imperfections but perhaps with some virtues, to the defense of the human spirit against nihilism, conflict, and despair.

The speech generated applause at the UN and electrified public opinion in Israel.[8] A week later, Israel became the fifty-ninth member of the UN, by a vote of 37–12. For the next decade, Eban served simultaneously as Israel's UN ambassador in New York and its U.S. ambassador in Washington (1950–1959). Then he was Israel's education minister for three years (1960–1963), deputy prime minister for three years (1963–1966), and foreign minister for eight years (1966–1974).

Eban's UN speeches—from the 1949 address on Israel's admission to the UN to his 1974 address after the Yom Kippur War—spanned twenty-five years. They are a record of eloquence unequaled by any diplomat during that period. Conor Cruise O'Brien, who sat next to Eban in the General Assembly representing Ireland, called him "the most brilliant diplomatist of the second half of the 20th century."[9] Alfred Friendly wrote in the *Washington Post* in 1977, three years after Eban completed his service, that "[n]o man in [Israel's] . . . history ever projected to the world its essence and its anguish, its vision and its spirit, in nobler and more exalted terms."[10]

But soon after his Yom Kippur War address, Eban lost his ministerial position in Yitzhak Rabin's new Israeli government, and he never again held an influential governmental post. He served in the Knesset, chairing its foreign affairs committee, but that position had no real power. By 1988, he was so low on the Labor Party electoral slate that he was not reelected to the Knesset.[11] Humiliated, he retired from political life, relocated to New York, and devoted himself to teaching, writing, and speaking.

Eban's meteoric rise and dramatic fall presaged a tragedy that extended beyond his personal political career, and it holds a lesson for today.

On May 10, 1951, Eban, along with Prime Minister David Ben-Gurion, spoke at a Madison Square Garden rally to initiate a three-year drive for Israel Bonds. Israel had a critical need for capital, after a devastating war and a massive influx of Holocaust survivors, together with hundreds of thousands of Jews immigrating from Arab countries, which had expelled them.[12] The event drew an audience of 20,000 people, with thousands in the overflow crowd outside.[13]

Eban titled his presentation "The Voice of the Trumpet Exceeding Loud," a phrase from *Exodus 19:19* when the Lord appeared in Sinai. In a single paragraph, Eban summarized the extraordinary events of the past three years:

> Here is a people which defended its life, its home and its open gates against the fury of a powerful foe; set up an oasis of democracy, liberty and progress in a wilderness of despotism and squalor . . . received into its shelter 600,000 of its kinsmen coming out of the depth of insecurity and want . . . began to explore and uncover the hidden resources of its soil which had lain neglected for long centuries past; caused water to gush forth in the most primeval wilderness of recorded time; extended the foundations of its industrial progress; embarked upon one of the great cultural adventures of history, to create out of diverse and remote citizens a unified society in the tongue and the spirit of Israel's past; established its banner in the family of nations and gave utterance to Israel's immemorial yearning for world peace. [14]

Eban's extraordinary eloquence and intelligence were evident not only in his prepared presentations, but also in his extemporaneous appearances. On April 12, 1958, Mike Wallace interviewed him for nearly half an hour on his popular primetime TV show, *The Mike Wallace Interview*.[15] Wallace introduced Eban as "a scholar . . . and a veteran statesman at the age of 43"—and then proceeded, in the prosecutorial style he later perfected on *60 Minutes*, to ask a series of increasingly hostile questions:

> Wallace: Mr. Ambassador, in its ten years as a nation, Israel has been involved in repeated violence—major border incidents, two open wars with the Arabs, the first in '48, the last in '56. What do you foresee for the next ten years: do you foresee continuing violence?
>
> Eban: Well, Mr. Wallace, the last 10 years have not only been years of violence; they have been incomparable years of joyous creation; of sovereignty restored; of the people gathered in; of the land revived; of democracy established. But there has also been violence imposed

> by the hostility of our neighbors. For our second decade, we devoutly hope . . . that we and our kindred neighboring people will devote all our efforts to the development of our respective countries and of our common region.

Wallace suggested that peace required the resolution of underlying issues with the Arabs, starting with refugees:

> Wallace: An estimated 700,000 Palestinian Arabs were left homeless during the Arab-Israeli war of '48. Israel refuses to re-admit them. They live in bitterness, and such men as historian Arnold Toynbee have said this: "the evil deeds committed by the Zionist Jews against the Arabs are comparable to crimes committed against the Jews by the Nazis." How do you feel about that?
>
> Eban: [I]t is a monstrous blasphemy. Here he takes the massacre of millions of our men, women, and children and he compares it to the plight of Arab refugees [who are] alive, on their kindred soil—suffering certain anguish but of course possessed of the supreme gift of life. . . . The refugee problem, Mr. Wallace, is not the cause of tension. The refugee problem is the result of an Arab policy . . . which created the problem by the invasion of Israel, which perpetuates it by refusing to accommodate [them] into their expanding labor market, and which refuses to solve a problem which they have the full capacity to solve . . . once the will to relieve it existed.[16]

One of Eban's greatest speeches came on the second day of the Six-Day War in 1967, when he gave an address to the UN that has been called "one of the great diplomatic speeches of all time."[17] The war broke out when Israel finally acted against the Arab military encirclement that had begun in mid-May with open Arab declarations of an imminent campaign to destroy the Jewish state, and with Arab troop movements becoming increasingly ominous. Eban had left Jerusalem the day the war began—June 5, 1967—and addressed the UN Security Council in New York the next day, with the speech carried live on television around the globe.[18]

Eban began by evoking "the point at which our fortunes stood" the day before, when an army "greater than any force ever assembled in history in Sinai" had massed on Israel's southern frontier:

> Nasser had provocatively brought five infantry divisions and two armored divisions up to our very gates; 80,000 men and 900 tanks were poised to move. . . . [A]n international route across the Strait of Tiran and the Gulf of Aqaba had been suddenly and arbitrarily choked. Israel was and is breathing only with a single lung.
>
> . . . Every house and street in Jerusalem . . . came into the range of fire. . . . [S]o also did the crowded and pathetically narrow coastal strip in which so much of Israel's life and population is concentrated. Iraqi troops reinforced Jordanian units in areas immediately facing vital and vulnerable Israeli communication centers. Expeditionary forces from Algeria and Kuwait had reached Egyptian territory. . . . Syrian units, including artillery, overlooked the Israeli villages in the Jordan Valley. . . . In short, there was peril for Israel wherever it looked.

Eban described the "apocalyptic air of approaching peril" that pervaded Israel as it watched its total encirclement with no significant response from the international community:

> With my very ears I heard President Nasser's speech on May 26. He said:
>
> *"We intend to open a general assault against Israel. This will be total war. Our basic aim will be to destroy Israel."*
>
> [O]n the morning of June 5 . . . [in] accordance with its inherent right of self-defense as formulated in Article 51 of the United Nations Charter, Israel responded defensively in full strength. Never in the history of nations has armed force been used in a more righteous or compelling cause.

Eban summarized the frantic efforts Israel had made to keep Jordan (and thus Jerusalem) out of the war. Israel had assured Jordan it would not be attacked unless it attacked Israel:

> But Jordan embarked on a . . . total assault by artillery and aircraft along the entire front, with special emphasis on Jerusalem, to whose dangerous and noble ordeal yesterday I come to bear personal witness.
>
> There has been bombing of houses; there has been a hit on the great new National Museum of Art; there has been a hit on the

> [Hebrew] University, and on Shaare Zedek, the first hospital ever to have been established outside the ancient walls. Is this not an act of vandalism that deserves the condemnation of all mankind? And in the Knesset building . . . the Israel Cabinet and Parliament met under heavy gunfire, whose echoes mingled at the end of our meeting with Hatikvah, the anthem of hope.

Eban said he would be "less than frank if I were to conceal the fact that the Government and people of Israel have been disconcerted" by the UN's role—particularly the sudden withdrawal of the UN Emergency Force in the Sinai without consulting Israel, which facilitated the Egyptian attack:

> I confess that my own attitude and those of my colleagues and of my fellow citizens . . . have been traumatically affected by this experience. . . . What is the use of a United Nations presence if it is in effect an umbrella which is taken away as soon as it begins to rain?

Eban argued that Jordan, backed by the Soviet Union, had no standing to demand that Israel return to the pre-war boundaries, because Jordan "gambled with destiny, [and thus] incurred the full responsibility of unprovoked war." But there was an even more compelling reason to reject a return to the pre-war boundaries:

> The Soviet proposal is for withdrawal to the same situation out of which the conflict arose: the same frontiers, and therefore the same insecurity, the same blockade of waterways, the same belligerent doctrine, the same divided city, the same choked access on vital roads, the same confrontation of unseparated armies, the same guns on Syrian hills threatening settlements in the valley, the same arms race and, above all, the same absence of peace treaties requiring mutual recognition of sovereignty. . . . Such proposals . . . are prescriptions for renewal of conflict.[19]

The *Jewish Chronicle* in London published a tribute to Eban's UN performance, writing that his diplomatic effort had been as important as Israel's military one: "Israel's victory in the Middle East war was applauded by a great part of the free world, not merely because she had performed an astonishing feat of arms but primarily because [through Eban] she had established the justice of her cause."[20]

Abba Eban at the UN Security Council, June 6, 1967

The *New York Times* profiled Eban two weeks later, with an extended excerpt from a speech he had given the day before, and the *Times* compared him to the most consequential orator of the century:

> More than one observer, peering down at the proceedings in the tall Assembly chamber, as Mr. Eban asserted his country's right to exist and to protect its borders and ports, thought of the comparison to Winston Churchill sending the English language to war in 1940.[21]

The Yom Kippur War began with a massive unprovoked attack by Egypt and Syria on Saturday, October 6, 1973—which was both Shabbat and Yom Kippur. In Washington, Eban received a telegram at 6:20 a.m. from Jerusalem, telling him Israel had learned the Egyptians and Syrians would launch an attack within hours. Eban's close working relationship with Secretary of State Henry A. Kissinger is apparent from the transcripts of their four telephone conversations that day. Kissinger later published the verbatim transcripts in his 2003 book, *Crisis: The Anatomy of Two Major Foreign Policy Crises.*

The first call was at 8:25 a.m., ten minutes after Egypt's foreign minister had called Kissinger to claim that Israel had just attacked Egypt in a naval action in the Suez. Eban told Kissinger he knew of no Israeli attack on any Egyptian forces. They spoke again twenty-five minutes later:

> Kissinger: I don't myself believe that you would start a general war with a naval attack in one place, but you always do surprising things. Could you get me the facts?
>
> Eban: They said the first move was a naval attack?
>
> Kissinger: South of the Canal. The Egyptian Foreign Minister called me and gave me a name, but it was an Arabic name. If you were attacking some place, you presumably knew where it was.
>
> Eban: Yes. That is not at all convincing.

Fifteen minutes later, Eban called Kissinger to deny definitively the Egyptian story. He told Kissinger:

> The P.M. [Prime Minister Golda Meir] asked me to tell you that the story of naval action by us at the Gulf of Suez is false. Her Hebrew vocabulary is very rich and she poured it out.

Later that day, in their fourth conversation, Eban called Kissinger to say he had received a report on Syria's actions, and Kissinger told him to "get it to me as soon as possible"—because "[i]f you give it to our people," there would be copies "in Damascus before I see it."

By 10 a.m. the next morning, Eban and Kissinger were discussing a joint strategy for proceedings before the UN Security Council. During the day, Egypt moved across the Suez Canal; Israel suffered heavy losses of aircraft and tanks; Defense Minister Moshe Dayan frantically told colleagues he thought Israel was about to be destroyed. At the UN the next day, Eban attacked Egypt and Syria's legal position and ridiculed their cover story for the new war:

> The premeditated and unprovoked assault . . . on the Day of Atonement . . . will surely rank . . . as one of the basest and most odious acts for which Governments have ever been responsible. . . . [The 1967 cease-fire] is an international agreement . . . accepted by Egypt, Syria and Israel, in response to a decision of the Security Council. . . . Egypt first invented an imaginary sea battle with imaginary Israeli ships, at an imaginary place, at an

Henry Kissinger and Abba Eban, January 17, 1974

> imaginary time: the most dramatic nonexistent battle in the history of war.[22]

Eban then told the UN what was "deeply impressed on our minds," and would be "engraved in our memories," was the "kind of adversaries we face":

> First, there is the choice of the day. There is only one day in the year . . . on which [Israel] turns aside from all material concern, unique in the spiritual calendar of mankind. . . . How idiotic would a man have to be to believe that on a day when there were no communications, no activity, no radio, no ability to summon reserves, when the vast majority of our soldiers were in their homes or synagogues, when even forward posts were manned at minimal level—that precisely on that day Israel would launch a war?

Eban said it was "vital that Egyptian and Syrian forces shall not be allowed to remain anywhere beyond the [1967] cease-fire lines," to reinforce the principle that they could only be modified "by negotiation and peace." And there were two other lessons from this war:

> First . . . The nature of that hostility [we face] is such that no security concern can be exaggerated. . . .
>
> Second . . . Imagine that in a mood of suicidal stupidity we had gone back to the previous armistice lines. . . . [T]hen the attacks of October 6 . . . would have done such destruction to our vital security that perhaps Israel and all its people, and all the memories, hopes and visions which have moved our history, might now all be lost. . . . How right we were to insist on negotiating with the utmost precision the boundaries of a peace settlement! How wrong were those who counseled us otherwise!

In the midst of the 1973 war, Eban had articulated the three principles that would guide Israel for the next half century: (1) Statements of Arab hostility would be taken at face value; (2) there could be no retreat to the pre-1967 "Auschwitz" borders; and (3) peace could be achieved only with defensible boundaries resulting from direct negotiations between the parties.

In April 1974, after an official report on the Yom Kippur War harshly criticized the Israeli failure to anticipate it, Golda Meir announced her resignation as prime minister. Eban—having represented Israel as UN ambassador, U.S. ambassador, and foreign minister for two-and-a-half decades, through four wars (in 1948, 1956, 1967, and 1973)—believed he was most suited to succeed her. His service had been stellar; he had an extraordinary international reputation; he had more diplomatic experience than any other potential successor; he was fluent in Arabic (as well as Farsi, French, and German in addition to English and Hebrew); and he was only fifty-nine years old.

But the very qualities that led to his success in the diplomatic arena—his British background, his speeches in refined English, his stately bearing, his long periods of residence in the United States—were political liabilities in Israel. For many, he was virtually a foreigner, a long-winded orator, fluent in Hebrew but speaking it formally, a person denigrated privately by his Labor colleagues as pompous and pretentious.[23] As Meir's successor, the party chose someone almost exactly the opposite: a Jerusalem-born *sabra*, a military hero from the 1967 war, a man of few words who silently projected strength: Yitzhak Rabin.[24]

After the 1974 election, Rabin formed a government with nineteen ministers in his cabinet—and pointedly excluded Eban. It was a humiliating dismissal, delivered in an insulting manner: Eban first heard of it on the radio.[25]

In his final speech at the Foreign Ministry, Eban said, "It matters very much, not only what Israel's policies are, but how they are expressed," and that policies presented without "moral incisiveness and intellectual elevation" would not succeed. Then he left the building—and it would be "over two years before I was emotionally capable of entering [it] again."[26]

In the years after 1974, Eban held a number of visiting professorships, wrote books and articles, and worked from 1979 to 1984 on a nine-part public television series, *Heritage: Civilization and the Jews*, which he both wrote and narrated, accompanied by a book of the same name. He wrote essays and op-eds in which he criticized Israel's course in the Lebanon war, and he urged Israel to take a conciliatory stance in negotiations with the Palestinians.[27]

By 2000, at the age of eighty-four, Eban was suffering from both Parkinson's disease and severe aphasia, a horrific condition that prevented him from communicating. In the following two years before his death, he was unable to leave his home.[28] In 2002, he received the Israel Prize, the state's highest honor—for "lifetime achievement"—twenty-seven years after leaving the Foreign Ministry. He was too ill to attend the ceremony, much less to write or deliver an acceptance speech, and his wife, Suzy, accepted the prize on his behalf.

Eban was, in the words of his biographer, Asaf Siniver, "one of the greatest communicators of his century."[29] In 1979, Kissinger, in the first volume of his memoirs, *White House Years*, wrote of Eban that:

> I have never encountered anyone who matched his command of the English language. Sentences poured forth in mellifluous constructions complicated enough to test the listener's intelligence and simultaneously leave him transfixed by the speaker's virtuosity. . . .
>
> Eban's eloquence . . . was allied to a first-class intelligence and fully professional grasp of diplomacy. He was always well prepared; he knew what he wanted. He practiced to the full his

> maxim that anything less than one hundred percent agreement with Israel's point of view demonstrated lack of objectivity.[30]

After losing reelection to the Knesset in 1988, Eban retired from public life and left the country. In an interview with *Ha'Olam Ha'Ze*, an Israeli news magazine, Eban recounted that:

> The party retired me against my wishes, and I found it mentally difficult to be there with no reason to wake up in the morning. Nothing was offered to me. They thought that I should retire, and that's it. I had nothing to contribute, and nobody asked me to, either. . . . If I had stayed there, I have no doubt that I would have suffered, mentally and physically. It was a tragic situation.[31]

Eban died a poor man, assisted financially in his last years by a small group of generous admirers; his extraordinary diplomatic eloquence—as important to Israel as its military prowess—was recognized with a prize awarded so belatedly that he had to receive it in total silence because of his medical condition. Eban's personal tragedy was that the talents that led to his diplomatic success in the world contributed to his political failure at home. His tragedy extends, however, beyond his personal one. It reaches into the center of Middle East history.

In September 1948, during his first year as Israel's UN representative, Eban published an essay in *Commentary* entitled "The Future of Arab-Jewish Relations: The Key Is the Cooperation of Equal and Separate States."[32] The 1948 war had demonstrated, Eban contended, that "Arabs and Jews need each other for any progress or any escape from deadlock," and he set forth the intellectual basis for partition of the land west of the Jordan River:

> The theory is that there are two peoples in Palestine, each with separate national aspirations; that neither can do without the full satisfaction of those aspirations, at least in a limited area; that each can best cooperate with the other on the basis of its own integrity and freedom.

The fact, Eban continued, that partition "offered something infinitely precious to the Jews" should not obscure the "gifts which it bestowed upon the Arabs"—ones that could have been obtained without a war:

> Nine hundred thousand [Palestinian] Arabs . . . were offered the chance of living in a purely Arab state. Two purely Arab states—Transjordan and Arab Palestine—were to be established on seven-eighths of the territory originally set aside . . . [for] a Jewish national home. . . . [M]any a Palestine Arab may come to compare this prospect, which was peacefully available, with the results of the "holy war." These results include the invasion and decimation of Arab Palestine; the panic-stricken flight of its population with its leaders in the van; occupation by rival Arab armies with frank aims of annexation; social and economic disintegration; and the collapse of all corporate Arab life. In this manner have Palestine Arabs been saved by their Arab "friends" from their Jewish "enemies."

Eban concluded that anyone who, in the future, helped the Arabs recognize Israel's permanence would be deemed "in the historic sense, a friend of the Arabs," because such recognition would free the Arabs to live in their own state and concentrate on their own welfare.

Three decades later—and after three more wars—with his career in the Foreign Ministry over, Eban published a 628-page memoir, *Abba Eban: An Autobiography* (1977), in which he claimed that the Palestinian issue was the key to solving the entire Arab-Israeli dispute, because Egypt and Syria had no national interests in Palestine (other than an inchoate feeling of "Arab solidarity"), and the Arab-Israeli dispute could thus be resolved, he thought, by a withdrawal from the disputed territories: "The territories are Judea and Samaria," he wrote, "but this does not make the Arab inhabitants Samaritans or Judeans."[33]

He became an outspoken advocate of the "peace process," pushing Israel to start it and then continually encouraging it once it did. In 1998, in his last book, *Diplomacy for the Next Century*, Eban asserted that "the Middle East had been irreversibly transformed" by the peace process, since it would now enable the Palestinians to "take possession of their destiny and go forward in peace and hope."

Given his medical condition in 2000 and his death two years later, we do not know what Eban would have said about Yasser Arafat's rejection of a Palestinian state at Camp David in 2000; or Arafat's rejection of the Clinton Parameters in 2000–01; or the barbaric suicide bombers Arafat sent thereafter to attack civilians in Jerusalem, Tel Aviv, and other Israeli cities; or the repeated rocket wars launched from Gaza after Israel removed every settlement and soldier in 2005; or Mahmoud Abbas's rejection of a Palestinian state in 2008, after the year-long "Annapolis Process"; or Abbas's repeated vows, throughout the Obama years, "never" to recognize a Jewish state; or Abbas's annual speeches at the UN demanding a British apology for the Balfour Declaration—an attempt to turn history back a century.

But in considering these things, Eban might have recalled his conversation in 1947 with Azzam Pasha, the Arab League secretary-general, which he recounted in his *Commentary* article. Regarding a Jewish state in any portion of Palestine, Pasha had told him:

> "By the logic of our history we shall fight it. . . . We once had Spain and Persia. If anyone had come . . . and asked us to surrender Spain or Persia he would have received the same negative response as I now give you." In a later moment [Pasha] confessed that the Arabs had become used to not having Spain and Persia. They might, he said, become used to not having part of Palestine—or else they might attempt a century-old irridentism and work up a crusade.

The century-long Palestinian *jihad* that Pasha foresaw has lasted three-quarters of a century. For the Palestinians, the peace process was never to create "two states for two peoples"—a formulation they repeatedly rejected.[34] They denied that Jews were a "people" entitled to a state, recognized them only as members of a religion rather than a national group, and refused to concede that the Jewish history in Palestine preceded theirs by at least a millennium. The formulation the Palestinians adopted as the goal of the process was "ending the occupation that began in 1967"—a phrase that involved no acknowledgment of Israel's legitimacy and obscured the fact that the Palestinians believed there was also another occupation that would be dealt with later: what they considered "the occupation that began in 1948."

For the Palestinians, it was thus not a peace process at all, but rather a "Pasha process"—an attempt to return to 1947, before there was a Jewish state, by pressing two interconnected demands: (1) an Israeli withdrawal to the pre-1967 lines (to reverse the outcome of the 1967 war), and (2) a "right of return" to Israel (to reverse the result of the 1948 one).[35] The Palestinians did not consider a Palestinian state to be a solution, because it required acceptance of a Jewish one as well. They sought to turn history back to a time when there was no Jewish state—not forward to a time when there could be two states for two peoples.[36]

Eban's most famous observation—that the Palestinians never missed an opportunity to miss an opportunity—thus missed the fundamental point: A Palestinian state in a portion of Palestine was not the opportunity the Palestinians sought. They viewed the creation of Israel—pursuant to a 1947 UN resolution that had recommended both a Jewish and an Arab state—as their catastrophe (their "*nakba*"), rather than their missed opportunity to create their own state, at the same time, pursuant to the same resolution.[37]

One of Eban's insights in his 1977 memoir proved prophetic, effectively anticipating the Abraham Accords that four Arab countries—the United Arab Emirates, Bahrain, Morocco, and Sudan—signed with Israel in 2020, bringing the total number of Arab nations formally at peace with Israel (along with Egypt and Jordan) to six, with various others reportedly interested in joining the Accords and normalization with Saudi Arabia visible on the horizon.[38] As Eban wrote in his memoir, the Arab countries have no national interests in Palestine—certainly not ones more important than their own national security or their critical economic needs—only an inchoate desire to support Arab unity where possible.

Given the existential threat of Iran, seeing the benefits of aligning with Israel's twenty-first-century economy, and watching the repeated failure of the Palestinians to accept any of the two-state solutions offered to them over three-quarters of a century—in 1937 (the Peel Commission), 1947 (UN Resolution 181), 2000 (Camp David), 2001 (the Clinton Parameters), 2008 (the Annapolis Process)—and observing the inability of Fatah and Hamas to live side by side in peace and security even with each other, much less with Israel; unable even to hold a presidential election in the Palestinian Authority in the last eighteen years, with no working legislative body either in the West Bank or in Gaza, and no rule of law in either location, much less the civil institutions—such as a free press and an independent judiciary—necessary for a successful state, it is no wonder that the Arab states no longer allow the Palestinians to hold a veto over their own national interests.

Eban's ultimate tragedy—and that of the 24,000 Jews and 91,000 Arabs killed or maimed, in war after war—was that while he spoke eloquently about peace in English, Hebrew, and Arabic, a Palestinian counterpart never emerged who shared the vision he laid out in *Commentary* in 1948.[39]

After Abba Eban, the second youngest Israeli ambassador to the United States was its eighteenth: Ron Dermer, appointed at the age of forty-two, who served from 2013 to 2021 during the Obama and Trump administrations.[40] Dermer gave a series of speeches that, taken together, are an enduring presentation of Israel's diplomatic, intellectual, and moral case, and in 2015, he played a key role in arranging and drafting a historic speech to a joint session of the U.S. Congress—one that would remain relevant more than seven years later.

EIGHT

Ron Dermer: The American Israeli Ambassador

"I left America to help another nation I love
defend the freedoms Americans have long taken for granted."

Ambassador Ron Dermer, 2014

As he ended his ambassadorship in 2021, Ron Dermer recalled that, when he graduated in 1993 from the Wharton School of Business at the University of Pennsylvania, he never imagined—having grown up in Miami Beach, where both his father and his older brother had served as mayor, and on his way to Oxford to earn a degree in Philosophy, Politics, and Economics (PPE)—that he would soon become an Israeli citizen, and then an Israeli diplomat: "If you had told me when I was twenty-one that one day I would be Israel's ambassador to the United States," he said, "I would have thought you should be committed."[1]

What "changed the trajectory of my life," he said, was that before proceeding to Oxford, he made a trip to Israel and became increasingly interested in the future of "a young country, with all its big decisions ahead of it, compared to an America that I loved [but] that seemed to have settled a lot of those issues." In the 1990s, America was living in the glow of a Cold War recently won; the country was flush with a "peace dividend" from reduced defense spending; and it faced a world having no other superpower. Some public intellectuals adopted the argument that the triumph of democratic capitalism over dictatorial centralized economies marked "the end of history."

Over the preceding century, the world had moved from (i) the imperial monarchies of the late nineteenth and early twentieth century, to (ii) the challenges of fascism and communism in the mid-twentieth century, to (iii) the world war initiated by Nazi Germany, to (iv) the Cold War after World War II and the American victory over the Soviet Union, with the seeming disappearance of the last authoritarian and totalitarian threats from history. But Jewish history has often taught that the "end of history" turns out to be simply the precursor of more history—and the possible return of the old.

Dermer possessed an exceptional ability in his speeches to bring history into the present, based on a recognition that it was not enough for Israel to rest on its extraordinary accomplishments. Once something has been achieved, it must be defended, intellectually and morally, politically and diplomatically, or it can be lost. Dermer would become an intellectual and diplomatic defender as significant as Abba Eban.

In contrast to the United States, in the 1990s Israel was a small country constantly struggling to survive, addressing issues relating to security, nationalism, and Zionism as difficult as any in Jewish history. Dermer was intrigued that in Israel these issues pervaded the consciousness of the entire country:

> [Israel] was forty-five years old [when I arrived in 1996]. . . . Israel is a very, very intense place, and the joke I used to tell is that if you want to know how intense Israel is—Israelis *go to Manhattan* to relax and unwind. . . . You feel this kind of emotional rollercoaster in Israel, where everybody has the ups and downs together. . . . It's not like in America, where you don't really have a huge block of the population watching the evening news . . . maybe 30 million, which is a very small share of the American population. In Israel, . . . you feel [current events] as a country together, and there was something that I found very attractive about that.[2]

After earning his Oxford degree, Dermer moved to Israel to work with Natan Sharansky as a political advisor, and in 2004 they coauthored *The Case for Democracy: The Power of Freedom to Overcome Tyranny and Terror*, a book that President George W. Bush read upon its publication and invited the authors immediately to the White House to discuss.[3] Two months later, Bush delivered his Second Inaugural Address, his response to the sudden return of history in the form of the September 11 attacks on New York and Washington. Bush began with these words:

> At this second gathering, our duties are defined not by the words I use, but by the history we have seen together. . . . After the shipwreck of communism came years of relative quiet, years of

> repose, years of sabbatical—and then there came a day of fire. . . . The best hope for peace in our world is the expansion of freedom in all the world. . . . Advancing these ideals is the mission that created our Nation. It is the honorable achievement of our fathers. Now it is . . . the calling of our time.[4]

In 2005, Benjamin Netanyahu was Israel's finance minister and appointed Dermer as Israel's economic attaché in Washington. Under American law, a U.S. citizen serving as a diplomat for a foreign nation must first relinquish his U.S. citizenship, and Dermer proceeded to do so by filing the necessary one-page form with the State Department.[5] He attached a 625-word essay to it, entitled "Proud to Have Been an American," which read in part:

> For 33 years I have felt America's warm embrace, and I am eternally grateful for it. I was born in America, raised in America, and formed in America. I have been educated by the wisdom of its founders, inspired by the words of its leaders, and protected by the sacrifices of its soldiers.
>
> When I think of freedom, I think of Lincoln. When I think of courage, I think of Normandy. When I think of justice, I think of Martin Luther King Jr. America has . . . shown me the power of freedom to change the lives of individuals, of nations, and of the world. . . .
>
> I left America because I wanted to help another nation I love defend the freedoms that Americans have long taken for granted. . . . In serving the State of Israel and in working to secure our common future, I will champion those ideals all of my life.
>
> May God forever bless America.[6]

In a later interview with the *Jerusalem Post*, Dermer further explained his decision to leave America for Israel:

> If you know history, you know that ["carrying the torch of freedom"] is not a cliché. . . . When the [Jewish] state was established, five percent of the world's Jews lived in Israel. Today, 45 percent of the world's Jews live here. It is the single largest Jewish community in the world. So this historical process is happening, and we are in it.[7]

After Netanyahu became prime minister in 2009, Dermer returned to Jerusalem to be his senior advisor and chief speechwriter, and in 2013, Netanyahu appointed him to be Israel's ambassador to the United States. When Dermer presented his credentials to President Obama at the White House, he wrote in the guest book: "America is a country to which the Jewish people owe so much and to which I, as a son of America, am so personally indebted."

As ambassador, Dermer frequently defended Israel from the tendentious misrepresentations of Zionist history common in the media.[8] He attributed the repeated failures of the Israeli-Palestinian "peace process" not to disagreements over specific issues, but rather to the Palestinian refusal to accept the Jewish connection to the land. The "core of the conflict," he said, "is that the Palestinians think we stole their house"—and "if you are dealing with a thief . . . you are not going to make peace." But the fact that Jews had been "historically connected to this place" for millennia should actually be, he argued, "a source of optimism":

> Because if this place were Uganda, I'd say there would be no chance of peace, because the other side would not recognize a claim that doesn't exist. But precisely because this is a land where the Patriarchs prayed, the Prophets preached, and the Kings of Israel ruled, and this is the land where we have had Jews living for 3,000 years, and where Jews were [always] dreaming of "Next year in Jerusalem" . . . [there can be] a reciprocal recognition of rights. But until you have that, you won't have peace.[9]

In another speech, Dermer said that the Balfour Declaration was itself a refutation of the frequent assertion by Arabs that Israel was the result of the Holocaust. The Declaration, Dermer noted, was issued a quarter century *before* Hitler and World War II, and the argument that Israel resulted from the Holocaust was thus "the exact opposite" of the truth:

> It is not that there is an Israel because of the Holocaust. It is that there was a Holocaust because there was no Israel—because there was no sovereign state to provide a voice, a refuge and a shield for a Jewish people targeted for annihilation.

In 2016, Dermer addressed antisemitism in a speech to the Anti-Defamation League (ADL), in which he proposed a simple test for deter-

Photo in the official announcement of Ron Dermer's appointment as Israel's ambassador to the United States (Israel Government Press Office, 2013)

mining whether boycotts of Israel by an academic or religious organization were antisemitic: the test was, is Israel the only country on their list?

> Is Israel the 51st, 91st or 131st state on their list of boycotted countries? If it is, then we should not accuse the members of that organization of antisemitism. We should assume that they are misinformed. . . . Our job should then be to engage this organization in dialogue . . . about our commitment to protect the inalienable rights of women, minorities, gays, and every citizen, and about our commitment to protect the sacred sites of Jews, Muslims, Christians and all faiths.

In other speeches, Dermer articulated the strategic case for Israel in terms that went beyond the arguments of the 1970s—which had focused on Israel as a dependable Middle East ally, described by former Secretary of State Alexander Haig as "the largest American aircraft carrier in the world that cannot be sunk, does not carry even one American soldier, and is located in a critical region for American national security."[10] Dermer argued that, in the future, Israel would become not simply an ally in a single region, but America's most important ally in the world:

> Now, that's a lot to say for an ambassador of a country the size of New Jersey. . . . But I'll explain why. . . . If you're the President of the United States and you're looking around the world and you say, "I need one security partner, I can only have one for the next 50 years." Who are you going to choose? . . .
>
> [T]hink about a military that can defend itself by itself, that you don't have to send your sons and daughters to go fight for it. Think about a country with a powerful intelligence capability, that can provide you valuable intelligence. . . . Think about a country with a cyber capability that's becoming more and more important in warfare. And think about a country that can develop weapons, offensive and defensive, with you. . . .
>
> America has many allies around the world: you've got French, and you've got Germans, and you've got Australia and you've got Canada—none of those countries match Israel in the categories that I just said. . . . And to the extent that you don't want to be in the Middle East, if you don't want to have troops in the Middle East, Israel is more important, not less important.[11]

In addition to the strategic, military, technological, and intelligence advantages of the American alliance with Israel, Dermer maintained that there was an overriding connection between the two countries, going beyond common interests and values. Speaking to B'nai B'rith International in 2016, he identified the connection as "a sense of purpose"—the recognition that America carries the torch of freedom, the Jewish contribution to the world in the biblical story of the Exodus, and that both countries share the advancement of freedom in the world as their central characteristic:[12]

> To truly appreciate the unique alliance between America and Israel you must appreciate what having such a sense of purpose means to both countries. . . . This sense of purpose is bigger than any leader or any issue. It is the DNA of both countries, and it lies at the bedrock of our unique alliance.
>
> That is why the real danger to this alliance will not come from disagreements over policy, demographic changes, or the numerous other reasons that are routinely cited as potential signs of trouble. The real danger would be for either America or Israel to lose its sense of purpose, for either country to no longer believe in its own exceptionalism.[13]

Dermer's speeches were consistently more than ceremonial; they were part of a basic belief he shared with Netanyahu that more important than *hasbara* (Israeli public relations) was the need for Israel to speak forcefully against those seeking to demonize it, because the issue was not obtaining favorable publicity for Israeli accomplishments, but rather defending the fundamental idea of the Jewish state.[14] Israel's rhetoric in the world was thus a national security issue, and the diplomatic eloquence of its representatives was a national security asset.

During his years as ambassador, Dermer gave a series of speeches on the root cause of terrorism,[15] Jewish-Christian solidarity,[16] Zionism and antisemitism,[17] the Palestinian denial of the Jewish connection to Jerusalem,[18] the central lesson of the assassination of Yitzhak Rabin,[19] Israel's historic achievements,[20] the Jews and African-Americans,[21] Jewish pessimism,[22] and other key issues. Taken together, the speeches are a compendium of the intellectual and moral force of the Zionist achievement.

But Dermer's most important speech was not one he delivered, but rather one he drafted: Prime Minister Benjamin Netanyahu's address before a joint session of Congress on March 5, 2015, as the United States prepared to enter into the Iran Deal.[23]

To understand the significance of that speech, and the unspoken but unmistakable historical message it conveyed, one needs to be conversant with two other speeches, and the history behind them: (1) Churchill's May 2, 1935, address to the British House of Commons, as German rearmament entered a danger zone; and (2) Churchill's December 30, 1941, address to the Canadian Parliament, known as the "Chicken Speech," at a key point in World War II.[24]

Netanyahu had previously quoted Churchill's 1935 speech in two major addresses: his 2006 speech to 3,000 people at the General Assembly of the United Jewish Communities (UJC), and his 2009 address to the United Nations after becoming prime minister that year. Churchill's 1935 address, together with Churchill's 1941 Chicken Speech, became the implicit foundation of Netanyahu's 2015 speech to Congress.

In early 1935, Hitler was in his third year as Germany's leader. His military plans had already "reached unheard of proportion," as a front-page story in the *New York Times* reported on April 21, 1935.[25] The day before, the *Times* reported that Hitler had "swiftly crystallized his leadership into a dictatorship without parallel in modern history."[26]

Forbidden under the post–World War I Versailles treaty from maintaining an army, Germany was nevertheless building one—as well as a large battle fleet, airplanes to make Germany equal to any nation in the air, a new conscription law, and a fleet of submarines that the *Times* described, in a lead editorial on the day of Churchill's May 2 speech, as having "larger tonnage and more terrible armament than any that old Germany ever had."[27]

In his speech, Churchill told Parliament that Britain could have avoided "the dangers into which we are steadily advancing," but "when the situation was manageable it was neglected, and now that it is thoroughly out of hand, we apply too late the remedies which then might have affected a cure." Churchill observed—in the paragraph Netanyahu would later read to both the UJC and the UN—that there was "nothing new in the story" of Britain's failure to act in time:

> It falls into that long, dismal catalogue of the fruitlessness of experience and the confirmed unteachability of mankind. Want of foresight, unwillingness to act when action would be simple and effective, lack of clear thinking, confusion of counsel until the emergency comes, until self-preservation strikes its jarring gong—these are the features which constitute the endless repetition of history.[28]

The need to act, and to do so before it was too late, was the central lesson Netanyahu had learned from his father, the Israeli historian Benzion Netanyahu, who had been Vladimir Jabotinsky's assistant in 1940. For the rest of his life, Benzion harbored a deep resentment at the failure of Jewish leadership in the 1930s to heed Jabotinsky's warnings of the coming disaster—and the failure to act once the danger was apparent to all.[29]

As of 2006, Iran was, in the words of the U.S. National Intelligence Estimate prepared in December 2005, "determined to develop nuclear weapons despite its international obligations and international pressure" for it to desist.[30] Netanyahu told the United Jewish Communities that history was repeating itself: "It is 1938; Iran is Germany; and it is racing to acquire nuclear weapons." "Too many times in our history we didn't see danger in time," he said, "and when we did, it was too late. Well, we see it now."[31]

At the end of 2006, Joshua Muravchik—a respected foreign policy analyst and a former aide to Senators Daniel Patrick Moynihan and Henry M. Jackson—published an op-ed in the *Los Angeles Times* entitled

Iran with Iraq immediately to its west and Afghanistan immediately to its east

"Bomb Iran," arguing for an air campaign to destroy Iran's nuclear facilities.[32] In 2007, John Bolton, former ambassador to the UN, who had dealt with nuclear proliferation as under secretary of state for arms control, said he saw no alternative to a preemptive attack on Iran.[33] Norman Podhoretz, the intellectual leader of the neoconservative movement, personally advised President George W. Bush to strike.[34] On January 23, 2008, the *Wall Street Journal* published an essay by Podhoretz, "Stopping Iran," in which he advocated military action because the consequences of Iranian nuclear weapons would extend far beyond Israel, and even beyond Europe. Such weapons would serve the purpose of a "far more ambitious aim":

> the creation of what [Iranian President] Ahmadinejad called "a world without America." . . . [N]o one imagined that Iran would acquire the capability to destroy the United States, [but] it was easy to imagine that the United States would be deterred from standing in Iran's way by the fear of triggering a nuclear war.[35]

In 2007, Senator John McCain said the only thing worse than bombing Iran was Iran with a bomb.[36] The threat of American military force was credible at that time: The United States had removed Saddam Hussein from power in Iraq and the Taliban from power in Afghanistan—which were the two countries immediately to the west and east of Iran. (Libya had given up its nuclear program in 2003 and Israel had bombed Syria's in 2007.) There were thus American military forces in both Iraq (150,000 troops) and Afghanistan (60,000 troops as 2009 began) that made it apparent to the Iranian rulers, situated between them, that their ambitions to obtain nuclear weapons might jeopardize their own rule as well.

Barack Obama became president in 2009, having pledged to fundamentally transform America. That goal included radically changing its foreign policy—indeed Obama saw the transformation of American foreign policy as essential to what he wanted to accomplish at home.[37]

During his campaign, Obama had told the *New York Times* that he believed Iran saw nuclear arms "in defensive terms, as a way to prevent regime change," and that Iran was thus deterrable, even if it had nuclear weapons.[38] His central foreign policy premise, he said, was that American safety was "best served when people in other nations are secure and feel invested."[39] Obama's approach was thus not to threaten Iran, but rather to convince Iran that America was no threat.[40]

In his inaugural address, Obama told foreign enemies he would "extend a hand if you are willing to unclench your fist"—a message he directed specifically at Iran in an interview during his first week in office.[41] In the campaign, he had endorsed negotiations with enemies without preconditions;[42] as president, he would make no demands before diplomatic discussions with Iran commenced; set no time limit for them once they had begun; and articulated no consequences for extended delay or failure. Iran put off talks throughout Obama's first term, while its nuclear program advanced unimpeded.

Obama's outreach to Iran reflected a consensus among a significant faction of the American foreign policy establishment. "The Iraq Study Group," a task force chaired by James Baker and Lee Hamilton (the former secretary of state and former House Foreign Affairs Committee chairman) issued a report in December 2006, as the United States remained bogged down in Iraq, asserting that "all key issues in the Middle East—the Arab-Israeli conflict, Iraq, Iran, the need for political and economic reforms, and extremism and terrorism—are inextricably linked." The report proposed a comprehensive diplomatic offensive—which it named "The New Diplomatic Offensive"—a move to "actively engage Iran . . . without preconditions."[43] Obama as a senator had opposed Bush's January 2007 "surge" in Iraq, saying it would "not in any imaginable way . . . accomplish any new progress."[44]

Two years later, Bush handed Obama a war largely won as a result of the surge.[45] The *New York Times* reported on January 18, 2009, that on his first full day in office, Obama would order U.S. military leaders to plan a speedy withdrawal of combat forces from Iraq.[46] An op-ed appearing in the *Times* that day called Bush's "winning the war . . . a remarkable gift to the incoming president, who now only has to sustain success."[47]

Obama proceeded to extend the approach of the Iraq Study Group a significant step further—not publicly acknowledged at the time—to make a "grand bargain" with Iran as the central goal of his foreign policy.[48] He envisioned turning Iran into part of a new regional security structure in the Middle East.[49] His policy was premised on the assumption that, in analyst Michael Doran's words, "Washington itself was the primary cause of the enmity," and that if the United States "were to adopt a less belligerent posture . . . Iran would reciprocate."[50] Moreover, détente with Iran would allow the United States to disengage from the Middle East and concentrate on its domestic goals.

In June 2009, the administration's extended-hand policy faced a moment of truth, as Iran held a presidential election on June 12 and announced, only two hours later, that its virulently anti-American president, Mahmoud Ahmadinejad, had been reelected in a landslide. The election result was transparently fraudulent—there had been huge public support for a different candidate in the weeks leading up to the election—and the announcement of the fraudulent result provoked massive demonstrations in Tehran, starting the following day, increasing in size to millions of Iranians during the following weeks.

Writing from Tehran, *New York Times* columnist Roger Cohen filed daily reports on ten days that shook Iran. On June 15, he described "an Iran close to the brink," unable to quell the uprising despite a massive show of force.[51] On June 17, he wrote that "[t]he Islamic Republic has lost legitimacy," and that the protest was "broader . . . than ever surfaced before," notwithstanding "the imposition of near-martial law."[52] On June 19,

Supporters of Iranian presidential candidate, Mir Hossein Mousavi, at a pre-election campaign rally on June 6, 2009

he reported whispers throughout the city: "Where's Obama?"[53] On June 20, he wrote that "the momentum is with [the new generation of Iranians]" and the government's authority was now "fragile."[54]

On June 21, the government shot several protestors, and the video of the murder of a student named Neda Agha Soltan went viral around the world. Cohen reported that there was now "a political earthquake in Iran":

> Ten days on [from the stolen election] . . . the brutal use of force and [Ayatollah Khamenei's] polarizing speech have drawn many more Iranians toward an absolutist stance. . . . [T]hey now want wholesale change. . . . Whatever happens now, all is changed utterly in Iran.[55]

On June 23, Cohen reported that "the June 12 ballot-box putsch" had broken Iran's social contract:

> The regime never had active support from more than 20 percent of the population. But acquiescence was secured by using only highly targeted repression (leaving the majority free to go about its business), and by giving a vote for president every four years. That's over.[56]

On June 26, Cohen devoted his column to the regime's treatment of women: their suffocation from "laws that can force a girl into marriage at 13; discriminatory laws on inheritance; the segregated beaches on the Caspian; the humiliation of arrest for a neck revealed or an ankle-length skirt. . . ."[57] On July 1, he reported: "[T]he Iran of today is not the Iran of three weeks ago; it is in volatile flux from without and within."[58] Cohen noted that "seldom had a fist been clenched more unequivocally, dissent silenced more harshly or deceit practiced with more brazenness than in Iran after June 12."[59]

Despite the daily indications that the Iranian theocracy had lost the support of the Iranian people, Obama decided to adhere to his preconceived course. On June 16, four days after the election, in the midst of the mass demonstrations, he told the press the election and the violence was "of concern to me and . . . to the American people," but that it was "not productive" for America "to be seen as meddling." Thus, he continued, how the situation "plays out over the next several days and several weeks is something ultimately for the Iranian people to decide."[60] In other words, the administration would stand aside, with no reaction other than an expression of "concern."[61]

Cohen remained in Tehran for as long as he could, staying there even after his press pass was revoked and becoming one of the last Western journalists to leave. Back in America, his July 4 column gave his recommendation about an American response:

> [T]he world is watching. As we Americans celebrate the Declaration of Independence, let's stand with Iran by recalling the first democratic revolution in Asia. It began in 1905 in Iran, driven by the quest to secure parliamentary government and a Constitution from the Qajar dynasty. Now, 104 years on, Iranians demand . . . a government accountable to the people.

But there was no further American response.[62] The silence and inaction—the things not said and done—had lasting consequences. This was the view of both Natan Sharansky, Israel's most prominent democracy advocate, and Leon Panetta, who was the director of the Central Intelligence Agency during these events. In 2014, Sharansky, serving as the head of the Jewish Agency, gave an extensive interview to the *Times of Israel* in which—according to the editor's summary of it—he "flatly blamed the president [Obama] for failing to support those dissidents who, across the region, were standing up against dictatorship":

Post-Election Protest in Iran, June 15, 2009

> And the original human rights sin, right at the beginning of Obama's presidency, Sharansky added, came with Iran. . . . "Iran is the saddest [instance], from my point of view, because everything starts from this. Everything starts from the fact that in 2009, when Iranians were ready for the revolution . . . they hear the message from the American president: Engagement with the government of Iran is more important than the replacement [of it]." . . . "That took all the energy out of this [movement]. . . ."[63]

Nearly a decade after the stolen 2009 election and the resulting near-revolution in Iran, with the Iranian theocracy now firmly ensconced and its nuclear weapons program much further advanced, Leon Panetta was asked, in a 2018 CNN interview, whether the Obama administration had "dropped the ball" by not aggressively standing with the protestors in 2009. Panetta responded that:

> I do think that was an appropriate time for the United States to have sent a clearer message that we stand by those who try to represent the rights of people. That's what the United States is all about. And it would have been important to have sent that message at the time.[64]

In 2009, Obama pledged to bring all American troops home from Iraq. In his first address to the UN General Assembly, he said "[n]o one nation can or should try to dominate another nation" and that "[n]o balance of power among nations will hold."[65] He vowed to put "daylight" between the United States and Israel, and later assured Iran that it could be "a very successful regional power."[66] He opposed Congressional efforts to impose stronger sanctions on Iran, fearing such sanctions would keep Iran from negotiating; he told Iran that the United States was not involved in assassinating its nuclear scientists; and he warned Israel not to strike at Iran's nuclear facilities.

In September 2009, Western intelligence sources discovered a secret, heavily fortified underground nuclear facility in Qom.[67] Iran continued to develop its Bushehr reactor and its heavy water facility in Arak and installed thousands of advanced new centrifuges in facilities that had no plausible peaceful use.[68] In 2011, Ehud Barak, a former Israeli prime minister from the Labor Party, who was serving as defense minister in Netanyahu's coalition government, warned that Iran was approaching a "zone of immunity" and that Israel might have no choice but to strike. The Saudi King had repeatedly urged the United States to "cut off the head of the snake" and destroy Iran's nuclear program.[69]

Netanyahu and Barak had concluded that Israel's extensive clandestine operations against the Iranian nuclear program would not ultimately shut it down, and that a massive aerial bombardment was necessary.[70] In January 2012, the *New York Times Magazine* published a story entitled "Will Israel Attack Iran?" by Ronen Bergman, the correspondent for military and intelligence affairs for one of Israel's largest newspapers.[71] Bergman predicted that Israel would strike at some point during the year.[72] But under Israeli law, an Israeli prime minister cannot order a military strike without the authorization of the fourteen-member security cabinet. Mossad's chief Meir Dagan strongly opposed a strike, as did a number of other Israeli military and intelligence officials, and the action was thus blocked.[73] Part of the reason was the opposition of the Obama administration to any military action, and the trust of the security cabinet in assurances that Obama was serious about stopping Iran.[74]

In 2012, the Obama administration and Iran opened secret negotiations, without informing Israel, in part out of concern about a possible Israeli attack.[75] When Israel learned of the talks, the administration assured it that any sanctions relief for Iran would be phased; that the sanctions would be dismantled only when Iran's illicit nuclear program was dismantled; that there would be "anytime, anywhere" inspections; and that Iran would first have to answer the long-pending questions about its nuclear program, posed by the International Atomic Energy Agency (IAEA) and never adequately answered.[76] None of those promises would be kept.

In early 2013, as Obama began his second term, the United States and its negotiating partners offered Iran a deal: in exchange for a temporary suspension of Iran's nuclear program, through restrictions that would automatically "sunset" within a fixed number of years, international sanctions would end and Iran would receive immediate financial relief exceeding $150 billion.[77] The prospective deal would leave Iran with its nuclear infrastructure virtually intact, with restrictions that could easily be reversed eventually, and in the meantime leaving Iran free to develop more advanced centrifuges and ballistic missiles, even during the term of the deal, with huge sums provided to Iran that would effectively finance both its nuclear program and its proxy armies in Iraq, Syria, Yemen, Lebanon, and Gaza.[78]

Even if Iran strictly observed the deal, Iran would have at its conclusion a completely legal, industrial-scale enrichment program capable of producing many nuclear weapons, with a breakout time that, Obama publicly acknowledged, would be "almost down to zero."[79]

Ron Dermer began his service as Israel's ambassador in October 2013, just as the United States was reaching the initial part of the Iran deal. In November 2013, the United States and Iran announced a "Joint Plan of Action," in which negotiations would proceed for six or twelve months to finalize a "Joint Comprehensive Plan of Action" featuring financial relief and international approval of Iran's ongoing nuclear program, in exchange for temporary restraints.[80]

On October 28, 2014, *The Atlantic*'s editor, Jeffrey Goldberg, interviewed "senior White House officials"—including, some believed, Obama himself—who exulted in having stopped Israel from attacking Iran. One official, Goldberg reported, said that "ultimately [Netanyahu] couldn't bring himself to pull the trigger" and "now it's too late." Another called Netanyahu "chickenshit."[81] Israel's ambassador at the time, the American-born Michael Oren, later recalled that:

> I spent the next day on Israeli television trying to translate *chickenshit* into Hebrew . . . [and trying to] explain how America's president could show more respect to Putin and Khamenei than he did to Netanyahu.[82]

Oren recognized that the comments of a "high official" of the Obama administration denigrating Israel's prime minister represented not only an extraordinary personal insult but, more importantly, a strategic problem for Israel itself:

> An America that slanders the democratically elected leader of its ally is one that is respected neither by its friends nor its enemies. And an Israel whose primary military supporters openly mock its deterrence is a target.[83]

Three months later, as the Obama administration worked to finalize its Iran deal, Speaker of the House John Boehner worked with Dermer to invite Netanyahu to address a joint session of Congress, with the speech set for March 3, 2015.[84] The decision to address Congress produced a major controversy not only among supporters of the Obama administration but also pro-Israel supporters in the United States.[85] The White House warned that the United States would no longer share intelligence with Israel on Iran and that no administration official would meet Netanyahu while he was in the United States.[86]

Obama refused to see Netanyahu during his visit, and fifty-eight Democrats boycotted his address. But the remaining Democrats and Republicans received Netanyahu warmly: The speech was interrupted by applause twenty-six times.[87] The *New York Times* reported it:

> had the trappings of the State of the Union address: a packed and rapt House chamber, suffocating security, lawmakers lining the aisles, a powerful world leader at the microphone—and

> a partisan chasm over the words and the man delivering them. . . . [Some lawmakers] said that Tuesday's appearance would be a moment they would long remember . . . while many Democrats condemned it as a polarizing and provocative challenge of President Obama's policy delivered in the very seat of American government. . . .
>
> Foremost among Democratic critics was Representative Nancy Pelosi of California, the party leader, who appeared incredulous and furious throughout the speech.[88]

Netanyahu told Congress there were two fundamental problems with the deal. First, it would be supervised by international inspectors, but "inspectors document violations; they don't stop them"—and Iran had built at least two secret nuclear facilities in the past.

Second—and far worse—was that, even if Iran did not violate the deal, the "sunset" provisions would leave Iran with an industrial-sized nuclear capability, much more enriched uranium, a new generation of advanced centrifuges, a zero-breakout time, and an international approval of an unrestricted nuclear program. As a result, Netanyahu warned, the deal "doesn't block Iran's path to the bomb; it paves Iran's path to the bomb."[89]

Netanyahu told Congress that the Iranian regime was "not merely a Jewish problem, any more than the Nazi regime was merely a Jewish problem." In a key portion of the speech, he reminded Congress that Iran had already taken over four countries:

> In the Middle East, Iran now dominates four Arab capitals, Baghdad, Damascus, Beirut and Sana. . . . [T]wo years ago, we were told to give [Iranian] President Rouhani and Foreign Minister Zarif a chance to bring change and moderation to Iran.
>
> Some change! Some moderation!

Those two paragraphs were an implicit reference to Churchill's 1941 Chicken Speech, as the commentator Belladonna Rogers observed at the time in "Echoes of Churchill Pervade Netanyahu's Speech."[90] In Churchill's speech, he had noted that in 1940 the Nazis had conquered four nations—Norway, Denmark, the Netherlands, and Belgium—after which France had abandoned its solemn pledge "not to make a separate peace." If France had stood with England, rather than capitulating to Germany, Churchill said, the war could have already been won by 1941.

Churchill addressing the Canadian Parliament, December 30, 1941

Then Churchill told the Canadian Parliament, in the passage of his speech that would give it its popular name in 1941 and the name by which it would be known to historians later:

> When I warned [the French] that Britain would fight on alone whatever they did, their generals told their Prime Minister, and his divided Cabinet, "In three weeks England will have her neck wrung like a chicken."
>
> Some chicken! Some neck! [Laughter and applause].[91]

Near the end of his speech, Churchill explained Britain's decision to stand alone, notwithstanding the French decision to sign its armistice with Germany—using language that would be echoed in Netanyahu's speech to Congress seventy-four years later:

> We did not make this war. We did not seek it. We did all we could to avoid it. We did too much to avoid it. We went so far at

Benjamin Netanyahu addresses the U.S. Congress, March 3, 2015

> times in trying to avoid it as to be almost destroyed by it when it broke upon us. . . . *[But] the peoples of the British Empire . . . are a tough and hardy lot. We have not journeyed all this way across the centuries, across the oceans, across the mountains, across the prairies, because we are made of sugar candy.* [Emphasis added.][92]

In his own speech, Netanyahu ended by telling Congress that "I can guarantee you this":

> [T]he days when the Jewish people remained passive in the face of genocidal enemies, those days are over. . . . We restored our sovereignty in our ancient home. And the soldiers who defend our home have *boundless courage*. For the first time in *one hundred generations*, we, the Jewish people, can defend ourselves. This is why, as a prime minister of Israel, I can promise you one more thing: *Even if Israel has to stand alone, Israel will stand.*[93] [Emphasis added.]

The cadences and phrases in Netanyahu's speech—the four conquered nations, the journey across the centuries, the courage of the people, the resolve to stand alone—precisely paralleled Churchill's address.[94] And if there were any doubt about the direct connection between the two speeches, Netanyahu's two-sentence paragraph—"Some change! Some moderation!"—made it virtually explicit.[95]

Netanyahu had used the ad hominem "chickenshit" attack on him to fashion a response that effectively invoked Churchill's call for national courage. Netanyahu was asking the Congress, in so many (Churchillian) words, to resist the Obama administration's push to make a separate peace with Iran, one that would come at the expense of America's Middle East allies and would finance their common enemy's preparation for war—as well as the acquisition of nuclear weapons to wage it. Netanyahu was employing language that silently evoked Churchill's condemnation of France's 1940 decision to make a separate peace.

There was one other historical reference underlying Netanyahu's address—reflected not in its language but in its setting. Days before the speech, Dermer had met in Washington with a skeptical group of Israeli supporters, who had questioned whether it was wise for Israel to challenge the Obama administration so openly and directly.[96] Dermer's response was to tell the group about Golda Meir in 1938:

> I told them a very simple story about what happened at Evian . . . that the future prime minister of Israel, on the eve of the destruction of European Jewry, was not allowed to speak. I said that, faced with a regime that is openly calling for the destruction of the one and only Jewish state, the current prime minister of Israel will speak. . . . We were a voiceless people; now we have a voice.[97]

Eighty-three years after Golda Meir, as a young leader of the Jewish community in Palestine, sat in compulsory silence at the back of the Evian Conference, Netanyahu stood at the podium before a joint session of Congress to oppose what Israelis across the political spectrum considered an impending historic capitulation by their American ally, one that would not bring peace, but rather fund their mutual enemy and facilitate its efforts to obtain weapons of mass destruction in due course, and threaten them both.[98]

Dermer later recalled that the environment changed dramatically once Israel's arguments were made not only by an ambassador in private dip-

Ambassador Ron Dermer in Congress after Netanyahu's address

lomatic conversations, but directly and publicly to the Congress by the Prime Minister, who was risking his standing both in the United States and at home to challenge the administration.[99] The Democrats in the Senate filibustered a vote on the Iran Deal under the Iran Nuclear Agreement Review Act of 2015, but it was clear that a bipartisan majority would have opposed it had a vote been held. Only 42 senators declared their support for the Iran Deal.[100]

Netanyahu's speech also had an unanticipated but significant impact on the Arab states who like Israel were threatened by Iran. They increased their ties with Israel after seeing it stand up for itself, as America was standing down. As Dermer later explained:

> [A]ll of a sudden, Israel was speaking out, and had an independent policy, and that gave [the Arab states] a great deal of confidence that Israel was willing to be a reliable actor, independent of what US policy would be in the region.
>
> And I can tell you that one of the leaders who we made peace with [in 2020 in the Abraham Accords] contacted the Prime Minister right after that speech. . . . [It] accelerated the ties that were happening beneath the surface between Israel and the Arab states. . . . So not only was it important in moral terms and his-

> toric terms to actually take that stand. In practical terms, I think it changed the trajectory.[101]

At the end of 2021, Benjamin Netanyahu—no longer Israel's prime minister—discussed his views of Herzl, Weizmann, Jabotinsky and other early Zionist leaders in an extensive interview with Gadi Taub, an Israeli historian at the Hebrew University of Jerusalem.[102] Netanyahu said that the essence of Jewish leadership was the ability to "identify the danger in time"—a quality he thought Herzl and Jabotinsky had in particular possessed—and that this was why he had "worked with everything I had for decades to prevent, to delay, to restrain [Iran's] moves towards this [nuclear] arsenal, because it threatens our very existence":

> And this is the mission. I say, "to identify the danger in time." . . . You can't accept or agree to the international agreement that is coming . . . where Iran can effectively create advanced centrifuges for enrichment of uranium, which effectively gives it the critical thing for creating a nuclear arsenal, for nuclear bombs which are aimed at this house, this city, of this small country. You can't.[103]

Netanyahu ended the interview by saying that, faced with such a threat, it was Israel's obligation to speak, and to act:

> And who will do it, if not us? And who will lead this fight, if not us? Who will speak among the nations, at Congress, at the UN, if not us? And who will act against them . . . if not us? "If I am not for myself, who will be for me? And if not now, when?" Just so, in those terms.

Netanyahu's quotation was from a portion of Hillel's epigram in *Pirkei Avot* ("Ethics of the Fathers"), written in the Mishnah two millennia ago.[104] Leo Pinsker used it as the epigraph for his 1882 book, *Auto-Emancipation*, the first great work of political Zionism.

Netanyahu thus was quoting ancient Jewish wisdom that had, at the end of the nineteenth century, marked the beginning of modern Jewish history—and was still relevant in the twenty-first, as Israel prepared to celebrate its seventy-fifth anniversary, simultaneously a stunning success and a state under existential threat.[105]

CONCLUSION

The Trusteeship of History

DANIEL GORDIS HAS WRITTEN that the rebirth of Jewish sovereignty transformed the Jews from "the nervous rabble about which Zionism's founding intellectuals wrote so compellingly just a century ago," to a people "with a sense of normalcy and pride that they now take for granted."[1] Gordis observed that the existence of Israel "transformed even the lives of Jews, like those in America, who chose not to make their lives in the Jewish state."

Over time, however, a sense of normalcy and pride can produce a historical amnesia. Few Jews today remember the world before Israel. Virtually none can recall a 1938 international conference, convened to assist Jewish refugees fleeing the Nazis, where the delegates avoided the word "Jews," because it might be counterproductive. Relatively few remember even the time before 1967, when the Jewish state lived behind indefensible borders, nine miles wide at its center, surrounded by states pledged to destroy it, armed by the Soviet Union.

Historic success can lead to a mistaken belief that history has "ended," or that it possesses an inherent "arc" that bends by itself, or that it has a "right side" on which it is only necessary to be.[2] The stories in this book are evidence that history is not an impersonal or inevitable process, but rather the record of what individuals do, some inspired by their belief in God, others by their unwillingness to await further divine tarrying, still others by a humanistic belief that they alone were there to act.[3] Whatever their inspiration, their actions made history. Perhaps these stories can help remedy the current deficiency in common memory about what it took to get us where we are.[4]

These stories are connected as well to a larger historical narrative. All of them—(a) Herzl's idea of a liberal Jewish home in a new/old land; (b) Brandeis's recognition that the Jewish and the American stories were related; (c) Weizmann's efforts to unite Jews and Arabs in their respective national pursuits; (d) Meir's move to Palestine after experiencing tyranny in Russia and freedom in America; (e) Jabotinsky's impassioned presentations to Churchill, British officials, and Members of Parliament; (f) Hecht's use of his literary and dramatic skill to convey a historic message; (g) Eban's defense of the Jewish state in the council of nations; and (h) Dermer's diplomacy for an adopted country, inspired by being "proud to have been an American"—are part of a broader saga: one of freedom and democracy; of Jewish and American ideas playing out in the world; of an invisible baton passed from generation to generation.[5]

The miracle of Jewish recovery in the twentieth century is not a cause for self-congratulation, nor an occasion to rest on the laurels of history—either Jewish or American. It is rather a reason for renewed commitment.[6] To navigate the challenges of our new/old world, it is not sufficient simply to have a knowledge of history: we need something more—a recognition that, in the words of Brandeis a century ago—we are the "trustees" of our history, with "a treasure to cherish," charged to "carry forward what others, in the past, have borne so well."[7] We need to ensure that the history does some work in the world.

BIBLIOGRAPHY

PRIMARY SOURCES

Autobiographies, Memoirs, and Diaries

Ben-Ami, Yitshaq. *Years of Wrath, Days of Glory: Memoirs from the Irgun.* New York: Shengold Publishers, 1983.

Davitt, Michael. *Within the Pale: The True Story of Anti-Semitic Persecutions in Russia*, 1903.

Eban, Abba. *Abba Eban: An Autobiography.* New York: Random House, 1977.

———. *Personal Witness: Israel Through My Eyes.* New York: G. P. Putnam's Sons, 1992.

Hitler, Adolf. *Mein Kampf.* Ralph Manheim, trans. Boston: Houghton Mifflin Co., 1945.

Hull, Cordell. *The Memoirs of Cordell Hull.* New York: The Macmillan Co., 1948.

Jabotinsky, Vladimir. *The Story of the Jewish Legion.* New York: B. Ackerman, Inc., 1945.

Jacobson, Dan. "A Memoir of Jabotinsky." *Commentary*, June 1961.

Kissinger, Henry. *White House Years.* Boston: Little, Brown and Co., 1979.

Lawrence, A. W., ed. *T. E. Lawrence by His Friends.* New York, Toronto, London: McGraw-Hill Book Co., Inc., 1937.

Lawrence, T. E. *T. E. Lawrence to His Biographer Robert Graves.* London: Faber & Faber, 1938.

Lipsky, Louis. *Memoirs in Profile.* Philadelphia: Jewish Publication Society of America, 1975.

Lowenthal, Marvin, ed. *The Diaries of Theodor Herzl.* New York: Grosset & Dunlap, 1962.

McDonald, James G. *My Mission in Israel 1948–1951.* New York: Simon and Schuster, 1951.

Medoff, Rafael. *America and the Holocaust: A Documentary History.* Philadelphia: Jewish Publication Society, 2022.

Naschauer, Ella. "In the Family Circle: An Intimate Glimpse of Theodor Herzl at Home," in Meyer W. Weisgal, ed., *Theodor Herzl: A Memorial.* Westport, CT: Hyperion Press, Inc., 1929.

Oren, Michael B. *Ally: My Journey Across the American-Israeli Divide*. New York: Random House, 2015.

Patai, Raphael, ed., and Harry Zohn, trans. *The Complete Diaries of Theodor Herzl*. New York and London: Herzl Press and Thomas Yoseloff, 1960.

Patterson, John. *With the Judeans in the Palestine Campaign*. New York: Sagwan Press, 2015.

Weizmann, Chaim. *Trial and Error: The Autobiography of Weizmann*. New York: Harper & Brothers, 1949.

Wise, Stephen S. *Challenging Years: The Autobiography of Stephen Wise*. New York: G. P. Putnam's Sons, 1949.

Government or Other Official Reports

"The Chief of the Division of Near Eastern Affairs (Murray) to the Consul General at Jerusalem (Wadsworth), July 2, 1938." *Foreign Relations of the United States Diplomatic Papers, 1938, General*, Volume 1, 867N.01/1106.

"Evian Conference on Political Refugees." *Social Service Review*, September 1938, 514–18. www.jstor.org/stable/30011106.

"Full Official Record: What the Mufti Said to Hitler." *Times of Israel*, October 21, 2015. Official German record of November 28, 1941, meeting in Berlin. Source: Documents on German Foreign Policy 1918–1945, Series D, Vol XIII, London, 1964.

"Full text of Iran-5+1 agreement in Geneva, 24 November 2013." www.globalsecurity.org/wmd/library/policy/int/iran-5-1-geneva-agreement_2013.htm.

Herzl, Theodor. Testimony Before the Royal Commission on Alien Immigration, 7 July 1902. Report of the Royal Commission on Alien Immigration, London, 1903, Minutes of Evidence, II: 211–221. Cmd. 1742, republished in Isaiah Friedman, *The Rise of Israel, Vol. 2, Herzl's Political Activity 1897–1904*. New York and London: Garland Publishing, Inc., 1987, 241–51.

Iraq Study Group Report, December 2006. web.archive.org/web/20100829020030 / www.media.usip.org/reports/iraq_study_group_report.pdf.

Jabotinsky, Vladimir. "The Threatened Partition of Palestine: Address to Members of Parliament on Monday, July 13th 1937." Jabotinsky Institute Archives, Document A-1c/8/50.

Lewis, Jeffrey. "2005 Iran NIE Details." https://www.armscontrolwonk.com/archive/202469/2005-iran-nie-details/, September 22, 2009.

"The Making of Transjordan." http://www.kinghussein.gov.jo/his_transjordan.html.

Minutes of British War Cabinet Meeting No. 261, Minute No. 12, 31 October 1917. http://www.balfourproject.org/war-cabinet-minutes-leading-to-the-balfour-declaration-1917/.

Orlan, Haiyim J. "The Participants in the First Zionist Congress." *Herzl Year Book*, Vol. II, 150.

Palestine Royal Commission. "Notes of Evidence Taken in London on Thursday, 11th February, 1937." London: His Majesty's Stationary Office, 1937.

Riemer, Michael J. *The First Zionist Congress: An Annotated Translation of the Proceedings*. Albany: State University of New York Press, 2019.

"SD on the Outcome of the Evian Conference Report of SD." Submitted to SS Gruppenfuehrer Heydrich, Yad Vashem Archive, 0.51/OSO/37 Berlin, 29 July 1938. www.yadvashem.org/odot_pdf/microsoft%20word%20-%203528.pdf.

U.S. 2007 National Intelligence Estimate, "Iran: Nuclear Intentions and Capabilities." www.dni.gov/files/documents/Newsroom/Reports%20and%20Pubs/20071203_release.pdf.

Speeches and Addresses

Biden, Joe. "Joe Biden on Iraq." www.latimesblogs.latimes.com/washington/2010/02/joe-biden-update-larry-king-iraq-obama-sarah-palin.html.

Brandeis, Louis D. *The Jewish Problem: How to Solve It.* New York: The Zionist Essays Publication Committee, 1915. www.law.louisville.edu/library/collections/brandeis/node/234.

———. "Speech at Young Men's Hebrew Association of Chelsea, Massachusetts." May 18, 1913, in *Brandeis on Zionism: A Collection of Addresses and Statements.* Washington, DC: Zionist Organization of America, 1942.

———. "The Jewish People Should Be Preserved." August 30, 1914, in *Brandeis on Zionism: A Collection of Addresses and Statements.* Washington, DC: Zionist Organization of America, 1942.

Brickner, Barnett. "Vindication and Triumph: The Theoretic and Practical Success of Herzl's Aims," in Meyer W. Weisgal, ed., *Theodor Herzl: A Memorial.* Westport, CT: Hyperion Press, Inc., 1929.

Churchill, Winston. White Paper Speech, May 23, 1939. www.alliedpowersholocaust.org/wp-content/uploads/2015/03/1939-May-Churchill-White-Paper-Speech.pdf.

Dermer, Ron. "The Danger of Returning to the Nuclear Deal with Iran," 2019. www.facebook.com/ambdermer/videos/453270461908315.

———. "Kemper Lecture 2018—Churchill and Israel," March 25, 2018. www.nationalchurchillmuseum.org/kemper-lecture-dermer.html; www.youtube.com/watch?v=tM9Log5Tof4.

———. "Remarks Delivered on July 7, 2016, at the B'nai B'rith World Center Award for Journalism ceremony in Jerusalem." http://blogs.timesofisrael.com/israeli-us-ties-the-dependence-is-mutual/.

Eban, Abba. "Statement to the Security Council by Foreign Minister Eban—6 June 1967," Israel Ministry of Foreign Affairs.

———. "Statement to the Security Council of the United Nations, May 26, 1948," reprinted in Abba Eban, *Voice of Israel.* New York: Horizon Press, 1957.

"Excerpts from Talks by Albanian and Israeli in U.N. and Text of Hussein Address." *New York Times*, June 27, 1967, 1.

Herzl, Theodor. *The Congress Addresses of Theodor Herzl.* New York: Federation of American Zionists, 1917.

Gottheil, Richard J. H. *Zionism.* Philadelphia: Jewish Publication Society of America, 1914.

Goldman, Solomon, ed. *The Words of Justice Brandeis.* New York: Henry Schuman, 1953.

Herzl, Theodor. *Zionist Writings: Essays and Addresses, Vol. 2* (August, 1898–May, 1904). Harry Zohn, trans. New York: Herzl Press, 1975.

Hitler, Adolf. "Text of Hitler's Address Reviewing the Course of the War and Explaining His Aims." *New York Times*, October 1, 1942.

"Israel to UN: You Never Hear Palestinian Leaders Say 'Two States for Two Peoples,'" January 26, 2012. https://matzav.com/israel-to-un-you-never-hear-palestinian-leaders-say-two-states-for-two-peoples/.

Netanyahu, Benjamin. "PM Netanyahu at the Official Ceremony for Benjamin Ze'ev Herzl." Israel Ministry of Foreign Affairs, July 26, 2016. mfa.gov.il/MFA/PressRoom/2016/Pages/PM-Netanyahu-addresses-official-memorial-ceremony-for-Benjamin-Zeev-Herzl-26-July-2016.

———. "PM Netanyahu's Remarks at the Official Memorial Ceremony for Benjamin Ze'ev Herzl." Israel Ministry of Foreign Affairs, July 13, 2017. www.gov.il/en/departments/news/speechherzel130717.

Obama, Barack. "A Way Forward in Iraq." Remarks to Chicago Council on Global Affairs, November 20, 2006. www.stltoday.com/news/local/govt-and-politics/obama-offers-his-plan-for-the-iraq-war/article_a83b95e9-0f66-516b-808d-63eb7f90d732.html.

———. "Floor Statement on Bush's Decision to Increase Troops in Iraq," January 19, 2007.

———. "Remarks by President Obama and President Lee of the Republic of Korea in Joint Press Availability." The White House, June 16, 2009.

Weizmann, Chaim. "Plea for Friendship and Peace." Address to Moslem and Christian Leaders, Jerusalem, April 27, 1918. Series B Papers, Paper 42, 182–86.

Correspondence

Browne, Malcolm D. *Lawrence of Arabia: The Selected Letters*. London: Little Books Ltd., 2005.

Churchill, Winston. Telegram to David Lloyd George, March 18, 1921, in Martin Gilbert, *The Churchill Documents, Vol. 9, Disruption and Chaos, July 1919–March 1921*. Hillsdale, MI: Hillsdale College Press, 2008.

Faisal, Emir. Letter to Felix Frankfurter, and Frankfurter reply, www.jewishvirtuallibrary.org/feisal-frankfurter-correspondence-march-1919.

Jabotinsky, Vladimir. Letter from President of the New Zionist Organization to Prime Minister Neville Chamberlain, September 4, 1939. *The Jabotinksy Institute in Israel*, Letter No. 4115, reference code A-1 2/29/2.

Lawrence, T. E. Letter, TEL 865, T. E. Lawrence Papers, The Huntington Library, San Marino, California.

———. Letter to Edward Marsh [Churchill's private secretary], January 17, 1921, in Martin Gilbert, *The Churchill Documents, Vol. 9, Disruption and Chaos, July 1919–March 1921*. Hillsdale, MI: Hillsdale College Press, 2008.

———. Letter to Robert Graves, February 12, 1921. www.telstudies.org/writings/letters/1921/210219_r_graves.html.

———. Letter to Robert Graves, February 16, 1921. http://www.telstudies.org/writings/letters/1921/210216_r_graves.html.

McMahon, Sir Henry. Letter to Sharif Hussein, 24 October 1915. *Report of a Committee set up to consider certain correspondence between Sir Henry McMahon and the Sharif of Mecca in 1915 and 1916*: Command Paper 5974 of 1939.

"Violet Bonham Carter to Winston S. Churchill" (Churchill papers: 2/316). Jabotinsky Institute Archives Letter No. 6696, A1-2/27, published in Martin Gilbert, *Winston S. Churchill, Companion Volume V, Part III: The Coming of War*. London: William Heinemann, 1982.

"Vladimir Jabotinsky to Winston S. Churchill" (Churchill papers: 2/316). Jabotinsky Institute Archives Letter No. 6696, A1-2/27, published in Martin Gilbert, *Winston S. Churchill Companion Volume V, Part III, The Coming of War*. London: William Heinemann, 1982.

Sykes, Mark. Letter dated November 14, 1917, to Lt. Col. Sir Maurice Haney, secretary to the War Cabinet, in Isaiah Friedman, ed., *The Rise of Israel, The Zionist Commission in Palestine 1918*. New York and London: Garland Publishing Inc., 1987, Doc 36.

"The Ambassador in France (Bullitt) to the Secretary of State, June 27, 1938." *Foreign Relations of the United States Diplomatic Papers, 1938, General*. Volume 1, 840.48 Refugees/413: Telegram.

Wasserstein, Bernard, ed. *The Letters and Papers of Chaim Weizmann*, Vol. XI, Series A, January 1922–July 1923. Jerusalem: Transaction Books, 1977.

Weizmann, Chaim. *Letters and Papers of Chaim Weizmann*. Vol. V, Series B Papers, II, December 1931–April 1952, 1984.

———. Letter to Vera Weizmann, June 17, 1918, Letter No. 213, in Dvorah Barzilay and Barnet Litvinoff, *The Letters and Papers of Chaim Weizmann*. Vol. VIII, Series A, November 1917–October 1918. New Brunswick and Jerusalem: Transaction Books/Rutgers University, Israel University Press, 1977.

Documents

Bush, George W. "Second Inaugural Address of George W. Bush, January 20, 2005." www.avalon.law.yale.edu/21st_century/gbush2.asp.

Council for German Jewry, the Jewish Colonisation Association, the HIAS-ICA Emigration Association, the Joint Foreign Committee of the Board of Deputies of British Jews and the Anglo-Jewish Association, the German Jewish Aid Committee, and the Agudath Israel World Organization, "Memorandum of Certain Jewish Organizations Concerned with the Refugees from Germany and Austria." www.nli.org.il/en/books/NNL_ALEPH990026644770205171/NLI.

Executive Order 9417, Establishing a War Refugee Board. www.presidency.ucsb.edu/documents/executive-order-9417-establishing-the-war-refugee-board.

FDR Statement, March 24, 1944, "The History Place—Holocaust Timeline: President Roosevelt Condemns War Crimes." www.historyplace.com/worldwar2/holocaust/h-roos-statement.htm.

"Franklin Roosevelt Administration: Jewish Organizations Press FDR to Act." www.jewishvirtuallibary.org/jewish-organizations-press-fdr-to-act-december-1942.

Friedman, Isaiah, ed. *The Rise of Israel, Vol. 2, Herzl's Political Activity 1897–1904, 1918*. New York and London: Garland Publishing Inc., 1987.

———. *The Rise of Israel, The Zionist Commission in Palestine 1918.* New York and London: Garland Publishing Inc., 1987.

Gilbert, Martin. *The Churchill Documents, Vol. 9, Disruption and Chaos, July 1919–March 1921.* Hillsdale, MI: Hillsdale College Press, 2008.

Jewish Electorate Institute, May 22, 2019 poll. https://www.jewishelectorateinstitute.org/poll-domestic-issues-dominate-the-priorities-of-the-jewish-electorate/.

"Paraphrase of Telegram," from American Minister, Bern, to Secretary of State, Washington, dated October 6, 1942. Sumner Welles Papers, Box 66, Folder OS, Office correspondence, Wise, Steph 1942, FDR Library. www.fdrlibrary.marist.edu/_resources/images/hol/hol00370.pdf.

"Report on the Visit to the President." Document 22 in David S. Wyman, ed., *America and the Holocaust: A Thirteen-Volume Set, Vol. 2.* Amherst: University of Massachusetts, 1990.

Shaoul, Jean. "100 Years Since the Balfour Declaration." Part One, November 7, 2017, *World Socialist Web Site.* www.wsws.org/en/articles/2017/11/07/balf-n07.html; Part Two, November 8, 2017, *World Socialist Web Site.* www.wsws.org/en/articles/2017/11/08/balf-n08.html.

Sumner Welles Papers, Box 66, Folder OS, Office correspondence, Wise, Steph 1942, FDR Library. www.fdrlibrary.marist.edu/_resources/images/hol/hol00370.pdf.

"Telegram from Gerhart Riegner (Via Samuel Silverman) to Stephen S. Wise, August 29, 1942," reprinted in Gary Phillip Zola and Marc Dollinger, eds. *American Jewish History: A Primary Source Reader.* Waltham, MA: Brandeis University Press, 2014.

"Telegram Received," dated Sunday, October 4, 1942, at 3:49 a.m. from "Wise" to Secretary Sumner Welles. Sumner Welles Papers, Box 66, Folder OS, Office correspondence, Wise, Stephen 1942, FDR Library. www.fdrlibrary.marist.edu/_resources/images/hol/hol00370.pdf.

Treasury Report to President Roosevelt, January 14, 1944. https://perspectives.ushmm.org/item/treasury-department-report-to-president-roosevelt.

Zola, Gary Phillip, and Marc Dollinger. *American Jewish History: A Primary Source Reader.* Waltham, MA: Brandeis University Press, 2014.

Newspaper and Magazine Articles

Ahad Ha'am. "The Wrong Way." www.jewishvirtuallibrary.org/quot-the-wrong-way-quot-ahad-ha-am.

"Army Pays Hitler Birthday Tribute—Fuehrer, 46 Today, Hailed as Private Who Led Nation Back to Military Power." *New York Times,* April 20, 1935.

"Ben Hecht Is Buried in Nyack Near Charles MacArthur Grave." *New York Times,* April 22, 1964.

Ben-Gurion, David. "Herzl's Dream—and the Reality." *New York Times,* May 1, 1960.

"Ben-Gurion Opens Israel Bond Campaign in New York." *JTA,* May 11, 1951, www.jta.org/1951/05/11/archive/ben-gurion-opens-israel-bond-campaign-in-new-york-35000000-raised-at-rally.

Birchall, Frederick T. "Germany Rejects Verdict of League on Arms Violations." *New York Times*, April 21, 1935.

Brooks, David. "Obama, Gospel and Verse." *New York Times*, April 26, 2007.

"Churchill Assails Palestine Tactics—Declares 'We Are Making Fools of Ourselves,' Blaming the Labor Government." *New York Times*, May 17, 1947.

Cohen, Roger. "City of Whispers." *New York Times*, June 19, 2009.

———. "The End of the Beginning." *New York Times*, June 23, 2009.

———. "Iran on a Razor's Edge." *New York Times*, June 15, 2009.

———. "Iran's Children of Tomorrow." *New York Times*, June 22, 2009.

———. "Iran's Second Sex." *New York Times*, June 26, 2009.

———. "Let the Usurpers Writhe." *New York Times*, July 1, 2009.

———. "The Making of an Iran Policy." *New York Times*, July 30, 2009.

———. "My Name Is Iran." *New York Times*, June 17, 2009.

———. "A Supreme Leader Loses His Aura as Iranians Flock to the Street." *New York Times*, June 20, 2009.

"A Dream of a Jewish State." *Jewish Chronicle*, January 17, 1896.

Eban, Aubrey S. "The Future of Arab-Jewish Relations: The Key Is the Cooperation of Equal and Separate States." *Commentary*, September 1948.

———. "Pursue Peace, Not Just Elections." *New York Times*, December 30, 1989.

"The Emir Faisal on Palestine and the Jews." *Jewish Chronicle*, October 3, 1919.

"Favors Zion Movement—Russia Gives Official Encouragement to the Jewish Project—Minister De Plehve's Letter to the Congress in Session at Basel, Switzerland." *New York Times*, August 26, 1903.

"40,000 Here View Memorial to Jews: Madison Square Garden Filled Twice for Mass Tribute to 2,000,000 Slain in Europe." *New York Times*, March 10, 1943.

Goldberg, Jeffrey. "The Crisis in U.S.-Israel Relations Is Officially Here." *The Atlantic*, October 28, 2014.

Greenberg, Meyer. "The Attitude of the Jewish Student at Yale Towards Judaism." *Yivo Bleter*, November–December 1945.

"Irgun Leader Skeptical of Solution for Palestine Through U.N. Inquiry—Begin Says Only British Withdrawal Can Bring Peace," *New York Times*, May 23, 1947.

"Israel's Chief Orator: Abba Eban." *New York Times*, June 21, 1967.

"Jewish National Movement—The Governmental Declaration—Great Thanksgiving Meeting—A Historic Gathering . . . Arab and Armenian Support." *Jewish Chronicle*, December 7, 1917.

Knowlton, Brian. "Economy and Iraq Are Set to Lead Obama Agenda." *New York Times*, January 18, 2009.

Kristol, William. "The Next War President." *New York Times*, January 18, 2009.

Kushner, Jared. "Opportunity Beckons in the Mideast." *Wall Street Journal*, March 14, 2021.

Muravchik, Joshua. "Bomb Iran." *Los Angeles Times*, November 1, 2006.

"Obama Says Ready to Talk to Iran." *Reuters*, January 27, 2009. www.reuters.com/article/us-obama-arabiya/obama-says-ready-to-talk-to-iran-idUSTRE50Q23220090127.

"Palestine for the Jews—Official Sympathy." *Times of London*, November 9, 1917.

"Palestine Royal Commission's Public Sitting in London—Mr. Jabotinsky Puts Jewish Defense Claim." *The Manchester Guardian*, February 11, 1937.
Pelcovits, N. A. "What About Jewish Anti-Semitism?" *Commentary*, February 1947.
Podhoretz, Norman. "The Case for Bombing Iran." *Commentary*, June 2007.
———. "Stopping Iran." *Wall Street Journal*, January 23, 2008.
"Rabbis Preach on President's Note—Theme of Wilson's Message on Zionist Movement Discussed in New Year Services Here." *New York Times*, September 7, 1918.
Ronen, Gild. "Bolton, Podhoretz Say: Bomb Iranian Nuclear Plants." *Israel National News*, September 30, 2007.
Roosevelt, Eleanor. "My Day" Column, April 14, 1943, Eleanor Roosevelt papers at FDR Library. www.fdrlibrary.marist.edu/_resourves/images/hol/hol00439.pdf.
"Roosevelt Awaiting Return of Churchill." *New York Times*, December 31, 1941.
"Security Council Votes to Admit Israel to U.N. Membership; Vote is 9 to 1." *Jewish Telegraph Agency*, www.jta.org/1949/03/06/archive/security-council-votes-to-admit-israel-to-u-n-membership-vote-is-9-to-1.
"Wise Gets Confirmations—Checks with State Department on Nazis' 'Extermination Campaign,'" *New York Times*, November 25, 1942, 10.
Zuckerman, Mortimer B. "3 Steps to Stop Iran from Getting a Nuclear Bomb." *U.S. News and World Report*, June 25, 2010.

Historical Background

Brickner, Barnett. "Vindication and Triumph: The Theoretic and Practical Success of Herzl's Aims," in Meyer W. Weisgal, ed., *Theodor Herzl: A Memorial*. Westport, CT: Hyperion Press, Inc., 1929.
Greiner, Bernhard. "'What Will People Say?' Herzl as Author of Comedies," in Mark H. Gelber and Vivian Liska, eds. *Theodor Herzl: From Europe to Zion*. Tübingen: Max Niemeyer Verlag, 2007.
Historical Society of Ottawa. "Some Chicken, Some Neck." https://www.historicalsocietyottawa.ca/publications/ottawa-stories/personalities-from-the-very-famous-to-the-lesser-known/some-chicken-some-neck.
International Churchill Society. "Winston Churchill 70 Years Ago: 'Some Chicken! Some Neck!'" www.winstonchurchill.org/publications/churchill-bulletin/bulletin-043-jan-2012/winston-churchill-70-years-ago-some-chicken-some-neck/.
Jabotinsky, Vladimir. "The Ethics of the Iron Wall." www.david-collier.com/ethics-iron-wall-zeev-jabotinsky.
———. "The Iron Wall." www.en.jabotinsky.org/media/9747/the-iron-wall.pdf.
National Churchill Museum. "Some Chicken; Some Neck, 1941." www.nationalchurchillmuseum.org/some-chicken-some-neck.html.
U.S. Holocaust Museum, Holocaust Encyclopedia. "The Nuremberg Race Laws." https://encyclopedia.ushmm.org/content/en/article/the-nuremberg-race-laws#:~.
"Vital Statistics: Jewish Population of the World: 1882–Present." Jewish Virtual Library. www.jewishvirtuallibrary.org/jewish-population-of-the-world.

"Vital Statistics: Total Casualties, Arab-Israeli Conflict," Jewish Virtual Library. www.jewishvirtuallibrary.org/total-casualties-arab-israeli-conflict.

Interviews

Abbas, Mansour. "Israel's Game-Changing Arab Politician Speaks." *Mosaic*, February 18, 2021.

Blum, Ruthie. "Mansour Abbas's 'Jewish State,' Bombshell." *Jerusalem Post*, December 23, 2021.

Dermer, Ron. "A Conversation with Ron Dermer." Hudson Institute, May 21, 2021. www.hudson.org/events/1964-virtual-event-a-conversation-with-ambassador-ron-dermer-52021.

Eban, Abba. Interview by CBS News correspondents Larry Lesueur and Winston Burdett. "Longines Chronoscope with Abba Eban," 1955. https://www.youtube.com/watch?v=vOKZZML-YW8.

———. "The Leon Charney Report," March 16, 1997. http://charneyreport.com/2015/05/24/avraham-ben-zvi-and-abba-eban/.

Horowitz, David. "Sharansky: If Obama Had Backed Iran's Dissidents, Arab Spring Might Have Looked Different." *Times of Israel*, January 30, 2014.

———. "Sharansky's Guide to the Region's Human Rights Dilemmas." *Times of Israel*, January 30, 2014.

Masri, Muhammad al-. "Three Hours with the PA President, December 25, 2021," quoted in Nan Jacques Zilberdik, "Abbas and PA." *Palestinian Media Watch*, January 4, 2022.

Nahmias, Omri. "Amb. Dermer, Elan Carr, Discuss Anti-Zionism vs. Antisemitism." *Jerusalem Post*, November 22, 2019.

Netanyahu, Benjamin. "Netanyahu: The Figures Who Formed Him, and the Duties of Jewish Leadership." *Mosaic*, December 21, 2021.

Shlaim, Avi. "Interview with Abba Eban, 11 March 1976." *Israel Studies*, Vol. 8, No. 1, Spring 2003. https://www.jstor.org/stable/30245611.

Contemporaneous Books

Ben-Gurion, David. Preface, in Ludwig Lewisohn, *Theodor Herzl: A Portrait for This Age*. Cleveland and New York: World Publishing Co., 1955.

Hecht, Ben. *Perfidy*. New York: Julian Messner Inc., 1961.

Herzl, Theodor. *The Jewish State: An Attempt at a Modern Solution of the Jewish Question*. New York: The Maccabaean Publishing Co., 1904.

———. *Old-New Land ("Altneuland")*. Lotta Levensohn, trans., with a Preface by Stephen S. Wise. New York: Bloch Publishing Co., 1941.

Seton-Watson, R. W. *The War and Democracy*, 1915.

Storrs, Ronald. *Orientations*. London, 1937.

Zimmern, Alfred. *The Greek Commonwealth*, 1912.

SECONDARY SOURCES

Biographies

Allawi, Ali A. *Faisal I of Iraq*. New Haven and London: Yale University Press, 2014.

Avineri, Shlomo. *Herzl: Theodor Herzl and the Foundation of the Jewish State.* London: Weidenfeld & Nicolson, 2013.

Bein, Alex. *Theodore Herzl: A Biography.* Philadelphia: The Jewish Publication Society of America, 1941.

Beller, Steven. *Herzl.* London: Peter Halban, 2012.

Burkett, Elinor. *Golda.* New York: Harper Perennial, 2008.

Cesarani, David. *Disraeli: The Novel Politician.* New Haven and London: Yale University Press, 2016.

Chouraqui, André. *A Man Alone: The Life of Theodor Herzl.* Jerusalem: Keter Books, 1970.

Cohen, Israel. *Theodor Herzl: Founder of Political Zionism.* New York and London: Thomas Yoseloff, 1959.

de Haas, Jacob. *Theodor Herzl: A Biographical Study.* Chicago and New York: The Leonard Company, 1927.

Elkins, Rabbi Dov Peretz. *Peter Bergson: The Jewish Lobbyist Who Advocated to Save Jews During the Holocaust.* Jerusalem: Mazo Publishers, 2022.

Elon, Amos. *Herzl.* New York: Holt, Rinehart and Winston, 1975.

Gorbach, Julien. *The Notorious Ben Hecht: Iconoclastic Writer and Militant Zionist.* West Lafayette, IN: Purdue University Press, 2019.

Halkin, Hillel. *Jabotinsky: A Life.* New Haven: Yale University Press, 2014.

Hoffman, Adina. *Ben Hecht: Fighting Words, Moving Pictures.* New Haven: Yale University Press, 2019.

Horowitz, Brian J. *Vladimir Jabotinsky's Russian Years, 1900–1925.* Bloomington: Indiana University Press, 2020.

Katz, Shmuel. *Lone Wolf: A Biography of Vladimir (Ze'ev) Jabotinsky*, Vols. 1 and 2. New York: Barricade Books, 1996.

Klagsbrun, Francine. *Lioness: Gold Meir and the Nation of Israel.* New York: Schocken Books, 2017.

Kornberg, Jacques. *Theodor Herzl: From Assimilation to Zionism.* Bloomington: Indiana University Press, 1993.

Korda, Michael. *Hero: The Life and Legend of Lawrence of Arabia.* New York: Harper Perennial, 2010.

Lewisohn, Ludwig. *Theodor Herzl: A Portrait for This Age.* Cleveland and New York: World Publishing Co., 1955.

MacAdams, William. *Ben Hecht: The Man Behind the Legend.* New York: Charles Scribner's Sons, 1990.

Mack, John E. *A Prince of Our Disorder: The Life of T. E. Lawrence.* Cambridge, MA: Harvard University Press, 1998.

Mosse, George L. "Max Nordau and His Degeneration." Introduction to Max Nordau, *Degeneration*. Lincoln and London: University of Nebraska Press, 1993.

Netanyahu, Benjamin. *A Place Among the Nations*. New York: Bantam Books, 1993.

Netanyahu, Benzion. *The Founding Fathers of Zionism*. Jerusalem and New York: Balfour Books, 2012.

Nordau, Anna and Maxa. *Max Nordau: A Biography*. New York: The Nordau Committee, 1943.

Paper, Lewis J. *Brandeis: An Intimate Biography of One of America's Truly Great Supreme Court Justices*. Secaucus, NJ: Citadel Press, 1983.

Pawel, Ernst. *The Labyrinth of Exile: A Life of Theodor Herzl*. New York: Farrar, Straus and Giroux, 1989.

Penslar, Derek. *Theodor Herzl: The Charismatic Leader*. New Haven: Yale University Press, 2020.

Rabinowicz, Oskar K. *Herzl, Architect of the Balfour Declaration*. New York: Herzl Press, 1958.

Rabinowitz, Ezekiel. *Justice Louis D. Brandeis: The Zionist Chapter in His Life*. New York: Philosophical Library, 1968.

Reinharz, Jehuda. *Chaim Weizmann: The Making of a Statesman*. New York and Oxford: Oxford University Press, 1993.

Roberts, Andrew. *Churchill: Walking with Destiny*. United States: Viking, 2018.

Schechtman, Joseph. *The Life & Times of Vladimir Jabotinsky: Rebel & Statesman: The Early Years*. New York: Thomas Yoseloff, 1956.

———. *The Vladimir Jabotinsky Story, Fighter and Prophet: The Last Years*. New York: Thomas Yoseloff, 1961.

Siniver, Asaf. *Abba Eban: A Biography*. New York: Overlook Duckworth, 2015.

St. John, Robert. *Eban*. New York: Doubleday & Co., 1972.

Wilson, Jeremy. *Lawrence of Arabia: The Authorized Biography of T. E. Lawrence*. New York: Atheneum, 1990.

Books

Anderson, Scott. *Lawrence in Arabia: War, Deceit, Imperial Folly and the Making of the Modern Middle East*. New York: Anchor Books, 2014.

Antonius, George. *The Arab Awakening: The Story of the Arab National Movement*. London and New York: Allegro Editions, 1939.

Arad, Gulie Ne'eman. *America, Its Jews, and the Rise of Nazism*. Bloomington: Indiana University Press, 2000.

Atkinson, Rick. *An Army at Dawn: The War in North Africa, 1942–1943*. New York: Henry Holt and Co., 2002.

Barr, James. *A Line in the Sand: The Anglo-French Struggle for the Middle East 1914–1948*. New York and London: W. W. Norton and Co., 2012.

Berenbaum, Michael, ed. *Not Your Father's Antisemitism: Hatred of the Jews in the Twenty-First Century*. St. Paul, MN: Paragon House, 2008.

———. *A Promise to Remember: The Holocaust in the Words and Voices of Its Survivors*. Boston: Bulfinch Press, 2003.

———. *Witness to the Holocaust*. New York: HarperCollins, 1997.

Bergman, Ronen. *Rise and Kill First: The Secret History of Israel's Targeted Assassinations*. New York: Random House, 2018.

Breitman, Richard, and Allan J. Lichtman, *FDR and the Jews*. Cambridge, MA: Harvard University Press, 2013.

Browning, Christopher R. *The Origins of the Final Solution: The Evolution of Nazi Jewish Policy, September 1939–March 1942*. Lincoln and Jerusalem: University of Nebraska Press and Yad Vashem, 2004.

Epstein, Lawrence J. *The Dream of Zion: The Story of the First Zionist Congress*. Lanham: Rowman & Littlefield, 2016.

Erbelding, Rebecca. *Rescue Board: The Untold Story of America's Efforts to Save the Jews of Europe*. New York: Anchor, 2018.

Feingold, Henry L. *The Politics of Rescue: The Roosevelt Administration and the Holocaust*. New Brunswick, NJ: Rutgers University Press, 1970.

———. *A Time for Searching: Entering the Mainstream*. Baltimore: Johns Hopkins University Press, 1992.

Friedman, David. *Sledgehammer: How Breaking with the Past Brought Peace to the Middle East*. New York: Broadside Books, 2022.

Gay, Peter. *The Cultivation of Hatred: The Bourgeois Experience, Victoria to Freud*. New York: W. W. Norton and Co., reprint edition, 1994.

Gilbert, Martin. *Churchill and the Jews: A Lifelong Friendship*. New York: Henry Holt and Company, 2007.

Gordis, Daniel. *The Promise of Israel*. Hoboken: John Wiley & Sons, 2012.

———. *We Stand Divided: The Rift Between American Jews and Israel*. New York: HarperCollins, 2019.

Hazony, Yoram. *The Jewish State*. New York: Basic Books, 2000.

Herf, Jeffrey. *Israel's Moment: International Support for and Opposition to Establishing the Jewish State, 1945–1949*. New York: Cambridge University Press, 2022.

Hilberg, Raul. *Sources of Holocaust Research: An Analysis*. Chicago: Ivan R. Dee, 2001.

Hoffman, Bruce. *Anonymous Soldiers: The Struggle for Israel, 1917–1947*. New York: Alfred A. Knopf, 2015.

Johnson, Paul. *A History of the Jews*. New York: Harper Perennial, 1988.

Julius, Anthony. *Trials of the Diaspora: A History of Anti-Semitism in England*. Oxford: Oxford University Press, 2010.

Karsh, Efraim. *Palestine Betrayed*. New Haven and London: Yale University Press, 2010.

———, and Inari Karsh. *Empires of the Sand: The Struggle for Mastery in the Middle East 1789–1923*. Cambridge and London, Harvard University Press, 1999.

Kertzer, David I. *The Pope at War: The Secret History of Pius XII, Mussolini, and Hitler*. New York: Random House, 2022.

Kranzler, David. *Thy Brother's Blood: The Orthodox Jewish Response During the Holocaust*. Brooklyn: Mesorah Publications, 1987.

Laqueur, Walter. *A History of Zionism*. New York: Schocken Books, 1972, 2003.

———. *The Terrible Secret: Suppression of the Truth About Hitler's "Final Solution."* Boston and Toronto: Little, Brown and Co., 1980.

Leff, Laurel. *Buried by the Times: The Holocaust and America's Most Important Newspaper.* New York: Cambridge University Press, 2005.

Lipstadt, Deborah. *Playing the Blame Game: American Jews Look Back at the Holocaust.* Ann Arbor: University of Michigan, Jean & Samuel Frankel Center for Judaic Studies, 2011.

Longerich, Peter. *Wannsee: The Road to the Final Solution.* New York: Oxford University Press, 2021.

Makovsky, Michael. *Churchill's Promised Land: Zionism and Statecraft.* New Haven: Yale University Press, 2008.

Mandelbaum, Michael. *The Frugal Superpower.* New York: PublicAffairs, 2010.

McCullough, David. *The American Spirit: Who We Are and What We Stand For.* New York: Simon & Schuster, 2017.

McMeekin, Sean. *The Berlin-Baghdad Express: The Ottoman Empire and Germany's Bid for World Power.* Cambridge, MA: Harvard University Press, 2010.

Mead, Walter Russell. *The Arc of a Covenant: The United States, Israel, and the Fate of the Jewish People.* New York: Alfred A. Knopf, 2022.

Medoff, Rafael. *The Jews Should Keep Quiet: Franklin D. Roosevelt, Rabbi Stephen S. Wise, and the Holocaust.* Philadelphia: The Jewish Publication Society, 2019.

Morse, Arthur D. *While Six Million Died: A Chronicle of American Apathy.* New York: Random House, 1968.

O'Brien, Conor Cruise. *The Siege: The Sage of Israel and Zionism.* New York: Simon and Schuster, 1986.

Olson, Jess. *Nathan Birnbaum and Jewish Modernity: Architect of Zionism, Yiddishism, and Orthodoxy.* Stanford, CA: Stanford University Press, 2013.

Oren, Michael B. *Six Days of War: June 1967 and the Making of the Modern Middle East.* Oxford: Oxford University Press, 2002.

Nagorski, Adam. *1941: The Year Germany Lost the War.* New York: Simon & Schuster, 2019

Richman, Rick. *Racing Against History: The 1940 Campaign for a Jewish Army to Fight Hitler.* New York: Encounter Books, 2018.

Sanders, Ronald. *The High Walls of Jerusalem: A History of the Balfour Declaration and the Birth of the British Mandate for Palestine.* New York: Holt, Rinehart and Winston, 1983.

Schneer, Jonathan. *The Balfour Declaration: The Origins of the Arab-Israeli Conflict.* New York: Random House, 2012.

Segev, Tom. *One Palestine, Complete: Jews and Arabs Under the British Mandate.* London: Abacus, 2001.

Shain, Yossi. *The Israeli Century: How the Zionist Revolution Changed History and Reinvented Judaism.* New York: Wicked Son, 2021.

Shapira, Anita. *Ben-Gurion—Father of Modern Israel.* New Haven, CT: Yale University Press, 2015.

———. *Israel: A History.* Boston: Brandeis University Press, 2012.

Simms, Brendan, and Charlie Laderman, *Hitler's American Gamble: Pearl Harbor and Germany's March to Global War*. New York: Basic Books, 2021.

Sinkoff, Nancy. *From Left to Right: Lucy S. Dawidowicz, the New York Intellectuals, and the Politics of Jewish History*. Detroit: Wayne State University Press, 2020.

Stein, Leonard. *The Balfour Declaration*. New York: Simon and Schuster, 1961.

Tuchman, Barbara W. *Bible and Sword: England and Palestine from the Bronze Age to Balfour*. New York: Random House, 1984.

Waldman, Nahum M., ed. *Community and Culture—Essays in Jewish Studies*. Philadelphia: Gratz College Seth Press, 1987.

Walzer, Michael. *Exodus and Revolution*. United States: Basic Books, 1986.

Wasserstein, Bernard. *Britain and the Jews of Europe 1939–1945*. London: Institute of Jewish Affairs, 1979.

Waxman, Dov. *The Israeli-Palestinian Conflict: What Everyone Needs to Know*. New York: Oxford University Press, 2019.

———. *Trouble in the Tribe: The American Jewish Conflict Over Israel*. Princeton and Oxford: Princeton University Press, 2016.

Weiss, Bari. *How to Fight Anti-Semitism*. New York: Crown, 2019.

Wyman, David S. *The Abandonment of the Jews: America and the Holocaust, 1941–1945*. New York: Pantheon Books, 1984; and an examination of the files of various participants in the archives of FDR Library.

Zipperstein, Steven J. *Pogrom: Kishinev and the Tilt of History*. New York: Liveright Publishing, 2018.

Articles

Abrams, Elliott. "If American Jews and Israel Are Drifting Apart, What's the Reason?" *Mosaic*, April 4, 2016.

Adler, Joseph. "Herzl's Philosophy of New Humanism," in *Herzl Year Book*, Vol. 3. New York: Herzl Press, 1959.

Adler-Rudel, S. "The Evian Conference on the Refugee Question," *The Leo Baeck Institute Year Book*, Vol. 13. London: Horovitz Publishing Co., 1968, 235–73.

Arkush, Allan. "Old-New Debate." *Jewish Review of Books*, Spring 2010.

———. "Zionism's Forgotten Father," *Jewish Review of Books*, Fall 2014.

Avineri, Shlomo. "Rereading Herzl's Old-New Land." *Jewish Review of Books*, Summer 2012.

Avishai, Bernard. "Netanyahu's Speech." *The New Yorker*, March 3, 2015.

Balsam, Mashav. "Bowing Out." *Haaretz*, May 3, 2010.

Barone, Michael. "Obama's Quest for a Grand Bargain with Iran Seems Unwise." *Washington Examiner*, February 12, 2015.

BBC News, "Iran Enriching Uranium at Fordo Plant near Qom," January 10, 2012. www.bbc.com/news/world-middle-east-16470100.

Bein, Alex. "The Origin of the Term and Concept 'Zionism,'" *Herzl Year Book*, Vol. 2. New York: Herzl Press, 1959.

Berenbaum, Michael. "Yehuda Bauer's Assessment of the US Government and American Jewry During the Holocaust: An Analysis," *The Journal of Holocaust Research*, Vol. 36, No 1, February 8, 2022, 77–88. DOI: 10.1080/25785648.2021.2023849.

Boyer, John W. "Karl Lueger and the Viennese Jews." *The Leo Baeck Institute Year Book*, Vol. 26, Issue 1, January 1981.

Breitman, Richard, and Alan M. Kraut. "Who Was the 'Mysterious Messenger'?" *Commentary*, October 1983.

Brinkley, Joel. "Eban Withdraws in Parliament Race." *New York Times*, June 16, 1988.

Browning, Christopher R. "When Did They Decide?" *New York Review of Books*, March 24, 2022.

Calder, John. "Abba Eban." *The Guardian*, November 17, 2002.

Caplan, Neil. "Feisal Ibn Husain and the Zionists: A Re-examination with Documents." *International History Review* 5, No. 4, November 1983.

Charney, Marc D. "Abba Eban, Eloquent Defender and Voice of Israel, is Dead at 87." *New York Times*, November 18, 2002.

Churchill, Winston. "Churchill and Lawrence." *Finest Hour* 119, Summer 2003. https://winstonchurchill.org/publications/finest-hour/finest-hour-119/churchill-and-lawrence-lawrence-of-arabia/.

Churchill Project. "Temper, Kennedy, and the Origin of Churchill's 'Wrung like a Chicken,'" May 24, 2021.

Citron, Atay. "Ben Hecht's Pageant-Drama: A Flag Is Born," in Claude Schumacher, *Staging the Holocaust: The Shoah in Drama and Performance*. Cambridge, UK: Cambridge University Press, 1998.

Clawson, Patrick. "New U.S. Tone on Iran," August 16, 2012. www.washington institute.org/ policy-analysis/new-us-tone-iran.

Cloud, David S., Dov Lieber, and Stephen Kalin. "Mideast Talks Seek Greater Unity on Containing Iran." *Wall Street Journal*, March 28, 2022.

Cotler, Irwin. "Combating Iran's Cycle of Denial, Deception, and Delay." *Jerusalem Post*, July 19, 2012.

Dershowitz, Alan. "Why Won't Abbas Accept 'Two States for Two Peoples'?" Gatestone Institute, June 12, 2017. www.gatestoneinstitute.org/10523/abbas-two-states.

Diniejko, Andrzej. "Benjamin Disraeli's *Tancred* as an Imperial Utopia." www.victorianweb.org/authors/disraeli/tancred.html.

Doran, Michael. "Obama's Secret Iran Strategy," *Mosaic*, February 2, 2015.

———, and Tony Badran. "The Realignment." *Tablet*, May 10, 2021.

Estorick, Eric. "The Evian Conference and the Intergovernmental Committee." *The Annals of the American Academy of Political and Social Science*. May 1939, 136–41. www.jstor.org/stable/1021894.

Feith, Douglas J. "The Forgotten History of the Term 'Palestine.'" *Mosaic*, December 13, 2021.

———. "Palestine and Zionism, 1904–1922." http://www.dougfeith.com/docs/Feith_Palestine_and_Zionism_1904-1922.pdf.

———. "Vladimir (Ze'ev) Jabotinsky—A Lecture Commemorating Him." *Jewish Current Issues*, August 22, 2010. www.jpundit.typepad.com/jci/2010/08/vladimir-zeev-jobotinsky-a-lecture-commemorating-him-by-douglas-feith-.html.

Fogelman, Shay. "Herzl, Swords and the Nazi Salute: The Curious History of Jewish Fencers," *Haaretz*, January 30, 2014.

"Founding Father Abba Eban, an Eloquent Statesman, Dies." *Jewish News of Northern California*, November 22, 2002. www.jweekly.com/2002/11/22/founding-father-abba-eban-an-eloquent-statesman-dies/.

Fraenkel, Josef. "The Jewish Chronicle and the Launching of Political Zionism," in *Herzl Year Book*, Vol. 2. New York: Herzl Press, 1959.

Gilbert, Martin. "Lawrence of Judea." *Azure Magazine*, No. 38, Autumn 5770/2009.

Golomb, Jacob. "Transfiguration of the Self in Herzl's Life and in His Literary Fiction." Philosophy Department, Hebrew University, Israel.

Gordis, Daniel. "How American Jews Have Detached Themselves from Jewish Memory." *Mosaic*, April 11, 2016.

———. "Symposium on the Jewish Future," *Commentary*, November 2015.

———. "Why Many American Jews Are Becoming Indifferent or Even Hostile to Israel." *Mosaic*, May 8, 2017.

Gordon, Evelyn. "How a Changing American Liberalism Is Pulling American Jews Away From Israel." *Mosaic*, May 17, 2017.

Gross, John. "Benjamin Disraeli by Adam Kirsch." *Commentary*, October 2008.

Guttentag, Gedalia. "Front-Row Seat to History." *Mishpacha*, December 9, 2020. www.mishpacha.com/front-row-seat-to-history/.

Halkin, Hillel. "Sacrifices." *The New Republic*, December 18, 2005.

Harel, Amos. "The Dramatic Moment When Israel Almost Struck Iran." *Haaretz*, March 24, 2022.

Harries, Owen. "A Reluctant Realist." *New York Times*, March 29, 1998.

Hold, Klaus. "Theodor Herzl and the Crisis of Jewish Self-Understanding," in Mark H. Gelber and Vivian Liska, eds., *Theodor Herzl: From Europe to Zion*.

Hulse, Carl. "Netanyahu Event Similar to a State of the Union Address, but More Electric." *New York Times*, March 3, 2015.

"The 100 Best and Most Influential Non-Fiction Books Written in English Since 1923." *Time Magazine*. http://entertainment.time.com/2011/08/30/all-time-100-best-nonfiction-books/slide/a-child-of-the-century-by-ben-hecht/.

Julius, Anthony. "Judaism's Redefiner." *New York Times*, January 23, 2009.

Kakutani, Michiko. "He Spoke of Art but Made His Money in Movies." *New York Times*, March 1990.

Karsh, Efraim. "The Palestinians and the Right of Return." *Commentary*, May 2001.

Keinon, Herb. "Netanyahu's Man in Washington." *Jerusalem Post*, May 14, 2016.

Kingsley, Patrick. "At Summit, Israel's Ties with Arabs Move from Ceremony to Substance." *New York Times*, March 27, 2022.

Kramer, Martin. "Netanyahu and Churchill: Analogy and Error." March 8, 2015. https://martinkramer.org/2015/03/08/netanyahu-and-churchill-analogy-and-error/.

———. "The Non-Israeli Ambassador," August 12, 2013. https://martinkramer.org/2013/08/12/the-non-israeli-ambassador/.

———. "Three Turning Points That Led to the Birth of the State of Israel." *Mosaic*, May 7, 2019.

Krystal, Arthur. "En Garde! The History of Dueling." *The New Yorker*, March 4, 2007.

Laqueur, Walter. "The Riegner Cable, and the Knowing Failure of the West to Act During the Shoah." *Tablet*, August 9, 2015.

Lazaroff, Tovah. "Lapid Warns That Israel Will Act Alone Against Iran if Needed." *Jerusalem Post*, December 27, 2021.

Leibovitz, Liel. "The 'New York Times' Violates My Protocol." *Tablet*, February 11, 2015.

Letters from Readers. "The Mysterious Messenger." *Commentary*, January 1984.

Libby, Lewis, and Douglas J. Feith. "Biden Shouldn't Underestimate Israel's Resolve in Face of Iranian Nuclear Threat." *National Review*, January 31, 2022.

Loewenberg, Peter. "Theodor Herzl: A Psychoanalytic Study," in Benjamin B. Wolman, *The Psychoanalytic Interpretation of History*. New York: Harper & Row, 1971.

Magnet, Myron. "The Founders' Priceless Legacy." *The New Criterion*, November 2020.

Makovsky, David. "A New Regional Role for Israel, as Washington Shows Signs of Stepping Back." *Jerusalem Post*, March 28, 2022.

Mandelbaum, Michael. "The Six-Day War: 1967's Gift to America." *American Interest*, June 2, 2017.

Marks, Jon. "Ambassador Optimistic About Israel's Future." *Jewish Exponent*, October 25, 2017.

McClay, Wilfred M. "The Claims of Memory." *First Things*, January 2022.

———. "History as a Way of Knowing," September 17, 2021. https://lawliberty.org/history-as-a-way-of-knowing/.

———. "The Mystic Chords of Memory: Reclaiming American History," December 13, 1995. www.heritage.org/note/9836/print-display.

———. "The Weaponization of History." *Wall Street Journal*, August 25, 2019.

Medoff, Rafael. "Ben Hecht's 'A Flag Is Born': A Play That Changed History." The David S. Wyman Institute for Holocaust Studies, www.wymaninstitute.org/2004/04/special-feature-ben-hechts-a-flag-is-born-a-play-that-changed-history/.

"Netanyahu Was Close to Attacking Iran in 2012 Despite Obama—NYT." *Jerusalem Post,* September 5, 2019.

Nolan, Rachel. "Behind the Cover Story: Ronen Bergman on Whether Israel Will Attack Iran." *New York Times*, January 30, 2012. 6thfloor.blogs.nytimes.com/2012/01/30/behind-the-cover-story-ronen-bergman-on-israeli-plans-to-strike-iran/?searchResultPosition=2.

Pearson, Richard. "Israeli Diplomat, Foreign Minister Abba Eban Dies." *Washington Post,* November 18, 2002.

Penslar, Derek J. "Theodor Herzl and the Palestinian Arabs: Myth and Counter-Myth." *Journal of Israeli History*, vol. 24, no. 1, 2005.

Polisar, Daniel. "Herzl's 'The Menorah,'" November 27, 2018. https://tikvahfund.org/library/podcastdaniel-polisar-herzls-menorah/.

———. "The Most Politically Significant Meeting of Any Group of Jews in the Last 1,800 Years." *Mosaic*, August 23, 2017.

Rabinowicz, Oskar K. "Herzl and England," in Raphael Patai, ed., *Herzl Year Book, Vol. III*, Herzl Centennial Issue. New York: Herzl Press, 1960.

Richman, Rick. "Anger Mismanagement." *Commentary*, February 2014.

———. "The 80th Anniversary of the Two-State Solution." *Mosaic*, October 2, 2017.

———. "Jabotinsky's Lost Moment, June 1940." *The Tower*, 2013. www.thetower.org /article/jabotinskys-lost-moment-june-1940/.

———. "Jabotinsky's Novels, and How They Relate to His Politics." *Mosaic*, August 5, 2021.

———. "Netanyahu Must Give That Speech." *Commentary*, February 12, 2015.

———. "Passover 2005—I." April 20, 2005. jpundit.typepad.com/jci/2005/04 /passover_2005_i.html.

———. "70 Years Ago Today." *Commentary*, August 3, 2010.

———. "Where Is Mahmoud Abbas's Bir Zeit Speech?" *Commentary*, June 15, 2010.

———. "Why Jabotinsky Still Matters." *The Tower*, June 2014.

Rindner, Sarah. "Tom Stoppard and Theodor Herzl in Jerusalem." *Mosaic*, March 3, 2022.

Rogers, Belladonna. "Echoes of Churchill Pervade Netanyahu Speech." *Real Clear Politics*, March 7, 2015.

Samuels, David. "The Aspiring Novelist Who Became Obama's Foreign Policy Guru." *New York Times Magazine*, May 5, 2016.

Schoenberg, Philip Ernest. "The American Reaction to the Kishinev Pogrom of 1903." *American Jewish Historical Quarterly*, Vol. LXIII, No. 3, March 1974.

Sheppard, Eugene R. "On Old Stones, a Black Cat, and a New Zion." *Jewish Review of Books*, Fall 2015.

Singh, Michael. "Axis of Abraham: Arab-Israeli Normalization Could Remake the Middle East." *Foreign Affairs*, Vol. 101, No. 2, March/April 2022.

Smith, Charles D. "The Invention of a Tradition: The Question of Arab Acceptance of the Zionist Right to Palestine During World War I." *Journal of Palestine Studies*, Vol. XXII, No. 2, Winter 1993.

Smith, Fred. "Remembering Abba Eban's Rousing Remarks: What He Said to the UN Security Council on Day 2 of the Six-Day War." *New York Daily News*, June 6, 2017.

Stein, Ludwig. "They Have Prevailed: A Tribute to Herzl and Nordau from One Who Was Skeptical," in Meyer W. Weisgal, ed., *Theodore Herzl: A Memorial.* Westport, CT: Hyperion Press, Inc., 1929.

Stults, Taylor. "Roosevelt, Russian Persecution of the Jews, and American Public Opinion." *Jewish Social Studies*, Vol. 33, No. 2, 1974.

Syrkin, Marie. "What American Jews Did During the Holocaust." *Midstream*, October 1982.

"T. E. Lawrence, Faisal and Weizmann: The 1919 Attempt to Secure an Arab Balfour Declaration." *Journal of the Royal Central Asian Society*, Vol. 56, Issue 2, 1969.

Tibor, Amir. "The Ambassador Who Came in from the Cold." *Atlantic*, February 15, 2017.

Tobin, Jonathan. "Netanyahu Must Not Give That Speech." *Commentary*, February 12, 2015.

TOI Staff. "Israel Reportedly Working on Air Defense Pact with Regional Allies." *Times of Israel*, March 29, 2022.

Weber, J. B. "The Kishineff Massacre and Its Bearing upon the Question of Jewish Immigration into the United States." New York, 1903.

Wistrich, Robert S. "Karl Lueger and the Ambiguities of Viennese Antisemitism," in Mark H. Gelber and Vivan Liska, eds., *Theodor Herzl: From Europe to Zion*. Tübingen: Max Niemeyer Verlag, 2007.

———."Theodor Herzl: Between Myth and Messianism," in Mark H. Gelber and Vivian Liska, eds., *Theodor Herzl: From Europe to Zion*. Tübingen: Max Niemeyer Verlag, 2007.

Ph.D. Theses

Kearney, Megan. "Disraeli and Religion." PhD diss., University of Oxford, 2016. https://ora.ox.ac.uk/objects/uuid:8e38d371-cebb-469f-9fab-acf7e81e4d5b.

Laffer, Dennis R. "The Jewish Trail of Tears: The Evian Conference of July 1938." PhD diss., University of South Florida, 2011. www.researchgate.net/publication/254706382_The_Jewish_Trail_of_Tears_The_Evian_Conference_of_July_1938.

PHOTOGRAPH AND IMAGE CREDITS

1. THE MYSTERY OF THEODOR HERZL

p. 6 Theodor Herzl in 1897. *Public Domain/Wikimedia Commons.*

p. 9 David Ben-Gurion reading Israel's Declaration of Independence, May 14, 1948. *Rudi Weissenstein, Israel Foreign Ministry.*

p. 40 First Page of Herzl's "Letter to the Jewish People," November 1903. Photo by Rick Richman. Source: *Jüdisches Lexikon*, Vol. II, facing 1572 (Berlin: Jüdischer Verlag, 1928).

2. LOUIS D. BRANDEIS: THE AMERICAN PROPHET

p. 46 Louis D. Brandeis, No Later Than 1916. *Harris & Ewing, Public Domain/Wikimedia Commons.*

p. 53 Louis Brandeis, Cover of "Call to the Educated Jew," Avukah American Student Zionist Federation pamphlet, 1936. Image by Rick Richman and David Richman.

p. 61 Balfour Declaration. *Public Domain/Wikimedia Commons.*

3. CHAIM WEIZMANN AND THE FIRST ARAB-ZIONIST ALLIANCE

p. 66 Chaim Weizmann, 1918. *Public Domain/Wikimedia Commons.*

p. 72 Weizmann Meets with Emir Faisal at his military headquarters, June 4, 1918. *Public Domain/Wikimedia Commons.*

p. 74 T. E. Lawrence map presented to the British War Cabinet in November 1918. *Public Domain/Wikimedia Commons.*

p. 76 Last Page of Faisal-Weizmann Agreement with T. E. Lawrence's Translation of Faisal's Caveat. *Public Domain/Wikimedia Commons.*

p. 77 Jewish National Home Boundaries Presented to the 1919 Paris Peace Conference. *Briangotts/Public Domain/Wikimedia Commons GNU Free Documentation License.*

p. 79 Faisal at the 1919 Paris Peace Conference. *Public Domain/Wikimedia Commons.*

p. 83 Churchill, Lawrence, and Abdullah in Jerusalem, 1921. *Public Domain/Wikimedia Commons.*

p. 85 British Mandate for Palestine, 1922. *Unknown source.*

p. 88 Weizmann testifying to UN Special Committee on Palestine. *Public Domain/Wikimedia Commons.*

4. VLADIMIR JABOTINSKY AND THE PEEL PROPHECIES

p. 92 Vladimir Jabotinsky in 1926. *Public Domain/Wikimedia Commons.*

p. 97 Jabotinsky with Jewish Legion soldiers, 1918. *Jabotinsky Institute in Israel.*

p. 99 Jabotinsky testifying before Peel Commission, 1937. *Jabotinsky Institute in Israel.*

p. 107 Peel Commission Proposed Partition of Palestine, 1937. *World History Archive, Alamy.*

p. 109 Jabotinsky Map I. Image by Rick Richman. Source: "The Threatened Partition of Palestine," Address to Members of Parliament, London, July 13, 1937. *Jabotinsky Institute in Israel.*

p. 109 Jabotinsky Map II. Image by Rick Richman. Source: "The Threatened Partition of Palestine," Address to Members of Parliament, London, July 13, 1937. *Jabotinsky Institute in Israel.*

p. 110 Jabotinsky Map III. Image by Rick Richman. Source: "The Threatened Partition of Palestine," Address to Members of Parliament, London, July 13, 1937. *Jabotinsky Institute in Israel.*

p. 114 UN Resolution 181 Partition Plan, November 29, 1947. Copyright 2005 by Eli E. Hertz. Published with permission.

p. 120 Jabotinsky with Menachem Begin in Poland, 1939. *Jabotinsky Institute in Israel.*

p. 121 Crowd at Jabotinsky funeral. *Jabotinsky Institute in Israel.*

p. 121 Crowds on both sides of Second Avenue for Jabotinsky funeral cortege. *Jabotinsky Institute in Israel.*

p. 121 Jabotinsky's grave on Mount Herzl. *Marco Plassio, Wikimedia Commons.*

5. GOLDA MEIR: PORTRAIT OF THE LIONESS AS A YOUNG WOMAN

p. 124 Golda Mabovitch in Milwaukee, 1914. *Public Domain/Wikimedia Commons.*

p. 127 Golda with her husband, Morris Meyerson. *UMW Libraries Digital Collections.*

p. 138 British Cartoon in *New York Times*, July 1938. www.collections.ushmm.org/search/catalog/pa4351, U.S. Holocaust Memorial Museum, copyright unknown. Source: Michael Berenbaum, *The World Must Know: The History of the Holocaust.*

p. 142 Myron C. Taylor addressing Evian Conference, July 1937. *Public Domain/Wikimedia Commons.*

p. 143 Lord Winterton speaking at Evian Conference, 1938. *Ullstein Bild Dtl. / Getty Images.*

p. 146 Henri Berenger (France), Myron C. Taylor (U.S.), Lord Winterton (Britain)

Evian 1938. *U.S. Holocaust Memorial Museum, National Archives and Records Administration, College Park, Md.*

6. BEN HECHT AND THE SOUL OF AMERICAN JEWS

p. 154 Ben Hecht, circa 1940. *Everett Collection, Alamy.*
p. 158 Frankfurt synagogue destroyed in Kristallnacht, 1938. *Chronicle, Alamy.*
p. 161 *New York Times* headline, March 1, 1942. Image by Rick Richman.
p. 163 *New York Times* headline, June 30, 1942. Image by Rick Richman.
p. 167 *New York Times* headline, December 9, 1942. Image by Rick Richman.
p. 171 "We Will Never Die" at Madison Square Garden, March 9, 1943. *Bettman, Getty Images.*

7. THE TRIUMPH AND TRAGEDY OF ABBA EBAN

p. 184 Aubrey S. (Abba) Eban with Foreign Minister Moshe Sharett at UN, 1949. *Israel Ministry of Foreign Affairs.*
p. 192 Abba Eban at UN Security Council, June 6, 1967. *Keystone Pictures USA, Alamy.*
p. 194 Henry Kissinger and Abba Evan, January 17, 1974. *Everett Collection, Alamy.*

8. RON DERMER: THE AMERICAN ISRAELI AMBASSADOR

p. 204 Ambassador Ron Dermer, 2014. *Facebook, Ambassador Dermer.*
p. 209 Ron Dermer with Netanyahu in Official Announcement photo, 2013. *Israel Government Press Office.*
p. 213 Map of Iran with Iraq and Afghanistan. *Peter Hermes Furian, Alamy.*
p. 216 Pre-Election Rally in Iran, June 5, 2009. *AFP Photo/Behrouz Mehri. Getty Images.*
p. 218 Post-Election Protest in Iran, June 15, 2009. *Getty Images/Stringer.*
p. 223 Churchill addressing Canadian Parliament, December 30, 1941. *Alamy.*
p. 224 Netanyahu addressing U.S. Congress, March 3, 2015. *Alamy.*
p. 226 Ambassador Ron Dermer in Congress after Netanyahu speech. *Jonathan Ernst/Reuters/Alamy.*

NOTES

Front Matter

The title of this book comes from Micah 4:4 (". . . they shall sit every man under his vine and under his fig tree; And none shall make them afraid"). The phrase also appears in Ezekiel 34:28 ("And they shall no more be a prey to the nations . . . and none shall make them afraid"); Isaiah 17:2 (prophesying that "the remnant of Aram shall be as the glory of the children of Israel . . . and none shall make them afraid"); Jeremiah 27:28 ("Jacob shall again be quiet and at ease, And none shall make him afraid"); and Zephaniah 3:13 ("The remnant of Israel . . . shall feed and lie down, And none shall make them afraid"); cf. Leviticus 26:6 ("And I will give peace in the land, and ye shall lie down, and none shall make you afraid; and I will cause evil beasts to cease out of the land, neither shall the sword go through your land").

President George Washington used the passage from Micah in his letter to the Touro Synagogue in Newport, Rhode Island, in 1790, welcoming Jews as citizens of the new United States of America. www.au.org/wp-content/uploads/migration/pdf_documents/washingtons-letter-to-touro.pdf.

The sources of the epigraphs are: (1) Bari Weiss, *How to Fight Antisemitism*, New York: Crown, 2019, 205–6; and (2) Dara Horn, "Dreams for Living Jews," *SAPIR*, Vol. 4, Winter 2022.

Introduction

The Ben-Gurion quotation is from his Foreword to the *State of Israel Government Yearbook, 5712 (1951/52)* (Jerusalem: Government Printer, 1951).

1. "Annual Address of the President of the American Historical Association, Minneapolis, December 29, 1931," *American Historical Review*, Vol. 37, No. 2, 221–36 (emphasis added).

2. See David Gelernter, *Americanism: The Fourth Great Western Religion* (New York: Doubleday, 2007).

3. Both Jewish and American historians have recognized that the function of history extends beyond scholarly study. Columbia University professor Yosef Hayim Yerushalmi, the preeminent Jewish historian of the twentieth century, emphasized the "value of Jewish history itself, not for the scholar, but for the Jewish people." Hillsdale College Professor Wilfred McClay, author of *Land of Hope: An Invitation to the Great American Story*, has similarly stressed the importance of American history

to the American people: we "have to learn, or relearn, our story. In so doing, we will discover that we also are learning about ourselves, and about all the things of which ordinary people are capable—even us. " Remarks by Wilfred M. McClay at the 18th Annual Bradley Prize Ceremony, Washington, DC, May 17, 2022.

4. See Anita Shapira, *Ben-Gurion—Father of Modern Israel* (New Haven, CT: Yale University Press, 2015); Neil Rogachevsky, "Ben-Gurion: The Man Who Willed a State." *Mosaic*, July 1, 2020; but see Benzion Netanyahu, *The Founding Fathers of Zionism* (Jerusalem and New York: Balfour Books, 2012), which lists the "founding fathers" of Jewish nationalism as Leo Pinsker, Theodor Herzl, Max Nordau, Israel Zangwill, and Vladimir Jabotinsky.

1. The Mystery Of Theodor Herzl

1. Diary entry for June 1, 1901, Paris. See Theodor Herzl, *The Complete Diaries of Theodor Herzl*, Raphael Patai, ed., Harry Zohn, trans. (New York: Thomas Yoseloff Ltd., 1960), Vol. III, 1151. The translation in the text is from Robert S. Wistrich, "Theodor Herzl: Between Myth and Messianism," Mark H. Gelber and Vivian Liska, eds., *Theodor Herzl: From Europe to Zion* (Tübingen: Max Niemeyer Verlag, 2007), 22.

2. "PM Netanyahu's Remarks at the Official Memorial Ceremony for Benjamin Zeev Herzl," July 13, 2017, https://www.gov.il/en/departments/news/speechherzel 130717.

3. Oskar K. Rabinowicz, "Herzl and England," in Raphael Patai ed., *Herzl Year Book,* Vol. III, Herzl Centennial Issue (New York: Herzl Press, 1960), 37.

4. "PM Netanyahu Addresses the Official Ceremony for Benjamin Ze'ev Herzl," July 26, 2016, https://mfa.gov.il/MFA/PressRoom/2016/Pages/PM-Netanyahu-addresses-official-memorial-ceremony-for-Benjamin-Zeev-Herzl-26-July-2016.aspx: "Even today, [Herzl's] tremendous boldness in approaching world leaders and influential people is astonishing."

5. There is a dispute among biographers as to whether Herzl had a bar mitzvah or a confirmation: *Cf.* Jacob de Haas, *Theodor Herzl: A Biographical Study* (Chicago and New York: The Leonard Company, 1927), Vol. I, 33 ("The announcement card used the word 'confirmation,' a term employed by the socially advanced Reform Jews. Actually he was 'Bar Mitzva,' according to orthodox usage."); Ludwig Lewisohn, *Theodor Herzl: A Portrait for This Age* (Cleveland and New York: World Publishing Co., 1955), 37 ("He was, it would appear, called to the Torah as a bar mitzvah, despite the word 'confirmation' . . . ").

6. See Herzl's diary entry for December 24, 1895, *Complete Diaries*, Vol. I, 285:

> I was just lighting the Christmas tree for my children when [Chief Rabbi of Vienna] Gudemann arrived. He seemed upset by the "Christian" custom. . . . I don't mind if they call it the Hanukah tree—or the winter solstice.

7. See, e.g., Jacques Kornberg, *Theodor Herzl: From Assimilation to Zionism* (Bloomington: Indiana University Press, 1993), 1, where Kornberg writes "that the Dreyfus case had no impact on Herzl's conversion to Zionism"; Shlomo Avineri,

Herzl: Theodor Herzl and the Foundation of the Jewish State (London: Weidenfeld & Nicolson, 2013), 66:

> During Herzl's time in Paris the trial had only begun and had not yet turned into a historic controversy. . . . While the common wisdom is that the Dreyfus affair triggered Herzl's Zionism, there is in fact no evidence of this, not in Herzl's voluminous diaries nor in the many articles he sent from Paris to his newspaper in Vienna.

8. Diary entry for September 3, 1897, *Complete Diaries*, Vol. II, 581. In another part of the same entry, Herzl explained what he meant by having "founded the Jewish state" at Basel:

> The foundation of a State lies in the will of the people for a State. . . . Territory is only the material basis; the State, even when it possesses territory, is always something abstract. . . . At Basel, then, I created the abstraction which, as such, is invisible to the vast majority of people. . . . I gradually worked the people into the mood for a State and made them feel that they were its National Assembly.

See Martin Kramer, "Three Turning Points That Led to the Birth of the State of Israel," *Mosaic*, May 7, 2019: "As [Herzl] writes these words, there are only about 50,000 Jews in the Land of Israel, fewer than half of one percent of the world's Jews." Perhaps Herzl was familiar with an 1882 lecture by the French historian Ernest Renan (1823–1892) titled "What Is a Nation?" Herzl's assertion that he "founded the Jewish state" at Basel is consistent Renan's assertion that a "nation" is not based on geography or race, but rather "is a soul, a spiritual principle" consisting of two things that are "really one and the same":

> One is the past, the other is the present. One is the possession in common of a rich legacy of memories; the other is present-day consent, the desire to live together, the desire to perpetuate the value of the heritage that one has received. . . . The nation, like the individual, is the culmination of a long past of endeavors, sacrifices, and devotion. . . . To have common glories in the past and to have a common will in the present; to have performed great deeds together, to wish to perform still more—these are the essential qualities.

Ernest Renan, "What Is a Nation?" in Geoff Eley and Ronald Grigor Suny, eds., *Becoming National: A Reader*, Martin Thom, trans. (Oxford and New York: Oxford University Press, 1996), 41–55.

9. David Ben-Gurion, Preface to Ludwig Lewisohn, *Theodor Herzl*, 11. See also, David Ben-Gurion, "Herzl's Dream—and the Reality," *New York Times*, May 1, 1960:

> For hundreds of years, throughout the world, the Jewish people had been no more than a pawn and a plaything—for chastisement or for kindness—in the hands of foreign political forces. Herzl took human dust, at the mercy of any capricious wind, and made it into a nation striving to mold its own destiny. . . .

10. Richard J. H. Gottheil, *Zionism* (Philadelphia: Jewish Publication Society of America, 1914), 95. Gottheil and his wife attended the Second Zionist Congress, where he served as a member of the Presidium and was elected to the Executive Committee. Haiyim J. Orlan, "The Participants in the First Zionist Congress, *Herzl Year Book*, Vol. II, 150.

11. The text of Nordau's address is in Michael J. Riemer, *The First Zionist Congress: An Annotated Translation of the Proceedings* (Albany: State University of New York Press, 2019), 97–109. See George L. Mosse, "Max Nordau and His Degeneration," Introduction to Max Nordau, *Degeneration* (Lincoln and London: University of Nebraska Press, 1993), xiii. At the First Zionist Congress, Nordau was elected as First Vice President.

12. Shlomo Avineri, *The Making of Modern Zionism: The Intellectual Origins of the Jewish State* (New York: Basic Books, 1981), 5.

13. Ibid., 5–6.

14. Carl E. Schorske, *Fin-de-Siècle Vienna: Politics and Culture* (New York: Vintage Books, 1981), 146.

15. Ibid., 147.

16. A historian (Adolf von Harnack) who joined another of the German dueling fraternities at a different university found that:

> the members were drawn from the sons of noble families, circles of the so-called literati (members of the free professions) and commercial circles. . . . [T]here was no aristocratic narrowness, but genuine liberality.

Quoted in Peter Gay, *The Cultivation of Hatred: The Bourgeois Experience, Victoria to Freud* (New York: W. W. Norton and Co., reprint edition, 1994), 17.

17. As a Zionist commentator noted in 1927, in an essay reviewing Herzl's early days:

> From the days of [Moses] Mendelssohn, Jews had been living under the seductive spell of political emancipation and cultural enlightenment. . . . In such a milieu it was inevitable that the Jewish problem should be conceived not as the problem of the Jewish people, but of the individual Jew.

Barnett Brickner, "Vindication and Triumph: The Theoretic and Practical Success of Herzl's Aims," in Meyer W. Weisgal, ed., *Theodor Herzl: A Memorial* (Westport, CT: Hyperion Press, Inc., 1929), 264.

18. Near the end of the novel, Tancred sets forth his newly informed religious views, telling another character that Jesus was "the descendant of King David as well as the Son of God," and:

> Through this last and greatest of [Jewish] princes it was ordained that the inspired Hebrew mind should mold and govern the world. Through Jesus God spoke to the Gentiles, and not to the tribes of Israel only. . . . Christianity is Judaism for the multitude, but still it is Judaism. . . . [*Tancred*, Kindle edition, 401].

19. Some biographers have speculated that Herzl chose the name "Tancred Herzl" because it was the name of a leader of the First Crusade that liberated Jerusalem. See e.g., Avineri, *Herzl and the Foundation of the Jewish State*, 57. But during his years as a student, Herzl saw the character of "Tancred" not as a historic conqueror of the Holy Land, but rather as a modern enlightened Christian; Herzl's ambition was to assimilate into the Viennese elite, not to liberate Palestine.

20. Leo Pinsker, *Road to Freedom: Writings and Addresses* (New York: Scopus Publishing Co., 1944).

21. More than 110 towns in Russia were subjected to pogroms. John Doyle Klier, *Russia, Jews and the Pogroms of 1881–1882* (New York and Cambridge: Cambridge University Press, 2011), xxii–xxiv (listing the towns).

22. David Ben-Gurion, Preface to Ludwig Lewisohn, *Theodor Herzl: A Portrait for This Age*, 10.

23. Amos Elon, *Herzl* (New York: Holt, Rinehart and Winston, 1975), 59.

24. Leo Pinsker, Letter to Dr. I. Ruelf, dated January 30, 1884, in Leo Pinsker, *Road to Freedom*, 137:

> [N]o sane person can speak of [Jewish government] at this time. . . .
> *This work, which still surpasses the ability of our generation, is most difficult of execution even in the established and foremost countries of Europe.* . . . [W]e first need to uproot old, established principles. . . . But who can give us the mythological Hercules to clean out the stables of Augeas? *Who—the trumpet of the Messiah, to arouse these half-alive people? For this there is needed a whole legion of prophets, in order to breathe a life-giving spirit of enthusiasm into this pile of debris.* [Emphasis added.]

25. Yoram Hazony, *The Jewish State: The Struggle for Israel's Soul* (New York: Basic Books, 2000), 84. See "Wilhelm Marr," Jewish Virtual Library:

> Marr's conception of antisemitism focused on the supposed racial, as opposed to religious, characteristics of the Jews. His organization, the League of Antisemites, introduced the word "antisemite" into the political lexicon and established the first popular political movement based entirely on anti-Jewish beliefs. Marr's often-reprinted political tract, "The Victory of Judaism over Germandom," warned that "the Jewish spirit and Jewish consciousness have overpowered the world." He called for resistance against "this foreign power" before it was too late.

See also "Marr, Wilhelm," https://www.britannica.com/biography/Wilhelm-Marr.

26. Avineri, *Herzl and the Foundation of the Jewish State*, 40:

> The new racial anti-Semitism, aimed at the Jews' economic success and their integration into European culture, did not emerge from the unschooled masses. It became popular among intellectuals, among professors and students at the universities. Racial anti-Semitism was from the start an intellectual movement, its claims grounded, according to its advocates, in the discoveries of biological and

anthropological sciences in the wake of Darwin's doctrine of the survival of the fittest.

27. Alex Bein, *Theodore Herzl* (Philadelphia: The Jewish Publication Society of America, 1941), 36–37 ("the reading of this book must have [had] the effect . . . of a blow between the eyes. The observations set down in his diary burn with indignation."). Elon, *Herzl*, 57 ("Dühring's book shocked him").

28. Quoted in Bein, *Herzl*, 38; Avineri, *Herzl and the Foundation of the Jewish State*, 54.

29. *Complete Diaries*, 4, May-June 1895.

30. Quoted in Bein, *Herzl*, 38. See also Ernst Pawel, *The Labyrinth of Exile: A Life of Theodor Herzl* (New York: Farrar, Straus and Giroux, 1989), 77:

> [M]ost Jews preferred to see [anti-Semitism] as a temporary aberration, the dying echo of medieval superstitions. They clung to their faith in progress and in the eventual triumph of the Enlightenment. . . . Herzl shared their illusions, and perhaps it was in order to preserve them that he never so much as mentioned Tisza-Eszlar [tried for ritual murder in 1882], which for nearly two years made headlines throughout Europe, just as he ignored the bloody Russian pogroms of 1881. . . .
>
> Herzl's reaction to Dühring—that peculiar mix of outrage, admiration, and denial—was an attitude rather typical of Austria's assimilated Jews and their refusal to acknowledge the unmistakable changes in the atmosphere.

31. Kornberg, *Theodor Herzl*, 50–51, quoting the *Neue Freie Presse* account of the event.

32. Herzl's letter to Albia read as follows:

> [F]rom the standpoint of liberty, non-Jews should also denounce this [anti-Semitic] tendency, since if you do not protest forcefully against these developments, you are actually identifying with them. *Qui tacet, consentire videtur* ["he who keeps silent is seen to consent"]. . . . There is no doubt that I myself, burdened with the defect of *Semitism*—a word yet unknown at the time of my entry into the fraternity—would not have now applied to Albia, nor would I have been accepted today. . . . I therefore ask you to release me from my membership.

Avineri, *Herzl and the Foundation of the Jewish State*, 56–57; Amos Elon, *Herzl*, 60, has a longer and slightly different translation:

> I would mention incidentally that as a lover of liberty, even as a non-Jew, I would have to condemn this [anti-Semitic] movement which my fraternity seems to have joined. I say "seems to," for when one does not protest audibly against such events, one shares responsibility for them. *Qui tacet, consentire videtur!* [He who keeps silent, seems to be consenting.] . . . It is pretty clear that handicapped as I am by the impediment of *Semitism* (the word was not yet known at the time of my entry), I would today refrain from seeking membership in the fraternity. It would probably refuse me anyway, for the above-mentioned

reason. It must therefore be obvious to every decent person that I do not wish to retain my membership.

33. Pawel, *Labyrinth of Exile*, 71.

34. Ibid., 70. Kornberg believes that Herzl hoped that assimilation would transform and perfect Jews. Kornberg, *Theodor Herzl*, 53:

> Antisemitism had not suddenly taken over Albia. It was not a turning point, and Herzl had long accepted Albia's animus toward the "Jewish spirit." Herzl was not protesting against anti-Jewishness, which was compatible with full assimilation, but against racial antisemitism, which sought to drive Jews back into the ghetto.

35. See Benzion Netanyahu, Introduction to Pinsker, *Road to Freedom*, 55:

> In 1882 . . . the situation seemed to be well in hand. . . . Nothing could shatter the deep-rooted illusion that [Jewish] equality was irrevocable, not even the riots that broke out in Germany the year before, nor the blood accusation hurled against the Jews of Hungary, nor the first anti-Semitic congress that convened in the same year at Dresden. These "new" manifestations were regarded by them as summer storms of short duration.

See Kornberg, *Theodor Herzl*, 22:

> In viewing Dühring's antisemitism as a remnant of the Middle Ages, Herzl had not yet grasped late-nineteenth-century antisemitism as a post-emancipation phenomenon, a backlash response to the entrance of Jews into European civil society, part of a rising tide of opposition to changes brought about by liberalism and capitalism in European politics and society. This view of antisemitism would come to him only a decade later.

36. Peter Gay, *The Cultivation of Hatred*, 544, note 19:

> In the course of the nineteenth century, the medieval caricature of the Jew as Christ-killer waned as racial anti-Semites began to draw another, if anything more lethal, caricature, the Jew by racial endowment always the same, no matter what his family history, his environment, his convictions.

37. Quoted by Elon, *Herzl,* 84 (citing Herzl, *Buch de Narrheit,* 243).

38. *Complete Diaries*, Vol. I, 7.

39. Herzl's play was produced in Israel for the first time in 2021. See Sarah Rindner, "Tom Stoppard and Theodor Herzl in Jerusalem," *Mosaic*, March 3, 2022. In *Herzl*, Amos Elon renders Jacob Samuel's dying words as having an additional phrase at the end: "Jews, my brothers, there'll come a time when they'll let you live—*when you know how to die*." [Emphasis added.] Rindner writes that Herzl had the phrase in the original draft of his play, but took it out at the suggestion of his friend Arthur Schnitzler: "Yehuda Moraly, who directed the [Israeli] production . . . felt it was important to put the phrase back in."

40. *Complete Diaries*, Vol. I, 11.

41. *The Diaries of Theodor Herzl*, trans. Marvin Lowenthal (New York: Grosset & Dunlap, 1962), 69. There is a slightly different translation in *Complete Diaries*, Vol. I, 244, which translates the final phrase as "the hearts of these people" rather than "the heart of the people."

42. *Complete Diaries*, Vol. I, 13.

43. Ibid., 14.

44. Ibid., 16. In his address to the Fifth Zionist Congress in Basel, on December 26, 1901, Herzl would address the failure of philanthropists to solve the Jewish Question:

> You know that many have tried their hand at this task which confronts us, animated by good intentions and moreover with great material means at their disposal. But you also know that these attempts came to nothing. Why? Because they all set out from a false premise. They said: "In the beginning is money." No! In the beginning is the idea! Money will secure hirelings, but it will not arouse a people. Only an idea will bring this to pass. And it has brought it to pass.

The Congress Addresses of Theodor Herzl (New York: Federation of American Zionists, 1917), 25/41.

45. *Complete Diaries*, Vol. I, 17. See Pawel, *Labyrinth of Exile*, 217–18.

46. *Diaries of Theodor Herzl,* 21. *Complete Diaries*, Vol. I, 27 translates the paragraph as follows:

> I still lack the aplomb which will increase in me with time, because it is necessary to someone who wants to break down opposition, stir the indifferent, comfort the distressed, inspire a craven, demoralized people, and associate with the lords of the world.

47. *Complete Diaries*, Vol. I, 38.

48. Ibid., 61.

49. Ibid., 94.

50. Ibid., 109–11, 118.

51. In *The Jewish State*, Herzl argued "[t]he world will be freed by our liberty." Herzl, *The Jewish State* (New York: Dover Publications, 1988), 157. Cf. Nahum Goldmann, "The Road Towards an Unfulfillable Idea," in *Herzl Year Book*, Vol. 3 (New York: Herzl Press, 1959), 131, 138:

> *Herzl's Zionism*—to put it very simply—*had two aspects: a Jewish one and a universal one.* The Jewish aspect consisted in ensuring the survival of the Jewish people; the universal one consisted in fulfilling by means of our own State and our own Jewish life and culture, the great basic ideas of our national existence. [Emphasis added.]

See also Barnett Brickner, "Vindication and Triumph: The Theoretic and Practical Success of Herzl's Aims," in *Herzl: A Memorial,* 264: "Herzl dared challenge not only the validity of the formulation of the Jewish problem by the assimilationists, but also its solution. He was the prophet of modern progressive Jewish nationalism." Robert S. Wistrich, "Theodor Herzl: Between Myth and Messianism."

52. *Complete Diaries*, 181, 183.

53. The title of Herzl's pamphlet "Der Judenstaat," is translated by some as "The State of the Jews." The subtitle was "Proposal of a modern solution for the Jewish question." The full text is available at no cost at https://www.gutenberg.org/files/25282/25282-h/25282-h.htm. For a description of the initial impact *The Jewish State* had among several royal figures in Europe, see Walter Russell Mead, *The Arc of a Covenant: The United States, Israel, and the Fate of the Jewish People* (New York: Alfred A. Knopf, 2022), 55–80.

54. Daniel Polisar, "The Most Politically Significant Meeting of Any Group of Jews in the Last 1,800 Years," *Mosaic*, August 23, 2017.

55. Herzl, "Judaism," https://herzlinstitute.org/en/theodor-herzl/.

56. "A Dream of a Jewish State," *Jewish Chronicle*, January 17, 1896.

57. Paul Johnson, *A History of the Jews*, 399. See Daniel Polisar, "The Most Politically Significant Meeting":

> Herzl willed the Congress into being through a remarkable set of traits and actions: single-mindedness, the willingness to invest all his resources, and the rapid making and acting on decisions. As one of his disciples put it:
>
> > We consulted, resolved, decided, and then we each left and went back to our own business. It was Herzl alone who organized the Congress, all by himself, with his own money and his own labor. . . . There were times when he sat up all night with the students, even addressing envelopes.

58. This was not the predecessor or forerunner of the current German newspaper of the same name, which was founded in 1946 in Hamburg.

59. In July 1895, Herzl had sought to persuade Benedikt to call a meeting of "important Jews" to whom Herzl would deliver a lecture on solving the Jewish Question, and he wanted the *Neue Freie Presse* to publish his article, "The Solution of the Jewish Question." Benedikt refused both requests. He didn't want the paper to get the reputation of being a "Jew's paper," even though both of the publishers were Jewish. Josef Fraenkel, "The Jewish Chronicle and the Launching of Political Zionism," in *Herzl Year Book*, Vol. 2 (New York: Herzl Press, 1959), 217.

60. *Complete Diaries*, Vol. II, June 8, 1897, 538.

61. The *Jewish Chronicle* had introduced him to its readers as "a distinguished journalist and litterateur of the first rank in Vienna . . . whose position on the staff of the *Neue Freie Presse* commands attention for all he writes." See Josef Fraenkel, "The Jewish Chronicle and the Launching of Political Zionism," in *Herzl Year Book,* Vol. 2 (New York: Herzl Press, 1959), 217 ("Herzl owed much of his reputation to this important Viennese paper, which was highly esteemed and had a large circulation at home and abroad").

62. In 1901, Herzl wrote that no one knew "how I suffered during my six years on that paper, having to tremble for the bread and butter of my children." But, he wrote, "[w]hat if I had allowed people to dissuade me? The world would be poorer by an

idea, and Judaism by this great movement." Quoted in J. Hodess, "The Real Herzl: An Appreciation of the Man as He Is Revealed in His Diaries," in *Theodore Herzl: A Memorial*, 83, 86.

63. *Complete Diaries*, Vol. II, 564, 6-16-97. See Reimer, *The First Zionist Congress*, 21.

64. *Complete Diaries*, Vol. II, 574 (August 14) and 575 (August 23).

65. Haiyim J. Orlan, "The Participants in the First Zionist Congress," 133. In addition, the Congress was attended by many guests in the gallery, their number estimated at more than one thousand. Ibid., 134. Daniel Polisar writes that "[t]here were somewhere between 196 and 246 delegates; it is impossible to know the exact number, in part because some delegates had their names removed from the official lists lest the Russian secret-police learn they had been there in an official capacity. Moreover, Herzl deliberately blurred the line between delegates and other participants in order to swell the impression of massive participation." Daniel Polisar, "The Most Politically Significant Meeting."

66. The five American delegates were: (1) Rosa Sonneschein from St. Louis, the founding editor of *The American Jewess*, the first English language magazine for Jewish women in the United States, which began publishing in 1895; (2) Adam Rosenberg, a New York lawyer; (3) Sabbatai Sheftl Schaffer, a Baltimore rabbi; (4) Davis Trietsch, a New York businessman; and (5) Cyrus Leopold Sulzberger (father of Arthur Hays Sulzberger, the publisher of the *New York Times*). Lawrence J. Epstein, *The Dream of Zion: The Story of the First Zionist Congress* (Lanham: Rowman & Littlefield, 2016), 51. Haiyim J. Orlan, "The Participants in the First Zionist Congress," 144. Rosa Sonneschein reported on the First and Second Zionist Congresses in *The American Jewess*. She wrote that "Almost the entire American Jewish press flanked against Zionism, almost the entire American Jewish pulpit antagonized it. . . ." Rosa Sonneschein, "Zionism," *The American Jewess*, September, 1898, 5, 6, https://quod.lib.umich.edu/a/amjewess/TAJ1895.0008.005/7:5?rgn=main;view=image.

67. "Basel Program—1897," https://azm.org/basel-program-1897. The entire statement adopted by the Congress, written primarily by Max Nordau, read as follows:

> Zionism aims at establishing for the Jewish people a publicly and legally assured home in Palestine. For the attainment of this purpose, the Congress considers the following means serviceable:
>
> 1. The promotion of the settlement of Jewish agriculturists, artisans, and tradesmen in Palestine.
> 2. The federation of all Jews into local or general groups, according to the laws of the various countries.
> 3. The strengthening of the Jewish feeling and consciousness.
> 4. Preparatory steps for the attainment of those governmental grants which are necessary to the achievement of the Zionist purpose.

68. Bein, *Herzl,* 229.

69. In *The Jewish State*, Herzl suggested "a white flag, with seven gold stars. The white field symbolizes our pure new life; the stars are the seven golden hours of our

working-day. For we shall march into the Promised Land carrying the badge of honor." Herzl, *The Jewish State*, 147.

70. Reimer, *The First Zionist Congress*, 97. De Haas, *Herzl*, Vol. 1, 172.

71. Reimer, *The First Zionist Congress*, 97. Walter Laqueur, *A History of Zionism* (New York: Schocken Books, 1972), 10.

72. Steven J. Zipperstein, *Elusive Prophet: Ahad Ha'am and the Origins of Zionism* (Berkeley and Los Angeles: University of California Press, 1993), 131, citing a letter by Leib Jaffe.

73. De Haas, *Herzl*, Vol. 1, 202. Herzl's short story has been called a "soulful essay" (Jacob de Haas); a "charming little autobiographical tale" (Amos Elon); a metaphor for Herzl's new appreciation of Jewish tradition (Steven Beller); and a story about what he had been able to achieve in two short years (Daniel Polisar). It was in fact all of these—and, as Herzl's own evaluation demonstrated, something more.

74. *Tancred*, Chapter 47, https://www.gutenberg.org/files/20004/20004-h/20004-h.htm.

75. *Complete Diaries*, Vol. III, 874.

76. Benzion Netanyahu wrote that "we should not assume even for a single moment that this idea [of a Jewish state] . . . was in any way unique to Herzl." Benzion Netanyahu, *The Founding Fathers of Zionism*, 71. Herzl's "uniqueness and greatness were not found in the idea of 'the Jewish state'" but rather in the minds of the Jews who heard it:

> Herzl saw the main flaw not in the absence of a feeling of nationhood, but in the presence of a feeling of inferiority which the Jewish nation had sunk into during the centuries of Exile . . . the people's low esteem for their own capabilities and their ubiquitous conviction that the harassed, scattered and fragmented people of Israel were weak, powerless and helpless.

Benzion Netanyahu, *The Founding Fathers of Zionism*, 72, 95. See Benjamin Netanyahu, *A Place Among the Nations* (New York: Bantam Books, 1993), 10–11.

77. Herzl was familiar with Descartes's epigram, "I think; therefore I am." At the Second Zionist Congress in Basel on August 28, 1898, Herzl summarized the status of Zionism as follows:

> The new Jewish movement came before the world as a strange apparition. . . . [W]as not the Jewish people dead and forgotten? . . . *In us the words of the thinker were paraphrased: "I suffer, therefore I am I."*
>
> . . . [T]he first Congress of the Zionists was a manifestation of our reanimated national consciousness. . . .
>
> It could not have been the historic import of our emancipation that we cease to be Jews, for we were repulsed whenever we wanted to intermingle with the others. The historic import of our emancipation was rather that we provide a home for our liberated nationality. . . . *We can do it now if we desire it with all our might. . . .*

> It is true that we aspire to our ancient land. But what we want in the ancient land is a new blossoming of the Jewish spirit.

The Congress Addresses of Theodor Herzl, 7/41, 8/41, 14/41 (emphasis added).

78. Benzion Netanyahu, *The Founding Fathers of Zionism*, 95 and 99:

> I would sum up Herzl's entire understanding of the internal conditions for the liberation of his people in three words: believe, dare and desire, and that is why he stated even at the start of his activity: "We are close to Jerusalem to the extent that we *desire* Jerusalem. It is a question of the will that beats within us. Our role is to awaken that will . . ." Therefore he . . . emphasized this point . . . and even raised it to the level of a first principle: If you will it, it is no dream.

Peter Loewenberg, "Theodor Herzl: A Psychoanalytic Study," in Benjamin B. Wolman, *The Psychoanalytic Interpretation of History* (New York: Harper & Row, 1971), 169, 171:

> The idea of the return of the Jews to Jerusalem is as old as the expulsion. Herzl's contribution was a new behavioral ethos. . . . Herzl postulated values in direct conscious contradiction to the ghetto way of life. . . . [He] expressed a deliberate effort to forge a new heroic national character (or to recapture a mythical Biblical racial character), create a flag and accessory symbols that would be honored and would win "respect in the eyes of the world."

79. No Jewish thinker before Herzl had placed the future of the Jewish people within this broad perspective of international politics. Avineri, *Making of Modern Zionism*, 85. See also Jacob Golomb, "Transfiguration of the Self in Herzl's Life and in His Literary Fiction," Philosophy Department, Hebrew University, Israel.

> Herzl's socio-political thought, unlike that of his Eastern European followers who were profoundly influenced by socialist and Marxist movements, was primarily based on the liberal British paradigm. . . . I concur with Jacob Talmon's perceptive observation "Herzl's Jewish nationalism derives from liberal and individualistic categories of thought." . . . Herzl was first among the Zionist thinkers who believed that Jewish nationhood is a very effective means to attain individual identity and personal authenticity.

80. Herzl had sent a special invitation to Ahad Ha'am in Odessa to attend the Congress. Lawrence J. Epstein, *The Dream of Zion: The Story of the First Zionist Congress* (Lanham: Rowman & Littlefield, 2016), 91.

81. Ahad Ha'am, "The Jewish State and the Jewish Problem," 1897, www.jewishvirtuallibrary.org/quot-the-jewish-state-and-jewish-problem-quot-ahad-ha-am.

82. Ahad Ha'am, "The Wrong Way," www.jewishvirtuallibrary.org/quot-the-wrong-way-quot-ahad-ha-am.

83. In America, Reform Judaism rejected Zionism. The July 1897 gathering of the Central Conference of American Rabbis declared that Herzl's effort was a total misunderstanding of Israel's mission. In the *Chicago Reform Advocate*, a rabbi expressed

the widespread Reform view: "Every land is our Palestine. Every city in which righteousness dwells is our Jerusalem." De Haas, *Herzl*, Vol. 1, 188–89. On September 8, 1987, *The American Israelite*, a prominent American Jewish newspaper, editorialized that a Jewish state was "no Jewish enterprise but . . . the hallucination of some overcharged Jewish brains." De Haas, *Herzl*, Vol. 1, 189. In a lengthy letter published in the *New York Times* on September 10, 1897, under the headline "A Jewish State Impossible," Rabbi Isaac M. Wise, the leader of Reform Judaism in America, wrote dismissively that the Zionist Congress in Basel had been "a gathering of visionary and impracticable dreamers, who conceived and acted a romantic drama, and applauded it, all by themselves."

84. Theodor Herzl, *Zionist Writings: Essays and Addresses,* Vol. 2 (August, 1898–May, 1904), Harry Zohn, trans. (New York: Herzl Press, 1975), 154. See Yoram Hazony, *The Jewish State*, 130. The paragraphs from Herzl's address read as follows:

> [We] believe that this desolate corner of the Orient has, like us, not only a past but also a future. On that soil, where so little grows at present, there grew ideas for all mankind. And for that very reason nobody can deny that there is a deathless relation between our people and that land. If there is such a thing as a legitimate claim to a portion of the earth's surface, all people who believe in the Bible must recognize the rights of the Jews. . . .
>
> Asia is the diplomatic problem of the coming decade. Let us recall in all modesty that we Zionists . . . foresaw and proclaimed this development of the European contest several years ago. . . . You know how closely every step which any one power takes in this direction is watched by the others. . . . The land in question cannot and will not ever pass into the possession of any one power, for it is guarded with extreme solicitude. Not only its present owner but all the powers watch over it carefully.

85. Herzl, *Zionist Writings,* 152–53.

86. Letter from Lord (Nathaniel Mayer) Rothschild to Theodor Herzl, 18 August 1902, C.Z.A. H VIII/708, reprinted in Isaiah Friedman, *The Rise of Israel,* Vol. 2, *Herzl's Political Activity 1897–1904* (New York and London: Garland Publishing, Inc., 1987), Document 44, 252–53. Herzl "did not regard contemporary British colonialism as imperialism with all its sinister connotations, but believed that it had both a modern cultural mission and the strengthening of her own power, a democratic modern power in the world." Rabinowicz, *Herzl: Architect of the Balfour Declaration*, 41. He sought moral, political, and diplomatic support from Britain, but as the Fourth Zionist Congress opened in London in 1900, he wrote that the "realization of our great goal must be expected only from the Jewish people's own strength." Ibid., 38–39.

87. *Complete Diaries*, Vol. I, 365.

88. Ibid., 366.

89. "Theodor Herzl's Testimony Before the Royal Commission on Alien Immigration, 7 July 1902," Report of the Royal Commission on Alien Immigration, London, 1903, Minutes of Evidence, II: 211–21, republished in Isaiah Friedman, *The Rise of Israel,* Vol. 2, 241–51.

90. Ibid., 249.

91. Ibid., 245–46.

92. *Complete Diaries*, Vol. I, 368.

93. Ibid., 370.

94. Ibid., 371.

95. Letter from Lord (Nathaniel Mayer) Rothschild to Theodor Herzl, 18 August 1902, C.Z.A. H VIII/708, reprinted in Isaiah Friedman, *The Rise of Israel,* Vol. 2, Document 44, 252–53. The full text of the key paragraphs reads as follows:

> I tell you very frankly that I should view with horror the establishment of a Jewish Colony pure and simple; such a Colony would be Imperium Imperio; it would be a Ghetto with the prejudices of the Ghetto; it would be a small petty Jewish state, orthodox and illiberal, excluding the Gentile and the Christian. And what would be the result; ten, fifteen or fifty thousand Jews would live in comparative happiness and ease, their habits and their example would be quoted and their co-religionists and brethren at home would be more oppressed and more ground down on the principle of "Do unto others as you would be done by."
>
> My aim and object must always be a different one from yours. I wish the Jew wherever he lives to be a prosperous and good citizen, and you cannot attain that object by establishing a few orthodox communities in scattered parts of the world. By all means encourage immigration. Find new homes for the Jews, but let them live amongst their Christian brethren, by the streams of Babylon or elsewhere, but let one and all of us beware of the impossible.

96. Theodor Herzl's reply to Lord Rothschild, 22 August 1902, *Diaries*, IV: 1347–48, reprinted in Isaiah Friedman, *The Rise of Israel,* Vol. 2, Document 45, 254–55. Cf. Martin Kramer, "Three Turning Points That Led to the Birth of the State of Israel": "Herzl's achievement was precisely to organize Zionism so that it wouldn't need a messianic savior like himself—just the right people in the right place at the right time."

97. *Complete Diaries*, Vol. I, 381, Vienna, Friday, November 7, 1902.

98. See Docs 53 and 54, in Isaiah Friedman, *The Rise of Israel,* Vol. 2, 283–90.

99. In February, the mutilated body of a Russian peasant boy had been found, murdered (it would be determined much later) by a relative. But the antisemitic newspaper in Kishinev, *Bessarabetz* ("The Bessarabian"), immediately blamed the Jews. *Bessarabetz* had propagandized against the Jews for years, accusing them of economic "exploitation," advocacy of "socialism," hatred of Christians, and "ritual murder." The newspaper asserted that the Jews had killed the boy for blood for their Passover matzah, and there were persistent rumors that the police would not react if there were a retaliatory riot against the Jews. After Easter services on April 19, rock-throwing by children expanded into escalating violence, involving about 2,000 people, including seminarians and workingmen, who chanted, "Death to the Jews!"

100. See Philip Ernest Schoenberg, "The American Reaction to the Kishinev Pogrom of 1903, *American Jewish Historical Quarterly*, Vol. LXIII, No. 3 (March 1974),

262 ("The Jews of Kishinev comprised approximately one-half of the city's estimated population of 110,000"). More than two months after the riots, 10,000 Jews were still homeless, and an equal number were still dependent on relief. Ibid., 262–63. For other background on the Kishinev pogrom, see Taylor Stults, "Roosevelt, Russian Persecution of the Jews, and American Public Opinion," *Jewish Social Studies*, Vol. 33, No. 2 (1974), 13; see also J. B. Weber, *The Kishineff Massacre and Its Bearing upon the Question of Jewish Immigration into the United States* (New York, 1903).

101. Steven J. Zipperstein describes the Bialik poem as "the finest—certainly the most influential—Jewish poem written since medieval times." Steven J. Zipperstein, *Pogrom: Kishinev and the Tilt of History* (New York and London: Liveright Publishing, 2018). The full text of the poem is at www.sazf.org/resources/in-the-city-of-slaughter.

102. Zipperstein, *Pogrom*, 138 (there was an "onslaught of press reports, ideological tracts, instantly crafted synagogue liturgy, protest meetings, and the like").

103. In 1904, the Jewish Publication Society of America published *The Voice of America on Kishineff*, edited by Cyrus Adler, a 500-page compilation of the extraordinary outpouring of editorials, sermons, resolutions, petitions and related reactions to the Kishinev massacre. The book proceeded city-by-city, in alphabetical order, reprinting the speeches given at large public gatherings. *The New York Times* alone published seventeen editorials on Kishinev, beginning on May 17, 1903 ("almost too horrible for belief and quite too horrible to be ignored").

In a typical example, Colonel John B. Weber, who had been the chairman in 1891 of a U.S. government special commission to investigate the conditions in Europe that were leading to a wave of immigration to the United States, gave this summary of the condition of the Jews to the public conference in Atlantic City, New Jersey, on July 12, 1903:

> Today the Jew in Russia is an alien in the land of his birth, one who bears an undue share of the burdens of government without the privileges of its meanest citizen. Fettered in his movements, handicapped in his vocation, restricted in his educational opportunities, unable to protect himself, and powerless to successfully invoke the protections of the authorities; a slave who has not even the master's self-interest to shield him from abuse, he stands helpless, friendless, and defenseless against brute force, egged on, not only by religious intolerance, but by contending forces which strive to strengthen the government on the one hand, and to destroy it, on the other—the irrepressible conflict of the age, between government by autocracy and government by the people. This makes the Jew the sport of the rabble, the spoil of the official, the football of fanaticism, the buffer against which strikes the brutal wrath of bigotry, intolerance and savagery. This in brief is the status of the Jew in Russia today.

Cyrus Adler, ed., *The Voice of America on Kishineff* (Philadelphia: Jewish Publication Society, 1904), 9. In Baltimore on May 17, 1903, Mayor Hayes addressed three thousand people, saying:

> To Marylanders whose very atmosphere is impregnated with religious liberty; to those whose very ancestors in 1634 brought with them to these shores religious liberty, it is difficult to believe that these Jews have been murdered in their homes and their women slain. . . . Think of it—in this twentieth century, and in a part of the world that claims the rank of a civilized nation, women and children have been butchered, while the Russian police stood idly by. It is an indelible disgrace to the government that did not prevent it, and will surely raise a protest that will be loudly heard in the imperial halls of St. Petersburg.

Ibid., 17–18. In Louisville, Kentucky, addresses were made by dignitaries who included Louis N. Dembitz, the uncle of a future Supreme Court Justice. The African American lawyers of the city adopted a resolution that read:

> *Resolved*, That we, the negro members of the Louisville bar, often occupied in defending the unfortunates of our own race—acquainted with sorrow, and knowing the poignancy of the oppressor's wrongs, do most solemnly enter our protest against the aforesaid outrageous and tender our sympathy and moral support to any movement looking to the amelioration of the hapless condition of our Hebrew brethren, and trust that the representatives of this enlightened Government may inaugurate steps to offer an asylum to these people in such a dignified manner as to command the attention of the civilized world.

Ibid., 95–96. In New York, 3,500 citizens attended a Wednesday evening rally, chaired by Mayor Seth Low, which was addressed by numerous dignitaries, including ex-President of the United States, Grover Cleveland. The Rev. Dr. Robert S. MacArthur told the crowd that, "[s]tanding beside the blackened homes of slaughtered Jews in Kishineff, sympathizing with widows and orphans and weeping over new-made graves, I denounce, in the name of civilization, and in the name of Christianity, and in the name of humanity, this atrocious crime." Ibid., 132.

104. Michael Davitt, *Within the Pale: The True Story of Anti-Semitic Persecutions in Russia*, 1903. Davitt supported Zionism, seeing political independence as the only solution to the "Jewish Question," in the same way that Irish independence was for the "Irish Question."

105. Adler, 476–78.

106. Ibid., 471–72.

107. See Taylor Stults, "Roosevelt, Russian Persecution of the Jews, and American Public Opinion," 13, 21. The Russian officials told Riddle that "the emperor whose will is the sole law of this land had no need of information from outside sources as to what is taking place within his dominions." On October 31, 1903, Secretary Hay wrote to B'nai B'rith to say that while the petition "did not reach the high destination for which it was intended, its words have attained world-wide publicity" and that the petition would "always be memorable . . . [given] the number and weight of the signatures attached to it, embracing some of the most prominent names of our generation . . . ." Adler, 481.

108. De Haas, *Herzl*, Vol. I, 132.

109. Isaiah Friedman, *The Rise of Israel,* Vol. 2, Introduction.

110. Steven J. Zipperstein, *Pogrom*, 94–96.

111. Isaiah Friedman, *The Rise of Israel,* Vol. 2, Introduction. In his diary entry for August 10, 1903, Herzl recorded the results of his meeting, writing that he fully understood Plehve's objective:

> I had understood all along that he attached much importance to the forthcoming Zionist Congress, obviously because he saw that the Kishinev business was bound to come up there for a frank airing. When that happens, I could be in the position of doing him a service by cutting the thing short.

112. *The New York Times* reported the Russian letter on August 26, 1903, on page six, under the headline "Favors Zion Movement—Russia Gives Official Encouragement to the Jewish Project—Minister De Plehve's Letter to the Congress in Session at Basel, Switzerland." Russia's letter became the cornerstone of Herzl's subsequent diplomacy. See Isaiah Friedman, *The Rise of Israel,* Vol. 2, Introduction.

113. Alex Bein, *Theodore Herzl*, 439–43. The British offer provided for a governor chosen by the British, but Jewish self-administration in local affairs and complete autonomy after five years.

114. Ibid., 443.

115. See *Complete Diaries*, Vol. IV, 1547, August 22, for Herzl's description of the reaction to the report he gave the members of the Zionist executive committee:

> I presented England and Russia. And it didn't occur to any of them for even a single moment that for these greatest of all accomplishments to date I deserved a word, or even a smile, of thanks. Instead, Messieurs Jacobson, Belkovsky, and Tschlenow criticized me a number of times.

116. Nordau told the delegates that the "night shelter" would also be "a political and historical means of education, which would accustom the Jews and the world to the idea that has become strange to them for thousands of years . . . that we Jews are a people, a people able, willing, and prepared to fulfill all the tasks of a civilized and independent people." Israel Cohen, *Theodor Herzl: Founder of Political Zionism* (New York and London: Thomas Yoseloff, 1959), 327–28.

One of Herzl's colleagues at the *Neue Freie Presse*, a close friend of Max Nordau, Professor Ludwig Stein, later recalled his own position at the time, rejecting Palestine as a location:

> I could never actively support the establishment of a Jewish state on the soil of the then absolute monarchy of Turkey. For if the Russian Jews were to flee from Czarist absolutism into that of the Caliphate they would be going from bad to worse. Like Zangwill, I preferred colonization on a large scale in the Argentine, or, later, in Texas, or in the British-ruled territory such as Uganda, rather than under the absolute government of Turkey.

Ludwig Stein, "They Have Prevailed: A Tribute to Herzl and Nordau from One Who Was Skeptical," in *Herzl Memorial*, 30, 32.

117. Israel Cohen, *Theodor Herzl*, 331–32.

118. Ibid., 333. Cohen was there as a press correspondent and had several conversations with Herzl. Ibid., 331, note 5.

119. de Haas, *Herzl*, Vol. 2, 183.

120. *Complete Diaries*, Vol. IV, 1547–48. Herzl told his friends Zangwill, Nordau, and Joseph Cowen that by the Seventh Zionist Congress, he would "either have obtained Palestine or realized the complete futility of any further efforts," and that in the latter case he would give this speech:

> "It was not possible. The ultimate goal has not been reached, and will not be reached within a foreseeable time. But a temporary result is at hand: this land in which we can settle our suffering masses on a national basis and with the right of self-government. I do not believe that for the sake of a beautiful dream or of a legitimistic banner we have a right to withhold this relief from the unfortunate. . . . Palestine is the only land where our people can come to rest. But hundreds of thousands need immediate help."

121. Quoted in de Haas, *Herzl*, Vol. 2, 188. The *Chronicle* supported the "Zionist-Zionists" in opposing the "end [of] the grand drama" that they thought would be the result of any place other than Palestine being considered. The London *Spectator* editorialized that the East African project would "divert attention . . . just at the moment when it is possible that, with the decline of Turkish power and wealth, the fate of Palestine may be within the power of collective Europe to decide." Ibid., 189.

122. Avner Falk, *Herzl, King of the Jews: A Psychoanalytic Biography of Theodor Herzl* (New York, London, Lanham: University Press of America, 1993), 522 (citing Pawel, *Labyrinth of Exile*, 511). Pawel sets forth a longer excerpt from Weizmann's critical article:

> Herzl is not a nationalist but a promoter of projects. . . . He only takes external conditions into account, whereas the power on which we rely is the psychology of the people and its living desires. We, for our part, always knew that we were incapable of gaining Palestine in the short term and we therefore were not discouraged when this or that attempt had failed. . . . Cultural work must be put before all else.

Stefan Zweig, writing in 1929, recalled the "attitude of disrespect which the very foremost of his followers adopted toward the person of Herzl":

> The East Europeans reproached him with understanding nothing of Judaism and with even being unfamiliar with its rites; the economists considered him a mere feuilletonist. Everyone had objections of his own—and they were not always very respectful.

Stefan Zweig, "'Konig Der Juden' ["King of the Jews"]: The Man of Letters and the Man of Action," in *Herzl Year Book*, Vol. III, 55, 57.

123. Diary entries for August 22 and August 31, 1903.

124. Herzl devoted several paragraphs to explaining his failure, starting with the

fact that many people "did not believe me or help me," necessitating consideration of an African location:

> I was not able to do it all by myself. At some future time, I shall make clear the details and the responsibility for this. Today I must say that for the foreseeable future, nothing can be done in Palestine. . . . [But] let us at least do something to ease the distress, continue to arouse the people, and strengthen those who have been aroused. This can only be done if one has firm ground beneath one's feet.

125. Theodor Herzl, *Zionist Writings*, 238–39. A facsimile of the letter was published in 1928 in *Jüdisches Lexikon*, Vol. II, facing p. 1572 (Berlin: Jüdischer Verlag, 1928).

126. Harvard professor Derek Penslar has attributed Herzl's early death to depression and disappointment. Derek Penslar, "What Zionism Did for Herzl," *Mosaic*, January 11, 2021. The more likely cause of Herzl's death, however, was his relentless pursuit of a Jewish state while suffering from a congenital heart condition. In a review of Ernst Pawel's Herzl biography, Peter Loewenberg, a UCLA historian, political psychologist, and practicing psychoanalyst, wrote:

> During the nine short years in which he built the Zionist movement, Herzl lived with the specter of his impending death. His letters and diaries frequently tell of fainting spells, loss of consciousness, blackouts, arrhythmias, shortness of breath. His self-imposed labor in the service of the Zionist cause acquires a heroic quality. He drove himself beyond any reserves of strength or resilience. Herzl died in 1904 at the age of only forty-four, his body exhausted, his heart worn out.

Peter Loewenberg, "The Private Life of a Nation Builder," *New York Times*, December 31, 1989.

127. Herzl, *Complete Diaries*, Vol. III, 1202 (Friday, early in the morning, January 24, 1902). Maurice Samuel (1895–1972) wrote in "Herzl's Diaries: An Explanation Which Deepens the Enigma," in *Theodor Herzl: A Memorial*, 125, 127, that Herzl wrote this "[t]oward the end of things, in the midst of heartbreaking failures, degrading needs, defections, worries of the most pitiful kind" and that "in such flashes the *Diaries* reveal a sublime Herzl; and for this reason they must remain a part of world literature."

128. See Rick Richman, "The Mystery of the So-Called 'New Moses' Endures," *Mosaic*, January 21, 2021:

> Many Herzl historians and biographers—including Shlomo Avineri, Alex Bein, Steven Beller, Jacques Kornberg, Peter Loewenberg, Ernst Pawel, and Daniel Polisar—have recognized the connection between Herzl's efforts in Britain and the issuance of the Balfour Declaration the following decade. Prime Minister Benjamin Netanyahu noted it in his 2017 remarks to a special Knesset session honoring Herzl and at an official memorial ceremony later that year.

Israeli historian Benzion Netanyahu concluded that:

> Had Herzl not prepared the consent of the major powers, had he not inculcated into the consciousness of the greatest statesmen that Zionism was *the only possible solution* to . . . the Jewish question and the question of Palestine—had he not made Zionism a known and accepted political factor, Palestine would have passed in time of war from hand to hand, as it had many times in its long history, and with it would have passed authority over the small Jewish settlement which survived within it after [World War I], and nothing would have changed concerning the fate of either the land or the Jewish people.

Benzion Netanyahu, *The Founding Fathers of Zionism*, 93 (emphasis in original).

See also Oskar K. Rabinowicz, *Herzl, Architect of the Balfour Declaration* (New York: Herzl Press, 1958), 5 ("it was Herzl who in England laid the foundations upon which Weizmann, Sokolow, and the other Zionist leaders were able to attain in 1917 the Balfour declaration").

129. Bernstein-Kohan, who was a physician, said that on two occasions during the week of the Sixth Zionist Congress, he had treated Herzl for "heart attacks." Pawel, *Labyrinth of Exile*, 512. Martin Buber, who spoke to him privately on one occasion that week, found him struggling for breath. Ibid. In December 1903, Herzl went to see Dr. Gustav Singer, a heart specialist and professor at the University of Vienna, who in a memoir later described Herzl as being:

> a pale, tired, sick patient. I was soon forced to realize that death was already lurking in the shadows. His pulse was irregular, the heart output greatly impaired as manifested by obvious congestive symptoms. In addition, there were the circles around his once so fiery eyes . . . we were forced to postulate a disease of the heart muscle, which implied a rapidly progressive heart failure.

Ibid., 523.

130. The dream was first published by Brainin in his Hebrew biography of Herzl. Bein, *Theodore Herzl*, 13–14, provided the first English translation of Brainin's account:

> At about the age of twelve—so Herzl told Brainin—he read somewhere in a German book about the Messiah-King whom many Jews still awaited. . . . The history of the Exodus and the legend of the liberation by the King-Messiah ran together in the boy's mind. . . . A little while thereafter Herzl was visited by the following dream:
>
> "The King-Messiah came, a glorious and majestic old man, took me in his arms, and swept off with me on the wings of the wind. On one of the iridescent clouds we encountered the figure of Moses. . . . The Messiah called to Moses: It is for this child that I have prayed. But to me he said: Go, declare to the Jews that I shall come soon and perform great wonders and great deeds for my people and for the whole world."
>
> This dream Herzl kept to himself. But a few days later there came to his hand one of the popular science books by Aaron Bernstein. There he read that the

> stream of electricity built a bridge over the entire world, that electricity was the real Messiah, and that its wonders would bring liberation to all nations and all enslaved human beings. . . . [Herzl said that] I said to myself: who knows, perhaps the electric stream is really the Redeemer whom we are awaiting and who will liberate us from the bondage of the body and the spirit.

See Robert S. Wistrich, "Theodor Herzl: Between Myth and Messianism," in *Theodor Herzl: From Europe to Zion,* 11. Joseph Patai, "Herzl's School Years," in *Herzl Year Book,* Vol. III, 59.

131. Dr. Stephen S. Wise, "The Epochal Herzl: His Influence Upon the Jews' Attitude to Themselves," in *Theodor Herzl: A Memorial,* 95–96. For Zionists who admired Ahad Ha'am and his cultural Zionism, Herzl inspired only mixed praise. See Gol Kalev, "Theodor Herzl vs. Ahad Ha'am Today," *Jerusalem Post,* April 16, 2018. Cf. Israeli author Hillel Halkin, in a colloquy with Prof. Ruth R. Wisse, saying he had long "had the attitude toward Herzl that many of his Eastern European critics had—that he wasn't really thoroughly Jewish enough, that he didn't have enough Jewish culture . . . that Zionism for him was simply an answer to anti-Semitism, that he didn't understand the deeper cultural and religious and social imperatives of Zionism." But, Halkin continued, "Today I think he was really a political genius":

> Herzl was extraordinary—the burden of history that he took upon himself, single-handedly, on his own shoulders, when there was no reason to think he could succeed. And he was generally, in his own lifetime, considered by sophisticated people, knowledgeable people, to be half-mad, and to be pursuing a total chimera, an unrealizable dream. And he knew it—he himself was a very sophisticated European Jew and he knew he was doing something crazy, suddenly trying to push this mad notion of a Jewish state. But he does it—and he does it defying all odds, flying in the face of all opinion of himself. He doesn't care anymore what people think of him, he just goes and he does it, and today it's clear to me that without Herzl there would have been no Israel.

"Ruth Wisse & Hillel Halkin on the Authors Who Created Modern Hebrew Literature," Tikvah Podcast, September 9, 2020, www.tikvahfund.org/library/podcast-ruth-wisse-hillel-halkin-on-the-authors-who-created-modern-hebrew-literature.

132. Theodor Herzl, *The Jewish State,* 102. Over the following century, Israel (i) established a democracy in a region long governed by dictators and royal families; (ii) extended civil rights to women, gays and Arabs; (iii) protected the holy sites of all religions; (iv) gave socialism a real world test both in its kibbutzim and its national economy; (v) created a modern entrepreneurial economy; (vi) produced more Nobel Prize winners per capita than any other country; (vi) sought peace with its neighbors and repeatedly offered the Palestinian Arabs a state of their own—something neither the Ottoman Empire in four centuries nor Jordan and Egypt in 1949–1967 had done. See Shlomo Avineri, "Rereading Herzl's Old-New Land," *Jewish Review of Books,* Summer 2012, in which he calls Herzl's *Old New Land* a "non-utopian novel" because Israel in fact exceeded Herzl's dreams.

133. In her magisterial 2012 book, *Israel: A History* (Boston: Brandeis University Press, 2012), Anita Shapira wrote that:

> As much as one tries to explain certain historical phenomena, they retain an inexplicable, mysterious, mystical element. Herzl's appearance in the Jewish world and his vigorous activity over less than a decade constituted one such phenomenon: a passing lightning storm that illuminated reality and shook it up, laying the groundwork for future changes. . . . Nothing in his personal history hinted at the mental fortitude, boundless energy, political acuity, and endless dedication he displayed in the last, amazing decade of his life.

2. LOUIS D. BRANDEIS: THE AMERICAN PROPHET

1. Brandeis was born in 1856 and entered Harvard Law School in 1875 at age nineteen. He graduated first in his class at age twenty, while working his way through school. He opened a law office in Boston with a classmate, established a very successful law practice, and eventually became known as "the People's Lawyer," because of his pro-bono actions against big companies and their monopolistic practices. He wrote a series of muckraking articles on the "money trusts" for *Harper's Weekly*, published in 1914 as *Other People's Money and How the Bankers Use It*. Throughout these years he had virtually no connection with Jewish institutions—religious or otherwise.

2. Brandeis's mother came from a religious Jewish family in Europe but joined the Unitarian Church in America. Lewis J. Paper, *Brandeis: An Intimate Biography of One of America's Truly Great Supreme Court Justices* (Secaucus, NJ: Citadel Press, 1983). Brandeis later wrote that "In the home of my parents there was no Jewish Sabbath, nor in my own home." Solomon, ed., *The Words of Justice Brandeis* (New York: Henry Schuman, 1953), 160.

3. For adjustments of historical dollars to current dollars, see www.dollartimes.com/inflation/inflation.php?amount=75000&year=1914. total income and gifts for each year from 1890 through 1940 can be found in Alpheus Thomas Mason, *Brandeis: A Free Man's Life* (New York: Viking Press, 1956), 691–92. In 1915, in his first full year as the head of the American Zionist movement, Brandeis gave $12,227 to Jewish charities and Zionist organizations, representing more than half his gifts for that year out of gross income of $135,735. His contributions in each year thereafter remained at that level, except for several years in the 1930s when he temporarily left the organized Zionist movement.

4. Louis D. Brandeis, "The Jewish People Should Be Preserved," August 30, 1914, reprinted in *Brandeis on Zionism: A Collection of Addresses and Statements* (Washington, DC: Zionist Organization of America, 1942), 44.

5. Ezekiel Rabinowitz, *Justice Louis D. Brandeis: The Zionist Chapter in His Life* (New York: Philosophical Library, 1968), 5:

> The low ebb of the Zionist movement in the United States was in 1914, confronted with the war in Europe which brought a crisis upon the Zionist World Organization. The members of the [Executive Committee] were scattered. . . .

The appearance at this critical period of the attorney Louis Dembitz Brandeis was a real miracle.

6. The influences that led Brandeis to Zionism, in addition to his conversations with Jacob de Haas and the study encouraged by de Haas, included: (a) Brandeis's discussions with Aaron Aaronsohn, an agricultural pioneer in Palestine; (b) Brandeis's involvement in the garment workers' strike in New York City—which pitted Jewish labor against Jewish management and left him admiring the values each side had shown; (c) his readings on cultural pluralism in articles by Horace Kallen; and (d) his reading about ancient Greece in Alfred Zimmern's 1912 book, *The Greek Commonwealth*, which made him think a Jewish state on the Mediterranean coast could replicate fifth-century Athens.

7. De Haas had been one of Herzl's first supporters in England, meeting him in 1896 when Herzl spoke in London a few months after publishing *The Jewish State*. The twenty-five-year-old de Haas attended the First Zionist Congress in 1897, addressed the Congress on the status of Jews in Britain, and was elected an officer. After he moved to the United States, he became the secretary of the Federation of American Zionists and the editor of *The Maccabean*, its publication.

8. Brandeis revered his uncle and later called him "a living university," whose deepest studies "were those allied to the Jewish religion":

> He was orthodox. He observed the law. But he was not satisfied with merely observing it. He sought to understand the law in order to find its reason; he studied deeply into the history of the Jewish people. . . . He recognized in the past the mirror of the future; a future which would be a noble and glorious one for his people. It was natural that he should have been among the first in America to support Herzl in his effort to build a new Palestine.

Brandeis recalled that he had witnessed "the joy and awe" with which his uncle "welcomed the arrival of the Sabbath day and the piety with which he observed it":

> I remember the extra delicacies, lighting of the candles, prayers over a cup of wine . . . and Uncle Lewis poring over the books of the day. I remember more particularly an elusive something about him, which was spoken of as the "Sabbath peace" which years later brought to my mind a passage from Addison in which he speaks of stealing a day out of life to live. . . . Uncle Lewis used to say that he was enjoying a foretaste of heaven.

Solomon Goldman, ed., *Words of Justice Brandeis*, 61, 150.

9. Louis Dembitz had served as Vice President of the Federation of American Zionists, and his article, "The Redemption of Palestine," had been published in 1901 in *The Maccabean*. Ezekiel Rabinowitz, *Justice Louis D. Brandeis*, 14.

10. Jacob de Haas, *Louis D. Brandeis: A Biographical Sketch* (New York: Bloch Publishing Co., 1929), 53. At the time, the principal Jewish organization in the U.S. was the American Jewish Committee, formed in 1906 in response to recent Russian pogroms. The AJC coordinated American Jewish support for Jews worldwide, but stressed assimilation and was in some ways anti-Zionist.

11. Max Nordau, "Zionism and Anti-Semitism," www.amazon.com/Zionism-Anti-Semitism-Cornerstone-Classic-Subject/dp/1480074497; manybooks.net/titles/nordauma2418624186-8.html. A slightly different translation can be found at "Zionism—Max Nordau—1905," www.zionism-israel.com/hdoc/Nordau_1905.htm.

12. References to Nordau and his books appeared regularly in the *New York Times*. In 1911, for example: The *Times* alerted its readers on January 11 to the imminent publication of a "new book by Max Nordau, 'The Interpretation of History,'. . . a sweeping criticism of history as it has been written thus far." The front-page review in the *New York Times Review of Books* on April 9 ended with: "As always with Dr. Nordau, the book is written in the most brilliant style, and is fascinating from the first page to the last." On July 2, the *Times* reported Nordau's speech on Zionism in New York, describing him as a "noted member of [the Jewish] race." On August 10, the *Times* reported that he had been elected president of the Tenth Zionist Congress in Basel, Switzerland and summarized his speech there. On September 4, the *Times* reported a new Nordau article in *The American Hebrew*, a weekly Jewish newspaper in New York, quoting him as writing that "The plague of anti-Semitism is at present marching around the earth as if it were an epidemic." On October 11, in an article on "Youngsters Over 60 Who Are Doing the World's Work," the *Times* described Nordau as "a great writer [and] an active leader of the political movement among the Jews."

Brandeis was thus likely familiar with Nordau and read his writings on Zionism once he began to study it seriously. He was demonstrably impressed with him as he became the head of the American Zionist movement. In a letter dated September 14, 1914, shortly after assuming the leadership of the movement, Brandeis wrote that Nordau "could be of the greatest service in spreading Zionistic education." Melvin I. Urosky and David W. Levy, *Letters of Louis D. Brandeis*, Vol. III (1913–1915): *Progressive and Zionist* (Albany: State University of New York Press, 1973), 302.

13. Goldmann, ed., *The Words of Justice Brandeis*, 51, 36. Brandeis said the Bible had "first attracted me because of its plainness of speech, its insistence on the righteousness of the individual and justice of the group, the unrestraint with which it arraigns the Jewish people and its patriarchs and chosen leaders":

> I wonder whether any government today would risk publishing a document depicting the nation's most favored ruler as the Bible does David. I doubt whether there is anything in the authorized and approved annals of the nations comparable to the rapid review of the lives of the kings found in the Book of Kings, particularly in that terrifying brief verse, "And he did that which was evil in the sight of the Lord. . . ."

14. The address was reprinted by Avukah (American Student Zionist Federation) in 1936 to mark the eightieth birthday of Justice Brandeis, with a preface by Stephen S. Wise, President of the Zionist Organization of America. Wise wrote in his preface that no one could read the address "without feeling anew that this utterance was touched by the quality or genius of prophecy" and that it was "like yet another chapter of Herzl's 'Judenstaat.'"

15. Louis Dembitz Brandeis, *The Jewish Problem: How to Solve It* (New York: The Zionist Essays Publication Committee, 1915), www.law.louisville.edu/library/collections/brandeis/node/234.

16. Brandeis argued that Jews should "make clear to the world that we too are a nationality striving for equal rights to life and self-expression." He cited a contemporary collection of essays, *The War and Democracy*, and quoted the analysis in it by a distinguished non-Jewish authority, R. W. Seton-Watson, who wrote of his hope that the war:

> will also give a new and healthy impetus to Jewish national policy, grant freer play to their splendid qualities, and enable them to shake off the false shame which has led men who ought to be proud of their Jewish race to assume so many alien disguises. . . .

17. *The Menorah Journal*, Vol. 1, No. 1 (January 2015) (New York: The Intercollegiate Menorah Association, 2015), www.gutenberg.org/files/22300/22300-h/meno-1.html.

18. In his 1949 autobiography, Stephen S. Wise wrote of Brandeis's leadership and "boundless personal generosity":

> Brandeis' public leadership of the Zionist cause lasted for only two years, up to the time of his accession to the Supreme Court. . . . but his leadership [thereafter] took the form of invaluable counsel to a small number of associates. . . . His own financial contributions were the greatest of any Zionist of his lifetime.

Stephen S. Wise, *Challenging Years: The Autobiography of Stephen Wise* (New York: G. P. Putnam's Sons, 1949), 186, 201. Brandeis's monetary contributions, measured in 2022 dollars, amounted to millions. See Mason, *Brandeis*, 691–92.

19. Louis Lipsky, *Memoirs in Profile* (Philadelphia: Jewish Publication Society of America, 1975), 204–5.

20. Ezekiel Rabinowitz, *Justice Louis D. Brandeis*, 6.

21. The annual budget of the Federation of American Zionists in 1914 was $12,150; by 1919, the successor organization, the Zionist Organization of America, had over 176,000 members. Melvin I. Urofsky, *Louis D. Brandeis: A Life* (New York: Schocken Books, 2009), 403, 418.

22. See A. L. Todd, *Justice on Trial: The Case of Louis D. Brandeis* (New York: McGraw-Hill, 1964); Rick Richman, "What the First Senate Hearing for a Supreme Court Nominee Shows about Today's Confirmation Process," *Mosaic*, October 6, 2020, www.mosaicmagazine.com/observation/history-ideas/2020/10/what-the-first-senate-hearing-for-a-supreme-court-nominee-shows/.

23. The text of the Balfour Declaration was published in *The Times of London* on November 9, 1917, under the headline "Palestine for the Jews—Official Sympathy," https://commons.wikimedia.org/wiki/File:Balfour_Declaration_in_the_Times_9_November_1917.jpg.

24. Historian Frank W. Brecher concluded that without Wilson's support the Declaration "almost certainly" would never have been issued.

25. The full text of the letter is reprinted in Rabinowitz, *Justice Louis D. Brandeis*, 11–12 (citing *The Lansing Papers*, Vol. II (p. 71).

26. The text of the letter was published in the *New York Times* and in Wise's autobiography, Stephen S. Wise, *Challenging Years.* Wise wrote that "[n]o more joyous greeting for the New Year could come to American Jewry and the Jews of the world than the utterance of the President" (Ibid., 194–95). Wise wrote to Weizmann that Wilson's statement on Zionism represented a "damaging blow" to the morale of the Central Powers [led by Germany] as the war continued (Ibid., 195).

27. On September 7, the *Times* reported on the previous day's Rosh Hashanah sermons under the headline, "Rabbis Preach on President's Note."

28. Herzl was aware of the Arab presence in Palestine but believed that there was room for both peoples and that Jewish development of Palestine would generate goodwill. His diaries reflect his concern for poor Arabs and an Arab character appears in his novel *Altneuland* (*Old-New Land*) as a cultured, liberal figure.

As Daniel Pipes has noted, it has long been documented that the assertedly mistaken notion that Palestine was "a country without a people" referred not to demographics but to nationhood. At all times, there were both Arabs and Jews in Palestine, but no national movement there prior to Zionism. See Daniel Pipes, review of *Legacy of Empire*, https://www.danielpipes.org/21192/legacy-of-empire; Adam M. Garfinkle, "On the Origin, Meaning, Use and Abuse of a Phrase," *Middle Eastern Studies*, Vol. 27, No. 4 (Oct. 1991), 539-550.

3. CHAIM WEIZMANN AND THE FIRST ARAB-ZIONIST ALLIANCE

1. Ali A. Allawi, *Faisal I of Iraq* (New Haven and London: Yale University Press, 2014), 125.

2. The list of factors included:

   1. The emergence in the latter part of the nineteenth century of nationalism as the principal movement in international politics.
   2. The intellectual, moral, and literary force of the Zionist writings, including those of Leo Pinsker, Theodor Herzl, Max Nordau, and Vladimir Jabotinsky.
   3. The Christian Zionism of various British leaders, and the influence on British thinking of the widely read Zionist novels by such English writers as Benjamin Disraeli (*Tancred*) and George Eliot (*Daniel Deronda*).
   4. The worldwide recognition of the plight of the Jews, particularly after the widespread pogroms in Russia, and the increasing scourge of antisemitism in Europe; and
   5. The strategic interests in World War I of Britain, France, and Germany as they competed for international dominance in a critical area of the world.

See Leonard Stein, *The Balfour Declaration* (New York: Simon and Schuster, 1961); Jonathan Schneer, *The Balfour Declaration: The Origins of the Arab-Israeli Conflict*

(New York: Random House, 2012); Ronald Sanders, *The High Walls of Jerusalem: A History of the Balfour Declaration and the Birth of the British Mandate for Palestine* (New York: Holt, Rinehart and Winston, 1983); Barbara W. Tuchman, *Bible and Sword: England and Palestine from the Bronze Age to Balfour* (New York: Random House, 1984).

3. The minutes of the British War Cabinet approving the Balfour Declaration state that:

> The Secretary of State for Foreign Affairs [Balfour] stated that he gathered that everyone was now agreed that, from a purely diplomatic and political point of view, it was desirable that some declaration favourable to the aspirations of the Jewish nationalists should now be made. The vast majority of Jews in Russia and America, as, indeed, all over the world, now appeared to be favourable to Zionism. If we could make a declaration favourable to such an ideal, we should be able to carry on extremely useful propaganda both in Russia and America.

"Minutes of War Cabinet Meeting No. 261, Minute No. 12, 31 October 1917," http://www.balfourproject.org/war-cabinet-minutes-leading-to-the-balfour-declaration-1917/.

See Jehuda Reinharz, *Chaim Weizmann: The Making of a Statesman* (New York and Oxford: Oxford University Press, 1993), 208, 212:

> [I]n the spring of 1917 . . . Britain's political and military fortunes were at a low ebb and the myth of Jewish power and influence in the United States and Russia, and the rumors of an impending German initiative to woo the Zionists, had reached new heights. . . . From the point of view of the British policymakers, the Balfour Declaration was a last-minute bid to tip the scales of the war in their favor.

4. Letter dated November 14, 1917, from Sir Mark Sykes to Lieutenant Colonel Sir Maurice Haney, secretary to the War Cabinet, published in Isaiah Friedman, ed., *The Rise of Israel: The Zionist Commission in Palestine 1918* (New York & London, Garland Publishing Inc. 1987), 106 (Doc 36).

5. "Jewish National Movement—The Governmental Declaration—Great Thanksgiving Meeting—A Historic Gathering . . . Arab and Armenian Support," *Jewish Chronicle*, December 7, 1917. Chaim Weizmann, in a letter dated December 6, 1917, to Jacobus H. Kann, a Zionist leader in The Netherlands, reported on the December 2 event:

> [S]peakers Lord Robert Cecil . . . Herbert Samuel, M.P. Colonel Sir Mark Sykes, M.P. Captain Hon. Ormsby Gore, delegates of all synagogues. Jewish institutions from all over England were present or sent messages . . . many M.P.s and prominent leading English leaders of opinion attended. Lord Robert Cecil . . . said: The wish of Great Britain was that Arabia should be for the Arabs, Armenia for the Armenians, Judea for the Jews, and real Turkey for the Turks. . . . The ultimate result of this great event he believed would have a far-reaching in-

> fluence on the history of the world. . . . Sir Mark Sykes said: Declaration marked turning point [not only] in history of Jewish race but of whole world. . . . Zionist Organization attached great importance to harmonious work in future with Arabs and Armenians. Representatives of Mohammedan and Christian Arabs and a delegate of Armenian National Council delivered speech of congratulations and sympathy. . . . Enthusiastic audience, thousands could not obtain admission.

Isaiah Friedman, ed., *The Rise of Israel, The Zionist Commission in Palestine,* 7 (Doc 3).

6. The dinner was attended by the Mufti of Jerusalem; the Arab mayor of the city; the archbishop of the Greek Orthodox Patriarchate; the acting Armenian bishop and various British officials. Weizmann addressed the group in English, with Storrs translating into Arabic. Weizmann Series B Papers, Paper 42, "Plea for Friendship and Peace," Address to Moslem and Christian Leaders, Jerusalem, April 27, 1918, 182–86. Storrs's account is in his book *Orientations* (1937).

7. Both Weizmann's view and that of the British officer assigned to the Zionist Commission, Major W. Ormsby-Gore, are shown in the minutes of the August 16, 1918, meeting of the London Zionist Political Committee, where Ormsby-Gore reported on the Zionist Commission in Palestine. He told the committee that:

> Zionists should recognize in the Arab movement, originally centered in the Hejaz but now moving north, a fellow movement with the fine ideals which had for its aim the rehabilitation of the Arab nation and the restoration of Damascus as a center of Arab learning and culture. . . .
>
> [He] did not share the view of those who desired a large Palestine. . . . *His idea of the boundaries was as follows: . . . [including] the whole of the Jordan Valley and the lower eastern slopes but not including the plateau of Ajlun. . . .*
>
> He referred to the cordial reception of Dr. Weizmann by the Christian and Moslem leaders, and of the obviously sincere sympathy between Armenians and Jews in Palestine. [Emphasis added.]

Isaiah Friedman, ed., *The Rise of Israel, The Zionist Commission in Palestine,* 378–83 (Doc 378).

8. The Balfour Project, "War Cabinet Minutes Leading to the Balfour Declaration, 1917," balfourproject.org/war-cabinet-minutes-leading-to-the-balfour-declaration-1917. In February 1918, Balfour was asked whether he viewed the Declaration "as a charter for ultimate Jewish sovereignty in Palestine" and responded that it was his hope "that the Jews will make good in Palestine and eventually found a Jewish State. It is up to them now; we have given them their great opportunity." Quoted in Douglas Feith, "Palestine and Zionism, 1904–1922," 225. http://www.dougfeith.com/docs/Feith_Palestine_and_Zionism_1904-1922.pdf. In his testimony in 1937 to the Peel Commission, Lloyd George said that "there could be no doubt as to what the cabinet then had in their minds" when the Balfour Declaration was issued:

> It was not their idea that a Jewish State should be set up immediately by the peace treaty. . . . On the other hand, it was contemplated that, when the time

> arrived for according representative institutions to Palestine, if the Jews had meanwhile responded to the opportunity afforded them . . . and had become a definite majority of the inhabitants, then Palestine would thus become a Jewish commonwealth.

Ibid., 41.

9. Temperatures in early June in the Sinai Peninsula typically reach ninety-nine degrees. In his letter to Vera Weizmann, dated June 17, 1918, in Dvorah Barzilay and Barnet Litvinoff, *The Letters and Papers of Chaim Weizmann*, Vol. VIII, Series A (November 1917–October 1918) (New Brunswick and Jerusalem: Transaction Books/ Rutgers University, Israel University Press, 1977), Letter No. 213. Weizmann wrote of watching the Turkish lines:

> I was in an Arab camp and watched the army's movements through field-glasses. . . . [T]he voyage along the Red Sea, which lasted about 5 days there and back, was pretty tiring. Sometimes the wind would blow for hours from the glowing mountains of the Sinai Peninsula and you'd feel as if you were actually standing near a red-hot oven. I saw the Sinai from a distance. It is a magnificent, menacing, bare rock. I saw it at sunset, and it was literally fiery red, somber and imposing. . . . [O]ne seems to hear the voices of the dead rising from the tomb, the voices of our prophets, sages and judges foretelling the future.

10. Ibid., 210.

11. On June 17, 1918, Weizmann gave a speech, with Ormsby-Gore and Rothschild present, to the Conference of Jews in Liberated Area of Palestine. He reported that "I have seen Sheref Faisal, the Arab Commander-in-Chief, and after my interview with him I am justified in stating that it is possible to find a modus vivendi for the thorny political Arab problem; for with the Arabs we wish to live on the best of terms." Weizmann Series B Paper, Paper 45, 190. Weizmann believed that Faisal and he "fully understood each other" and that "all these misinterpretations have totally disappeared." Weizmann Paper 47, 201–2.

12. The Jewish Virtual Library shows the following population for Palestine as of 1916: total population, 660,000, with 60,000 Jews. The 1920–21 *American Jewish Year Book* "Statistics of Jews" shows the total population of Palestine for that year as 700,000, with 85,000 Jews. The Jewish population thus was about 10–13 percent of all of Palestine at that time. Today, more than 12 million people live in the area consisting of the land west of the Jordan River.

13. Statistics from various sources show that there were more Jews than Muslims in Jerusalem ever since 1882. A British census of Palestine in 1922 showed a total population of 62,578 for Jerusalem—33,971 Jews, 13,413 Muslims, and 14,669 Christians. As of the time of the Balfour Declaration and Weizmann's later meetings with Faisal, Jerusalem was thus a Jewish-majority city. An August 22, 1918, report on Palestine by W. Ormsby-Gore provides an extensive review of the situation as of that time:

> *In Jerusalem the Jews form the majority of the population, outnumbering all the Christians and Mahommedans combined.* . . . [T]he bulk of Jerusalem Jewry con-

sists of the orthodox Jews, either devoted entirely to the religious life or dependent upon the religious devotees. . . .

The majority of the population of Judea, taken as a whole, is of course still Moslem. The Moslem population of Palestine is anything but homogeneous. . . . The bulk of the population are fellaheen; that is to say, agricultural workers. . . . In the Gaza district they are mainly of Egyptian origin. Elsewhere they are of the most mixed race. They have for centuries been ground down, overtaxed, and bullied by the Turk, and still more by the Arab-speaking Turkish minor official.

There is so much unoccupied and uncultivated land in the occupied parts, and also, I understand, in the remainder of Palestine, that there is plenty of room for Zionist development without ousting the existing Moslem population. The plains of Sharon and Shephelah can support a population ten times that which exists at present.

. . . *I am quite satisfied that neither [the King of Hedjaz] nor Sherif Feisal are seriously upset by the Zionist movement, nor have they any desire to include cis-Jordan Palestine in their dominions.* [Emphasis added.]

Isaiah Friedman, ed., *The Rise of Israel, The Zionist Commission in Palestine,* 387, 390–91, (Doc. 103).

14. "Excepts from an article by Sharif al-Hussein Ibn Ali al-Husseini, published in 'al-Qiblah' (the daily newspaper of Mecca al-Mukarramah) on March 23, 1918," web .archive.org/web/20110514052041/http:/amislam.com/feisal.htm:

The resources of the country [Western Palestine] are still virgin soil and will be developed by the Jewish immigrants. One of the most amazing things until recent times was that the Palestinian used to leave his country, wandering over the high seas in every direction. His native soil could not retain a hold on him, though his ancestors had lived on it for 1,000 years. At the same time we have seen the Jews from foreign countries streaming to Palestine from Russia, Germany, Austria, Spain, America. The cause of causes could not escape those who had the gift of a deeper insight. They knew that the country was for its original sons [*abna'ihi-l-asliyin*], for all their differences, a sacred and beloved homeland. The return of these exiles [*jaliya*] to their homeland will prove materially and spiritually an experimental school for their brethren who are with them in the fields, factories, trades, and in all things connected with toil and labor.

15. For a map showing where the Jews of Palestine lived for more than 1,600 years, from 1000 BC to 636 AD, on both sides of the Jordan River, before the Arab conquest, see Martin Gilbert, *The Routledge Atlas of the Arab-Israeli Conflict,* 7th ed. (London and New York: Routledge, 1996, 2002), 1. The division of the Promised Land west and east of the Jordan River, and the allocation to the east (Transjordan) to the Reubenites, Gadites and half of the tribe of Manasseh, is described in Deuteronomy 3 and Numbers 32.

16. See Douglas J. Feith, "The Forgotten History of the Term 'Palestine,'" *Mosaic,* December 13, 2021.

17. Weizmann spoke at a Zionist demonstration at the Great Assembly Hall in London on December 7, 1918, with about 7,000 in attendance. The transcript published in the *Jewish Chronicle* on December 13, 1918, quoted him as saying:

> People were asking what shall the Jews demand from the Peace Conference? And what could they get from the Peace Conference? . . . There were some who argued that the Jews must get a Jewish state. [Cheers.] If the Poles, Jugo Slavs, and Czech-Slovaks, could get a State, why not the Jewish people, it was asked. Surely Jews were as noble descent and of ancient a life as any of these newly formed States. Very true. If length of pedigree and nobility of lineage counted they should long ago have had their rights. But they were not enough. To have a Jewish State in Palestine, the Jews must first be in Palestine. . . . There were only 100,000 Jews as against more than 600,000 non-Jews. . . .
>
> It was his moral duty to state that it was not only unwise but positively unjust to ask the Peace Conference for a Jewish State. What should they demand? In the first place, that the world should recognize that Palestine, which was the Jewish land in the past, would again be the Jewish land in the future. Their claim to it had not lapsed. They had never left it of their own accord; it was wrenched from them. . . . Their right had endured for 2,000 years and it was none the weaker on account of its antiquity, but rather strengthened by it. The right having been recognized, they would ask for opportunities and conditions to enable them to bring the Jews back to Palestine . . . to create in a relatively short time a great Jewish community of three or four million.

18. "Memorandums by the Emir Feisal Jan. 1 and 29 1919," www.scribd.com/document/72247338/Memorandums-by-the-Emir-Feisal-Jan-1-and-29-1919.

19. The translation of Faisal's proviso is taken from George Antonius, *The Arab Awakening: The Story of the Arab National Movement* (London and New York: Allegro Editions, 1939), 439.

20. Department of State, "Papers Relating to the Foreign Relations of the United States, the Paris Peace Conference, 1919, Volume III," Paris Peace Conf. 180.03101/31, BC–24, "Secretary's Notes of a Conversation Held in M. Pichon's Room at the Quai d'Orsay, Paris, on Thursday, 6 February, 1919, at 3 p.m.," history.state.gov/historicaldocuments/frus1919Parisv03/d61:

> EMIR FEISAL said that . . . Palestine, for its universal character, [should] be left on one side for the mutual consideration of all parties interested. With this exception he asked for the independence of the Arabic areas enumerated in his memorandum.

21. "Zionist Organization Statement on Palestine at the Paris Peace Conference, February 1919," www.jewishvirtuallibrary.org/zionist-organization-statement-on-palestine-at-the-paris-peace-conference.

22. "PRINCE OF HEDJAZ WELCOMES ZIONISTS; Feisal Assures 'Cousins' of the Arabs of Co-operation in Palestine. ROOM FOR BOTH IN SYRIA Working for a Reformed Near East, He Says, 'Our Two Movements Complete Each Other,'"

New York Times, March 5, 1919, timesmachine.nytimes.com/timesmachine/1919/03/05/97080071.pdf. Among the eight other American Jews who attended the Paris Peace Conference was the chief Orthodox rabbi of the United States and founder of the Orthodox Union, Bernard Louis Levinthal, representing the American Jewish Committee—the great-grandfather of Anne Mandelbaum, the editor of this book.

23. On March 7, 1919, Weizmann explained to the *Jewish Chronicle* the background to the Faisal-Frankfurter correspondence. Faisal's interview with *Le Matin*, he said, had "depressed us very much on account of its hostile tone":

> On Saturday we met Feisal's Secretary, and he disavowed the interview. He said that all that the Emir had said was that if the Zionists wished to found a Jewish State *at the present moment*, they would meet with difficulties from the local population. Mr. Frankfurter asked that a [clarification] should be published, whereupon the Emir wrote the [letter to Frankfurter].

Jewish Chronicle, March 7, 1919. The full text of Faisal's letter, and Frankfurter's reply, is at https://www.jewishvirtuallibrary.org/feisal-frankfurter-correspondence-march-1919.

24. The Faisal-Frankfurter letter is discussed in Simcha Berkowitz, "The Faisal-Frankfurter Letters: An Unending Story," in Nahum M. Waldman, ed., *Community and Culture—Essays in Jewish Studies* (Philadelphia: Gratz College Seth Press, 1987), 1–17; Charles D. Smith, "The Invention of a Tradition: The Question of Arab Acceptance of the Zionist Right to Palestine during World War I," *Journal of Palestine Studies*, Vol. XXII, No. 2 (Winter 1993); "T. E. Lawrence, Faisal and Weizmann: The 1919 Attempt to Secure an Arab Balfour Declaration," *Journal of the Royal Central Asian Society*, Vol. 56, Issue 2 (1969); Neil Caplan, "Feisal Ibn Husain and the Zionists: A Re-examination with Documents," *International History Review*, Vol. 5, No. 4 (November 1983); and "The Emir Faisal on Palestine and the Jews," *Jewish Chronicle*, October 3, 1919.

25. The text of the July 2, 1919, resolution of the Syrian Congress can be found in George Antonius, *Arab Awakening*, Appendix G, 440–42.

26. *The Letters and Papers of Chaim Weizmann*, Series B Papers, II, December 1931 to April 1952 (1984), 264, Doc. 27, "On T. E. Lawrence," first published in Arnold W. Lawrence, ed., *T. E. Lawrence by His Friends* (New York, Toronto, London: McGraw-Hill Book Co., Inc., 1937):

> Lawrence never regarded the policy of the Jewish National Home as in any way incompatible with assurances given to the Arabs. He did not think the aims and aspirations of the Jewish people in Palestine contrary to the interests of the Arabs. . . . This long and memorable talk with Lawrence [in 1918] was the foundation of . . . a lasting friendship between us. . . . Lawrence readily gave not only his advice, but his personal help in furthering both the Zionist aspirations and an understanding with the Arabs.

27. A. W. Lawrence, ed., *T. E. Lawrence by His Friends.*

28. See also, Chaim Weizmann, *Trial and Error: The Autobiography of Weizmann* (New York: Harper & Brothers, 1949), 294. Weizmann wrote:

> I had met Lawrence fleetingly in Egypt, with Allenby, and later in Palestine. I was to meet him quite often later and he was an occasional visitor to our house in London. His relationship to the Zionist movement was a very positive one in spite of the fact that he was strongly pro-Arab and he has mistakenly been represented as anti-Zionist.

For his part, Lawrence appears to have held Weizmann in high regard. Lawrence wrote to Rt. Rev. Rennie MacInnes, the Anglican Bishop of Jerusalem, that Weizmann was "a great man whose boots neither you nor I, my dear Bishop, are fit to black." Bernard Wasserstein, ed., *The Letters and Papers of Chaim Weizmann*, Vol. XI, Series A, January 1922–July 1923 (Jerusalem: Transaction Books, 1977), Letter No. 44, note 4, 14.

See also Sean McMeekin, *The Berlin-Baghdad Express: The Ottoman Empire and Germany's Bid for World Power* (Cambridge, MA: Harvard University Press, 2010), 352: "'Lawrence of Arabia' was, improbably, a closet Zionist. Despite his reputation as the patron saint of English Arabists, Lawrence . . . felt that only with a Jewish state would the Arabs make anything of themselves." Martin Gilbert considered Lawrence "a serious Zionist." Martin Gilbert, "Lawrence of Judea," *Azure*, No. 38 (Autumn 5770/2009): "Lawrence's friendship with the Arab leaders, with whom he had fought during the Arab Revolt, and his knowledge of their weaknesses as well as their strengths, was paralleled by his understanding of Zionist aspirations."

29. Ali A. Allawi, *Faisal I of Iraq*, 282, 296, 311. Lawrence blamed the British policies and administration in Iraq for the outbreak of the rebellion. Ibid., 311.

30. TEL 865, T. E. Lawrence Papers, The Huntington Library, San Marino, California.

31. Martin Gilbert, *The Churchill Documents,* Vol. 9, *Disruption and Chaos, July 1919–March 1921* (Hillsdale, MI: Hillsdale College Press, 2008), 1295, note 1: "On 4 December 1920 Churchill's Private Secretary, Edward Marsh, had written to Lawrence: 'When can you come and see him? He would like very much to have a talk with you.'"

32. Winston S. Churchill to David Lloyd George (Churchill papers: 17/2), 12 January 1921, in Martin Gilbert, *The Churchill Documents,* Vol. 9, 1306.

33. Ibid., 1305.

34. *Seven Pillars,* 21. Quoted in James Barr, *A Line in the Sand: The Anglo-French Struggle for the Middle East 1914–1948* (New York and London: W. W. Norton and Co., 2012), 109. See Scott Anderson, *Lawrence in Arabia: War, Deceit, Imperial Folly and the Making of the Modern Middle East* (New York: Anchor Books, 2014), 492:

> At least initially, Lawrence had little interest in rejoining the fray. Immersed in writing his memoirs, and undoubtedly still smarting over this shabby treatment by Lloyd George's government the previous year, he told Churchill he was too busy and that he had left politics behind. He only relented when the new colo-

> nial secretary assured him that he would have a virtually free hand in helping fundamentally reshape the British portion of the Middle Eastern chessboard.
> . . .

See also Jeremy Wilson, *Lawrence of Arabia: The Authorized Biography of T. E. Lawrence* (New York: Atheneum, 1990), 644:

> Although Churchill had been given responsibility for a large part of the Middle East in early January . . . [h]e knew very little about the Arab world and, if he was to succeed in his difficult assignment, he would need expert assistants. Lawrence would be valuable both for his knowledge of the region and for his friendship with Feisal. Lawrence did not agree very willingly . . . and he later wrote that he had only accepted because "Winston . . . offered me direct access to himself on every point, and a free hand, subject to his discretion."

35. Letter from Lawrence to Robert Graves, February 16, 1921, written close to midnight, http://www.telstudies.org/writings/letters/1921/210216_r_graves.shtml:

> We sit late at the office. . . . We are making a most ambitious design for the Middle East: a new page in the loosening of the Empire tradition, and are working like beavers to end it by Wednesday.

36. Allawi, *Faisal I of Iraq*, 321–22.

37. "T. E. Lawrence to Edward Marsh [Churchill's private secretary]," January 17, 1921, Martin Gilbert, *The Churchill Documents*, Vol. 9, 1314. See Efraim Karsh and Inari Karsh, *Empires of the Sand: The Struggle for Mastery in the Middle East 1789–1923* (Cambridge and London: Harvard University Press, 1999), 307–8.

38. Martin Gilbert, *Churchill and the Jews: A Lifelong Friendship* (New York: Henry Holt and Company, 2007), 47–48. The "promise" was the letter from Sir Henry McMahon to Sharif Hussein, 24 October 1915. See *Report of a Committee set up to consider certain correspondence between Sir Henry McMahon and the Sharif of Mecca in 1915 and 1916*: Command Paper 5974 of 1939. Gilbert wrote that:

> To ensure that Britain had not promised the same area to both the Jews and the Arabs, Churchill's senior advisor at the Middle East Department, Sir John Shuckburgh, asked Sir Henry McMahon why neither Palestine nor Jerusalem had been specifically mentioned in his letters as part of the future Arab sovereignty. McMahon replied that his reasons for "restricting myself" to specific mention of Damascus, Hama, Homs and Aleppo were "(1) that these were places to which the Arabs attached vital importance and (2) that there was no place I could think of at the time of sufficient importance for purposes of definition further south of the above." McMahon added, "It was as fully my intention to exclude Palestine as it was to exclude the more northern coastal tracks of Syria." [Letter of 12 March 1922: Foreign Office papers, 371/7797.]

See also Efraim Karsh, *Palestine Betrayed* (New Haven and London: Yale University Press, 2010), 40–41, which reaches the same conclusion. See also Tom Segev, *One Palestine Complete: Jews and Arabs Under the British Mandate* (London: Abacus,

2001), 158; Segev asserts that the British belief that they had fulfilled their obligations to the various parties left some on both sides dissatisfied:

> The Arabs felt [Palestine] had been torn away from Syria. The Zionists were bitter because Transjordan had been torn away from Palestine and the northern border differed significantly from the Zionist map. Arabs and Jews would thus claim for many years afterward that a national injustice had been perpetrated on them.

39. Michael Makovsky, *Churchill's Promised Land: Zionism and Statecraft* (New Haven and London: Yale University Press, 2007), 111.

40. Andrew Roberts, *Churchill: Walking with Destiny* (United States: Viking, 2018), 283.

41. Martin Gilbert, *Churchill and the Jews*, 52. Churchill later described his efforts as follows:

> Accompanied by Lawrence [and others], I set out for Cairo. We stayed there and in Palestine for about a month. We submitted the following main proposals to the Cabinet: First, we would repair the injury done to the Arabs by placing the Emir Feisal upon the throne of Iraq as King, and by entrusting the Emir Abdullah with the government of Trans-Jordania. . . . [and] we suggested an adjustment of the immediate difficulties between the Jews and Arabs in Palestine which would serve as a foundation for the future.

"Churchill and Lawrence—Lawrence of Arabia," *Finest Hour* 119, Summer 2003, 20, https://winstonchurchill.org/publications/finest-hour/finest-hour-119/churchill-and-lawrence-lawrence-of-arabia/. As to Lawrence's efforts, see Michael Korda, *Hero: The Life and Legend of Lawrence of Arabia* (New York: Harper Perennial, 2010), 515–16.

> [Lawrence] anticipated by more than fifty years Henry Kissinger's "shuttle diplomacy," using aircraft to fly from one leader to another throughout the Middle East in intensive bursts of negotiating and persuasion. . . .
>
> Lawrence worked in the Middle Eastern Department of the Colonial Office for just over a year, yet in that short time he not only managed to help create the borders of modern Iraq, and place his friend Feisal on its throne as its first king, but also managed to create a kingdom in all but name for Feisal's brother Abdullah in what was then known as Trans-Jordan and later became the Kingdom of Jordan. . . .

42. Telegram from Winston S. Churchill to David Lloyd George, March 18, 1921, in Martin Gilbert, *The Churchill Documents*, Vol. 9, 1401, 1403.

43. Churchill further told the delegation that Zionism would bring "prosperity and happiness to the people of the country as a whole," that there would be "more freedom, better health, more food and more people," and that "[a]bove all there will be respect for religions." His remarks to the Palestinian Arab delegation were published in *The Egyptian Gazette* on April 2, 1921. The text is in Martin Gilbert, *The Churchill Documents*, Vol. 9, 1419–21.

44. "The Making of Transjordan," http://www.kinghussein.gov.jo/his_transjordan.html.

45. In a cable to the British Foreign Office in London sent from Jeddah, Lawrence wrote that the King "has announced his abandonment of position founded on McMahan letters." Malcolm Brown, ed., *Lawrence of Arabia: The Selected Letters* (London: Little Books Ltd., 2005), 200. Andrew Roberts, *Churchill*, 283, note 90. See Scott Anderson, *Lawrence in Arabia*, 492:

> By the time Lawrence returned to England [from the Middle East] in the autumn of 1921, his one-year service to the Colonial Office nearly over, he had quite literally become the unseen kingmaker of the Middle East.

46. https://winstonchurchill.org/publications/finest-hour/finest-hour-119/churchill-and-lawrence-the-writing-of-seven-pillars/, citing Lawrence, T. E. Lawrence, "Introductory Chapter," *Seven Pillars of Wisdom: A Triumph* (Harmondsworth, England: Penguin, 1962), 283. See Efraim Karsh and Inari Karsh, *Empires of the Sand*, 307–8, citing Martin Gilbert, *Winston S. Churchill*, 1295, 1300, 1314.

47. The quotations in this paragraph are found in Wilson, *Lawrence of Arabia*, 651, citing *T. E. Lawrence to His Biographer Robert Graves* (London: Faber & Faber, 1938), 112, 127, and 114. In 1929, Lawrence wrote to Professor Yale that:

> It is my deliberate opinion that the Winston Churchill settlement of 1921–22 (in which I shared) honorably fulfills the whole of the promise we made to the Arabs, in so far as the so-called British spheres are concerned.

See John E. Mack, *A Prince of Our Disorder: The Life of T. E. Lawrence* (Cambridge, MA: Harvard University Press: 1998), 314–15:

> In his final statement on the subject in 1935, Lawrence wrote to Robert Graves how well the Middle East had done: "it more than any part of the world has gained from that war." Late in 1922 he wrote that he "must put on record my conviction that England is out of the Arab affair with clean hands." In 1927 he wrote . . . "The Arabs have now a place where they can obtain their full freedom, if they're good enough to use it." He said that "[m]y part of the Middle East job was done by 1922 and on the whole well done."

Arnold Lawrence wrote in 1936, after his brother's death, that when Lawrence left the Colonial Office he "anticipated a Jewish majority . . . after a long process of British administration of Palestine." See *T. E. Lawrence by His Friends*, "Epilogue."

48. "Churchill White Paper Speech, May 23, 1939," http://www.alliedpowersholocaust.org/wp-content/uploads/2015/03/1939-May-Churchill-White-Paper-Speech.pdf.

49. "The British White Paper of 1922," avalon.law.yale.edu/20th_century/brwh1922.asp.

50. The United States was not a member of the League of Nations, since the U.S. Senate rejected President Wilson's plan to join it. But in 1925, the Unite States consented to Britain's administration of Palestine under a British-American treaty that

provided that the United States would not recognize any modifications of the terms of the Mandate unless the United States consented to the modifications.

51. David Garnett, ed., *The Letters of T. E. Lawrence* (London, 1938), 345.

52. "Winston S. Churchill to Colonel Lawrence (Churchill papers: 17/26)," July 8, 1922. The full text is in Martin Gilbert, *The Churchill Documents*, Vol. 10, *Conciliation and Reconstruction, April 1921–November 1922* (Hillsdale, MI: Hillsdale College Press, 2008), 1930.

53. Ali A. Allawi, *Faisal I of Iraq* (New Haven: Yale University Press, 2014).

54. The specious charge that Zionism was an instance of imperialism is succinctly rebutted by Dov Waxman in *The Israeli-Palestinian Conflict: What Everyone Needs to Know* (New York: Oxford University Press, 2019), 42:

> Zionism . . . was not driven by imperialism. It was not motivated by the political, economic, or strategic interests of any European state (although it received support from some, who had their own motives). Jewish settlers were not sent to Palestine by any imperial power—in fact, they were fleeing the Russian and Austro-Hungarian empires—nor were they acting on behalf of any imperial power. They did not even come from a single country. They chose to settle in Palestine not because of its strategic value or natural resources but solely because of its historic, religious, and cultural value to Jews. . . . Rather than conquering or stealing the land, before 1948 the Zionist movement legally purchased it, often at exorbitant prices, from its owners, who were mostly absentee Arab landowners. . . . Crucially, Zionist settlers saw themselves as the indigenous people of the land, who were returning to it after a long, forced exile. Instead of trying to recreate the societies and cultures they left behind in Europe, they wanted to create a new kind of Jewish society focused on Hebrew culture.

55. Fifteen Arab countries currently have full or partial diplomatic ties with Israel. See "BDS: 15 Arab, Islamic Countries Cooperate with Israel," www.middleeastmonitor.com/20181030-bds-15-arab-islamic-countries-cooperate-with-israel/. For the alleged lack of enthusiasm in the Biden administration for the Abraham Accords, see Michael Doran and Tony Badran, "The Realignment," *Tablet*, May 10, 2021.

56. "The Abraham Accords," https://www.state.gov/the-abraham-accords/. See "David Friedman on What He Learned as U.S. Ambassador to Israel," https://mosaicmagazine.com/observation/politics-current-affairs/2022/04/podcast-david-friedman-on-what-he-learned-as-u-s-ambassador-to-israel/.

See Michael Singh, "Axis of Abraham: Arab-Israeli Normalization Could Remake the Middle East," *Foreign Affairs*, Vol. 101, No. 2 (March/April 2022), 40 (the Accords are "opening up new avenues for cooperation and heralding a dramatic reordering of the Middle East . . . with major economic and geopolitical consequences"); Zohar Palti, who held several senior Mossad and Defense Ministry posts, called the Accords an "amazing achievement" and said "[w]e are building agreements here for years"), interview in Amos Harel, "The Dramatic Moment When Israel Almost Struck Iran," *Haaretz*, March 24, 2022.

57. See David S. Cloud, Dov Lieber, and Stephen Kalin, "Mideast Talks Seek Greater Unity on Containing Iran," *Wall Street Journal*, March 28, 2022, A10 ("A historic summit . . . bringing Arab, Israeli and U.S. officials together for the first time on Israeli soil for talks on expanding their budding partnerships . . . discussing unprecedented, formal defense partnerships, as well as new military and economic ties and a joint strategy for Iran"); Patrick Kingsley, "At Summit, Israel's Ties with Arabs Move from Ceremony to Substance," *New York Times*, March 27, 2022, 19 ("groundbreaking meeting"); (David Makovsky, "A New Regional Role for Israel, as Washington Shows Signs of Stepping Back," *Jerusalem Post*, March 28, 2022 ("One can feel the tectonic plates in the Mideast shifting . . . a testament to Israel's increasing centrality in the region"); TOI Staff, "Israel reportedly working on air defense pact with regional allies," *Times of Israel*, March 29, 2022 ("Israel and its regional allies are working on developing a joint defense system to protect against the threat of Iranian drones and missiles").

58. The Emirati foreign minister made a remarkable statement to the other participants at the Summit, viewable at www.youtube.com/watch?v=u9szaSj_qt4.

4. VLADIMIR JABOTINSKY AND THE PEEL PROPHECIES

1. Pierre van Paassen was sent to Palestine to investigate the disturbances and concluded that it had been "a mere subterfuge on which the Arabs had seized to bring their long-smoldering revolt to a head." Pierre van Paassen, *Days of Our Years* (New York: Hillman-Curl, Inc., 1939), 360. He recalled the situation as follows in his 1939 memoir:

> [C]ertain influential Palestinian Arabs were not in agreement with King Faisal of Iraq, who, as chief spokesman of the Arabic peoples at the peace conference in Paris, had expressed his entire satisfaction with the international plan to set aside Palestine as a national home for the Jewish people. . . .
> The Mufti said "the Jews want to tear down [our sanctuary]. They plan to rebuild the temple of Solomon." "Do they?" I asked him in surprise. "I have never heard of that. . . . They hope that a new social order that the Jews plan to institute here will be a temple of humanity, a model of justice in human relationships. I cannot see a man like Dr. [Albert] Einstein advocating a restoration of the ancient sacrificial ceremonies with oxen and bullocks slaughtered. . . . The Jews have outgrown that bloody business centuries ago."

Van Paassen noted that the "most influential paper in Egypt, *La Bourse Egyptienne*" had just reported that "'the murder of the Palestine Jews is an echo of the Mufti's inflammatory exhortations in the mosque.'" Ibid., 361–69.

2. See Ricki Hollander, "Anti-Jewish Violence in Pre-State Palestine/1929 Massacres," *CAMERA*, August 23, 2009.

3. For the history of the Peel Commission, see generally, Rick Richman, "The 80th Anniversary of the Two-State Solution," *Mosaic*, October 2, 2017.

4. See Palestine Royal Commission, *Minutes of Evidence Heard at Public Sessions* (London: H.M. Stationery Office, 1937). The Commission held sixty-six pub-

lic meetings, all in Jerusalem except for the last, which was held in London. Chaim Weizmann testified at the eighth meeting; Goldie Meyerson (later named Golda Meir) at the thirty-eighth; David Ben-Gurion at the forty-ninth; and Vladimir Jabotinsky at the final session. Ibid., 30–40, 224–37, 288–91, 369–79. The Mufti of Jerusalem, Haj Amin al-Husseini, testified at the forty-ninth, immediately after Ben-Gurion. Ibid., 292–99.

5. When World War II broke out, Haj Amin al-Husseini went to Nazi Germany to urge Hitler to bring the war to Palestine as soon as possible. In 1941, he reached a secret agreement with Hitler to work together in a "common cause": the elimination of the "Jewish element" in Palestine. TOI Staff, "Full official record: What the mufti said to Hitler," *Times of Israel*, October 21, 2015 (official German record of the meeting between Adolf Hitler and the Grand Mufti of Jerusalem, Haj Amin al-Husseini, on November 28, 1941, at the Reich Chancellery in Berlin).

6. There have been two major biographies of Jabotinsky, each comprising two volumes: (1) Joseph Schechtman, *The Life & Times of Vladimir Jabotinsky: Rebel & Statesman: The Early Years* (New York: Thomas Yoseloff, 1956), and Joseph Schechtman, *The Vladimir Jabotinsky Story, Fighter and Prophet: The Last Years* (New York: Thomas Yoseloff, 1961); and (2) Shmuel Katz, *Lone Wolf: A Biography of Vladimir (Ze'ev) Jabotinsky*, Vols. 1 and 2. The Yale University Jewish Lives series has a short biography, Hillel Halkin, *Jabotinsky: A Life* (New Haven: Yale University Press, 2014), reviewed by Rick Richman, "Why Jabotinsky Still Matters," *The Tower*, June 2014, www.thetower.org/article/why-jabotinsky-still-matters/:

> Although little-known in the English-speaking world today, Vladimir (Ze'ev) Jabotinsky (1880–1940) is a towering figure in the history of Zionism whose influence pervades Israel, and whose political descendants dominate its politics. His life was as dramatic and heroic as that of any figure in the annals of 20th century history, from Theodor Herzl to Theodore Roosevelt, from Winston Churchill to the other giants of the age.

See also, "Vladimir (Ze'ev) Jabotinsky—A Lecture Commemorating Him by Douglas Feith," *Jewish Current Issues*, August 22, 2010, www.jpundit.typepad.com/jci/2010/08/vladimir-zeev-jobotinsky-a-lecture-commemorating-him-by-douglas-feith-.html; Rick Richman, "70 Years Ago Today," *Commentary*, August 3, 2010. For an analysis of Jabotinsky as novelist, see Rick Richman, "Jabotinsky's Novels, and How They Relate to His Politics," *Mosaic*, August 5, 2021, http://www.mosaicmagazine.com/response/israel-zionism/2021/08/jabotinskys-novels-and-how-they-relate-to-his-politics/. A useful survey of the literature on Jabotinsky can be found in Yisrael Medad, "Jabotinsky Resurgent: The Man, His Thought, His Legacy," Doc Emet Productions, May 31, 2022, https://docemetproductions.com/jabotinsky-resurgent-the-man-his-thought-his-legacy/. See also *Jabotinsky Centennial Dinner, The Waldorf Astoria, New York City, November 11, 1980*, a dinner tribute book published by The Jabotinsky Foundation (New York), with essays by Joseph Klausner, Menachem Begin, Col. John Patterson, and Pierre van Paassen.

The Israeli political scientist Shlomo Avineri, in *The Making of Modern Zionism*, wrote that Jabotinsky "towered high above all the other Zionist leaders between both world wars in his culture, sensibilities, and intellectual horizons." Hillel Halkin described Jabotinsky as "one of the most intelligent, talented, honest, and likeable of all twentieth-century politicians." Hillel Halkin, "Sacrifices," *The New Republic*, December 18, 2005, https://newrepublic.com/article/62680/sacrifices.

7. Jabotinsky's effort to build a military force to join World War I on the side of the British was hugely controversial within the Zionist movement. See Brian J. Horowitz, *Vladimir Jabotinsky's Russian Years, 1900–1925* (Bloomington: Indiana University Press, 2020), 136–37, 151:

> The majority of Jabotinsky's colleagues opposed the Legion idea as a "crazy scheme," a "dangerous" plan that would "ruin the Jewish people." Complaints came from the Russian Zionist leadership, which feared that a special alliance with Britain would put the Yishuv at risk because Germany might win. Many of the leading Russian Zionists felt strongly toward Germany, having spent years studying in German speaking cities. . . . [Some Zionists] were eager to see Russia lose the war: they hoped the defeat would stimulate political reforms in Russia. Therefore, they considered Jabotinsky's support for Britain, Russia's ally, as a betrayal. . . .
>
> He argued that [the Great Powers] would only regard Jews with respect if they could fight for themselves. In fact, Jabotinsky was the first Zionist to see the essential need for an army. In this way, he understood the value of Jewish armed forces for the sake of politics rather than merely to protect belongings and life and limb.

8. In *The Founding Fathers of Zionism*, 192, Benzion Netanyahu wrote that "no phenomenon like the Legion creation had ever appeared during the long years of Jewish existence in Exile. . . . [W]e would need to go back in history 1300 years to find it even in the Jews' own land." But Jabotinsky's Jewish Legion "was created by him as a private person without any support from the Jewish leadership. . . . Who could have imagined that such a project could be brought off, and who but Jabotinsky could have done it?"

9. John Patterson, *With the Judeans in the Palestine Campaign* (New York: Sagwan Press, 2015).

10. See Bernard Wasserstein, *Britain and the Jews of Europe 1939–1945* (London: Institute of Jewish Affairs, 1979), 272 (the Jewish Legion "helped to secure the favorable atmosphere towards Zionism in which the Balfour Declaration had been issued in 1917"); see generally, Vladimir Jabotinsky, *The Story of the Jewish Legion* (New York: B. Ackerman, Inc., 1945).

11. See Vladimir Jabotinsky, "The Iron Wall," www.en.jabotinsky.org/media/9747/the-iron-wall.pdf. In that essay, Jabotinsky wrote that only an unbreachable "iron wall" could provide the basis for an eventual peace agreement between the Arabs and the Jews:

> As long as the Arabs feel that there is the least hope of getting rid of us, they will refuse to give up this hope in return for either kind words or for bread and but-

ter, because they are not a rabble, but a living people. And when a living people yields in matters of such a vital character it is only when there is no longer any hope of getting rid of us, because they can make no breach in the iron wall.

Not till then will they drop their extremist leaders whose watchword is "Never!" And the leadership will pass to the moderate groups, who will approach us with a proposal that we should both agree to mutual concessions. Then we may expect them to discuss honestly practical questions, such as a guarantee against Arab displacement, or equal rights for Arab citizen, or Arab national integrity.

And when that happens, I am convinced that we Jews will be found ready to give them satisfactory guarantees, so that both peoples can live together in peace, like good neighbors. But the only way to obtain such an agreement, is the iron wall.

In a second essay, "The Ethics of the Iron Wall," www.david-collier.com/ethics-iron-wall-zeev-jabotinsky/, Jabotinsky argued it was a mistake to offer concessions before the Arabs were prepared to recognize the Jews as equals in Palestine: "It is incredible what political simpletons Jews are. They shut their eyes to one of the most elementary rules of life, that you must not 'meet halfway' those who do not want to meet you." He believed that negotiations with the Arabs were possible only if they would first consent to the creation of a Jewish Palestine, and he gave an example from the Talmud about the dangers of negotiations before that happened:

Two people walking along the road find a piece of cloth. One of them says: "I found it. It is mine." But the other says: "No: that is not true: I found the cloth, and it is mine." . . . It is only one of the two claimants who is obstinate: the other . . . has determined to make the world wonder at his magnanimity. So he says: "We both found the cloth, and therefore I ask only a half of it, because the second belongs to B." But B insists that he found it, and that he alone is entitled to it. In this case, the Talmud recommends a wise judgment that is, however, disappointing to our magnanimous gentleman. The judge says: "There is agreement about one half of the cloth. A admits that it belongs to B. So it is only the second half that is in dispute. We shall therefore divide this into two halves." And the obstinate claimant gets three-quarters of the cloth, while the gentleman has only one-quarter, and serves him right. It is a very fine thing to be a gentleman, but it is no reason for being an idiot. Our ancestors knew that. But we have forgotten it.

12. Palestine Royal Commission, "Notes of Evidence Taken in London on Thursday, 11th February, 1937" (London: H.M. Stationary Office, 1937).

13. The account the next day in *The Manchester Guardian*, titled "Palestine Royal Commission's Public Sitting in London—Mr. Jabotinsky Puts Jewish Defense Claim," reported that:

Hundreds of Jews lined up outside the main entrance to the House of Lords yesterday afternoon in the hope of gaining admission to the first sitting in London of the Palestine Royal Commission.

14. Joseph Schechtman, *The Vladimir Jabotinsky Story, Fighter and Prophet: The Last Years* (New York: Thomas Yoseloff, 1961), 306, note 29.

15. The full text of the Peel Commission Report can be found in Aaron S. Klieman, *The Rise of Israel, Vol. 24, The Royal Commission Report 1937* (New York and London: Garland Publishing, Inc., 1987). It was "an impressive document, 404 pages in length, well-written, containing a wealth of useful information and intelligent analysis. It remains one of the most important sources for the study of the period." Tom Segev, *One Palestine, Complete: Jews and Arabs Under the British Mandate* (London: Abacus, 2001), 401–2.

16. David Lloyd George—who had been prime minister at the time of the Balfour Declaration—called the report "scandalous" and "a lamentable admission" of British failure. Viscount Herbert Samuel—who had been the British High Commissioner for Palestine in the 1920s—harshly criticized the partition idea in the House of Lords debate. In the House of Commons, Sir Archibald Sinclair, James de Rothschild, and Winston Churchill all opposed it.

17. In America, both Louis D. Brandeis and Stephen S. Wise opposed the partition of Palestine. In a July 26, 1937, letter to his fellow Zionist and close friend, Felix Frankfurter, Brandeis wrote that Colonel Wedgwood had said that "Weizmann was selling us for a mess of porridge." Rabbi Stephen S. Wise criticized the plan as striking "at the very heart of Jewish hopes" and called it "an affront to the League of Nations."

18. Mr. V. Jabotinsky, "The Threatened Partition of Palestine: Address to Members of Parliament on Monday, 13th July, 1937" (Johannesburg: New Zionist Organization, 1937), Jabotinsky Institute Archives, Doc. A-1c/8/50, www.infocenters.co.il/jabo/jabo_multimedia/a%201/115488.pdf.

19. "Polish Jews Protest Partition," *New York Times*, July 19, 1937. The official *Gazeta Polska* of the Polish government stated that Poland "is vitally interested in large-scale Jewish emigration" and "Poland considers Vladimir Jabotinsky's plan for evacuating 75,000 Jews annually to be of the utmost importance and therefore strongly supports it." "Partition Opposed by Official Polish Paper," *JTA*, July 4, 1937.

20. "Violet Bonham Carter to Winston S. Churchill (Churchill papers: 2/316)," Jabotinsky Institute Archives Letter No. 6696, A1-2/27, published in Martin Gilbert, *Winston S. Churchill Vol. 5, Document Volume III, The Coming of War* (London: William Heinemann, 1982).

21. "Vladimir Jabotinsky to Winston S. Churchill," ibid.

22. Ibid.

23. The managing editor of the *New York Journal-American* forwarded a copy of Churchill's article the day before publication to President Roosevelt. Letter from Tom Wrigley, Manager, Washington Bureau, to Stephen Early, Secretary to the President, dated July 24, 1937.

24. The Commission reported that during the first seven months of 1938, 258 Arab and Jewish civilians died, and another 613 Jewish and Arab civilians were wounded.

25. See "Israel's Game-Changing Arab Politician Speaks," *Mosaic,* February 18, 2021, quoting Mansour Abbas in an interview with The Washington Institute:

> If we look at Arab politics inside the state of Israel, we have seen ourselves always as an opposition party. . . . Now Ra'am, my party, says the exact opposite. . . . We say that [Arabs] cannot expect a change if [Arabs and Jews] are always opposed to each other and if we don't talk to each other in a serious way. . . . Jews and Arabs can live together when this state incorporates the Arab minority without sacrificing our identity or forgoing the initial rights of Jews.

See also, Ruthie Blum, "Mansour Abbas's 'Jewish State' Bombshell," *Jerusalem Post*, December 23, 2021, quoting Mansour Abbas as saying that "Israel was born as a Jewish state" and "that's how it will remain." He said he was changing Israeli politics and society and that "from now on, it will be natural for Arab parties to be members of the government," vowing to put legislative work for his community above Islamism and Palestinian activism. Blum noted that Abbas had uttered his words "unapologetically, publicly and in Arabic," which made him "not only courageous, but credible."

See also, Einat Wilf, "Israeli-Arab MK Mansour Abbas is What Zionism Intended," *State of Tel Aviv*, June 17, 2002, in which Wilf, a former Israeli Member of the Knesset, suggests that Jabotinsky would have welcomed the emergence of Mansour Abbas's Arab party and its participation in the Israeli government.

26. "Address delivered by Vladimir Jabotinsky at a Banquet given in his honor at the Carlton Hotel, Johannesburg, on Saturday, March 26th, 1938," Jabotinsky Archives, 115510, Reference Code A1-8/54. See Dan Jacobson, "A Memoir of Jabotinsky," *Commentary*, June 1961; see Geraldine Auerbach, "Jabotinsky's Visit to Kimberley in 1938," www.kehilalinks.jewishgen.org/kimberley/Jabotinsky.html. In his address, Jabotinsky described the efforts he had made in Europe:

> We went to the centers of the storm, to Poland, to Roumania, to other countries. We knocked at the highest doors. We spoke to kings and presidents and ministers, who received us and invited us again, and listened to the voice of truth. And we told them, "Is it really true that you want to drag the fair names of your countries into the same mud as somewhere else? Is it really true that you, you, you, brought up in the great schools of the liberal thought of the great 19th century, you want to dirty your hands, you want to drag your banners in the destruction of the people who made men of your ancestors, the people who gave you what we gave you? Why not go and look for some solution in the name of the old principle, expressed for the first time in Polish national rising of 1863, 'for your freedom and ours'? Go this way, there is a country called Palestine where, if it is open, there is room enough for the Arabs who live there, for their children, for millions of Jews, for peace and prosperity."

27. Jabotinsky recounted that the world knew two things about the Jews: "First, that the Jews have been turned out ofPalestine by force; and second, that the Jews have never ceased claiming Palestine back." He concluded that:

> History is not against us, and the world is not against us. The horizon is black, but behind the horizon there is the sun. . . . We are carrying today the great-

> est truth of Jewish history. We are a few steps from the threshold of victory . . . truth will win.

28. Quoted by Benzion Netanyahu in Benzion Netanyahu, *The Founding Fathers of Zionism* (Jerusalem: Balfour Books, co-published with Gefen Publishing House Ltd., 2012), 229–30.

29. Letter from Vladimir Jabotinsky, President of the New Zionist Organization, to Prime Minister Neville Chamberlain, September 4, 1939, The Jabotinksy Institute in Israel, Letter No. 4115, reference code A-1 2/29/2. See Rick Richman, *Racing Against History: The 1940 Campaign for a Jewish Army to Fight Hitler* (New York: Encounter Books, 2018), 75.

30. On January 15, 1940, the *New York Times* reported that Jewish refugees were marooned on the Danube, after an intense cold had frozen the river all the way down to the Black Sea. Jabotinsky's letter to Churchill read in part as follows:

> I appeal to you to intervene to save the 2,000 refugees marooned on small barges in the ice on the Danube. . . . It would be cruelly futile now to argue whether the refugees were "right" or "wrong" in trying to escape from hell. They have tried, in the only direction they (or you, or anybody) could think of. Today they must be saved, and as Roumania will not allow them to land, the only way to save them on the brink of a hideous hecatomb is to lift—for them at least—the Palestine ban.
>
> No argument of "policy" can be invoked in the face of such misery, where only the argument of humanity has the right to be heard.

Letter No. 4177, A1-2/30/1, Jabotinsky Archives. Churchill at the time was First Lord of the Admiralty but had no power to change the government's Palestine policy. He forwarded the letter to the Secretary of State for the Colonies, Malcolm MacDonald, who did nothing. Jabotinsky sent identical letters to every member of the British cabinet, and received this cruel (and inaccurate) reply from Lord Halifax, Britain's foreign minister:

> It is understood that these unfortunate people were induced to embark upon their present journey by unscrupulous tourist agents who concealed from them the fact that persons not having immigration permits are prohibited from entering Palestine.

Shmuel Katz, *Lone Wolf: A Biography of Vladimir (Ze'ev) Jabotinsky* (New York: Barricade Books, 1996), 1745. The refugees eventually were able to board a ship that made its way toward Palestine, with Jabotinsky's son Eri on board for moral support. When the ship arrived, the British arrested Eri Jabotinsky and imprisoned him for six months. Ibid.

Vladimir Jabotinsky's last cable to Churchill, sent June 21, 1940, asked him to help seek Eri's release after British authorities released a large number of Jews from prison other than Eri. Letter 4299, A1-2/30/2, Jabotinsky Institute Archives ("My son still jailed in Palestine despite wide measure of liberating detainees. While doing here my utmost to serve common cause I earnestly urge you to forbid this persecution of genuine patriot for deed of mercy"). Eri was still in British prison when his father died on August 3, 1940.

31. See Rick Richman, "Jabotinsky's Lost Moment, June 1940," *The Tower*, 2013, www.thetower.org/article/jabotinskys-lost-moment-june-1940/.

32. Raymond Daniell, "CHURCHILL IN PLEA; Urges French People to Stay in Fight as His Own Nation Will," *New York Times,* June 19, 1940.

33. Western Union Telegram to Winston Churchill, dated June 15, 1940, Jabotinsky Institute Archives, Letter No. 4294, Document A1-2/30/2. The day after Churchill became prime minister in May 1940, Jabotinsky had sent a cablegram to him that read as follows:

> Wishing success in your formidable mission I as spokesman of movement principally identified with Jewry's revived military tradition offer you plan of cooperation. Stop. I am cabling upon assumption that you realize necessity to reverse all those features of previous policy which nearly killed magnetism of allied cause abroad. Stop. One feature was absurd shrinking from Jewish aspects of present crisis forgetful that when in anti-Nazi war even Jews are forced into indifference gentile isolationism feels doubly justified. Stop. I offer to raise Jewish Army for all allied fronts provided status similar to Polish Army's and provided [Malcolm] MacDonald policy stopped leaving Palestine's destiny officially unprejudiced till peace conference. Stop. Discounting at present farther possibilities foresee 130,000 recruits in eastern hemisphere alone plus world wide network of centers radiating new attitude to allied cause among all creeds. Stop. Details in memorandum submitted to War Office by New Zionist presidency last March. . . .

Western Union Cablegram to Winston Churchill, dated May 12, 1940, Jabotinsky Institute Archives, Letter No.4252, Document A-1-2/30/2.

34. Arthur Koestler, at work in 1940 on his masterpiece *Darkness at Noon,* who had headed Jabotinsky's organization in Berlin during the 1920s, wrote in his diary after learning about Jabotinsky's death:

> Exit one of the great tragic figures of this century. . . . Adored hero of the Jewish masses in Russia and Poland; creator of the first Jewish legion which helped conquer Palestine; sentenced to fifteen years hard labor for organizing Jewish resistance against Arab pogrom in Jerusalem; translated Dante and Shakespeare into modern Hebrew; wrote and spoke eight languages; most fascinating orator I ever heard.

A decade and a half after Jabotinsky's death, the Zionist leader Louis Lipsky—an opponent of Jabotinsky during his life—wrote a poignant tribute of him:

> Jabotinsky never lived in the regular time of day. He had his own time. While we Zionists saw the clock at six, he saw it at twelve. He did not know what was meant by premature; whatever was true was timely. . . .
>
> He came to the United States when it was frozen in the spirit of isolation,

> and died before American isolation became defense and aid for Britain. He preached to his last days for a Jewish army and Jewish flag (Jews as allies of the fighters against Hitler). . . . He was dazzled by a light. He saw his people once more like the other peoples of the earth, at home in freedom, the masters of their own land, no longer suppliants and pariahs, no longer enduring inferiority, but bravely and courageously fighting for their freedom. That light never got out of his eyes. . . . He was a bold, imaginative, brave man. Practically alone he marched ahead. He was sure the army would follow him some day.
>
> Louis Lipsky, *Memoirs in Profile*, 154–55.

35. For a more extensive description of Jabotinsky's death and funeral in New York, including photographs of the cortege after the funeral service, and Jabotinsky's reburial in Jerusalem in 1964, see Rick Richman, *Racing Against History*, 93–98 and 147–51.

5. GOLDA MEIR: PORTRAIT OF THE LIONESS AS A YOUNG WOMAN

1. In addition to Golda Meir's 1975 autobiography, Golda Meir, *My Life* (New York: G. P. Putnam's Sons, 1975), there are two excellent biographies of her: Elinor Burkett, *Golda* (New York: Harper Perennial, 2008) and Francine Klagsbrun, *Lioness: Gold Meir and the Nation of Israel* (New York: Schocken Books, 2017).

2. As of 1912, approximately 1,200 members of the Socialist Party of America held offices in 340 cities and towns in America, with Socialist mayors in Buffalo, Minneapolis, Reading, Schenectady, and Berkeley, www.dissentmagazine.org/online_articles/what-milwaukee-can-teach-the-democrats-about-socialism.

3. "100 Women of the Year: 1956 Golda Meir," *Time Magazine*, time.com/5793561/golda-meir-100-women-of-the-year: "After she raised $50 million for Israel's war of independence, founding Prime Minister David Ben-Gurion wrote that Meir was the 'Jewish woman who got the money which made the state possible.'"

4. Quoted in Rebecca Erbelding, *Rescue Board: The Untold Story of America's Efforts to Save the Jews of Europe* (New York: Anchor, 2018). See www.penguinrandomhouse.ca/books/553635/rescue-board-by-rebecca-erbelding/9780525433743/excerpt.

5. Ibid.

6. Adolf Hitler, *Mein Kampf*, Ralph Manheim, trans. (Boston: Houghton Mifflin Co., 1945), 1. Writing in 1925 from prison, Hitler began his autobiography with sentences that made his perspective and ambitions clear:

> Today it seems to me providential that Fate should have chosen Braunau on the Inn as my birthplace. For this little town lies on the boundary between two German states which we of the younger generation at least have made it our life work to reunite by every means at our disposal. . . . One blood demands one Reich.

In the following pages, he offered a long quasi-intellectual analysis of why "one blood" required the destruction of Jewish blood in German states.

7. The *Times*'s coverage of Hitler and the Nazis also presaged the type of journalism that would later produce *People Magazine*. On January 13, 1938, in "Goering Marks 45th Birthday," the *Times* reported breezily that "Chancellor Hitler led the list of those sending congratulations and the entire Cabinet . . . called personally." On February 19, a *Times* headline read: "Hitler Gives Musicale, Raises 1,050,000 Marks," in a story that reported the "contributions" that "leading industrialists and other rich men" had made at the end of the evening to Hitler's "Winter charities campaign." On February 25, the *Times* reported that Hitler was building "Adolf Hitler University" in Berlin, with the first building dedicated to "the faculty of military science."

8. "PROTESTS ATTACK BY DODD ON HITLER; German Ambassador Visits Hull, Who Says Free Speech Is Guaranteed to Citizens," *New York Times*, January 15, 1938, page 1.

9. Ferdinand Kuhn Jr., "British Minimize Vienna Surrender; Relieved That Clash Was Avoided," *New York Times*, February 16, 1938, page 1. The *Times* report explained that:

> For the British are trying to discover at the moment whether they can make "deals" with both Germany and Italy. It would have been awkward, to say the least, if Austro-German bloodshed had interrupted the present Anglo-German flirtation, or if the threat of bloodshed in Austria overhung Anglo-German negotiations.

10. On February 17, the *Times* reported that "London now regards it as only a matter of months before the swastika clasps Czechoslovakia in its arms, just as it has gripped Austria" and "as German expansion throws its shadow across the Continent Britain seems more and more anxious to come to terms." Ferdinand Kuhn Jr., "British 'Write Off' Austrian Question . . . Czechs Held Next Victims," *New York Times*, February 17, 1938.

On March 20, the *Times* reported that "Washington would like to see how Prime Minister Neville Chamberlain makes out with his new program of separate negotiations on a realistic basis with Germany and Italy. If he should succeed . . . there would be influential voices raised in the Administration to . . . make a fresh start in international relations on what some are pleased to describe as a basis of realism." Bertram D. Holland, "Foreign Problems Now Press on US—Hull Accepts Disappearance of Austria, but Fundamentals of Policy are Unchanged," *New York Times*, March 20, 1938.

11. The *New York Times* quoted British Foreign Minister Halifax as saying "Horrible! Horrible! I never thought they would do it." "Europe Under Ultimatums," *New York Times*, March 19, 1938. The *Times* reported that the "vast majority of Conservative members of Parliament felt that it might not hurt Britain after all if Chancellor Hitler of Germany were allowed to push farther into Central Europe," and their "overwhelming impulse was to 'write off' Czechoslovakia and Spain and wash British hands of future trouble on the Continent." Ferdinand Kuhn Jr., "British Now Favor Isolation Policy," *New York Times*, March 22, 1938. In "Austria Enlarges Big German Army," the *Times* reported that "Hitler has gone far toward accomplishment of one of

his primary ambitions as expressed in his book 'Mein Kampf'—the military domination of the continent of Europe."

12. "Fey, Foe of Nazis, Commits Suicide—Austrian Ex-Vice Chancellor, Fearing Arrest, First Killed His Wife and Son—Many Others End Lives . . . Baron Lois Rothschild is Arrested," *New York Times*, March 17, 1938.

13. "Vienna Jews Beaten; Stores Plundered," *New York Times*, March 14, 1938. See also "Jews Humiliated by Vienna Crowds—Families Compelled to Scrub Streets . . . Nazis Seize Big Stores—Total of Arrests Enormous," *New York Times*, March 19, 1938: "All Jewish executives in Vienna's largest department stores . . . were arrested. . . . Shops, cafes and restaurants were raided and large numbers of Jews were arrested."

14. "Goering Is Acclaimed in Vienna; Warns Jews Must Quit Austria," *New York Times*, March 27, 1938.

15. Dorothy Thompson, "Refugees: A World Problem," *Foreign Affairs*, Vol. 16, No. 3 (April 1938), www.jstor.org/stable/20028859.

16. See "80 years ago: An international conference to discuss Jewish refugees ends in failure," USC Shoah Foundation, https://sfi.usc.edu/news/2018/06/22491-80-years-ago-international-conference-discuss-jewish-refugees-ends-failure.

17. "The Ambassador in France (Bullitt) to the Secretary of State, June 27, 1938," *Foreign Relations of the United States Diplomatic Papers, 1938, General*, Volume 1 (840.48 Refugees/413: Telegram), https://history.state.gov/historicaldocuments/frus1938v01/d728.

18. A "Memorandum of Certain Jewish Organizations Concerned with the Refugees from Germany and Austria," submitted by various Jewish organizations, addressed "Palestine as a Country of Immigration" in part as follows:

> Palestine has a special status as a country of Jewish immigration, because Great Britain, the Mandatory, together with the League of Nations and the American Government, have endorsed the policy of facilitating there the establishment of a Jewish national home. . . . Palestine, moreover, is a country with which Jewish hope has been associated from time immemorial, and a large proportion of the refugees would prefer to settle there for idealistic reasons, if they had the opportunity. Jewish immigration has been the chief factor in the remarkable development of the country during recent years; and the coming of the German Jews has contributed to an eminent measure to the economic and cultural development.

19. "The Chief of the Division of Near Eastern Affairs (Murray) to the Consul General at Jerusalem (Wadsworth), July 2, 1938," *Foreign Relations of the United States Diplomatic Papers, 1938*, https://history.state.gov/historicaldocuments/frus1938v01/d730. In the document, Wallace Murray answers a question about the U.S. position at the coming Conference "on the matter of Jewish immigration into Palestine" by providing an extract from the "confidential memorandum furnished for the guidance of the American delegation," which read:

> It is highly probable that various groups will endeavor to induce the representatives . . . to take up the question of immigration into Palestine. It is felt that the

> Committee should reject any attempts to interject into its considerations such political issues as are involved in the Palestine, the Zionist and the anti-Zionist questions. These questions would stir up bitter passions and might even lead to a disruption of the committee's labors.

Richard Breitman and Allan J. Lichtman, *FDR and the Jews* (Cambridge, MA: Harvard University Press, 2013), 109, attribute the Evian Conference solely to a humanitarian motive of Roosevelt:

> The Evian conference was an extraordinary undertaking for a president facing a nasty recession, ongoing struggles with Congress over recovery measures, internal battles against conservatives in his party, and a difficult midterm election. No hidden political motive underlay Roosevelt's humanitarian initiative. To the contrary, with the Jewish vote secure for his party, he had little to gain and much to lose politically from potentially antagonizing anti-Semites and restrictionists.

Breitman and Lichtman note that in June 1938, on the eve of the conference, a Gallup poll showed that FDR's popularity had declined to 54 percent from 63 percent eight months before, and that the American Jewish Committee commissioned polls that showed that 45 percent of the public felt Jews had too much power in the United States. They thus assert that, if anything, the Evian initiative was counter to Roosevelt's political interests.

But the restrictions Roosevelt placed on the Conference, set forth in the invitation to it, doomed it from the beginning, making it effectively only a public relations effort. The Evian Conference's sole action was to establish a follow-on committee, whose chairman, George Rublee, later said Roosevelt's true intention in calling the Conference was not to rescue the refugees, but rather "to assuage the indignation excited by the persecution of the Jews." Quoted in Rafael Medoff, *The Jews Should Keep Quiet: Franklin D. Roosevelt, Rabbi Stephen S. Wise, and the Holocaust* (Philadelphia: The Jewish Publication Society, 2019), 80, citing "Rublee Oral History (1951), Columbia University, 283–84."

The conclusion Breitman and Lichtman reach at the end of their book seems closer to the mark:

> Even Jewish advocates close to FDR recognized that he often failed to turn humanitarian principles into action to benefit Jewish victims of Nazism, especially during his first term and the period from the outbreak of World War Two through the formation of the War Refugee Board [in 1944].

Breitman and Lichtman, *FDR and the Jews*, 329.

20. For a comprehensive article on the Evian Conference, see S. Adler-Rudel, "The Evian Conference on the Refugee Question," Leo Baeck Institute, *Year Book XIII* (London: Horovitz Publishing Co., 1968), 235–73.

21. The Jewish Agency for Palestine, "Memorandum Submitted to the Inter-Governmental Conference on Refugees, 6th July, 1938."

22. JTA Archive, "Winterton Appointment Stirs Comment," June 26, 1938:

> The Jewish Chronicle demanded editorially that Palestine be given an opportunity to afford the maximum possibility to assist in solving the immediate refugee problem. It expressed the hope that Lord Winterton's appointment would not prejudice the possibility. . . . "The appointment of Winterton cannot fail to arouse serious misgivings," the editorial declared, pointing to Lord Winterton's pro-Arab utterances and statements as creating the impression that he was "out of sympathy with the Jews in general."

23. At the beginning of the Conference the next morning, the Chairman read the telegram of the Conference to President Roosevelt:

> The Intergovernmental Committee on Refugees addresses to President Roosevelt the tribute of its gratitude for the initiative taken by him on March 25th last with a view to securing a practical solution of the problem raised by the movement of refugees throughout the world, and in particular by the movement of refugees from Germany, including Austria. The Committee expresses the hope that this initiative may, with the collaboration of all governments concerned, lead to successful results.

Intergovernmental Committee—Evian—July 1938, "Verbatim Report of the Second Meeting held on Thursday, July 7th, 1938."

24. William Shirer, *Berlin Diary, 1934–1943* (London: Hamish Hamilton, 1941), 101.

25. The representative from Colombia, Jesús María Yepes, articulated the problem as follows:

> The problem of political refugees . . . [presents] a question of principle. . . . Can a State, without upsetting the basis of our civilization, and indeed, of all civilization, arbitrarily withdraw nationality from a whole class of its citizens, thereby making them Stateless Persons whom no country is compelled to receive on its territory? . . . The whole tragedy . . . lies in the fact that this preliminary question was not settled in time.

The core problem, in fact, went deeper. The conditions set for the Conference—no change in law, no financial obligations, no discussion of Palestine—ensured that nothing could be done; the countries that participated were more concerned about not offending Germany than saving Jews; and none of the participants was interested in an academic discussion about a "question of principle"—only in simply satisfying the Roosevelt administration by their presence.

26. Intergovernmental Committee, Evian, July 1938, "Verbatim Report of the Sixth Meeting (Public) held on Friday, July 18th, 1938." For other documents relating to the Evian Conference, see the Myron C. Taylor Papers—Evian Intergovernmental Committee Conference at the Franklin D. Roosevelt Presidential Library and Museum, FDRlibrary.marist.edu/archives/collections/franklin, "Selected Digitized Documents Related to the Holocaust and Refugees, 1933–1945."

27. Ibid.

28. Michael Berenbaum, "Yehuda Bauer's Assessment of the US Government and American Jewry During the Holocaust: An Analysis," *The Journal of Holocaust Research*, Vol. 36, No 1 (February 8, 2022), 77–88, DOI: 10.1080/25785648.2021.2023849.

29. Henry Feingold, *The Politics of Rescue: The Roosevelt Administration and the Holocaust* (New Brunswick, NJ: Rutgers University Press, 1970), 35. Feingold writes further that "Roosevelt was anxious to conceal the largely Jewish character of the refugee crisis" and the administration preferred the label "political refugees" or "involuntary immigrants":

> While Berlin was converting all "enemies," including Roosevelt, to the Jewish faith, the Roosevelt Administration was reconverting Jews, caught in the Nazi net, to a bland category called "political refugees." Washington's bureaucracy, like Berlin's, invented a terminology to camouflage what was happening and in doing so helped to muffle the rumbles of the final solution.

30. See "The Chairman of the American Delegation (Taylor) to the Secretary of State," July 14, 1938:

> [T]he Latin Americans . . . have told us in great frankness that the pressure brought upon them by Germany through compensation agreements and other commercial arrangements was such that they did not dare join in any action which might seem to be even in the smallest respect critical. . . . They told me frankly after the meeting this morning that unless I could find some formula which would seem to release them from any obligation in this matter they would have to vote against the resolution.

State Department, Office of the Historian, Foreign Relations of the United States Diplomatic Papers, 1938, General, Vol. I, history.state.gov/historicaldocuments/frus1938v01/d736.

31. Ibid.

32. Aaron Klieman, ed., *The Letters and Papers of Chaim Weizmann,* Vol. XVIII—Series A (Jerusalem: Transaction Books, 1979), 431, Letter 372.

33. Van Paassen, *Days of Our Years*, 410. The book was named one of the ten most important non-fiction books of 1939. "Best Non-Fiction of 1939 Selected," *New York Times*, January 18, 1940, 21.

34. "SD on the Outcome of the Evian Conference Report of SD," Submitted to SS Gruppenfuehrer Heydrich, Yad Vashem Archive, 0.51/OSO/37 Berlin, 29 July 1938, www.yadvashem.org/odot_pdf/microsoft%20word%20-%203528.pdf.

35. "Evian Conference," www.encyclopedia.com/religion/encyclopedias-almanacs-transcripts-and-maps/evian-conference.

36. T. R. Ybarra, "Dorothy Thompson's Plea for the Exiles," *New York Times*, August 14, 1938.

37. The latest history, a 990-page book, makes no reference to Evian. Richard Overy, *Blood and Ruins: The Last Imperial War, 1931–1945* (United States: Viking, 2022).

In his two-volume, 1,804-page memoir, FDR's secretary of State, Cordell Hull, devoted a single page to the Evian Conference, writing that "[a]t the State Department . . . we believed it necessary to . . . take stronger international action lest these victims of persecution be exterminated, and lest the unsettled state of Europe be further disturbed by the wholesale wanderings of these hapless people from country to country":

> With the President's approval, I therefore sent out invitations to a number of other governments to cooperate in setting up a special refugee committee. In announcing this move on March 24, 1938, we made it clear that the financing of the emergency emigration would be done by private organizations, and that no country would be expected to receive a greater number of immigrants than its existing legislation permitted.

Cordell Hull, *The Memoirs of Cordell Hull*, Vol. I (New York: The Macmillan Co., 1948), 578. There is no reflection in Hull's memoir on the contradiction between the necessity of "stronger international action" to avoid "extermination" and the emphasis in the Evian invitation that no governmental funds would be discussed, nor any change in immigration law.

38. Dennis R. Laffer, "The Jewish Trail of Tears: The Evian Conference of July 1938," www.researchgate.net/publication/254706382_The_Jewish_Trail_of_Tears_The_Evian_Conference_of_July_1938.

39. Ernst Marcus, "The German Foreign Office and the Palestine Question," *Yad Vashem Studies*, 194.

40. Golda Meir, *My Life*, 159.

41. Ibid.

42. Jean Shaoul, "100 years since the Balfour Declaration," Part One, November 7, 2017, World Socialist Web Site, www.wsws.org/en/articles/2017/11/07/balf-n07.html; Jean Shaoul, "100 years since the Balfour Declaration," Part Two, November 8, 2017, World Socialist Web Site, www.wsws.org/en/articles/2017/11/08/balf-n08.html. The two-part essay concluded that Israel should be replaced by a "United Socialist States of the Middle East":

> The Zionist state that the Balfour Declaration and the subsequent machinations of the major powers spawned has been a terrible and failed experiment. . . . The only way out of the current impasse is the development of a political movement to unite Arab and Jewish workers and intellectuals in a common struggle against capitalism and for the building of a socialist society.

43. Quoted in Golda Meir, *My Life*, 160. The article was written for the Women's Labor Council in July 1939.

44. Ibid.

6. BEN HECHT AND THE SOUL OF AMERICAN JEWS

1. "Ben Hecht, 70, Dies at His Home Here," *New York Times*, April 16, 1964.
2. Ibid.

3. "All-Time 100 Nonfiction Books," http://entertainment.time.com/2011/08/30/all-time-100-best-nonfiction-books/slide/a-child-of-the-century-by-ben-hecht/. *Moment Magazine*'s "Five Books Project" asked various authors, "What five books should you read to be an educated Jew?" Yossi Klein Halevi listed *A Child of the Century*, because Hecht was "one of the most significant Jewish figures of the 20th century," embodying "assimilation, professional success, and then a return to Jewish identity and a powerful if ambivalent relationship with Israel." www.momentmag.com/what-five-books-should-you-read-to-be-an-educated-jew/.

4. Hecht devoted 110 pages of his memoir to his efforts to save "the doomed Jews of Europe and his support for the Irgun; Hollywood merited only 49 pages." Adina Hoffman, *Ben Hecht: Fighting Words, Moving Pictures* (New Haven: Yale University Press, 2019), 4. Julien Gorbach, *The Notorious Ben Hecht: Iconoclastic Writer and Militant Zionist* (West Lafayette, IN: Purdue University Press, 2019), 132: "Revisionism [was] the cause Hecht took up in the 1940s that would change his life and legacy."

5. Adina Hoffman, *Ben Hecht*, 6.

6. Julien Gorbach, *Notorious Ben Hecht*, 56, citing "Popular Arts Project: The Reminiscences of Ben Hecht," Columbia Center for Oral History Research, 1959, 736.

7. Gorbach, *Notorious Ben Hecht*, 108, citing a 1972 interview by William MacAdams.

8. In his autobiography, *A Child of the Century*, Hecht wrote that:

> The movies are one of the bad habits that corrupted our century. [They are] an eruption of trash that has lamed the American mind and retarded Americans from becoming a cultured people. [They have fed the American public] naïveté and buncombe in doses never before administered to any people. They have slapped into the American mind more human misinformation in one evening than the dark ages could muster in a decade.

Hecht wrote about the failure of his novels to generate a serious readership, as opposed to his films, which were widely celebrated by film buffs and scholars:

> Had I contented myself with writing books, as I started out to do when I was 17, I might have acquired a more definite identity than I seem to have, among the critics, if nowhere else. I can understand the literary critic's shyness toward me. It is difficult to praise a novelist or a thinker who keeps popping up as the author of the new Marvel Movie melodramas. It is like writing about the virtues of a preacher who keeps fearlessly getting himself arrested in bordellos.

Quoted in Michiko Kakutani, "Books of the Times: He Spoke of Art but Made His Money in Movies," *New York Times*, March 1990 [a review of William Macadams, *Ben Hecht: The Man Behind the Legend* (New York: Charles Scribner's Sons, 1990)].

9. Haskel Lookstein, *Were We Our Brothers' Keepers? The Public Response of American Jews to the Holocaust* (New York: Random House, 1985), 57–59, 71–73.

10. Stephen S. Wise, *Challenging Years*, 264–65.

11. Fred T. Marsh, "Miracles by Hecht," *New York Times*, June 18, 1939.

12. Hecht would later write of this period in *A Child of the Century* that:

> I write of Jews today, I who never knew himself as one before, because that part of me which is Jewish is under violent and apelike attack. My way of defending myself is to answer as a Jew.

13. "Peter Bergson" was the pseudonym adopted by Hillel Kook for his activities in America. He was a nephew of Palestine's first Chief Rabbi, Abraham Yitzak Kook, and he adopted the pseudonym to avoid embarrassing his rabbinical family with his Zionist activities. See generally, Rabbi Dov Peretz Elkins, *Peter Bergson: The Jewish Lobbyist Who Advocated to Save Jews During the Holocaust* (Jerusalem: Mazo Publishers, 2022).

14. Ben Hecht, *Child of the Century,* 517.

15. The fundraiser is described in Julien Gorbach, *Notorious Ben Hecht*, 165, 396, note 12.

16. Ben Hecht, *Child of the Century*, 540.

17. On January 19, the *New York Times* published an article titled "Palestine Called a Vital War Base," reporting a speech by Rear Admiral Yates Stirling, Jr., former Chief of Staff of the U.S. Fleet, to a National Conference for Palestine, attended by more than 1,200 Jewish leaders. Admiral Stirling asserted that control of Palestine could affect the outcome of the war:

> "The fanwise spread of Allied airplanes can begin in Palestine and reach out to these lands in Southeastern Europe which now lie under Hitler's domain" [Stirling said]. "It is not inconceivable that one of the major offensives into Hitler's Europe can be undertaken by troops which have their starting point in Palestine."

Navy Secretary William Franklin Knox sent a cable to the Conference stating that "Palestine looms large on the horizon as a strategic key to the Middle East," because "Hitler must capture it if he is to reach Iran and the Mosul oil field he needs."

18. "Nazis Blame Jews for Big Bombings—Goebbels Says 'Extermination' of All in Europe 'and Perhaps Beyond' Will Result," *New York Times*, June 13, 1942.

19. Rick Atkinson, *An Army at Dawn: The War in North Africa, 1942–1943* (New York: Henry Holt and Co., 2002), 11.

20. Wise ended by agreeing that it "would be far better to make any statement general, though inclusive of specific reference to this threat against the Jews, than to make it solely a statement in defense of Jews." Sumner Welles Papers, Box 66, Folder OS Office Correspondence, Wise, Stephen 1942, www.fdrlibrary.marist.edu/_resources/images/hol/hol00370.pdf.

21. "1,000,000 Jews Slain by Nazis, Report Says—'Slaughterhouse' of Europe Under Hitler Described at London," *New York Times*, June 30, 1942.

22. On July 7, 1942, the *Times* reported that the Nazi occupation authorities would begin evacuating all Jews from the Netherlands.

23. After the war, Jews would look back and try to explain why they had not fully

realized what was happening. See, e.g., Marie Syrkin, writing in 1982 that the inability reflected incomprehension rather than indifference:

> Today when genocide, gas chamber, and mass extermination are the small coin of language, it is hard to reconstruct the innocent state of mind when American Jews, like the Jews of Europe's ghettos, could not immediately grasp that the ascending series of Nazi persecutions had reached this apex.

Marie Syrkin, "What American Jews Did During the Holocaust," *Midstream*, October 1982, 6. See also Deborah Lipstadt: "It is a-historic, if not facile, to expect from the wartime American Jewish community a level of organization, political clout, and impact characteristic of political behavior of the Baby Boom/Vietnam-era protest generation." Deborah Lipstadt, *Playing the Blame Game: American Jews Look Back at the Holocaust* (Ann Arbor: University of Michigan, Jean & Samuel Frankel Center for Judaic Studies, 2011), 27.

24. See Walter Laqueur, *The Terrible Secret: Suppression of the Truth About Hitler's "Final Solution"* (Boston and Toronto: Little Brown and Co., 1980), 65, describing the period from July 1941 to the end of 1942:

> [N]o intelligence service in Europe could possibly not help hearing about the "final solution" in 1942 for the simple reason that it was common knowledge on the continent. Details were perhaps shrouded in mystery, but the picture in general was not: as Hitler had predicted, the Jews were disappearing. The Allied governments heard about this from a variety of sources.

Laqueur wrote that beginning in June 1942, press reports made it clear what was happening:

> [A]uthors and editors had realized that from the various news items from Eastern Europe a sinister new pattern emerged: these were no longer pogroms in the traditional sense. The first dispatch began as follows: "More than 700,000 Polish Jews have been slaughtered by the Germans in the greatest massacres in the world's history." It then announced that "the most gruesome details of mass killings even to the use of poison gas" were revealed in a report sent secretly to [the Jewish representative on the Polish National Council].

Ibid., 72–73.

25. The description of the Riegner telegram incident comes from Richard Breitman and Alan M. Kraut, "Who Was the 'Mysterious Messenger'?" *Commentary*, October 1983; Letters from Readers, "The Mysterious Messenger," *Commentary*, January 1984; Walter Laqueur, "The Riegner Cable, and the Knowing Failure of the West to Act During the Shoah," *Tablet*, August 9, 2015; Arthur D. Morse, *While Six Million Died: A Chronicle of American Apathy* (New York: Random House, 1968); Walter Laqueur, *The Terrible Secret*; David S. Wyman, *The Abandonment of the Jews: America and the Holocaust, 1941–1945* (New York: Pantheon Books, 1984); and an examination of the files of various participants in the archives of FDR Library.

26. The U.S. Holocaust Museum summary recounts that Riegner arrived at the American consulate "in great agitation" and met with vice-consul Howard Elting, Jr., who forwarded the message, adding that Riegner's information "may well contain an element of truth." Leland Harrison, the highest-ranking U.S. diplomat in Switzerland, thought the mass murder plan was likely only a "war rumor," but forwarded the message to the State Department in Washington—which withheld it from Wise. "The Riegner Telegram," enyclopedia.ushmm.org/content/en/article/the-riegner-telegram.

27. Riegner also went to the British consulate in Geneva, which forwarded his message to London, for transmittal to Samuel Sydney Silverman, who was a member of Parliament and the World Jewish Congress's representative in London:

> Though Foreign Office officials debated whether to forward the message to Silverman since it might have "embarrassing repercussions" if the public learned the news, they ultimately decided to do so. Riegner requested that Silverman "consult New York." Silverman, therefore, sent a copy of Riegner's message directly to Rabbi Wise, which arrived on Saturday, August 29th, three weeks after Riegner met with [U.S. Vice-Consul] Elting.

Ibid.

28. "Telegram from Gerhart Riegner (Via Samuel Silverman) to Stephen S. Wise, August 29, 1942," reprinted in Gary Phillip Zola and Marc Dollinger, eds., *American Jewish History: A Primary Source Reader* (Waltham, MA: Brandeis University Press, 2014), 254–55. A facsimile of the telegram is in Michael Berenbaum, *A Promise to Remember: The Holocaust in the Words and Voices of Its Survivors* (2003), 26.

29. See "Who Was the 'Mysterious Messenger'?" *Commentary*, October 1983.

30. Rabbi Wise held a meeting on September 6 for the heads of thirty-four American-Jewish organizations at the WJC office in New York. According to David Kranzler in *Thy Brother's Blood: The Orthodox Jewish Response During the Holocaust* (Brooklyn: Mesorah Publications, 1987), 92–93, Wise extracted a promise of silence from those present, to be lifted only if the State Department confirmed the facts. See also, Laurel Leff, *Buried by the Times: The Holocaust and America's Most Important Newspaper* (New York: Cambridge University Press, 2005), 149–63 for a detailed account.

31. E.g., the *New York Times* in a September 11, 1942, article titled "War on Judaism by Nazis Related . . . Record Is Documented," reported Rosh Hashanah services would be denied for the 7,000,000 Jews under Nazi rule—"already the victims of a barbarous war upon their existence." The article cited a "documented record [released by the Institute of Jewish Affairs] of the Hitler attempt to extirpate the Jewish religion," reporting that "the methods and the tempo established in Poland have now traveled to and have been duplicated in every country of Nazi occupation."

32. The *New York Times* carried its report of Hitler's speech on its front page and a transcript on page 8. "Text of Hitler's Address Reviewing the Course of the War and Explaining His Aims," *New York Times*, October 1, 1942.

33. See Christopher R. Browning, "When Did They Decide?" *New York Review*

of Books, March 24, 2022, 29; Adam Nagorski, *1941: The Year Germany Lost the War* (New York: Simon & Schuster, 2019), 294–96:

> Contrary to popular belief, the Wannsee Conference was not the key moment of decision about launching the full-scale Holocaust. The decision to substitute the Shoah by bullets with the Shoah by gas, thereby moving to industrialized-style mass murder, had already been taken in late 1941—not in a single moment but as a product of the evolution of Hitler's and Himmler's thinking on the subject. The Wannsee Conference's purpose was to coordinate the complex logistics . . . which could happen only once the fundamental decision about the fate of the Jews had been made.

One major historian, however, concludes that the policy of total eradication of the Jews was not finally determined until April–May of 1942. Peter Longerich, *Wannsee: The Road to the Final Solution* (New York: Oxford University Press, 2021). See also Christopher R. Browning, *The Origins of the Final Solution: The Evolution of Nazi Jewish Policy, September 1939–March 1942* (Lincoln and Jerusalem: University of Nebraska Press and Yad Vashem, 2004).

34. See Brendan Simms and Charlie Laderman, *Hitler's American Gamble: Pearl Harbor and Germany's March to Global War* (New York: Basic Books, 2021): "In 1939, Hitler had delivered his infamous warning that the consequences of a world at war would be the annihilation of the Jews. In the subsequent two years, he had repeatedly invoked his 'prophecy' . . ."

35. The Vatican archives dealing with the activities during World War II of Pope Pius XII, who became Pope in 1939 and served until his death in 1958, were sealed until recently. Pope Francis opened the archives to researchers in 2020. The first full account of the thousands of pages, which included internal memoranda prepared at Pope Pius's request, as he considered Hitler's attempt to exterminate the Jews and received reports from church leaders in Nazi-occupied Europe about the atrocities they witnessed, is contained in David I. Kertzer, *The Pope at War: The Secret History of Pius XII, Mussolini, and Hitler* (New York: Random House, 2022). Reports of widespread Nazi atrocities were provided to the Vatican by the White House in September 1942. See footnote 36 below. However, Professor Kertzer did not come across anything in the Vatican archives dealing with the Riegner telegram. Email from David I. Kertzer to the author, July 7, 2022.

36. On September 19, Myron Taylor—President Roosevelt's friend, who had been his emissary to the Evian Conference in 1938—met with Pope Pius XII to discuss a wide range of issues. Three days later, Taylor handed the Pope a report that documented German atrocities, with a longer memorandum for Cardinal Luigi Maglione, the Vatican's secretary of state, that noted the ongoing slaughter of Poland's Jews and the deportation of Jews from Germany, Belgium, Holland, France and Slovakia "to be butchered," with "a large part of the Jewish population deported to Lithuania and Lublin" already executed. Taylor's memorandum asked "whether the Vatican has any information that would tend to confirm the reports."

The Vatican's staff counseled the Pope to delay in responding to the American request, even though the Vatican had also received accounts of the mass murder of Jews in Ukraine and elsewhere; had been told by the Polish ambassador that "[t]he Germans' massacres of the Jews in Poland are of public notoriety"; and had been informed by the Roman military chaplain that "[t]he elimination of the Jews, with mass killing, is almost total. . . . It is said that over two million Jews have been killed." On October 10, the Vatican noted only that it had received reports of "severe measures" but that "up to the present time it has not been possible to verify the accuracy thereof." As early as a year before, however, the Pope had received one of the first credible accounts that Europe's Jews were being systematically murdered.

Kertzer, *The Pope at War,* 214, 224, 238–43. The post-trip report by Taylor can be found in the archives of the Franklin D. Roosevelt Library. See "Report to Honorable Franklin D. Roosevelt, President of the United States, by Myron Taylor, on His Trip to the Vatican, Europe and British Isles, September 12–October 12, 1942." See pages 125–27 of the Report. www.fdrlibrary.marist.edu/_resources/images/psf/psfa0494a.pdf.

37. "Telegram Received," Sunday, October 4, 1942, at 3:49 a.m. from "Wise" to Secretary Sumner Welles. After quoting the "strong new evidence" wire from Geneva, Wise stated he would be in Washington on Monday and "feel we should see you any time excepting three." They met the next afternoon. Sumner Welles Papers, Box 66, Folder OS, Office correspondence, Wise, Stephen, 1942, www.fdrlibrary.marist.edu/_resources/images/hol/hol00370.pdf.

38. "Paraphrase of Telegram," from American Minister, Bern, to Secretary of State, Washington, dated October 6, 1942, Sumner Welles Papers, Box 66.

39. World Jewish Congress, "Note Regarding the German Policy of Deliberate Annihilation of European Jewry," October 22, 1942, perspectives.ushmm.org/item/note-regarding-the-german-policy-of-deliberate-annihilation-of-european-jewry. The United States Holocaust Memorial Museum summary states that:

> This joint memo was written by Gerhart Riegner of the WJC and Richard Lichtheim of the Jewish Agency, which also had an office in Geneva. It was drafted to submit to Leland Harrison—the US envoy in Bern—along with other reports. Riegner and Lichtheim had a meeting with Harrison that same day.

40. Sumner Welles Papers, Box 66. For other correspondence between Zionist sources in Palestine and Geneva during this period, see Jewish Virtual Library, "The Riegner Report: Correspondence Regarding the 'Riegner Cable' (August–October, 1942)," www.jewishvirtuallibrary.org/correspondence-regarding-the-ldquo-riegner-cable-quot-august-october-1942. On October 8, Lichtheim wrote that:

> What has happened to the deportees and the ghetto inhabitants, and what is happening to them every day, has been confirmed by so many sources that there can be no doubt about the intentions of Hitler and the Gestapo. . . . [T]here is no doubt that mass murder and deportation to unknown destinations has indeed occurred in Poland, especially in the ghettos of Warsaw and Lodz. . . . When we combine all the reports, we cannot doubt that the deliberate destruction of Polish Jewry has already advanced from the stage of planning to that of execution.

41. On November 24, 1942, the *New York Times* reported that Berlin and Vienna were virtually empty of Jews other than elderly ones.

42. "Wise Gets Confirmations—Checks with State Department on Nazis' 'Extermination Campaign,'" *New York Times*, November 25, 1942, 10. The *Times* reported the news on page 10, at the end of a report titled "Himmler Program Kills Polish Jews," reporting that—as set forth in the subheadings—"Slaughter of 250,000 in Plan to Wipe Out Half in Country This Year Is Reported . . . Officials of Poland Publish Data."

Three days later, the *Times* reported the formation of a new organization, the "American Council for Judaism," backed by distinguished rabbis in ten cities, including David Philipson, the dean of the Reform movement; Rabbi Samuel Goldenson of Temple Emanu-El in New York; and Rabbi Louis Wolsey of Rodeph Shalom in Philadelphia. The chairman of the new group stated that it was "definitely opposed to a Jewish state, a Jewish flag, or a Jewish army." Its goal, he said, was to "bring Christian and Jew together." *New York Times*, December 12, 1942.

43. Department of State, Telegram Sent, November 25, 1942, from M. J. McCermott, Chief, Division of Current Information, to Editor, The Christian Century," reprinted in David S. Wyman, ed., *America and the Holocaust: A Thirteen-Volume Set Documenting the Editor's Book, The Abandonment of the Jews* (Amherst: University of Massachusetts, 1990), Vol. 2, *The Struggle for Rescue Action*, 31.

44. Letter dated December 2, 1942, from Stephen S. Wise to the President, Document 16 in David S. Wyman, ed., *America and the Holocaust*, Vol. 2, 46. The letter, addressed to "Dear Boss" and signed "Stephen," stated:

> I have had cables and underground advices for some months, telling of these things. *I succeeded, together with the heads of other Jewish organizations, in keeping these out of the press* and have been in constant communication with the State Department, particularly Under Secretary Welles. The State Department has now received what it believes to be confirmation of these unspeakable horrors and has approved of my giving the facts to the press. The organizations banded together in the conference of which I am chairman, feel that they wish to present to you a memorandum on this situation, so terrible that this day is being observed as a day of mourning and fasting throughout the Jewish world. . . . As your old friend, I beg you will somehow arrange to do this. [Emphasis added.]

45. Documents 20 and 21 in David S. Wyman, ed., *America and the Holocaust*, Vol. 2, 50–71. The cover letter stated:

> Already almost two million Jews . . . have been cruelly done to death, and five million more Jews live under the threat of a similar doom. The record of these heinous crimes against the Jews in Nazi Europe is detailed in the attached memorandum. . . . The result is a crime so monstrous as to be without parallel in history.

The final paragraph of the memorandum stated that:

> Ultimate German plans, as they are already being tested upon the Jews, spell a depopulated and debilitated Europe where the process of elimination would make Germans the master race. . . . [T]he Jews of Europe, whom Hitler has marked out as the first to suffer utter extinction, have no assurance at present that a United Nations victory will come in time to save them from complete annihilation.

Rabbi Wise read aloud a two-page letter that stressed that "[u]nless action is taken immediately, the Jews of Hitler's Europe are doomed." The letter asked Roosevelt "to warn the Nazis that they will be held to strict accountability for their crimes." Wise then handed Roosevelt a twenty-page condensation of the extermination data.

46. The cover letter for the memorandum given to FDR at the meeting can be found at Jewish Virtual Library, "Franklin Roosevelt Administration: Jewish Organizations Press FDR to Act," www.jewishvirtuallibary.org/jewish-organizations-press-fdr-to-act-december-1942.

47. There is a facsimile of the memorandum as translated from the Yiddish in David S. Wyman, ed., *America and the Holocaust* (Amherst: University of Massachusetts, 1990), Vol. 1, 72–74. It is described in Raul Hilberg, *Sources of Holocaust Research: An Analysis* (Chicago: Ivan R. Dee, 2001), 119–21. The proverb Roosevelt quoted was: "When a river you reach and the devil you meet, with the devil do not quarrel until the bridge you cross." "Report on the Visit to the President," Document 22 in David S. Wyman, ed., *America and the Holocaust*, Vol. 2, 72, 74.

48. The number had been deliberately understated. In the December 26, 1942, issue of *The New Republic,* Varian Fry—who had spent 1940 and 1941 in France secreting thousands of Jews out of the country—wrote on "The Massacre of the Jews," detailing the Nazi methods—starvation of local Jewish populations, deportations in packed cattle cars without food or water (arriving with one-third already dead), and "extermination centers, where Jews are destroyed by poison gas or electricity." Fry reported that the Nazi program was "already far advanced," with another five million Jews "scheduled to be destroyed."

49. House of Commons debate on United Nations Declaration, hansard.millbanksystems.com/commons/1942/dec/17/united-nations-declaration#S5CV0385P0-19421217_HOC-280.

50. David Kranzler, *Thy Brother's Blood*, 71, recounts that:

> The Bergson Group was reviled by almost every segment of American Jewry for their radical approach to rescue. Their provocative advertisements and rhetoric angered the Roosevelt camp and the non-revisionist Zionists, especially Stephen Wise, who considered them fascists or worse.

51. Ben Hecht, "The Extermination of the Jews—Remember Us!" *American Mercury*, February 1943, 194–98, www.unz.com/print/AmMercury-1943feb-00194. The same issue carried an article by the American journalist and writer Eugene Lyons, which began as follows:

> Two million "entirely innocent men, women and children" of the Jewish race, in the words of a joint declaration of the United Nations, have been murdered by the Nazis and five million more face extinction hourly. It is the blackest, most horrifying massacre in all human history. . . . The massacres are no sudden burst of bestiality. They represent a planned, cold-blooded project in mass murder.

Eugene Lyons, "Horror Unlimited," *American Mercury*, February 1943, 199–202.

52. Ben Hecht, *Child of the Century*, 564.

53. Quoted in "40,000 HERE VIEW MEMORIAL TO JEWS; Madison Square Garden Filled Twice for Mass Tribute to 2,000,000 Slain in Europe," *New York Times,* March 10, 1943.

54. Eleanor Roosevelt, "My Day" Column, April 14, 1943, in the Eleanor Roosevelt papers at the FDR Library, www.fdrlibrary.marist.edu/_resourves/images/hol/hol00439.pdf.

55. Ben Hecht, "Ballad of the Doomed Jews of Europe," mystical-politics.blogspot.com/2014/04/ben-hecht-ballad-of-doomed-jews-of.html. Photographs of the various newspaper ads that Hecht wrote for the Bergson Group can be found at www.hirhome.com/israel/bergson_ads.pdf.

56. Morgenthau met with Roosevelt on January 16, 1944, and handed him a four-page memorandum titled "Personal Report to the President," labeled "Secret," signed by Morgenthau personally at the bottom. The first three paragraphs read as follows:

> One of the greatest crimes in history, the slaughter of the Jewish people in Europe, is continuing unabated.
>
> This government has for a long time maintained that its policy is to work out programs to save those Jews and other persecuted minorities of Europe who could be saved.
>
> You are probably not as familiar as I with the utter failure of certain officials in our State Department, who are charged with actually carrying out this policy, to take any effective action to prevent the extermination of the Jews in German-controlled Europe.

See the photograph of the memorandum at https://perspectives.ushmm.org/item/treasury-department-report-to-president-roosevelt. Morgenthau told Roosevelt that the "gross procrastination" of the State Department was not only evident from the public record, but from "facts which have not yet been made public." The memorandum warned that:

> [T]here is a growing number of responsible people and organizations today who have ceased to view our failure as the product of simple incompetence on the part of those officials in the State Department charged with handling this problem. They see plain antisemitism motivating the actions of these State Department officials and, rightly or wrongly, it will require little more in the way of proof for this suspicion to explode into nasty scandal.

57. Executive Order 9417, www.presidency.ucsb.edu/documents/executive-order-9417-establishing-the-war-refugee-board. See FDR Statement, March 24, 1944, "The History Place—Holocaust Timeline: President Roosevelt Condemns War Crimes," www.historyplace.com/worldwar2/holocaust/h-roos-statement.htm. In his memoir, Cordell Hull argued that the State Department "fully cooperated" in the formation and administration of the War Refugee Board, and asserted the Department had made "strenuous efforts" to save the Jews:

> Naturally the more extreme sympathizers in this country, especially among the Jews, and some in high positions such as Secretary of the Treasury Morgenthau, found grievous fault with the State Department. . . . It was but natural that, in their anguish over the projected extermination of their race in Europe, they should feel that even the strenuous efforts we were making were inadequate. Nevertheless, it can be safely said that the results accomplished by the State Department, up to the time of the creation of the War Refugee Board, were at least equal those of all other countries combined, and that some hundreds of thousands of Jews are now alive who would probably have fallen victim to Hitler's insane enmity had not the Department begun so early and so comprehensively to deal with the refugee problem. President Roosevelt at no time complained to me that the Department had not done enough.

Cordell Hull, *The Memoirs of Cordell Hull* (New York: The Macmillan Co., 1948), 1539–40. The memoir does not detail the "strenuous efforts."

58. In her 2018 book, *Rescue Board: The Untold Story of America's Efforts to Save the Jews of Europe*, Rebecca Erbelding notes the formation of the Board was an effort "born in part out of public pressure," which included Hecht's nationwide pageant and an October 6, 1943, march by 400 rabbis in Washington organized by the Bergson Group. See also Edward White, "The Hollywood Darling Who Tanked His Career to Combat Anti-Semitism," *Paris Review*, November 3, 2017 ("When President Roosevelt announced the formation of the War Refugee Board a few months later, Hecht's pageant seemed like a turning point, the moment when it became impossible to ignore Europe's abandoned Jews"). Yitshaq Ben-Ami, a member of the Bergson Group, later wrote that:

> No one helped us more in our new campaign than Ben Hecht. . . . [T]he little that was ultimately achieved by the United States' War Refugee Board was due mostly to his militant involvement. . . . Our mission in the United States would not have attained the scope and intensity it did if not for Hecht's gifted pen.

Yitshaq Ben-Ami, *Years of Wrath, Days of Glory: Memoirs from the Irgun*, Second Expanded Edition (New York: Shengold Publishers, Inc., 1983), 283, 284.

59. In *Rescue Board*, Erbelding estimates the lives saved were in the thousands. There are frequent references in secondary sources to "up to 200,000" being saved, but they cite no evidence to support this number. Even those instrumental in forming the Board recognized that it was too little, way too late. Like the Evian Conference, it appears to have been formed primarily out of Roosevelt's fear of the political

consequences of inaction in an election year. In a memorandum dated March 10, 1944, prepared for Under Secretary of State Edward Stettinius Jr., the Board's director John Pehle wrote of problems "of major importance" facing it, especially:

> There is good reason to believe that the British are not yet convinced that there has been a real change in this Government's attitude toward this matter—rather that they feel that the creation of the War Refugee Board was primarily a political move in an election year.

In a section of the memorandum titled "Palestine Issue," Pehle noted that Palestine was a key place for finding temporary refuge for the Jews:

> From the standpoint [of refuge], with which we are concerned, of saving the Jews in Europe from death, bringing them into Palestine and placing them in camps, to be returned to their homelands at the end of the war, is just as effective as admitting them to Palestine on a permanent basis.

60. The Talmud states that "whoever destroys a single life . . . [is] as if he destroyed an entire world. And whoever saves a single life . . . [is] as if he saved an entire world." *Mishna Sanhedrin* 4:5, www.jewishvirtuallibrary.org/the-oral-law-talmud-and-mishna. See Gideon Frieder, "To Save the World Entire," November 1, 2013, www.ushmm.org/remember/holocaust-reflections-testimonies/echoes-of-memory/to-save-the-world-entire.

61. In a poll of Jewish students at Yale in late 1945, less than half regarded Jewishness as favorable, while 34 percent said it was a burden; one-quarter favored complete assimilation, and only half thought it worthwhile for American Jews to maintain a group identity. Meyer Greenberg, "The Attitude of the Jewish Student at Yale Towards Judaism," *Yivo Bleter*, November–December, 1945," referenced in N. A. Pelcovits, "What About Jewish Anti-Semitism?" *Commentary*, February 1947, http://www.commentary.org/articles/n-pelcovits/what-about-jewish-anti-semitism/. Pelcovits wrote that:

> Louis Finkelstein, President of the Jewish Theological Seminary . . . sums up the evidence of hundreds of rabbis, teachers, parents, and community leaders in an article which appeared in *Hadoar* last March [1946]. Rabbi Finkelstein found an ominous trend of active hostility towards Jewishness in the United States, particularly on the part of college students, intellectuals, and professional people. Judaism was normally regarded as the supreme obstacle to advancement, rarely as the source of religious values.

Pelcovits's article contained an incisive analysis of the cause and effect of antisemitism:

> Louis Golding illuminated the entire problem with his description of Paddy, the Irish terrier, who became possessed of a neurotic dislike for Scotch terriers, deafening the neighborhood with mad barking and canine challenge whenever the inoffensive Scottie appeared. Clearly the patient, the "problem," was Paddy, and

> not his victim. But while this judgment is unquestionably accurate . . . it failed to point out that the effect of anti-Semitism on its victim has been to produce a new problem, a specifically Jewish problem.
>
> To illustrate, it is only necessary to carry Golding's analogy a step further. . . . [T]he other neighborhood dogs . . . soon join in the collective barking at Scottie and occasionally chase him around the block. Quite innocently, Scottie becomes the provocation to disturbance of the neighborhood peace. He begins to feel uneasy and conspicuous. Surely there must be something wrong with him; fifty dogs can't be wrong. . . . And is there not something foreign about those Scottie whiskers? He studies in-conspicuousness, holing up during the day and slinking along alleys at night. This strange behavior is remarked by the other dogs, who now suspect that there is something uncanine about Scottie. The poor dog . . . removes his whiskers and practices arching his belly. . . . In dreams he sees himself as an English setter or Irish terrier (like Paddy!) . . . In short, he is faced with a Scottie problem.

"Thus," Pelcovits concluded, "[t]he heart of the problem of Jewish anti-Semitism is that *the victim has accepted the judgment of his persecutor*." (Emphasis in original.)

See also, Irving Howe, "The Lost Young Intellectual," *Commentary*, October 1946. Howe wrote of the typical "young American Jew" who "teeters between an origin he can no longer accept and a desired status he cannot attain" and of the contemporary intellectuals who found it "difficult to be a Jew and just as difficult not to be one." Howe acknowledged that some had suggested Zionism as a means of restoring Jewish meaning, but Howe pronounced himself "very skeptical . . . of any familiar pat solution" and ended his essay by pronouncing the Jewish intellectual as doomed "to continue as what he is: the rootless son of a rootless people."

The American Jews, although safe in America, found that in 1946 they still suffered from an identity crisis, perhaps exacerbated by a combination of survivor's guilt, bystander's guilt, sheer shock at the details of the Holocaust as they became known, and uncertainty about their status in the United States. It would not be until 1948, when Israel was established, that things began to change.

62. Ben Hecht, "Tales of Capering, Rueful Laughter," *New York Times*, July 7, 1943.

63. See Rafael Medoff, "Ben Hecht's 'A Flag Is Born': A Play That Changed History," The David S. Wyman Institute for Holocaust Studies, www.wymaninstitute.org/2004/04/special-feature-ben-hechts-a-flag-is-born-a-play-that-changed-history/.

64. David's speech can be found in Atay Citron, "Ben Hecht's Pageant-Drama: A Flag Is Born," in Claude Schumacher, *Staging the Holocaust: The Shoah in Drama and Performance* (Cambridge, UK: Cambridge University Press, 1998), 87.

65. "Letter to the Terrorists of Palestine," *New York Post*, May 14, 1947, http://thomassuarez.com/hecht.html.

66. The Irgun raid on Acre is described in detail in Bruce Hoffman, *Anonymous Soldiers: The Struggle for Israel, 1917–1947* (New York: Alfred A. Knopf, 2015), 409–12.

67. A partial text is in Hoffman, *Anonymous Soldiers*, 179–80. A more complete

version can be found in William MacAdams, *Ben Hecht: The Man Behind the Legend* (New York: Charles Scribner's Sons, 1990), 249.

68. "Churchill Assails Palestine Tactics—Declares 'We Are Making Fools of Ourselves,' Blaming the Labor Government." *New York Times*, May 17, 1947.

69. "Irgun Leader Skeptical of Solution for Palestine through U.N. Inquiry—Begin Says Only British Withdrawal Can Bring Peace," *New York Times*, May 23, 1947.

70. See Jeffrey Herf, *Israel's Moment: International Support for and Opposition to Establishing the Jewish State, 1945–1949* (New York: Cambridge University Press, 2002), 155–57. The British government formally protested Hecht's sentence to the State Department, informing it that Britain regarded it as "intolerable that such a statement should apper in the press of a friendly country" and requesting that the U.S. government immediately put a stop to such advertisements. On May 27, Secretary of State Marshall replied that he could not legally stop them but "deeply regret[ted]" the appearance of Hecht's advertisement. Ibid., 156.

71. Hecht had written a biography of Mickey Cohen, entitled "The Soul of a Gangster," which was never published.

72. In 2014, the *Jewish Review of Books* published the text of Hecht's speech, which the Israeli writer Stuart Schoffman had found in the Hecht Papers at the Newberry Library in Chicago—21 typewritten pages. Ben Hecht/Stuart Schoffman, "A Stone for His Slingshot," *Jewish Review of Books*, Spring 2014. Schoffman described it as "one of the most riveting and remarkable Jewish fundraising speeches ever delivered."

73. For various reasons, the Jewish Army did not materialize during World War II. Britain eventually allowed a Jewish Brigade of about 5,000 men to fight in northern Italy in 1944. It was not the army Jabotinsky and Bergson had envisioned, but it illustrates the observation Holocaust scholars have made about these years: "The Jews were *powerless*, but they were not *passive*." Indeed, they tried to build an army.

74. Adina Hoffman, *Ben Hecht*, 6–7.

75. Ben Hecht, *Perfidy* (New York: Julian Messner Inc., 1961), 13–14.

76. See Daniel Gordis, "How American Jews Have Detached Themselves from Jewish Memory," *Mosaic*, April 11, 2016 ("So this is where we find ourselves today: widespread ignorance about the Jewish past"); Dov Waxman, *Trouble in the Tribe: The American Jewish Conflict over Israel* (Princeton and Oxford: Princeton University Press, 2016); Elliott Abrams, "If American Jews and Israel Are Drifting Apart, What's the Reason?" *Mosaic*, April 4, 2016; Daniel Gordis, "Why Many American Jews Are Becoming Indifferent or Even Hostile to Israel," *Mosaic*, May 8, 2017; Evelyn Gordon, "How a Changing American Liberalism Is Pulling American Jews Away from Israel," *Mosaic*, May 17, 2017.

77. See David Litt, "How Obama Was Our Most Jewish President and Trump Our Least," *Forward*, September 28, 2017; David Rothkopf, "In Search of the Real Barack Obama," *Foreign Policy*, June 1, 2015. For the contrary view, see David Friedman, *Sledgehammer: How Breaking with the Past Brought Peace to the Middle East* (New York: Broadside Books, 2022).

78. Jewish Electorate Institute, May 22, 2019, poll, https://www.jewishelectorate institute.org/poll-domestic-issues-dominate-the-priorities-of-the-jewish-electorate/.

79. See generally, Yossi Shain, *The Israeli Century: How the Zionist Revolution Changed History and Reinvented Judaism* (New York: Wicked Son, 2021). See Daniel Gordis, *The Promise of Israel* (Hoboken: John Wiley & Sons, 2012), 172, observing that the danger for Jews in America is:

> not that a new Charles Lindbergh may emerge in the United States but that [they forget that] the very Jewish life that American Jews take for granted is actually a product of the existence of a Jewish state–the very state from which many young Jews are now distancing themselves.

80. See Daniel Gordis, *We Stand Divided: The Rift Between American Jews and Israel* (New York: HarperCollins, 2019), 212–13:

> The idea that a flourishing Jewish community can proceed without Israel as a core part of its identity is simply not realistic. Demography suggests that American Jewish literacy levels require Israel as a fulcrum for passionate discourse. . . . American Jews cannot flourish without Israel, but the reverse is also true. It is critical that Israeli leaders, who are often far too quick to dismiss the importance of Diaspora Jewry to Israel, understand that Israel, too, desperately needs that relationship.

81. The first part of the Begin quote comes from https://reformjudaism.org/jewish-life/arts-culture/literature/ben-hecht-fighting-words-moving-pictures. The second comes from "Ben Hecht Is Buried in Nyack Near Charles MacArthur Grave," *New York Times*, April 22, 1964, 47. The *Times* reported that "several hundred" people attended the funeral in New York, and the *JTA* reported that Begin and others had flown in from Israel for it. https://www.jta.org/1964/04/23/archive/revisionist-leaders-flew-from-israel-to-speak-at-ben-hechts-funeral/amp.

82. Hecht deserves a higher place in the history of American literature. In 1963, the University of Chicago republished his first novel, *Erik Dorn*, which he wrote in 1921 at the age of twenty-seven. Nelson Algren's introduction noted "the curiously prophetic shadow that a book, written half a century ago, now casts across our own strange time." Hecht's 1939 book of novellas, *A Book of Miracles*, remains impressive nearly a century later, as does his *Guide for the Bedeviled* on antisemitism. See also William MacAdams, *Ben Hecht* ("he was the most influential writer in the history of American movies, creating a new and exciting language for the screen"). As a writer of fiction and nonfiction, plays and movies, and essays of extraordinary power and impact, Hecht is almost unique.

A documentary about Ben Hecht by the acclaimed filmmaker Aviva Kempner is currently in production. See https://benhechtfilm.org/.

7. THE TRIUMPH AND TRAGEDY OF ABBA EBAN

1. "Statement to the Security Council of the United Nations, May 26, 1948," reprinted in Abba Eban, *Voice of Israel* (New York: Horizon Press, 1957), 16. In a June 1953 address to a United Jewish Appeal conference in Washington, Eban compared the relative positions of the Jews and Arabs after 1948—with many new Arab states created during the twentieth century over a huge area of land, and a single, minuscule Jewish state still struggling for existence:

> Look at the Arab map with its endless stretches of fertile land, its huge rivers yet unharnessed, its oil wells brimming with wealth and power, its manifold sovereignties and strong international representation.
>
> Then look at Israel, developing within the smallest possible margin of territorial and economic resources available to any state and ask yourselves frankly: Are the Arab peoples the fair objects of condolence or of congratulations? Does the world owe an apology to them; or do they owe gratitude, forbearance, and moderation to the world?

Quoted in Marc D. Charney, "Abba Eban, Eloquent Defender and Voice of Israel, Is Dead at 87," *New York Times*, November 18, 2002, http://www.nytimes.com/2002/11/18/world/abba-eban-eloquent-defender-and-voice-of-israel-is-dead-at-87.html.

2. "U.N. and the Negev," *Jewish Chronicle*, October 22, 1948.

3. Editor's note to Aubrey S. Eban, "The Future of Arab-Jewish Relations: The Key Is the Cooperation of Equal and Separate States," *Commentary*, September 1948.

4. John Calder, "Abba Eban," *The Guardian*, November 17, 2002.

5. Jewish Telegraph Agency, "Security Council Votes to Admit Israel to U.N. Membership; Vote is 9 to 1," www.jta.org/1949/03/06/archive/security-council-votes-to-admit-israel-to-u-n-membership-vote-is-9-to-1.

6. Eban later wrote that he had been encouraged by the "massive" Security Council vote in favor of Israel and had hoped that Israel's membership would be quickly ratified by the General Assembly, as in the case of all previous UN membership decisions. But "I should have known better. Israel, after all, is the exception to every rule." Abba Eban, *Personal Witness: Israel Through My Eyes* (New York: G. P. Putnam's Sons, 1992), 190.

7. Ibid., 193.

8. Abba Solomon Eban, *Abba Eban: An Autobiography* (New York: Random House, 1977), 142–43.

9. Quoted in Marc D. Charney, "Abba Eban, Eloquent Defender and Voice of Israel," *New York Times*, November 18, 2002.

10. Richard Pearson, "Israeli Diplomat, Foreign Minister Abba Eban Dies," *Washington Post*, November 18, 2002.

11. The Labor Party had failed to place Eban among its top twenty candidates. In prior years, the candidates were appointed rather than elected by party members, and Eban had previously been ranked at number five, even though his views were to the left of the party's mainstream opinion. Eban told the *New York Times* that Israel's

changing demography (more than half of North African rather than European origin) also led to his defeat. Joel Brinkley, "Eban Withdraws in Parliament Race," *New York Times*, June 16, 1988.

12. See "Israel Business and Economy: State of Israel Bonds," Jewish Virtual Library, www.jewishvirtuallibrary.org/state-of-israel-bonds.

13. See "Ben-Gurion Opens Israel Bond Campaign in New York," *JTA*, May 11, 1951, www.jta.org/1951/05/11/archive/ben-gurion-opens-israel-bond-campaign-in-new-york-35000000-raised-at-rally.

14. Abba Eban, *Voice of Israel* (New York: Horizon Press, 1957), 62–63. In October 1953, Eban led the final phase of the three-year drive for the bond sales. See "Israel Sets Highest Record in Foreign Bond Sales in U.S.," *JTA*, October 6, 1953: "Ambassador Eban addressed 2,000 Jewish community leaders at 11 breakfast meetings held throughout the city to launch the campaign and to formulate plans for the celebration of the 3,000th anniversary of Jerusalem. . . ."

In a June 26, 1955, address to the UN Commemorative Assembly in San Francisco, on the tenth anniversary of the UN, Eban titled his remarks "Ten Years Ago We Were Not Here":

> Never in all recorded history had any family of the human race been overwhelmed by such a tidal wave of grief and havoc as that which engulfed the Jewish people during the Nazi decade. . . . [After the war] [i]t seemed seriously possible that every people would be established in sovereignty except the first and most sorely ravaged amongst the victims of persecution. Every culture and civilization would be embodied in free political and social institutions except that culture and civilization which had conceived the revolutionary message of individual morality, social justice and universal peace. . . . The presence of Israel in San Francisco today . . . illustrates the sudden recuperation of the Jewish people from the lowest point in its fortunes to the dignity and opportunity it had tenaciously pursued for 2000 years.

Eban, *Voice of Israel*, 206, 207.

15. Mike Wallace, "Interview with Abba Eban," April 12, 1958, hrc.contentdm.oclc.org/digital/collection/p15878coll90/id/56/.

16. Ibid. Arnold Toynbee was a famous historian in his day, better described more recently as the "best example of an intellectual and writer whose antagonistic stance towards the Jews is thematic in his or her work." Anthony Julius, *Trials of the Diaspora: A History of Anti-Semitism in England* (Oxford: Oxford University Press, 2010), 412–14. In Julius's words, Toynbee's work "has left no trace on historical writing; . . . it is now mentioned only to be dismissed." Ibid., 414.

17. See Fred Smith, "Remembering Abba Eban's rousing remarks: What he said to the UN Security Council on Day 2 of the Six-Day War," *New York Daily News*, June 6, 2017:

> The most riveting speech I ever heard was delivered 50 years ago—on June 6, 1967—to the Security Council of the United Nations. In its beauty of language

> and immediacy, it rivals Churchill's eloquence during World War II. . . . And the speech proved to be a diplomatic, oratorical and political counterpart to what soon became a victory for the survival of the Jewish state—an outcome that was in grave doubt only the day before.

18. "Statement to the Security Council by Foreign Minister Eban—6 June 1967," Israel Ministry of Foreign Affairs.

19. "Excerpts from Talks by Albanian and Israeli in U.N. and Text of Hussein Address," *New York Times*, June 27, 1967.

20. "Careless Talk," Editorial, *Jewish Chronicle*, July 14, 1967.

21. "Israel's Chief Orator: Abba Eban," *New York Times*, June 21, 1967. Eban told the UN that on May 23, Radio Damascus had officially announced that it had (in the words of the Arab broadcast) "prepared everything necessary in order to engage in battle with Israel," and the following day the Syrian prime minister had announced Syria's intention to (in its prime minister's words) "wipe Israel off from the face of the earth." Eban suggested members of the General Assembly "might wish to compare [those remarks] with the terms of the United Nations Charter."

22. "Statement to the General Assembly by Foreign Minister Eban, 8 October 1973," Israel Ministry of Foreign Affairs. Eban continued:

> No, there is no doubt: Egypt and Syria exploited the physical vulnerability arising from a spiritual vocation which the Jewish people can never renounce.
>
> Egypt concentrated for this assault more than 3,000 tanks, 2,000 guns, nearly 1,000 aircraft and, according to Egyptian spokesmen, 600,000 men, all armed with weapons of Soviet manufacture of the most modern type, including bombers, ground missiles, missile boats. Against them, on the first day, were regular Israeli garrisons in the most defensive posture that a nation can ever dream of allowing itself in a situation of regional tension.
>
> And on the Syrian side, 1,000 tanks and corresponding numbers of weapons in the air. Now all that brutal force crashed unprovoked across the cease-fire line. We have suffered tragic losses of life and blood. . . . I admit that the sacrilegious exploitation of the Day of Atonement, and Israel's renunciation, during those critical hours, of preventive action, have cost us dear, but the Egyptian and Syrian advantage has been and will be brief. . . .
>
> At this very solemn and tragic hour, we cannot help but think back upon the waste and the anguish and the avoidable suffering of the past two decades. All our Arab neighbors together, which are developing countries, have spent in this period something like 20,000 million dollars on War. The result: nothing. The achievement: nothing. . . . [T]he tiniest fraction of that expenditure would have been sufficient to solve all the refugee problems in the Middle East fifty times over.

23. See Michael B. Oren, *Six Days of War: June 1967 and the Making of the Modern Middle East* (Oxford: Oxford University Press, 2002), 100:

> For many in the country . . . he remained the ungainly Aubrey Solomon of Capetown, a foreigner hopelessly out of step with Israeli ways and mentality,

> long-winded and dull. "He doesn't live in reality" [Prime Minister Levi] Eshkol once sniped; "he never gives the right solution, only the right speech." Privately, the prime minister referred to him, in Yiddish, as "der gelernter naar"—"the learned fool."

See also Martin Kramer, "The Non-Israeli Ambassador," August 12, 2013, https://martinkramer.org/2013/08/12/the-non-israeli-ambassador/, describing Eban as "the non-Israeli ambassador" who "brilliantly represented the State of Israel in its first decade, without having lived there at all." The 2,800-word obituary in *The New York Times* noted that Eban:

> would send his supremely cultured voice using the King's English into forensic combat. His orations, fierce in their defense of his country, were also marked by rich appeals to history, soaring visions of a peaceful Middle East and withering scorn for Israel's enemies. . . . What was commanding in the halls of diplomacy did not resonate the same way at home. His compatriots' style was rough and egalitarian. They were outgoing, not aloof like Mr. Eban, and famously rude, even in the halls of Parliament. Increasingly, Israelis came to judge him pompous and, eventually, isolated from the political mainstream.

Marc D. Charney "Abba Eban, Eloquent Defender and Voice of Israel, Is Dead at 87," *New York Times*, November 18, 2002.

These political liabilities had been evident as early as 1967, when Prime Minister Levi Eshkol left office and Eban was not considered a likely successor:

> Mr. Eban . . . has lost some of his popularity on account of what many consider to be his haughty manners and stilted style of speech. . . . Israelis . . . now find his Hebrew style rhetorical and pompous, when simplicity and clarity are called for. One of the jokes about him—and not the most cruel—going the rounds is that a special interpreter had to be found by the UN Secretariat to translate Mr. Eban's English speech at the General Assembly into . . . English.

Jewish Chronicle, June 23, 1967, "As Yet, No Victory Parade"; see also *Jewish Chronicle*, Editorial, August 4, 1967 ("Eban's Oxford Union type of repartee does not translate well into Hebrew and is not always understood, and it is all too cool, too calm and delivered at too low a pitch").

Robert St. John, in his admiring biography of Eban, written while Eban was foreign minister, described Eban's effect as follows:

> Close associates have used various expressions to describe his supreme egoism: overly self-confident, exceedingly selfish, somewhat narcissistic, given to pomposity, often guilty of intellectual snobbism. They point to his sensitivity about criticism, his desire for an audience, his love of applause, his occasional reference to himself in the third person, his habit of listening to his own voice on a tape recorder, his obsession with personal publicity, his conceit about his own bon mots, his refusal to share credit with others.

Robert St. John, *Eban* (New York: Doubleday & Co., 1972), 507.

24. Even Eban's physical appearance hurt him, since he differed dramatically from the macho image of the Israeli sabras: he was, his fellow diplomat and admirer Conor Cruise O'Brien said, "portly in appearance, and rather plummy in public discourse; he looked like Beach the Butler, and sounded like an archbishop." Quoted in Owen Harries, "A Reluctant Realist," *New York Times*, March 29, 1998. Eban once joked that, "I could have been elected prime minister if people abroad could vote in Israeli elections." "Founding Father Abba Eban, an Eloquent Statesman, Dies," *Jewish News of Northern California*, November 22, 2002, www.jweekly.com/2002/11/22/founding-father-abba-eban-an-eloquent-statesman-dies/.

25. Asaf Siniver, *Abba Eban: A Biography* (New York: Overlook Duckworth, 2015), 318–20. See Abba Solomon Eban, *Abba Eban: An Autobiography*, 578, 579, 581, 605:

> I had heard all this for the first time on radio. . . . [My party] had laid every possible burden on me. It had never found me wanting; yet it now acted toward me with a lack of normal courtesy. . . . There was nothing particularly dignified about the way in which my party dispensed with me in the summer of 1974. . . .

26. Abba Eban, *Personal Witness*, 573.

27. See Abba Eban, "Pursue Peace, Not Just Elections," *New York Times*, December 30, 1989 ("U.S. officials tell us there has been no 'ripening' of conditions for discussing peace, security, boundaries and constitutional structure. Contrary to conventional wisdom, our region has never been as ripe as it is today for large visions and hard facts.").

28. Siniver, *Abba Eban*, 358.

29. Ibid. A CD of Eban's greatest speeches at the UN, "Great Speeches of Abba Eban," was eventually produced, with four of his speeches between 1948 and 1967. www.amazon.com/Great-Speeches-Abba-Amazon-Exclusive/dp/B000R34BIC.

30. Henry Kissinger, *White House Years* (Boston: Little, Brown and Co., 1979), 358–59. Eban later returned the compliment, describing him as "the only U.S. Secretary of State under whom two Presidents served." Owen Harries, "A Reluctant Realist," *New York Times*, March 29, 1998. In 1990, Kissinger hosted a seventy-fifth birthday party for Eban at the UN and said that Eban was "the greatest spokesman the Jewish people had ever had." Quoted in Asaf Siniver, *Abba Eban*, 355.

For an example of Eban's ability to dismiss a loud group of protestors trying to disrupt his speech, using sheer extemporaneous eloquence, see "Abba Eban at UCLA, 11-12-1970," www.youtube.com/watch?v=KqgMouDULf8. For a biographical portrait of Eban, see "A Tribute to Abba Eban," a ten-minute video narrated by Eban, with comments by Arthur Schlesinger, Jr., and Henry Kissinger: www.youtube.com/watch?v=sFEFEfb1rOM. A fascinating, extended interview of Eban is at "The Leon Charney Report," March 16, 1997, http://charneyreport.com/2015/05/24/avraham-ben-zvi-and-abba-eban/, beginning at minute 20. A 1955 interview by CBS correspondents Larry Lesueur and Winston Burdett with Abba Eban, "Longines Chronoscope with Abba Eban," is at www.youtube.com/watch?v=vOKZZML-YW8.

31. Quoted in Asaf Siniver, *Abba Eban*, 354.

32. Aubrey S. Eban, "The Future of Arab-Jewish Relations: The Key Is the Cooperation of Equal and Separate States," *Commentary*, September 1948.

33. Eban, *Abba Eban*, 608.

34. See "Israel to UN: You Never Hear Palestinian Leaders Say 'Two States for Two Peoples,'" January 26, 2012, https://matzav.com/israel-to-un-you-never-hear-palestinian-leaders-say-two-states-for-two-peoples/. Alan M. Dershowitz, "Why Won't Abbas Accept 'Two States for Two Peoples'?" Gatestone Institute, June 12, 2017, www.gatestoneinstitute.org/10523/abbas-two-states. The other ubiquitous phrase used to describe the goal of the peace process—"two states living side by side in peace and security"—likewise avoided the necessity of recognizing that one of them would be Jewish. The Palestinian position was that the Jewish state would be subject to a "right of return" for Palestinian refugees and their descendants, ultimately rendering the Jews a minority in their own state, with the two states effectively both becoming Palestinian.

35. On the "right of return," see Efraim Karsh, "The Palestinians and the Right of Return," *Commentary*, May 2001.

36. In his September 25, 2016, address to the UN General Assembly, the Palestinian president Mahmoud Abbas demanded that Britain apologize for the Balfour Declaration. He repeatedly asserted (in 2011, 2014, and 2016) that he would "never" recognize a Jewish state.

37. See Barry Rubin, "Why Did the Arabs Suffer 'Nakba' (Disaster) in 1948 and Every Day Since? The Surprising View of the Man Who Coined That Term," P. J. Media, February 5, 2013, pjmedia.com/barryrubin/2012/02/05/why-did-the-arabs-suffer-a-nakba-disaster-in-1948-and-every-day-since-the-surprising-view-of-the-man-who-originated-that-term-n132748.

38. Jared Kushner, "Opportunity Beckons in the Mideast," *Wall Street Journal*, March 14, 2021: "Eliminating the ISIS caliphate and bringing about six peace agreements—between Israel and the United Arab Emirates, Bahrain, Sudan, Morocco and Kosovo, plus uniting the Gulf Cooperation Council—has changed the paradigm."

39. "Vital Statistics: Total Casualties, Arab-Israeli Conflict," Jewish Virtual Library, www.jewishvirtuallibrary.org/total-casualties-arab-israeli-conflict. See Rick Richman, "Where Is Mahmoud Abbas's Bir Zeit Speech?" *Commentary*, June 15, 2010.

40. Even more important than Dermer's youth and length of service was his relationship with the prime minister, which gave him more influence than Eban enjoyed with David Ben-Gurion or Golda Meir. Dermer became Netanyahu's most-influential adviser. See Amir Tibor, "The Ambassador Who Came In From the Cold," *Atlantic*, February 15, 2017. See also "Interview with Jerusalem Post," https://t.co/1SkEaIjvQ:

> Dermer, 45, has the complete confidence and trust of Netanyahu, as well as unfettered access to him. The Americans know that when they speak to him, their messages will be directly related back to Netanyahu; and—more importantly—

they know when he speaks, he is reflecting—more accurately than probably anyone else on the planet—the positions of the prime minister.

8. RON DERMER—THE AMERICAN ISRAELI AMBASSADOR

1. Ron Dermer, "Podcast: Ambassador Ron Dermer Looks Back on His Years in Washington," December 9, 2020, tikvahfund.org/library/podcast-ambassador-ron-dermer-looks-back-on-his-years-in-washington.

2. Ibid. Today, there are about 7 million Jews in Israel and slightly over 7 million in the United States. "Vital Statistics: Jewish Population of the World: 1882—Present," Jewish Virtual Library, www.jewishvirtuallibrary.org/jewish-population-of-the-world. Some surveys put the number of Jews in the United States as less than those in Israel. Jewish News Syndicate, "Jewish World Population Increases to 15.2 million with 45.3 percent living in Israel," September 5, 2021. www.jns.org/jewish-world-population-rises-to-15-2-million-45-3-live-in-israel.

3. Natan Sharansky and Ron Dermer, *The Case for Democracy* (New York: PublicAffairs, 2006), Preface to the 2006 paperback edition, xii.

4. The Avalon Project at Yale Law School, "Second Inaugural Address of George W. Bush; January 20, 2005," www.avalon.law.yale.edu/21st_century/gbush2.asp.

5. U.S. State Department Form DS-4080, "Oath of Renunciation of the Nationality of the United States."

6. Reprinted in *The New York Sun*, March 17, 2005, https://www.nysun.com/article/opinion-proud-to-have-been-an-american.

7. Herb Keinon, "The Full Text of the Interview with Ron Dermer," *Jerusalem Post*, July 2, 2009.

8. In 2017, on the centennial of the Balfour Declaration, Dermer said:

> The tragedy for the Palestinians was not that the Balfour declaration was issued. It was that they rejected it. That rejection . . . has been the cause of our conflict for a century. And until the Palestinian national movement accepts the legitimate grounds for the permanence of the Jewish state, our conflict with the Palestinians will not end—no matter how many envoys are sent and no matter how many peace plans are proposed.

www.facebook.com/ambdermer/posts/2387664904792514.

In focusing on the Palestinian rejection of any Jewish sovereignty in Palestine (as opposed to a state withdrawn to the indefensible 1949 borders, subject to a Palestinian "right of return" to the state that would delegitimize it as a Jewish-majority entity), Dermer identified the critical issue. The absence of Israeli-Palestinian peace is not the result of an absence of peace plans. Twenty-seven plans proposed through 2014 are listed in Dov Waxman, *The Israeli-Palestinian Conflict*, 42:

The Faisal-Weizmann Agreement (1919)
The Peel Partition Plan (1937)
The Morrison-Grady Plan (1946)

The UN Partition Plan (1947)
The Lausanne Conference (1949)
The Husni al-Zaim Initiative (1949)
The Alpha Plan (1954–1955)
The Rogers Plan (1969)
The Geneva Plan (1973)
The Begin Plan (1977)
The Fez Initiative (1982)
The Reagan Plan (1982)
The Brezhnev Plan (1982)
The London Agreement (1987)
The Schultz Initiative (1988)
The Shamir Plan (1989)
The Madrid Conference (1991)
The Oslo Accords (1993–1995)
The Beilin-Abu Mazen Agreement (1995)
The Camp David Summit (2000)
The Clinton Parameters (2000)
The Taba Summit (2001)
The Arab Peace Initiative (2002)
The Geneva Initiative (2003)
The Road Map for Peace (2003)
The Annapolis Conference (2007)
The Kerry Initiative (2013–2014)

One might also count the Bernadotte Plan (1948), the Zinni Plan for Peace (2002), the Mitchell Plan (2002), and the Trump Administration "Peace to Prosperity Plan" (2020), https://trumpwhitehouse.archives.gov/wp-content/uploads/2020/01/Peace-to-Prosperity-0120.pdf, for a total to date of thirty-one peace plans, over a period extending a full century.

For a description of the Kerry Initiative, see Walter Russell Mead, *The Arc of a Covenant*, 542–43:

> Kerry relied on the traditional ham-and-eggs negotiating pattern: if only we had some ham, then we could have ham and eggs once we get some eggs. . . . During the nine months of the Kerry-led peace process, he would meet more than one hundred times with Netanyahu and Mahmoud Abbas. The process collapsed with little to show for this effort. . . .

Palestinian President Mahmoud Abbas repeatedly stated (in 2011, 2014, and 2016) that he would "never" recognize a Jewish state, and in his 2016 address to the UN General Assembly he demanded that Britain apologize for the Balfour Declaration from ninety-nine years before. In 2020, he rejected the Trump Administration Plan out-of-hand, before seeing it.

9. In that speech, Dermer continued: "The good news is that a century after Bal-

four there are hopeful signs that leaders in the Arab world are increasingly showing a willingness to cross that Rubicon, which may ultimately convince some Palestinian leaders to do the same."

In a November 15, 2015, speech at the historic Ebenezer Baptist Church, Dermer addressed the argument that terrorist attacks kept happening "because of the occupation, or because there's no peace process, or because the Palestinians don't have a state."

> Most people believe this despite the fact that, for nearly half a century before there was any so-called occupation, hundreds of Jews were murdered by Palestinian terrorists, and despite the fact that both when the peace process was racing ahead and when it was at a standstill, hundreds of Jews were murdered by Palestinian terrorists. . . .
>
> The great tragedy for Israelis and Palestinians alike has been that for the past century . . . [the Palestinian] goal has not been to establish a Palestinian state; it has been to destroy a Jewish state. And rather than abandon the path of terrorism, many Palestinian leaders have embraced it—not only by perfecting terror but by glorifying it—by naming public squares after mass murderers, by inciting violence in their media, inculcating hatred in their schools.
>
> The hope for peace between Israelis and Palestinians does not depend on who sits in the Oval Office or on what decisions are made at the United Nations. The hope for peace depends on what is in the minds and hearts of young Palestinians.

10. In 2019, the eminent American foreign policy scholar, Michael Mandelbaum, Christian A. Herter Professor Emeritus of American Foreign Policy at The Johns Hopkins School of Advanced International Studies, used an equally perceptive metaphor, describing Israel as the equivalent of a shot-blocker in basketball—the player whose statistics do not appear in the box score, but who is essential to the team, preventing shots that would otherwise score. See Michael Mandelbaum, "The Six-Day War: 1967's Gift to America," *The American Interest*, June 2, 2017.

11. "A Conversation with Ron Dermer," May 21, 2021, www.hudson.org/events/1964-virtual-event-a-conversation-with-ambassador-ron-dermer-52021. See Yonah Jeremy Bob, "UK Ambassador to Israel: We Have a Big Appetite for Israeli Military Tech," *Jerusalem Post*, March 31, 2022:

> England has a "big appetite" for Israel's military technology, UK Ambassador to Israel Neil Wigan said Thursday at *The Jerusalem Post* Conference in London. . . . "I think it is a fit," he added. "Israeli use of technology and how to do security and military operations, we are very interested in this. Our armed forces has a big appetite to learn and profit from that."

12. Ron Dermer, "Remarks Delivered on July 7, 2016, at the B'nai B'rith World Center Award for Journalism ceremony in Jerusalem," http://blogs.timesofisrael.com/israeli-us-ties-the-dependence-is-mutual/. On the "world-historical meaning" of the Book of Exodus, see Michael Walzer, *Exodus and Revolution* (United States: Basic Books, 1985), 21 et seq.

13. "Remarks Delivered on July 7, 2016, at the B'nai B'rith, http://blogs.timesofisrael.com/israeli-us-ties-the-dependence-is-mutual/. See also Dermer's speech on December 3, 2018, at a joint Poland-Israel Chanukah reception:

> We live in a world in which many believe, particularly young people, that all that separates us must be eliminated. They believe that our different faiths and nationalities, cultures and traditions, are merely artificial barriers that sow hatred and conflict. But we must never forget that what separates us is also what makes us. It makes us Poles and Israelis. It makes us Christians and Jews. It gives meaning to our lives and purpose to our future. . . . We must never abandon our unique identities. For a nation that does not embrace what makes it unique will not long survive as a nation.

www.facebook.com/ambdermer/posts/2706296782929323.

14. Amir Tibon, "The Ambassador Who Came In From the Cold," *Atlantic*, February 15, 2017, http://www.theatlantic.com/international/archive/2017/02/netanyahu-dermer-israel-washington/516684/.

> Robert Danin, a former U.S. diplomat who worked with Dermer in Jerusalem when the latter served as Netanyahu's political adviser, said that . . . "They don't think about it in terms of *hasbara*, but as a national security issue, almost an existential one. They think Israel is involved in a war of ideas, requiring it to speak strongly against unjust critics to help ensure the country's survival."

15. Ron Dermer, speech at the Zionist Organization of America dinner, November 24, 2015:

> The root cause of terrorism has always been the same—a totalitarian mindset. It is a mindset that takes root when people are poisoned by ideologies which devalue human life. . . . Seventy-five years ago, this totalitarian mindset came in the form of the ideology of Nazism, the belief in a master race. Today, this totalitarian mindset comes in the form of the ideology of militant Islam, the belief in a master faith. . . . We know that we stand on the frontline in the battle between modernity and medievalism. And no matter whether the world stands with us or not as we face this evil, rest assured, Israel will hold that line and defend itself.

www.facebook.com/ambdermer/posts/1914336232125386.

16. See Ron Dermer, speech at the Israeli Embassy's "Eighteenth Annual Christian Solidarity Event," May 8, 2020:

> The backbone of Israel support in the world is the support of the United States of America. And the backbone of that backbone is the unequivocal support for Israel of tens of millions of devout Christians throughout this great country. . . . [Israel] is the land where Abraham, Isaac and Jacob prayed, where David and Solomon ruled, where Isaiah and Jeremiah prophesied, and where a young Rabbi from Nazareth preached a universal message of love and peace. . . .

> [W]hen Jews come to the Land of Israel, we are not going to a foreign land. We are returning home.

www.facebook.com/ambdermer/posts/3192442224314774. In his speech on July 23, 2018, to the annual Washington summit of Christians United for Israel (CUFI), Dermer said:

> I want to thank CUFI and its over 4,000,000 members for unabashedly standing by Israel's side. . . . I want to thank the person whose vision and leadership made all this possible—Pastor John Hagee. . . . Israel gave Pastor Hagee a special honor this year. As we celebrated our 70th Independence Day, our embassy recognized 70 Americans who made a unique contribution strengthening the alliance between America and Israel. That list includes President Harry Truman, Justice Louis Brandeis and Albert Einstein. That list also includes Pastor John Hagee. . . .
>
> There is no people on earth with a stronger connection to a city than the Jewish people's connection to Jerusalem. The power of that connection proved itself during 2,000 years in exile. Three times a day, we turn to Jerusalem in prayer. Under wedding canopies, and in houses of mourning, people remember Jerusalem. . . . You are standing up for a country that proudly holds up the torch of liberty in a dark and dangerous region. You are standing up for the one place in the Middle East where Christians are free and where Christian communities are thriving.

www.facebook.com/ambdermer/posts/2588789948013341.
In his speech on July 13, 2015 to CUFI, Dermer noted that:

> As the Middle East continues its descent into barbarism and chaos, life for Christians there has become nasty, brutish, and short. A century ago, 20% of the region's population was Christian. Today, Christians account for less than 4% of the population. . . . Israel is proud to be a light in the darkness—a shining city on a hill with a growing and thriving Christian community—five times as large as it was in 1948, the year the modern state of Israel was born.

www.facebook.com/ambdermer/posts/1857677837791226.

17. See Omri Nahmias, "Amb. Dermer, Elan Carr, Discuss Anti-Zionism vs. Antisemitism," *Jerusalem Post*, November 22, 2019, quoting Dermer as follows:

> In 120 years, since the days of the First Zionist Congress, we have come full circle. Then, people thought the reason for antisemitism is that the Jews did not have a state. Now, many people think the reason for antisemitism is that the Jews do have a state. Then, the enemies of the Jewish people said, "Jews go to Palestine." Now, the enemies of the Jewish people say "Jews get out of Palestine." Israel is neither the cause nor the cure for antisemitism. But Israel has given the Jewish people something that we did not have in all those centuries of antisemitism, and that is the power to fight back . . . not just on the battlefield but also in the battle of ideas.

18. Herb Keinon, "Dermer: Trump's Jerusalem Move Is 'Shock Therapy' for Palestinians," *Jerusalem Post*, March 15, 2018. Dermer discussed why the Palestinians deny any historical connection between the Jewish people and Jerusalem:

> "Because to admit this connection is to admit that the Jewish people aren't foreign colonialists in the land of Israel; that Israel for the Jewish people is not India for the British, or Algeria for the French, or the Congo for the Belgians—but that this is the land of our ancestors." The minute the Palestinians recognize a Jewish connection to Jerusalem, he said, the whole edifice of Palestinian rejectionism would begin to collapse, because it would mean that the Jewish people are in Israel "not merely by might, but by right."

19. In 1995, on the twentieth anniversary of the assassination of Israeli Prime Minister Yitzhak Rabin, Dermer held a memorial dinner at the Israeli embassy, attended by President Obama's chief of staff, Denis McDonough, Treasury Secretary Jack Lew, Justice Ruth Bader Ginsburg, former Secretaries of State Albright and Kissinger, and Israeli Defense Minister Moshe Ya'alon. www.facebook.com/ambdermer/photos/a.1451178395107841.1073741826.1450515471840800/1904280153130994/. Dermer called November 4, 1995, "the darkest night in Israel's history":

> The sages of our people tell us that baseless hatred led to the destruction of the Second Temple and the loss of Jewish sovereignty at the hands of the Romans. It took the Jewish people 2,000 years to return to our land and restore that sovereignty. And yet within a few decades of Israel's rebirth, a Jew—a religious Jew no less—murders the Prime Minister of Israel. . . .
>
> Every year, observant Jews across the world fast on the day after Rosh Hashana—it is called the fast of Gedalia. . . . Gedalia was the Jewish governor of Judea who was assassinated by another Jew. And 2,500 years later, millions remember him. I hope Yitzhak Rabin will be remembered not just in another 20 years but in another 2,000 years. I hope his memory will remind us that political opponents are not enemies and that there is no cause that justifies murder.

20. Ron Dermer, speech at Israel's 71st Independence Day celebration in Washington, May 22, 2019:

> We celebrate the incredible story of how, in only seven decades, a poor country, with virtually no natural resources, became a global technological power. . . . where a powerless nation was transported from 2,000 years of statelessness into a sovereign future; where an exiled people return to the same land where their patriarchs prayed . . . where the laws of history were defied, and where an ancient dream became a modern miracle.

21. In his November 15, 2015, speech at Ebenezer Baptist Church, Dermer noted the connections in America between Jews and African Americans:

> I was born in Miami Beach. It's a great city, where both my father and brother served as mayors. But it was once a place steeped in antisemitism. Jews could

> not live north of 5th street and hotels in Miami Beach used to advertise to vacationers that there were "no dogs, no Jews and no blacks allowed." Because of our long history of persecution, the Jewish people could empathize with the plight of African Americans as few others could. . . . Dr. King called [Israel] "one of the great outposts of democracy in the world, a marvelous example of what can be done . . ."

22. On October 18, 2017, Dermer addressed the annual gala of the Friends of the Israel Defense Forces (FIDF):

> As Jews, we like to see the glass as being one-sixteenth empty," Dermer said. "We have a hard time being optimistic about the future we face. But the glass is full, and it's overflowing. . . . So for those of you who worry—and that's our national sport—I hope you remember that your grandparents and their parents and their parents going back three generations would have given anything to trade their problems with us. . . .

See Jon Marks, "Ambassador Optimistic About Israel's Future," *Jewish Exponent*, October 25, 2017: "Generations of Jews have dreamed of the privilege of living in a sovereign Jewish state," Dermer said. "With that privilege comes a great responsibility to secure that dream for future generations."

23. In 2020, as he was ending his service as ambassador, Dermer was asked to name the highlight of his time in Washington. His answer, he said, could have been: (a) the ten-year, thirty-eight-billion-dollar agreement with the Obama administration on long-term military assistance; (b) the recognition of Jerusalem as Israel's capital and the relocation of the American embassy there; (c) the acknowledgment of Israeli sovereignty over the Golan Heights and support for the legal right to settle in the West Bank; or (d) the historic Abraham Accords with four Arab countries, brokered by the Trump administration in its final eighteen months. But, in fact, Dermer said, it was none of these stellar achievements. It was Netanyahu's 2015 address to Congress.

24. www.nationalchurchillmuseum.org/some-chicken-some-neck.html. International Churchill Society, "Winston Churchill 70 Years Ago: 'Some Chicken! Some Neck!'" www.winstonchurchill.org/publications/churchill-bulletin/bulletin-043-jan-2012/winston-churchill-70-years-ago-some-chicken-some-neck/.

25. Frederick T. Birchall, "Germany Rejects Verdict of League on Arms Violations," *New York Times*, April 21, 1935.

26. "Army Pays Hitler Birthday Tribute—Fuehrer, 46 Today, Hailed as Private Who Led Nation Back to Military Power," *New York Times*, April 20, 1935, 6.

27. "The Great Misunderstood," *New York Times*, May 2, 1935, 20.

28. Winston Churchill, "Air Parity Lost," May 2, 1935, International Churchill Society, www.winstonchurchill.org/resources/speeches/1930-1938-the-wilderness/air-parity-lost/. At the UN in 2009, Netanyahu, after quoting this paragraph from Churchill's speech, said:

"I speak here today in the hope that Churchill's assessment of the 'unteachability of mankind' is for once proven wrong. I speak here today in the hope that we can learn from history—that we can prevent danger in time."

29. In 1940, Benzion Netanyahu was thirty years old. Writing in *Haaretz* after Benzion's death, Israeli writer Ari Shavit noted that:

> [Benzion Netanyahu] never forgave the Zionist leadership for ignoring the warnings of Ze'ev Jabotinsky and failing to evacuate Europe's Jews from the killing fields in time. He never forgot that the United States didn't heed his warnings about the Holocaust in the 1940s.

Ari Shavit, "Benzion Netanyahu's Death—Researching the Past, Predicting the Future," *Haaretz*, May 1, 2012, www.haaretz.com/2012-05-01/ty-article/ari-shavit-benzion-netanyahu-studying-the-past-predicting-the-future/.

30. National Intelligence Estimates (NIE) are the classified assessments of the Director of National Intelligence (DNI) expressing the collective judgments of the eighteen U.S. intelligence agencies. Iran's nuclear weapons activities in the period 1980 to 2007 were described in detail in the U.S. 2007 National Intelligence Estimate (NIE), "Iran: Nuclear Intentions and Capabilities," www.dni.gov/files/documents/Newsroom/Reports%20and%20Pubs/20071203_release.pdf. For the 2005 NIE, see Jeffrey Lewis, "2005 Iran NIE Details," www.armscontrolwonk.com/archive/202469/2005-iran-nie-details/, September 22, 2009.

31. Netanyahu argued that there was "time to act in a variety of ways, and all ways must be considered . . . because we cannot let this thing happen again." It would require, he told the General Assembly, something "particularly difficult . . . what I call pre-emptive leadership":

> And of all the activities required in the political, economic and military fields, pre-emption is the most difficult. You can never prove to people what the situation would be if you do not move. . . . For us the Jewish people, too many times in our history we didn't see danger in time, and when we did, it was too late. Well, we see it now. . . . But can the world wake up? Can we wake up the world? . . .
>
> A man I very much admire—he said "no." This is what Winston Churchill said in the House of Commons in 1935, about this tendency of democracies to sleep, while dangers lurk and gather up:
>
> "There is nothing new in the story. It is as old as Rome. It falls into that long, dismal category of the fruitlessness of experience and the confirmed unteachability of mankind. Want of foresight, unwillingness to act when action would be simple and effective, lack of clear thinking, confusion of counsel until the emergency comes, until self-preservation strikes its jarring gong, these are the features which constitute the endless repetition of history."

32. Joshua Muravchik, "Bomb Iran," *Los Angeles Times*, November 1, 2006. The op-ed began with this sentence: "WE MUST bomb Iran." Muravchik argued that

even tough sanctions would not stop Iran, because Iran was "a country on a mission": "There is simply no possibility that Iran's clerical rulers will trade [its] ecstatic vision for a mess of Western pottage in the form of economic bribes or penalties."

33. Gild Ronen, "Bolton, Podhoretz Say: Bomb Iranian Nuclear Plants," *Israel National News*, September 30, 2007.

34. Ibid. During this period, President George W. Bush said more than once that if we permitted Iran to build a nuclear arsenal, people fifty years later would look back and wonder how we could have allowed such a thing to happen, and would judge us as harshly as we judge the British and the French for their failures in 1938.

35. Norman Podhoretz, "Stopping Iran," *Wall Street Journal*, January 23, 2008. The essay was also published in *Commentary*'s February 2008 issue, as a follow-up to Podhoretz's June 2007 *Commentary* article, "The Case for Bombing Iran," http://www.commentary.org/the-editors/from-2007-norman-podhoretzs-the-case-for-bombing-iran/.

36. "On the Issues: Iran," *New York Times*, May 23, 2012. See Mortimer B. Zuckerman, "3 Steps to Stop Iran from Getting a Nuclear Bomb," *U.S. News and World Report*, June 25, 2010:

> The Arab states see clearly what is happening. A new study of public opinion shows that most Arabs in the Gulf see their region as a more likely target than Israel from an Iranian bomb. If we wait for that threat to fully materialize, we will have waited too long. As the French president, Nicolas Sarkozy, has said, we might be left with a choice of "an Iranian bomb or bombing Iran." The only thing worse than bombing Iran, according to Sen. John McCain, is letting Iran get the bomb.

37. One of the most perceptive observers of American foreign policy, Professor Michael Mandelbaum of Johns Hopkins University, predicted in 2010 that the American role abroad would be hampered not only by President Obama's domestic focus but by the inherent limitations on American power abroad arising from America's economic situation. See Michael Mandelbaum, *The Frugal Superpower* (New York: PublicAffairs, 2010), 4:

> When Barack Obama was elected in 2008 he and his supporters expected that his presidency would transform the United States. . . . Mounting domestic economic obligations will narrow the scope of American foreign policy in the second decade of the 21st century and beyond. Because the United States will have to spend so much more than it has in the past on obligations at home—particularly caring for the ever-increasing ranks of its older citizens—it will be able to spend less than in the past on foreign policy. Because it will be able to spend less, it will be able to do less. *Just what the United States will and will not do will be the most important issue in international relations in the years ahead.* [Emphasis added.]

38. David Brooks, "Obama, Gospel and Verse," *New York Times*, April 26, 2007:

> When you ask about ways to prevent Iran from developing nuclear weapons, [Obama] talks grandly about marshaling a global alliance. But when you ask specifically if an Iranian bomb would be deterrable, he says yes: "I think Iran is like North Korea. They see nuclear arms in defensive terms, as a way to prevent regime change."

In his February 2008 *Commentary* article, Norman Podhoretz argued that deterrence would not suffice with respect to Iran:

> I argued that deterrence could not be relied upon with a regime ruled by Islamofascist revolutionaries who not only were ready to die for their beliefs but cared less about protecting their people than about the spread of their ideology and their power. If the mullahs got the bomb, I said, it was not they who would be deterred, but we.

Hashemi Rafsanjani, a former president of Iran who was reputedly a moderate, had said plainly that Iran would not be deterred by fear of retaliation:

> If a day comes when the world of Islam is duly equipped with the arms Israel has in its possession . . . application of an atomic bomb would not leave anything in Israel, but the same thing would just produce damages in the Muslim world.

Bernard Lewis, the leading contemporary authority on the culture of the Islamic world, explained that "mutual assured destruction" (MAD), which had been effective during the Cold War, would not work with those who believed the use of nuclear weapons would lead to a higher religious result, at the cost of only a sustainable loss to them.

39. David Brooks, "Obama, Gospel and Verse," *New York Times*, April 26, 2007.

40. As a senator, Obama had proposed a regional conference with Iran to forge a new relationship in the Middle East. Senator Obama, "A Way Forward in Iraq," Remarks to Chicago Council on Global Affairs, November 20, 2016, www.stltoday.com/news/local/govt-and-politics/obama-offers-his-plan-for-the-iraq-war/article_a83b95e9-0f66-516b-808d-63eb7f90d732.html. Obama called for a phased withdrawal of U.S. troops from Iraq to become an "over-the-horizon force" and said he "firmly believe[d] that we should convene a regional conference with the Iraqis, Saudis, Iranians, Syrians, the Turks, Jordanians, the British and others."

41. "Obama says ready to talk to Iran," *Reuters*, January 27, 2009, www.reuters.com/article/us-obama-arabiya/obama-says-ready-to-talk-to-iran-idUSTRE50Q23220090127.

42. In July 2007, in a presidential debate, Barack Obama was asked if he would be "willing to meet separately, without preconditions, during the first year of your administration, in Washington or anywhere else, with the leaders of Iran, Syria, Venezuela, Cuba and North Korea?" He answered, "I would."

43. "The Iraq Study Group Report," December 2006, web.archive.org/web/20100829020030/ www.media..usip.org/reports/iraq_study_group_report.pdf, 36. The Report asserted that Iran's reluctance to respond to American diplomatic efforts

was based on Iran's belief "that the United States seeks regime change in Iran." Report, 37.

44. Senator Barack Obama, "Floor Statement on Bush's Decision to Increase Troops in Iraq," January 19, 2007.

45. William Kristol, "The New War President," *New York Times*, January 18, 2009. A year-and-a-half later, in mid-2010, Vice President Biden predicted that the withdrawal from Iraq "could be one of the great achievements" of the Obama administration. "You're going to see a stable government in Iraq that is actually moving toward a representative election." See www.latimesblogs.latimes.com/washington/2010/02/joe-biden-update-larry-king-iraq-obama-sarah-palin.html.

46. Brian Knowlton, "Economy and Iraq Are Set to Lead Obama Agenda," *New York Times*, January 18, 2009.

47. William Kristol, "The Next War President," *New York Times*, January 18, 2009. The following day, the *Times* reported that nearly 75 percent of Iraqis said they planned to vote in elections set for January 31—the first of several that would be held in Iraq as it began to move toward a representative government.

48. For a detailed evaluation of President Obama's strategic approach to the Middle East, see Michael Doran, "Obama's Secret Iran Strategy," *Mosaic*, February 2, 2015; "What They're Saying About 'Obama's Secret Iran Strategy,'" *Mosaic*, February 19, 2015; Michael Barone, "Obama's Quest for a Grand Bargain with Iran Seems Unwise," *Washington Examiner*, February 12, 2015; Michael Doran and Tony Badran, "The Realignment," *Tablet*, May 10, 2021.

49. In testimony on May 17, 2016, before the House Committee on Oversight and Government Reform, Michael Doran testified that:

> The Iran nuclear deal, we can now see, was but the most visible piece of a much larger policy—namely, rapprochement with Iran as a means of furthering American disengagement from the Middle East. . . . In 2012, [Obama] opened secret, bilateral negotiations with the Iranians on the nuclear question in Oman. Simultaneously, he quietly brought his policies in Lebanon, Iraq, and, especially, Syria into alignment with Iranian interests.
>
> . . . [Obama] sold the agreement publicly as a narrow arms control agreement, the only goal of which was to sever Iran's "pathways to a nuclear weapon." In actual fact, it was but one piece of a much larger regional vision. In that vision, the United States would recognize the legitimacy not just of Iran's nuclear program but also of its interests in the Arab world.

50. See Michael Doran and Tony Badran, "The Realignment," quoting from Robert Malley's 2019 article in *Foreign Affairs* suggesting that President Obama's "ultimate goal" had been:

> "to help the [Middle East] find a more stable balance of power that would make it less dependent on direct U.S. interference or protection." That is a roundabout way of saying that Obama dreamed of a new Middle East order—one that relies more on partnership with Iran.

51. Roger Cohen, "Iran on a Razor's Edge," *New York Times*, June 15, 2009.

52. Roger Cohen, "My Name Is Iran," *New York Times*, June 17, 2009.

53. Roger Cohen, "City of Whispers," *New York Times*, June 19, 2009.

54. Roger Cohen, "A Supreme Leader Loses His Aura as Iranians Flock to the Street," *New York Times*, June 20, 2009.

55. Roger Cohen, "Iran's Children of Tomorrow," *New York Times*, June 22, 2009.

56. Roger Cohen, "The End of the Beginning," *New York Times*, June 23, 2009.

57. Roger Cohen, "Iran's Second Sex," *New York Times*, June 26, 2009.

58. Roger Cohen, "Let the Usurpers Writhe," *New York Times*, July 1, 2009.

59. Roger Cohen, "The Making of an Iran Policy," *New York Times*, July 30, 2009.

60. The White House, "Remarks by President Obama and President Lee of the Republic of Korea in Joint Press Availability," June 16, 2009, http://www.obamawhitehouse.archives.gov/the-press-office/remarks-president-obama-and-president-lee-republic-korea-joint-press-availability. In his February 2008 article in *Commentary*, Norman Podhoretz had outlined the strategic case for supporting, covertly or overtly, the protests in Iran as a nonmilitary solution to the Iranian threat—regime change:

> Those who had been urging Bush to launch such a program, and who were confident that it would succeed, pointed to polls showing great dissatisfaction with the mullocracy among the Iranian young, and to the demonstrations against it that kept breaking out all over the country.

61. On June 22, ten days into the Iranian revolt, President Obama began a press conference by saying:

> First, I'd like to say a few words about the situation in Iran. The United States and the international community have been *appalled and outraged* by the threats, beatings, and imprisonments of the last few days. I *strongly condemn* these unjust actions, and I join with the American people in *mourning* each and every innocent life that is lost.
>
> I have made it clear that the United States respects the sovereignty of the Islamic Republic of Iran, and is not at all interfering in Iran's affairs. But we must also *bear witness* to the courage and dignity of the Iranian people, and to a remarkable opening within Iranian society. And we *deplore violence* against innocent civilians anywhere that it takes place. . . .
>
> *This is not about the United States and the West; this is about the people of Iran, and the future that they and only they will choose. The Iranian people can speak for themselves.* That is precisely what has happened these last few days. . . . [W]e also know this: those who stand up for justice are always *on the right side of history.* [Emphasis added.]

Reuters Staff, "Obama Comments on Iran," Reuters, June 23, 2009. For a caustic criticism of Obama's words and inaction, see James Bowman, "Negative Side Effects," *New Criterion*, April 2014 ("the best thing about being on the right side of history is that you don't actually have to do anything. You don't even have to threaten to do anything") and James Bowman, "Stumbling Through the Fog," *New Criterion*, April 2022:

> Mr. Obama had offered, in lieu of helping the liberal and anti-theocratic demonstrators in Tehran, the usual consolation that, though defeated, they had been "on the right side of history." Though his words were no doubt of unspeakable comfort to the demonstrators in their prison cells, we're still waiting for history to avenge them.

62. While there was no response from the Obama administration, worldwide protests against Iran continued. On July 25, 2009, one of the largest protests held outside Iran was organized by "United for Iran" and hosted in over 100 major cities around the globe. In New York, there were major demonstrations in the streets. See CBS News, "Global Protests Demand End of Iran Abuses," July 25, 2009, www.cbsnews.com/news/global-protests-demand-end-of-iran-abuses/.

63. David Horowitz, "Sharansky's Guide to the Region's Human Rights Dilemmas," *Times of Israel*, January 30, 2014. Sharansky told the *Times* that Obama's decision not to provide encouragement for those confronting the ayatollahs' regime "doomed those protests, which might otherwise have led to a revolution ousting the hardline Islamist regime." David Horowitz, "Sharansky: If Obama Had Backed Iran's Dissidents, Arab Spring Might Have Looked Different," *Times of Israel*, January 30, 2014.

64. Quoted in Joel B. Pollak, "Leon Panetta: Obama Should Have Helped Iran Protests in 2009," *Breitbart News*, January 2, 2018, www.breitbart.com/politics/2018/01/02/leon-panetta-obama-helped-iran-protests-2009/.

65. "Remarks by the President to the United Nations General Assembly," September 23, 2009, obamawhitehouse.archives.gov/the-press-office/remarks-president-united-nations-general-assembly. Obama's remarks in context read as follows:

> In an era when our destiny is shared, power is no longer a zero-sum game. *No one nation can or should try to dominate another nation*. No world order that elevates one nation or group of people over another will succeed. *No balance of power among nations will hold*. The traditional divisions between nations of the South and the North make no sense in an interconnected world; nor do alignments of nations rooted in the cleavages of a long-gone Cold War. [Emphasis added.]

66. "Transcript: President Obama's Full NPR Interview," *NPR*, December 29, 2014, www.npr.org/2014/12/29/372485968/transcript-president-obamas-full-npr-interview.

67. The Obama administration stayed silent about its existence, which did not become public until the IAEA confirmed it in January 2012. BBC News, "Iran Enriching Uranium at Fordo Plant Near Qom," January 10, 2012, www.bbc.com/news/world-middle-east-16470100.

68. Iran reportedly believed that, through its acquiescence, the West had effec-

tively accepted its nuclear program. Irwin Cotler, "Combating Iran's Cycle of Denial, Deception, and Delay," *Jerusalem Post*, July 19, 2012.

69. Ross Colvin, "'Cut Off Head of Snake' Saudis Told U.S. on Iran," Reuters, November 28, 2010, www.reuters.com/article/us-wikileaks-iran-saudis-idUSTRE6AS02B20101129:

> King Abdullah of Saudi Arabia repeatedly exhorted the United States to "cut off the head of the snake" by launching military strikes to destroy Iran's nuclear program, according to leaked U.S. diplomatic cables. . . .
>
> The April 2008 cable detailed a meeting between General David Petraeus, the top U.S. military commander in the Middle East, and then U.S. ambassador to Iraq, Ryan Crocker, and King Abdullah and other Saudi princes.
>
> At the meeting, the Saudi ambassador to the United States, Adel al-Jubeir "recalled the King's frequent exhortations to the U.S. to attack Iran and so put an end to its nuclear weapons program," the cable said.
>
> "He told you to cut off the head of the snake," Jubeir was reported to have said.

70. Ronen Bergman, *Rise and Kill First: The Secret History of Israel's Targeted Assassinations* (New York: Random House, 2018), xix, 622–23. The epigraph of Bergman's book, from which he chose his title, is a verse from the Talmud: "If someone comes to kill you, rise up and kill him first."

Bergman described targeted killings that had "slowed the [Iranian] program's progress considerably" and international sanctions that "had flung Iran into a grave economic crisis that threatened to bring down the regime entirely." On November 29, 2010, motorcyclists blew up the cars of two senior figures in the Iranian nuclear project; in July 2011, a motorcyclist shot a nuclear physicist and senior researcher; in November 2011, a huge explosion obliterated nearly an entire Revolutionary Guard base near Tehran, killing the general who headed Iranian missile development; on January 12, 2012, a motorcyclist killed a chemical engineer at the Natanz uranium enrichment facility. But:

> [Barak] and Netanyahu both concluded that Iran was nearing the moment when the project's installations would be indestructible, and they agreed that Israel should act to destroy the facilities before that happened. They ordered the IDF and the intelligence arms to prepare for Operation Deep Waters: an all-out air attack, supported by commando forces, in the heart of Iran. Some $2 billion was spent on preparations for the attack and for the anticipated ensuing war. . . .

Meir Dagan, head of Israel's Mossad, used an analogy to describe the difference between covert action against critical parts of Iran's nuclear structure and a large military strike on the heads of it:

> In a car there are 25,000 parts on average. Imagine if 100 of them are missing. It would be very hard to make it go. On the other hand, sometimes it's most effective to kill the driver, and that's that.

Bergman, *Rise and Kill First*, xxi. There was ample precedent for an Israeli preemptive strike: In 1981, Israel had destroyed Saddam Hussein's reactor; in 2007, Israel had destroyed Syria's nuclear reactor. But in 2012, the Israeli defense establishment opposed a strike on Iran, given the opposition of the Obama administration and its assurances to Israel about the administration's ultimate willingness to use force. Once American negotiations with Iran began, Netanyahu "postponed an attack again and again, and when the final [deal] was signed, he canceled it altogether, at least for the near future." Ibid., 624–29.

71. Ronen Bergman, "Will Israel Attack Iran?" *New York Times*, January 29, 2021, www.nytimes.com/2012/01/29/magazine/will-israel-attack-iran.html.

72. Rachel Nolan, "Behind the Cover Story: Ronen Bergman on Whether Israel Will Attack Iran," *New York Times*, January 30, 2012, 6thfloor.blogs.nytimes.com/2012/01/30/behind-the-cover-story-ronen-bergman-on-israeli-plans-to-strike-iran/.

73. See "Netanyahu Was Close to Attacking Iran in 2012 Despite Obama—NYT," *Jerusalem Post*, September 5, 2019: "In an interview, Prime Minister Benjamin Netanyahu confirmed that Israel was close to attacking Iran in 2012 but stopped after he did not have enough support in his cabinet. . . . 'If I'd had a majority, I would have done it.'" See also "Israel Called Off 2012 Strike on Iran Because It Coincided with Joint US Drill," *Times of Israel*, August 21, 2015 ("Relying on tape recordings of former defense minister Ehud Barak and other unnamed foreign reports, the TV report [by Israel's Channel 2] made clear that the US was opposed to the strike on Iran, but Israel was going to go ahead with it anyway").

74. See David Samuels, "The Aspiring Novelist Who Became Obama's Foreign Policy Guru," *New York Times Magazine*, May 5, 2016, in which Samuels described an interview with Leon Panetta about the efforts in 2012 to preclude Netanyahu from striking Iran:

> As secretary of defense, he tells me, one of his most important jobs was keeping Prime Minister Benjamin Netanyahu of Israel and his defense minister, Ehud Barak, from launching a pre-emptive attack on Iran's nuclear facilities. "They were both interested in the answer to the question, 'Is the president serious?'" Panetta recalls. "And you know my view, talking with the president, was: If brought to the point where we had evidence that they're developing an atomic weapon, I think the president is serious that he is not going to allow that to happen." . . .
>
> "But would you make that same assessment now?" I ask him.
>
> "Would I make that same assessment now?" he asks. "Probably not."

75. See Amos Harel, "The Dramatic Moment When Israel Almost Struck Iran," *Haaretz*, March 24, 2022, an interview with Zohar Palti, who held senior Mossad and Defense Ministry posts and "was a central part of the opposition [in 2012] to attacking Iran." He recalled, "what happened when Netanyahu and Barak ordered the army to prepare an Iran strike—within 16 days":

> "What very much hastened the American progress toward an interim agreement with Iran, in 2013, and then the nuclear accord in 2015, was in part actually our behavior. We gave them a certain feeling of urgency [because of the threat of an attack], and that is what prompted the Obama administration to create a secret back channel of negotiations with Iran. A year later the interim agreement was signed, and the idea of an attack was dropped."

76. Ron Dermer, speech to Christians United for Israel (CUFI) on the negotiations with Iran, July 13, 2015, https://www.facebook.com/ambdermer/posts/1857677837791226.

77. In his address to CUFI on July 13, 2015, Dermer described the magnitude of the American and European concessions to Iran:

> In a few months, this deal would give Iran 150 billion dollars. Iran has a 300-to-400-billion-dollar economy. A 150-billion-dollar infusion of cash into Iran's coffers is like 8 trillion dollars flowing into the U.S. treasury. . . . The truth is that billions of dollars will be used to replenish the Iranian regime's ATMs in the region. Those ATMs are the Ayatollah Terror Machines—the Shiite militia in Iraq, Assad's regime in Syria, Hezbollah in Lebanon, the Houthis in Yemen, Hamas and Islamic Jihad in Gaza, and the many other Iranian terror proxies throughout the region.

78. The rationale for agreeing to a time-limit on Iran's obligations was the optimistic belief that the deal itself would be a moderating influence on Iran, because Iran was arguably "less a terrorist state than a turbulent one," which would moderate itself once the international "turbulence" involving it disappeared. A prominent proponent of the Iran Deal argued at the time that:

> [Iran's] continued isolation poses far greater dangers to the international community than a process that draws it closer to the rest of the world—with monitors on the ground, regular diplomatic exchanges, and greater economic integration. . . . bring[ing] the middle class into the global economy—exposing élites to foreign travel, and to scientifically trained entrepreneurs and scholars. This opening to the international community might well create new national interests for the regime to protect, and perhaps ultimately transform it.

Bernard Avishai, "Netanyahu's Speech," *New Yorker*, March 3, 2015. The Israelis believed that this was wishful thinking, and that ending sanctions on Iran would lead not to moderation, but instead to the expansion of Iran's nuclear program—particularly if ending sanctions was not conditioned on Iran ending its missile production, nuclear weapons research, support for terrorist proxies in the region, etc. See also Walter Russell Mead, *The Arc of a Covenant*, 538, describing the Obama administration's belief that, if it ended American hostility to Iran, "the hardliners would retreat" and the region would become "more stable, more peaceful, and, who knows, perhaps more democratic."

79. "Transcript: President Obama's Full NPR Interview on Iran Nuclear Deal," National Public Radio, April 7, 2015. In the interview, Obama acknowledged that by the end of the Iran Deal, when the restrictions on Iran would lapse, advanced centrifuges would mean "the breakout times would have shrunk almost down to zero." www.npr.org/2015/04/07/397933577/transcript-president-obamas-full-npr-interview-on-iran-nuclear-deal.

80. The "Joint Plan of Action" was adopted on November 24, 2013. "Full text of Iran-5+1 agreement in Geneva, 24 November 2013,"www.globalsecurity.org/wmd/library/policy/int/iran-5-1-geneva-agreement_2013.htm.

81. Jeffrey Goldberg, "The Crisis in U.S.-Israel Relations Is Officially Here," *Atlantic*, October 28, 2014.

82. Michael B. Oren, *Ally: My Journey Across the American-Israeli Divide* (New York: Random House, 2015), 365.

83. Ibid., 366.

84. Netanyahu and Dermer were accused of seeking to use the Congressional platform for political purposes. But it was not self-evident that picking a fight with Israel's most important ally was an advantageous strategy for a prime minister running for reelection.

85. Abraham Foxman, head of the Anti-Defamation League (ADL), counseled canceling the speech; Morton Klein, head of the Zionist Organization of America (ZOA), supported it. Two writers at *Commentary* took opposite positions on the advisability of the impending address. Cf. Jonathan Tobin, "Netanyahu Must Not Give That Speech," *Commentary*, February 12, 2015, and Rick Richman, "Netanyahu Must Give That Speech," *Commentary*, February 12, 2015. From the Richman post:

> The speech will be [Netanyahu's] attempt to say what Churchill would have said if he had seen America heading down the road Kissinger and Shultz described [in their cautionary testimony] to the Armed Services Committee. A head of state must come to Washington to say it, and to say it not simply in private discussions, nor simply before pro-Israel advocates at AIPAC, but directly to the representatives of the American people, and before it is too late.
>
> It is not going to be David Cameron, Angela Merkel, or François Hollande, the leaders of a Europe that is no longer strategically serious. If it is going to be anyone, it will have to be Benjamin Netanyahu.

Some speculated that Obama's displeasure with Netanyahu's plan to speak to Congress was not the diplomatic slight to Obama as president but rather "concern that it may upset his plan for a grand bargain with Iran." See Michael Barone, "Obama's Quest for a Grand Bargain with Iran Seems Unwise," *Washington Examiner*, February 12, 2015; Liel Leibovitz, "The 'New York Times' Violates My Protocol," *Tablet*, February 11, 2015 (arguing that the "true rift between Netanyahu and Obama is about policy, not politesse").

86. Michael B. Oren, *Ally*, 366. Oren wrote that he had supported Netanyahu's position on Iran, but had disagreed with his decision to address Congress:

> This would insinuate himself—and Israel—between Republicans and Democrats and exacerbate our differences with the White House. . . . The same speech could have been given at that week's AIPAC conference, I suggested, or postponed until after the Israeli elections, removing the impression of grandstanding. "It's incumbent on every Israeli leader to do the utmost to prevent Iran from getting the bomb," I told the media. "But it's just as vital to preserve bipartisan support for Israel in America. The first goal should not be attained at the latter's expense."

National security adviser Susan Rice called the speech "destructive of the fabric of US Israel relationship," and Thomas Friedman in the *New York Times* urged Netanyahu to take the "intelligent advice of his previous ambassador in Washington." Ibid., 368.

87. "Transcript of Netanyahu's Speech to Congress," as delivered, with instances of applause noted, www.nytimes.com/2015/03/04/us/politics/transcript-of-netanyahus-remarks-to-congress.html. It shows that Netanyahu was interrupted by applause twenty-six times.

88. Carl Hulse, "Netanyahu Event Similar to a State of the Union Address, but More Electric," *New York Times*, March 3, 2015. Hulse's report noted further that:

> As she rose and sat during standing ovations, Ms. Pelosi wore a piqued expression that made it clear she was rising only out of obligation. She occasionally shook her head in disapproval and repeatedly turned to make remarks to her colleagues as Mr. Netanyahu spoke. In a statement after Mr. Netanyahu finished, Ms. Pelosi said that his tone left her "near tears throughout" and that she was "saddened by the insult to the intelligence of the United States."

89. Appearing on *Meet the Press* on March 22, 2015, Dermer was asked to define a "bad deal" with Iran and responded as follows:

> A bad deal has a short breakout time. Right now, they're talking about a year breakout time. That leaves Iran with a vast nuclear infrastructure in place. That breakout time has to be much longer. And a very bad deal is a deal that would automatically remove restrictions on Iran's nuclear program after only about a decade. That would be a terrible deal, because it would create a situation where you'd have a deal that wouldn't block Iran's path to the bomb, it would pave it. They won't have to sneak into the nuclear club. They wouldn't need to break into the nuclear club. They could just walk into the nuclear club. . . .

90. Belladonna Rogers, "Echoes of Churchill Pervade Netanyahu Speech," *Real Clear Politics*, March 7, 2015. Ms. Rogers wrote that:

> Churchill only had to rally his listeners; Netanyahu had to educate his. The address to the Canadian Parliament was . . . one of the most consequential in World War II. In his unmistakable reference to it, Netanyahu sought to urge America to stand by its allies in the Middle East.

91. The Churchill Project has written that this section of the speech "brought down the house in words which will live as long as his story is told." The Churchill Project, "Temper, Kennedy, and the Origin of Churchill's 'Wrung Like a Chicken,'" May 24, 2021. The full text of the speech is at America's National Churchill Museum, "Some Chicken; Some Neck, 1941," www.nationalchurchillmuseum.org/some-chicken-some-neck.html. A description of the atmosphere can be found at The Historical Society of Ottawa, "Some Chicken, Some Neck," https://www.historicalsocietyottawa.ca/publications/ottawa-stories/personalities-from-the-very-famous-to-the-lesser-known/some-chicken-some-neck:

> Almost 2,000 people, including MPs, Senators, privy councilors, provincial premiers, judges, clergy, high-ranking military leaders, and heads of Commonwealth and foreign delegations, sat on the parliamentary benches and on temporary seats set up on the Commons' floor. The galleries too were packed. . . .
>
> Churchill's arrival was the signal for minutes of near-frantic cheering from the assembled multitude. . . . In his speech, one of his most memorable, Churchill thanked the Canadian people for all they have done in the "common cause." . . . Alluding to defeatist comments made by French generals who in 1940 had said that in three weeks England would have her neck rung like a chicken, Churchill famously said "Some Chicken! Some Neck!" Simple words, but ones that captured the resolve of a people to fight on to victory. The House erupted into cheers.

92. Churchill's speech was broadcast around the world by shortwave radio and carried by the CBC, BBC, and major American radio networks. The following day, the *New York Times* reported that President Roosevelt, along with "many millions of other Americans," had listened to it on their radios. The *Times* quoted Roosevelt as describing the speech as "perfectly wonderful." "Roosevelt Awaiting Return of Churchill," *New York Times*, December 31, 1941.

On December 26, 1941, four days before the speech, Churchill had addressed the U.S. Congress, and had ended by observing how World War II might have been avoided by a unified response to Germany's violation of its post–World War I treaty obligations:

> If we had kept together after the last war, if we had taken common measures for our safety, this renewal of the curse need never have fallen upon us. . . . Five or six years ago it would have been easy, without shedding a drop of blood, for the United States and Great Britain to have insisted on the fulfillment of the disarmament clauses of the treaties which Germany signed after the Great War. . . . The chance has passed, it is gone. Prodigious hammer strokes have been needed to bring us together today.

93. The following are additional excerpts from Netanyahu's address to Congress:

> Iran's nuclear program can be rolled back well-beyond the current proposal, by insisting on a better deal and keeping up the pressure on a very vulnerable

regime. . . . [F]or over a year, we've been told that no deal is better than a bad deal. Well, this is a bad deal. It's a very bad deal. We're better off without it.

Now we're being told that the only alternative to this bad deal is war. That's just not true. The alternative to this bad deal is a much better deal. A better deal that doesn't leave Iran with a vast nuclear infrastructure and such a short breakout time. A better deal that keeps the restrictions on Iran's nuclear program in place until Iran's aggression ends. A better deal that won't give Iran an easy path to the bomb. A better deal that Israel and its neighbors may not like, but with which we could live, literally. And no country . . . has a greater stake than Israel in a good deal that peacefully removes this threat.

94. It is not clear whether invoking Churchill's Chicken Speech was Netanyahu's or Dermer's idea, but both were well versed in Churchill's speeches. Dermer's deep knowledge of Churchill can be seen in his 2018 Kemper Lecture, "Churchill and Israel," March 25, 2018; www.nationalchurchillmuseum.org/kemper-lecture-dermer.html; www.youtube.com/watch?v=tM9Log5Tof4.

95. See Martin Kramer, "Netanyahu and Churchill: Analogy and Error," March 8, 2015, https://martinkramer.org/2015/03/08/netanyahu-and-churchill-analogy-and-error/. Charles Krauthammer called Netanyahu's speech "Churchillian . . . a speech of, I think, extraordinary power but great desperation." Colonel Richard Kemp wrote that:

Like Churchill . . . Netanyahu is taking a risk. For Churchill the risk was to his life—he had to make a hazardous transatlantic voyage . . . through stormy, U-boat infested waters. For Netanyahu the risk is to his own political life and to his country's relationship with the United States, given the intense presidential opposition to his speech. . . . And in both cases, the stakes could not be higher, greater than their own lives, political fortunes or rivalries and affecting not just their own countries and the United States, but the whole of the world.

Richard Kemp, "Netanyahu, Churchill and Congress, Trying to Avert War," March 1, 2015, www.gatestoneinstitute.org/5302/netanyahu-congress-speech.

96. See Gedalia Guttentag, "Front-Row Seat to History," *Mishpacha*, December 9, 2020, www.mishpacha.com/front-row-seat-to-history/, quoting Dermer saying:

"There was about six weeks between the time Bibi's speech was announced in mid-January to the time it was given in early March. Many people within the Jewish community here in Washington opposed the prime minister coming, and the government wanted me to speak to a group of the leadership here in town, 80 percent of whom were against the forthcoming speech."

97. Dermer told another story, about the Czech ambassador who asked him, two weeks before the speech, "What's the story with this controversy?"

So I said I have . . . two questions: if the British parliament would have invited the Czech Prime Minister in 1938 to come and speak before the British parliament and the British nation about why you oppose the Munich agreement, against the wishes of Chamberlain at the time . . . would your Prime Minister have come? And second, if your Prime Minister refused to come would your country have ever forgiven him? And [the Czech ambassador] says, "I understand your point."

98. At the annual Holocaust Memorial Day ceremony at the Yad Vashem Holocaust Memorial, Netanyahu used biblical language to reinforce that message:

> "Seventy years ago we were a people of war refugees, powerless and voiceless. Today we express what we have to say. . . . It is our duty to fight those who wish to destroy us, not to bow down to them nor to downplay reality. We will not allow the state of Israel to be a passing episode in the history of our nation." . . . Netanyahu ended by invoking . . . Isaiah 52: 2, "Shake thyself from the dust; put on thy beautiful garments my people."

Israel 365 News, "Netanyahu Invokes Biblical Prophecy to Open World's Eyes to 'Darkness' of Iran," April 16, 2015, www.israel365news.com/36483/netanyahu-invokes-prophet-isaiah-warning-iran-hope-future-jerusalem/.

99. Hudson Institute, "A Conversation with Ron Dermer," May 21, 2021, www.hudson.org/events/1964-virtual-event-a-conversation-with-ambassador-ron-dermer-52021:

> I saw that the environment in the United States changed overnight after the Prime Minister's speech in Congress. . . . Before then, it was like I was just talking to a wall. And then after that speech, it changed everything. It's absolutely remarkable. I hesitate to say these things because it makes me sound like a sycophant, but it's just true. It's just true. It absolutely changed the environment.

100. United States Institute of Peace, "The Final Tally: How Congress Voted on Iran," September 17, 2015, iranprimer.usip.org/blog/2015/sep/11/congress-votes-deal. See also Julie Hirschfeld Davis and Ashley Parker, "Ambassador Tries to Bridge Gap with U.S., but on Israel's Terms," *New York Times*, March 25, 2015.

101. Hudson Institute, "A Conversation with Ron Dermer," www.hudson.org/research/16936-transcript-a-conversation-with-ambassador-ron-dermer:

> But one thing that I did not anticipate, a positive development that I did not foresee, was the impact that it was going to have on the Arab states. . . . [A]ll of a sudden, Israel was speaking out, and had an independent policy, and that gave them a great deal of confidence that Israel was willing to be a reliable actor, independent of what US policy would be in the region.
>
> [T]hat speech . . . accelerated the ties that were happening beneath the surface between Israel and the Arab states. And when you had a US administration that was confronting Iran, that's how you were able to surface under the wings of the United States to allies in the region. . . . All of a sudden it was ready to break out because they understood that it was in their strategic interest to move into this public alliance with Israel.

See also Dennis Ross, "The Abraham Accords And The Changing Shape Of The Middle East," The Hoover Institution, *The Caravan*, June 21, 2002:

> Arab leaders increasingly came to view cooperation with Israel as in their interests. It may have begun exclusively in the security domain, with security cooperation becoming even more important as America's Arab partners became increasingly convinced that the US was withdrawing from the region and was inherently less reliable. As Arab officials told me, "Israel, unlike the US, isn't going anywhere"—and, certainly as importantly, "Israel actually acts and doesn't talk about it."

See also Mead, *The Arc of a Covenant*, 549, 575:

> Israel and its Arab neighbors increasingly saw America's new Iran policy as their gravest security threat . . .
>
> Geopolitically speaking, the Arabs and the Israelis were turning into strategic allies. . . . In the view of Egypt and most Gulf states, the Palestinian issue was small potatoes compared to the urgent need to build in Arab-Israeli alliance to prevent the submergence of the Arab world under a renewed Ottoman or Persian Empire.

102. "Netanyahu: The Figures Who Formed Him, and the Duties of Jewish Leadership," *Mosaic*, December 21, 2021.

103. The reasons the Israeli government believed "you can't" accept it were summarized by Dermer in his July 2015 speech to CUFI, shortly after the Iran Deal was reached:

> Israelis across the political spectrum are united in their view that this deal is a disaster. Now for a country where every two Jews have three opinions, that's saying something. Your Arab allies also think this is a very bad deal. And when Israel and the Arab states are on the same page, which happens about once a century, pay attention. . . . The reason why we oppose this deal is because . . . it doesn't block Iran's path to the bomb. It makes Iran's illegal nuclear program legal. It provides billions in sanctions relief for Iran to fuel the fires of war that it is spreading across the Middle East. And it rolls out the red carpet for Iran to become a military nuclear power. . . .

On Netanyahu's definition of the mission as "identifying the danger in time," cf. Daniel J. Mahoney, "Churchill, Political Judgment, and the 'Courage to See'," *American Greatness*, May 28, 2022.

104. The full quotation, from Hillel the Elder in *Pirkei Avot*, Chapter 1:14, is: "If I am not for myself, who will be for me? If I am only for myself, what am I? And if not now, when?"

105. The determination to act alone, if necessary, spans the Israeli political spectrum. See Tovah Lazaroff, "Lapid Warns That Israel Will Act Alone Against Iran if Needed," *Jerusalem Post*, December 27, 2001. See Lewis Libby and Douglas J. Feith, "Biden Shouldn't Underestimate Israel's Resolve in Face of Iranian Nuclear Threat," *National Review*, January 31, 2022. Ron Dermer, "The Danger of Returning to the Nuclear Deal with Iran," a ten-minute video, June 14, 2019, American Jewish Committee, www.facebook.com/ambdermer/videos/453270461908315; see also, Patrick

Clawson, "New U.S. Tone on Iran," August 16, 2012, www.washingtoninstitute.org /policy-analysis/new-us-tone-iran:

> US policymakers often fail to appreciate how deeply Israelis mistrust the notion of relying on foreign security guarantees. A formative experience for Israeli security doctrine came at a time of great need in June 1967, when President Lyndon Johnson refused to honor his predecessor's explicit, written pledge guaranteeing security of navigation through the Straits of Tiran—a firm promise that had been central to Israel's agreement to withdraw from the Sinai Peninsula in 1957. That episode reinforced the state's founding principle: that the Jewish people can never rely on others to protect them. For many Israelis, this principle is the single most important guide to foreign policy.

CONCLUSION: THE TRUSTEESHIP OF HISTORY

1. Daniel Gordis, "Symposium on the Jewish Future," *Commentary*, November 2015.

2. See Wilfred M. McClay, in an Encounter Books Interview: "[Popular historians] tend almost reflexively to see modern phenomena . . . as the inevitable forces of nature, 'the arc of history,' and such. . . . Almost nothing in history is inevitable, and almost nothing in history is permanent. . . . In short, whenever you hear someone begin to speak of 'the judgment of History,' grab a spoonful of salt, since what is coming next is likely nothing more than the judgment of the smug and self-satisfied Present." "Wilfred McClay on Teaching American History, the Trouble with Howard Zinn, and 'Land of Hope'," An Interview with Wilfred McClay, May 15, 2019, https://www.encounterbooks.com/features/wilfred-mcclay-teaching-american-history-trouble-howard-zinn-land-hope/.

3. For a portrayal of the foundation of the state of Israel as "a highly contingent event" facilitated by a unique two-year period, when both the Soviet Union and the United States, for different reasons, supported the formation of the Jewish state, see Jeffrey Herf, *Israel's Moment: International Support for and Opposition to Establishing the Jewish State, 1945–1949* (New York: Cambridge University Press, 2022), 1–23. For a view of Jewish history as one with a religious meaning and the restoration of Israel as a miracle, see "The Miraculous Case for God: A View from Jewish History: A Conversation with Rabbi Meir Soloveichik and Eric Cohen," The Tikvah Fund, December 3, 2020, https://tikvahfund.org/cfg-event/.

4. This is an issue not only in Jewish history but in American history as well. In an address in 2005 entitled "American History and America's Future," reprinted in his 2017 book, *The American Spirit*, David McCullough argued that the general ignorance of the stories of the Founders of the United States endangered the American experiment itself:

> We have to value what our forebears . . . did for us, or we're not going to take it very seriously, and it can slip away. . . . If you've inherited some great work of art that is worth a fortune and you don't know that it's worth a fortune, you don't

> even know that it's a great work of art, and you're not interested in it—you're going to lose it.

David McCullough, *The American Spirit: Who We Are and What We Stand For* (New York: Simon & Schuster, 2017), 110–11.

See also Wilfred M. McClay, "History as a Way of Knowing," September 17, 2021, https://lawliberty.org/history-as-a-way-of-knowing/:

> History constantly reminds that we did not invent ourselves, and that the formative influences of our origins linger on in us. . . . It reminds us that historicity is a central part of the human condition. . . . [History] is not merely an academic subject or an accumulated body of knowledge, but a discipline formative of the soul.

Myron Magnet has called the heritage from the American Founders an "exceptional treasure," something "precious, something worth defending." Myron Magnet, "The Founders' Priceless Legacy," *New Criterion*, November 2020, 4, 11.

For a Jewish perspective on this issue, see *Jewish Current Issues*, "Passover 2005—I," April 20, 2005, jpundit.typepad.com/jci/2005/04/passover_2005_i.html.

See also Wilfred McClay, "The Claims of Memory," *First Things*, January 2022:

> The American people can be blamed if we abandon the requirement to know our own past, and if we fail to pass on that knowledge to the rising generations. We will be responsible for our own decline. And our society has come dangerously close to this very state. Small wonder so many young Americans now arrive at adulthood without a sense of membership in a society whose story is one of the greatest enterprises in human history. That this should be so is a tragedy. It is also a crime, the squandering of a rightful inheritance.

The vitality of Americanism and Zionism in the twenty-first century may depend in significant part on the ability of the beneficiaries of these great movements to appreciate their inheritance—which may depend on the restoration to common memory of stories such as those in this book.

5. In a September 22, 2016, interview at the Hudson Institute, Prime Minister Netanyahu had the following colloquy with Tikvah Fund Chairman Roger Hertog:

> HERTOG: . . . So for over 3,000 years, Jews have prayed to God for the reestablishment of Zion and Jerusalem, yet Israel was established largely by men and women who were uncertain about God. What role do you think God played in the miracle, in the creation of the Jewish state?
>
> NETANYAHU: Well, evidently a very good one, because we've beaten the odds. (Applause). Now, if you want me to question God, you know, based on experience I could be stricken down. And I'm not going to take that risk.
>
> I think that there are reservoirs of faith and culture that are very powerful in our people. You know, the founding fathers of Zionism, they may not have been religious people, [but] they were cognizant of religion—they even knew what they were challenging. One thing they weren't—they weren't ignorant. That's the important thing. You know, you want to reject something, know

> what you're rejecting. The thing that I worry about is we'd have a world where people don't even know what they're embracing and what they're rejecting. They should know our traditions. They're powerful. They've brought us here.

Netanyahu described what he called "the unique power of the Jewish people and the unique power of the Jewish state"—resulting from the "primary Internet system" that the Jewish people established in exile:

> You know, when we had the Diaspora, we had, you know, these scholars and sages in Yemen writing letters to the sages in Spain, writing letters to the sages in Germany and so on, asking questions about law, truth, justice. And truth was never finite, it always expanded, you always built on what you knew into what you didn't know. And I think when the walls of the ghettos and the enlightenment came, that same discipline was transferred to physics, mathematics, chemistry. It's a very powerful tradition for this constant question that the Jewish tradition encourages.
>
> But I think that if that were it, we wouldn't be here and Israel wouldn't be here. I think it also is grounded in deep faith. So our feet are planted in the soil and we came back—to our ancient land, and at the same time, you know, the branches go up and up and up, and I think it's this unique combination of faith and reason that has made the Jewish people so remarkable and the Jewish state so successful. And God is watching over us as we speak. (Applause).

Quoted in Rick Richman, "Rosh Hashanah 5777," *Commentary*, October 2, 2016, www.commentary.org/rick-richman/rosh-hashanah-5777-israel/.

6. See "Netanyahu: The Figures Who Formed Him, and the Duties of Jewish Leadership," *Mosaic*, December 21, 2021:

> GADI TAUB: . . . Zionism is something no nation has tried to do, let alone succeeded in doing. And after the state was founded, the population was tripled in seven years, and Zionism succeeded in a democratic form, *and a whole generation grew up here as though that's all a given.*
>
> BENJAMIN NETANYAHU: This needs to be acquired and renewed all the time. We are still a small nation, a small state. With enormous powers, but you need all the time to be focusing on the fact that you are a miracle. *You have to.* And it's not obvious. [Emphasis added.]

Rabbi David Wolpe of Sinai Temple in Los Angeles has said that the "trick of life" is to value something while you have it, the way you will value it when it is gone. And thus, he said, if you appreciate the existence of Israel, "think about what you would do to have it—if you did not already have it—and then *do that*, so you can keep it." See Rick Richman, "Visiting Israel at War," *Jewish Press*, August 23, 2006, www.jewishpress.com/indepth/visiting-israel-at-war/2006/08/23/.

7. Louis D. Brandeis, May 18, 1913, before the Young Men's Hebrew Association of Chelsea, Massachusetts, quoted in "Brandeis on Zionism: A Collection of Addresses and Statements by Louis D. Brandeis," www.wzo.org.il/index.php?dir=site&page=articles&op=item&cs=3276.

INDEX

A NOTE ABOUT THE TYPEFACE

This book is set in Garamond, first created in the early sixteenth century by Claude Garamond (c. 1500–1561), a French type designer, based on his inspiration from the type of Aldus Manutius, a fifteenth-century Italian scholar. The typeface was further developed by Jean Jannon in the seventeenth century and has today evolved into a variety of modern versions. The one used in this book is Adobe Garamond Premier Pro, which was created by Robert Slimbach in 1989 and is one of the most popular versions in fine printing, because of its clarity and elegance.